HOMOSEXUALITY
IN PERSPECTIVE

cultural impediments to doing such research have been immense when one considers the deeply ingrained senses of sin and shame the West has associated with sexuality. On the other hand, it is striking that it took so long to turn seriously to the study of a function so central to human life. Given the widespread incidence of at least minor sexual dysfunction, it is amazing that it was so difficult to approach the systematic study of the physiologic bases of the treatment of sexual dysfunction. Yet now such research seems commonplace. One can talk easily of heterosexual function and the treatment of its dysfunction. For this newly won ease in approaching the study of sexual function, and for the initial substantial data in the field, we are as a culture indebted to William Masters and Virginia Johnson.

This contribution can be placed in perspective only if it is in fact recognized not simply as a scientific achievement, but as a contribution to the culture of the West. Masters and Johnson have afforded a set of insights concerning ourselves as sexual beings. They have shed light on an area that has been surrounded by myths, fear, and shame. Yet this element of our lives is the foundation that supports some of our tenderest emotions and affections. In establishing in detail the role of the clitoris in orgasm, the multiorgasmic capacity of women, the continuation of sexual function into old age, and the exact physiology of sexual arousal, orgasm, and resolution, Masters and Johnson have sketched the physical framework within which one soul can touch another in pleasure and love.

After years of embarrassed ignorance, knowledge has become available in *Human Sexual Response* and *Human Sexual Inadequacy*. These works have conveyed to our culture a willingness to assay our sexual function as a prudent prelude to talking about sexual normality, abnormality, and treatment. They have conveyed a concern for complaints regarding sexual function without invoking notions of underlying disease states. And most important, these books have reminded us that to understand ourselves as bodily beings, we will have to look, at least as a first step, at our bodies and see how they work. On such a passionately discussed topic concerning the roots of some our strongest passions, the work of Masters and Johnson has shown the scientific virtue of quiet concern for the truth, for the facts of the matter.

FOREWORD

For over a millennium and a half the West has shown a marked ambivalence regarding sexual relations, including sexual intercourse within marriage. Pope Gregory the Great, for example, in his *Pastoral Rule*, warned that married couples who sought pleasure from intercourse "transgressed the law of marriage" and as a consequence "befouled their intercourse with pleasure." Concerns about sexual pleasure and excessive sexual activity have remained a preoccupation of the West and have at times taken special expression in particular movements such as the Bogomils of the tenth and eleventh centuries and the Cathars, who followed them, as well as such recent groups as Ann Lee's Shakers. The established cultural attitude regarding sexual function reflected a sense of shame beyond one of modesty. One should note that the etymology of the word *pudendum* derives from the Latin *pudere* "to be ashamed." Such attitudes have persisted. In the nineteenth century, for example, physicians concerned with sexual attitudes still announced in medical journals that "not one bride in a hundred, of delicate, educated, sensitive women accept matrimony from any desire of sexual gratification; when she thinks of this at all, it is with shrinking, or even with horror, rather than with desire." Marriage manuals of this period often contained seriously inaccurate information, such as that the peak fertility of women was during menstruation and that in midcycle women were most infertile. Attempts to do research concerning the physiology of sexual response were met with condemnation, as a St. Louis physician discovered, when in the early 1870s he studied the physiology of orgasm.

Only very slowly, through the work of individuals such as Sigmund Freud, Alfred Charles Kinsey, William H. Masters, and Virginia E. Johnson, has there been an acceptance in our culture of the importance of studying sexual function and dsyfunction. The

In *Homosexuality in Perspective* Masters and Johnson have continued their attempts to understand the phenomena associated with human sexuality and to learn the ways to help individuals with their complaints of sexual dysfunction. The study of the sexual response of homosexuals, and the comparison of that response with the sexual response of heterosexuals, is obviously even more difficult in terms of our cultural barriers. Though a sizable number of persons in all Western cultures have been occasionally if not predominantly homosexual, homosexuality has attracted scorn, condemnation, and punishment. Unlike Plato's *Phaedrus* and *Symposium*, which depict homosexuality as a paradigm of love and the erotic, English law characterizes it as a sin one should not even name. The result is the loss of the candor of Plato's dialogues in speaking of and comparing heterosexual and homosexual love. This volume contributes importantly to a return to that candor, a candor required in order to understand the human condition and to help with the treatment of those who fail to function in the intimacies of their sexuality.

By approaching and comparing the physiology and the therapy of both homosexuals and heterosexuals with equal attention to facts and to a concern for their needs, Masters and Johnson have again provided a volume of facts that will have an impact upon the humane understanding of our sexuality. By showing that there are no physiologic norms clearly distinguishing homosexual and heterosexual function, and that the sexual dysfunctions of homosexuals can be treated as can those of heterosexuals, they invite an abandonment of many of the stereotypes of normal versus abnormal function. Without advocating a particular view of an acceptable sexual life, this work suggests an attitude of quiet tolerance for the range of ways individuals express their divergent sexual needs with fellow humans on the basis of very similar physiologic responses. In fact, one can see in this attitude an ethic of tolerant care, which must be cognate even with religious traditions that disapprove of active homosexuality.

In reading this volume one will surely find important new information concerning the physiology of homosexual response and the ways to resolve dysfunction between homosexual partners. One will also find critical reflections on human attention and sloth in the most rapturous of dramas. Sex is, after all, always a fact of life, and yet always more than just a fact of life.

H. Tristram Engelhardt, Jr., Ph.D., M.D.
The Kennedy Institute of Ethics
Georgetown University
Washington, D.C.

PRINTED IN THE UNITED STATES OF AMERICA

M V

Homosexuality in Perspective

W I L L I A M   H.   M A S T E R S
CO-DIRECTOR

V I R G I N I A   E.   J O H N S O N
CO-DIRECTOR

THE MASTERS & JOHNSON INSTITUTE
ST. LOUIS, MISSOURI

LITTLE, BROWN AND COMPANY
BOSTON

PREFACE

Millions of men and women have interacted sexually with same-sex partners. A significant percentage of these individuals, like those interacting with opposite-sex partners, have developed varying symptoms of sexual distress, but for them adequate treatment has not been readily available.

A homosexual man or woman who is sexually dysfunctional or dissatisfied is entitled to evaluation and treatment with the same clinical objectivity currently accorded the sexually dysfunctional heterosexual individual. If health-care professionals are to meet these responsibilities, much more must be known and much less presumed of the psychophysiologic aspects of homosexual function.

As multiple aspects of homosexual interaction are opened to scientific scrutiny, inadequacies, discrepancies, and errors in prior laboratory and clinical research will be identified. A better perspective of homosexuality as it relates to heterosexuality inevitably will be an important byproduct of these multidimensional laboratory and clinical investigations. To date, research efforts have been directed toward establishing psychosocial perspectives between the two sex preferences. This report is only an initial step in developing equally important psychobiological perspectives. It must not be construed as a statement of social, legal, or religious position.

As these progressive changes come to pass, the study of human sexual function assuredly will grow into a field of unrestricted scientific inquiry and develop into a mature health-care discipline.

W. H. M.
V. E. J.

St. Louis

ix

ACKNOWLEDGMENTS

There were many contributions from the hundreds of study subjects who trusted the intent and the conduct of the research programs, and from the sexually troubled men and women who had confidence in the therapy concepts. Without their support, this investigation of homosexual function, dysfunction, and dissatisfaction could not have been conducted.

The skills of Robert C. Kolodny, who carefully critiqued this text and contributed the section on endocrinology in Chapter 18, are warmly acknowledged. Beyond this we are openly in debt to Raymond W. Waggoner, Sandra K. Webster, Rhea L. Dornbush, Mark F. Schwartz, Mary Jane Rosenfeld, Judy Yates, Chris Busby, and to the entire Institute staff.

To these, our friends, and to all who have contributed, our respect and gratitude.

W. H. M.
V. E. J.

CONTENTS

CLINICAL STUDY, 1968-1977

PRECLINICAL STUDY, 1957–1970

I

PRECLINICAL
INVESTIGATION

Much has been written, discussed, declaimed, or just whispered about human homosexual function. Libraries bulge with tomes on the subject. Personal attestations abound. Famous figures in history have been assiduously identified as homosexual, either in defense of or as an attack upon not only their sexual orientation but also the totality of their personalities. Theological discussions have ranged from learned to demagogic levels on the status of the homosexual in our society. And psychosocial aspects of homosexuality have been exhaustively reported, but rarely without observer bias.

As a natural consequence of society's continuing obsession with the subject of sex, there are thousands of self-appointed or professionally annointed experts on the subject of homosexuality. Yet, despite this proliferation of assumed or presumed expertise, conscientious health-care professionals are embarrassed by the lack of a secure information base from which to respond to the multiplicity of problems encountered by the millions of homosexual men and women in our society.

For many years the oppressive weight of professional ignorance, combined with the intellectually debilitating pressures of public reprobation, has effectively immobilized health-care professionals in their legitimate search for accurate facts about homosexuality. How does one start to separate fact from fiction? How does scientific objectivity grow when public opprobrium still remains unbridled? Literally, so little is actually known of the physiologic and psychosexual aspects of homosexuality that it is uncertain just how ignorant we are about the subject.

As health-care professionals we will only develop a culturally

3

unbiased perspective of homosexuality from continued basic science research and from accepting the clinical responsibility for treating problems of sexual dysfunction or dissatisfaction within the homosexual population.

In the midsixties, when considering the logical expansion of the Institute's investigation of human sexual function and dysfunction by initiating a physiologically and psychosexually oriented homosexual research program, the need for an objective investigation was so great that the research team's understandable reluctance to face both public and professional condemnation was quickly resolved. Since a significant percentage of this country's population had existed in a quagmire of sexual misconception and had been subjected to the unending trauma that public misinformation, phobia, and taboo create, and since it was possible that to some modest degree these levels of ignorance and prejudice might be lessened by a definitive research effort, there was no question of not activating the investigative programs designed to focus on homosexuality.

PRECLINICAL STUDY GOALS

From the onset, it was clear that a multidimensional investigation was needed in order to compile objective information, to resolve various unsettled disputes, and to demystify profoundly muddled public and professional concepts of homosexual interaction. In short, definitive research programs were (and still are) indicated to provide clearer perspectives of homosexuality. Several different areas for study were defined by the research team as logically falling within the Institute's parameters of investigative expertise developed over the years in heterosexual research programs.

1. Laboratory investigation of the physiology of homosexual response was an obvious extension of prior research of heterosexual physiology. It was presumed that once reliable descriptive information about homosexual physiology had been established, legitimate comparisons could be drawn between homosexual and heterosexual sexual response cycles. Any significant physiologic differences found

between these alternative forms of sexual expression might have direct clinical application in the treatment of heterosexually or homosexually oriented problems of sexual dysfunction.

On the other hand, if no significant physiologic differences could be established between sexual response patterns of homosexuals and heterosexuals, a number of sexual myths and misconceptions would be exploded and the investigative material derived might still be of major clinical value. It should be stated at this point that while significant physiologic differences between heterosexual and homosexual response were not anticipated, the need for an objective investigation into the issue was recognized. For if variations in human sexual patterning could only be identified on an individual, subjective basis, without regard to sexual preference, any presumed physiologic support for the recurrent arguments of "my way" versus "your way" would be reasonably neutralized.

2. It was anticipated that the functional efficiency of a homosexual study-subject population could be evaluated in the laboratory environment. Any difference in ability of homosexual men or women to attain orgasm in the laboratory as compared to that of heterosexual study subjects in a similar setting would be of investigative interest, just as would the absence of such differences. This evaluation of homosexual functional efficiency * was planned to include reports both of frequency of orgasmic response and of failures to achieve orgasmic release with a particular sexual technique. It was presumed that this information would be of value whether or not significant differences could be established between heterosexual and homosexual response patterns.

3. In order to provide truly multidimensional perspectives of homosexual function, it was decided that description and analysis of the fantasy patterning of homosexual male and female study subjects would provide an additional bank of resource material. The experience of the research team in the original heterosexual research project had indicated that study subjects participating in the laboratory investigation were, after becoming comfortable with

---

* It must be acknowledged that sexual proficiency is not synonymous with orgasmic responsiveness and that sexual gratification, sexual maturity, and sexual interest are phenomena to be considered somewhat apart from orgasmic frequency or orgasmic failure alone. The objectivity of documenting orgasm as a precise, definable physiologic event made it a useful parameter to reflect one dimension of functional efficiency.

the research team and secure in the research environment, willing to share subjective material with unusual freedom and spontaneity. It was presumed that there would be returns of major clinical value if fantasy content collected in interviews with homosexual study subjects could be compared to previously unpublished data describing the fantasy patterns of members of the heterosexual study groups.

4. Any investigation of homosexual response patterns gains particular perspective when related to equivalent data reflecting heterosexual response patterns. Although an extensive heterosexually oriented study had been conducted, it had been initiated 10 years previously. Therefore, it was believed that a contemporary investigation of heterosexual function would provide another important measure of comparison for the contemplated homosexual study. While data obtained in the original research project would serve as a means of investigative check and balance, the recruitment of a second, contemporary group of heterosexual study subjects for further investigation was necessary for two additional reasons. First, the stimulative techniques of cunnilingus and fellatio had not been evaluated in the original heterosexual research project. Such a study was not deemed prudent in the 1950s, but by 1966 it was possible to conduct such research in a laboratory environment. It was obvious that if any meaningful comparisons were to be drawn between homosexual and heterosexual response patterns, the stimulative techniques usually employed by both sexual preference groups must be evaluated.

Second, heterosexual response needed to be reevaluated in the laboratory without an atmosphere of untoward social pressure placed upon the research team. Although security problems were more complex during the homosexual research program (see Chapter 4), the extreme social and professional pressures to discontinue the research programs that existed during the original heterosexual study were markedly reduced. When the homosexual program was initiated, the researchers no longer were contending with an ever-present possibility that permission to continue the research might be withdrawn at any moment. This is explained by the facts that an independent research foundation had been established and the work was not dependent on outside funding. Thus, the investigation of homosexual function was conducted at a much slower pace than had been evident a decade earlier. The same pace was present when the contemporary heterosexual study group was recruited and evaluated.

THE STUDY-SUBJECT GROUPS

It was decided that two new study-subject groups would be recruited: a homosexual population of men and women, and a heterosexual population of men and women (designated study group A). As a final step in study-subject analysis, data were drawn from the original group of heterosexual study subjects described in *Human Sexual Response* (1966). For purposes of comparison with the two new study-subject groups, this original group of heterosexual study subjects was reduced to those members whose participation was similar to that requested of members of study group A (see Chapter 2). This reduced group was designated study group B.

The same criteria used to recruit the original heterosexual study population (selected members of which had been newly designated study group B) were retained as basic recruitment guidelines for the two new groups in terms of age distribution, levels of education, and Kinsey sexual preference ratings (Kinsey *et al.*, 1948). In addition, no homosexual male study subjects were selected without a history of facility to respond at orgasmic levels to the sexual excitation in masturbation, partner manipulation, and fellatio, and no female homosexual study subjects were recruited who were not capable of attaining orgasm through masturbation, partner manipulation, and cunnilingus. Selection of study subjects for study group A was restricted to heterosexual men and women who were readily capable of achieving orgasm in masturbation, partner manipulation, fellatio or cunnilingus, and with intercourse.

The homosexual research group and heterosexual study group A were composed deliberately of individuals who were highly functional sexually. This selective approach to the constitution of a research population was established during the original heterosexual research project (study group B) and was chosen again for several reasons. First, protection of the welfare of study subjects had always been of the utmost concern, and past experience had taught that individuals who had a great deal of confidence in their sexual facility were the least likely to experience any negative consequences from participation in a research study involving sexual function in a laboratory environment. Second, if research interest is directed toward physiologic response to sexual stimulation, the investigation is most efficiently conducted with male and female study subjects who react regularly and effectively at orgasmic levels to sexual stimuli. Third, reports of behavioral patterning and descriptions of subjectively oriented material gathered from successfully functioning men and women are vital in providing a comparative basis for clinical interpretation of similar material collected from men and women considered to be sexually dysfunctional.

It must always be kept in mind that due to specific selectivity toward highly effective sexual function and above-average levels of formal education, the Institute's study-subject groups are *not* representative of the population as a whole. The extent to which these groups differ from the general population is discussed more fully in Chapter 2.

The Kinsey classification was used as a frame of reference in rating study-subjects' sexual preference. In brief review, and using a liberal rather than literal interpretation, Kinsey 0 orientation means that the man or woman has never had overt homosexual experience. A Kinsey 1 identification describes an individual whose minimal amount of homosexual experience has been far overshadowed by the degree of his or her heterosexual experience. The classification of Kinsey 2 suggests a person with a significantly higher level of homosexual experience than a Kinsey 1, but still with a predominant background of heterosexual interaction.

A rating of Kinsey 3 represents an individual with a history of approximately equal homosexual and heterosexual experience. Despite obvious ambivalence as to partner gender, there usually is a history of periods of partner identification. An individual rated as Kinsey 4 is one who has had a significant amount of heterosexual experience but whose sexual outlets have been predominantly homosexual. A man or woman with a Kinsey 5 preference rating is an individual whose homosexual experience fully dominates his or her history and whose heterosexual activity is minimal. Finally, a Kinsey 6 describes a man or woman whose sexual preference is the exact opposite of a Kinsey 0—that is, an individual who has no history of overt heterosexual experience.

Only the reported history of sexual experience, not described fantasy patterns or dream sequences, was used in this study to determine a Kinsey classification of sexual preference. Obviously, classification based on historical recall is not always a reliable data-gathering method. But while this system has been criticized, it is easy to apply, and if used only as a preference rating scale as originally intended, it is a valuable means of classification.

In recruiting the homosexual study group it was decided to select subjects representing the full range of homosexual preference. While it was anticipated that Kinsey 5 and 6 volunteers would be the most easily recruited, a broad spectrum of homosexual preference was desired, including men and women predominantly heterosexual in prior experience. Therefore, a major effort was expended to develop a representative population of men and women with sexual histories reflecting Kinsey 1 through 4 sexual preferences. If Kinsey 5 and 6 subjects had been the only men and women evaluated, this bias toward exclusive homosexual orientation could have obscured some of the theoretically possible variations in sexual response patterns that might have been present in study subjects whose sexual experience had been mixed or predominantly heterosexual. It should be emphasized that, regardless of their preference ratings, all of the study subjects selected for the homosexual research group were involved in homosexual activity at the time of recruitment.

The two heterosexual research populations (study groups A and B) were limited to men and women with no higher than a Kinsey 1 preference rating. All of these study subjects were living heterosexually active lives when recruited.

Obviously, there was a discrepancy in the recruitment of the men and women for the two heterosexual groups as opposed to those who formed the homosexual study group, since heterosexual volunteers leading heterosexual lives with sexual preference ratings of 2 through 5 were not recruited for the program. Consistency in recruiting practice was not maintained because the concept of assembling a heterosexual study group that included individuals with a history of a significant amount of homosexual experience simply never occurred to the research team 23 years ago when study group B was originally assembled. Since for comparative purposes study group A was recruited in adherence to standards established 10 years previously, the discrepancy was deliberately maintained for methodologic consistency. The obvious variation in distribution of sexual preference that exists between the two heterosexual groups and the homosexual group is emphasized at the outset of this report. The extent to which this difference in subject selection may have influenced the resulting data is not known.

It was believed that in order to evaluate sexual interaction patterns with greatest accuracy, the focus should be on couples in committed relationships of reasonably long standing. Thus, most of the study subjects selected were members of "committed" couples of either heterosexual or homosexual orientation. For the purposes of this investigation, the definition of a committed heterosexual relationship was the existence of a state of marriage, while committed homosexual couples were defined as partners who had lived together for a minimum of one year. The lack of parallelism in these definitions was recognized at the outset of this work, but no realistic unitary set of criteria was available to resolve this difference. There were certain necessary exceptions to these definitions that will be described in Chapter 2. The obvious fallacies in the empirical assumption that either a year's conjoint residency or a state of marriage is secure evidence of a couple's mutual commitment need no further discussion. Such selection criteria were simply the best that could be imposed under the circumstances. Reasonably stable relationships were identified on the basis of in-depth personal interviews; in some cases, evidence of instability in a relationship was obtained sufficient to warrant rejection of the couple as potential study subjects.

Despite specific research concentration on committed couples, it was believed that men and women without established relationships should also be represented. Therefore, a small number of volunteers of heterosexual and of homosexual orientation who described sexual histories with a striking absence of committed relationships and who expressed no current interest in forming such relationships were recruited to represent "uncommitted" men and women of the two major sexual preferences. In the laboratory, these men and women were designated as "assigned partners" and arbitrarily paired with each other to create "assigned couples" (see Chapters 4 through 6). By comparing their sexual behavior patterns, physiological responses, functional efficiency, and fantasy patterning with those of homosexual and heterosexual committed couples, another interpretative dimension was added to the research program, and broader perspectives inevitably were created for homosexual interaction. The concept of commitment and the consequences of commitment in laboratory interaction are further discussed in Chapter 11.

Criteria for study-subject age distribution and educational levels were based upon standards previously established by the original heterosexual study group. These are reported in detail in Chapters 2 and 3. There was a bias toward higher than average levels of education in the population of the original study group, and therefore the bias was continued in the new study groups. This educational selectivity was purposefully based on the prior experience of the research team, in which it was observed that in general, the higher the degree of formal education of the study subject, the more informative and thoughtful would be his or her communicative response to questioning. Since as much, if not more, was learned of ultimate clinical value from the study-subjects' presentation of subjective material as was gathered from observation of physical responses or sexual behavior patterns in the laboratory, the educational bias of the research population was important.

The investigative techniques and research results of the different areas of study will be presented in detail in the following chapters. Briefly, in order to gather the multidimensional data sought, each study subject was observed and interviewed on several occasions. Each homosexual subject was observed in at least one episode of masturbation, manual stimulation, and fellatio or cunnilingus, and each heterosexual study subject was observed in the equivalent stimulative situations as well as during at least one episode of coitus. Most study subjects were observed in repeated interactions using the different stimulative techniques.

All of the study subjects were interviewed during the screening process, and data relating to general attitudes and fears or preferences oriented to sexual function were compiled. During and after sexual activity in the laboratory there was opportunity for the subjects to express subjective reactions to the specific experience. In case of failure to achieve orgasm or the occurrence of any problems, the subject was questioned immediately in order to determine his or her feelings about the incident.

In addition, in-depth interviews with a selected number of study subjects of both homosexual and heterosexual orientations were conducted to obtain information about fantasy patterning. The results of this investigative program are presented in Chapter 9.

Several secondary projects were conducted in conjunction with the major investigations. Rectal intercourse was evaluated with a small number of homosexual and heterosexual subjects, and dildo usage was studied with a similarly constituted research group. The results of these secondary research projects are presented in Chapter 5.

An unanticipated research project that initially developed under the impetus of the homosexual study programs evolved into a separate investigative effort. This was the study of a previously unidentified group of men and women whose lack of any sexual preference and whose total disinterest in even identifying with, let alone forming, a committed relationship with a partner of either gender required formal group designation. The investigation into the subject of ambisexuality is reported in Chapter 8.

2

SELECTION PROCESS FOR
STUDY POPULATIONS

There were numerous problems associated with recruitment and screening of the committed and assigned study groups in the homosexual research program. Recruiting techniques and results of the screening program used to establish the homosexual study population and comparative heterosexual study group A are considered in detail in this chapter. In addition, there is a description of the process by which the original heterosexual study group reported in *Human Sexual Response* was reduced to those subjects (study group B) whose participation provided another dimension to the homosexual study and allowed legitimate comparisons of sexual preference groups to be drawn within the overall investigation of human sexual function.

RECRUITMENT OF HOMOSEXUAL
STUDY GROUP

Committed Study Subjects. The homosexual study group was recruited in an ongoing process over a four-year period, from 1964 to 1968. Recruitment of stable, committed homosexual couples during the 1960s was difficult. The usual local resources for investigative referral of homosexual study subjects, such as homophile organizations, activist groups, homosexual bars, correctional institutions, or medical resources were deemed inadequate in that if recruiting had been conducted through these sources it would have been impossible to provide study-subject anonymity and research security. In addition, committed homosexual couples infrequently

13

surfaced in a public declaration of sexual preference or even circulated openly among their peers during the decade of the sixties. At that time, the local community of known committed homosexual couples certainly was not of sufficient magnitude to provide a satisfactory number of study subjects for the Institute's research purposes. Therefore, a decision was made to recruit the committed homosexual research group on a national rather than on a local level.

Following the pattern established when the original heterosexual research population was recruited in 1957, initial contacts were developed in the local community with stable homosexual couples and were disseminated through the framework of local educational institutions into immediately adjacent geographic areas. As work progressed, word was spread through the cooperation of local couples to committed couples in other communities. Problems initially encountered in contacting responsible and interested homosexual couples were progressively overcome as stable couples, after cooperating with the laboratory investigation, referred friends or acquaintances whose homosexual relationships also were long-standing.

Another factor in assembling homosexual subjects that was not present in the recruitment of heterosexual study groups (Chapter 1) was the decision to find subjects whose Kinsey sexual preference ratings represented the full range of personal homosexual orientation, from Kinsey Scale 1 through Kinsey 6. Subjects with preference ratings reflecting predominantly homosexual experiences, those rated Kinsey 5 and 6, were relatively easy to recruit. There were more volunteers in these grades than in the other classifications, but only a limited number could be accepted in order to maintain the balance in sexual preference ratings originally planned.

The most difficult type of subject to recruit for study participation was the Kinsey 1 volunteer. Although only a relatively minimal amount of prior homosexual experience was reported by these men and women, their sexual responses in the laboratory were to be entirely to homosexual stimuli. Due to the predominance of heterosexual experience in the backgrounds of these men and women, criteria for selecting this group were very strict. The Kinsey 1 representatives were accepted into the program only if they could document that they were currently living in a homosexual relationship of at least three months' duration. This was the only exception made to the criterion of a minimum of one year's established relationship before acceptance of a homosexual couple in a committed status. Thus, the Kinsey 1 volunteers, who reported a minimal amount of homosexual interaction compared to the predominance of their heterosexual experience, had concentrated their homosexual activities in the immediate past prior to recruitment. Obviously, they also were likely to be in their late thirties or into their forties and to have been quite active heterosexually in order to have a history of three months' experience in a committed homosexual relationship and still be classified as Kinsey 1 men and women.

There was also concern in arbitrarily selecting the specific classification of Kinsey grades 2 through 4 for any individual who had had a large number of both homosexual and heterosexual experiences. The ratings (described in Chapter 1) were assigned by the research team after detailed history-taking, but it is difficult for any individual to be fully objective in assessing the amounts of his or her heterosexual versus homosexual experience when there has been a considerable amount of both types of interaction. Some of these preference ratings might well be subject to different interpretation by other health-care professionals. Generally, the Kinsey 2, 3, and 4 individuals had an estimated number of sexual contacts that impressed the interviewer as far above the typical range of age-related sexual experience.

The Kinsey 3 classification was the most difficult to assign of the ratings. Relative equality in any form of diverse physical activity is hard to establish. Particularly was this so when the interviewer, in attempting to separate mature sexual experience into its homosexual and heterosexual components, was faced with a history of a multiplicity of partners of either sex. This problem was augmented by the subjects' frequently vague recall of the average number of sexual interactions with each partner. This lack of a clearly defined sex history is an almost inevitable hazard when conducting retrospective interviews, particularly with men and women who have had a large number of sexual partners.

It should be emphasized that just as was true for the Kinsey 1 grade of sexual preference, men and women with 2, 3, and 4 grades were only accepted as members of the homosexual study group if they currently were living homosexually oriented lives.

Assigned Study Subjects. Recruitment of assigned study subjects for the homosexual group was done through word of mouth. Prostitutes were never employed to function as assigned partners in any of the Institute's study groups. A sufficient number of volunteers were available, so the vast majority of the men and women who formed the assigned couples came from the local area. All of the men and women recruited as assigned partners currently lived lifestyles in which committed relationships were viewed with disinterest. Their expressed purpose in sexual interchange was one of sexual satisfaction, and their interest usually was directed to quantity rather than quality of sexual opportunity. These homosexual men and women saw the invitation to interact in the laboratory as simply another variation in sexual encounter, one about which they evidenced an honest curiosity. They were accepted on these terms.

SCREENING

Once potential study subjects were identified, screening steps followed established patterns. First, the potential study subject was contacted by telephone. The referral source was identified at this time. The research program's concepts and purposes were explained in detail, and the study subject's age group, formal education, and degree of committed relationship, if any, were ascertained. If interest in cooperating with the research program was expressed, a personal interview was scheduled.

If the person interviewed initially evidenced a sense of comfort with his or her sexual orientation, the next step during the interview was to develop a detailed psychosocial history. Psychosocial histories were taken from each study subject in separate interviews by both members of the research team. This was followed by a complete physical examination, a routine laboratory evaluation, and a detailed medical history. If the detailed history-taking and the physical and laboratory evaluations did not identify the presence of major psychopathology or severe neurosis, and if no physical or metabolic pathology was detected, the study subject was invited to participate in the research program. All potential subjects were informed as fully as was possible about potential risks and inconveniences of study participation. At the time this work was begun, formal institutional review boards for the protection of human subjects were not yet in use, but the Board of Directors of the Institute gave approval to the overall research program.

ELIMINATION OF SUBJECTS

Evidence of social stability was a key factor in study-subject selection. Obviously, social stability had to be related to age in all of the study groups. For the younger males in the homosexual population, socially secure relationships were of little importance in the midsixties when this research program was conducted. Except for the 51–60-year-old homosexuals, of whom there were too few to draw valid comparisons, no other age group evidenced as high a percentage of elimination of potential study subjects as that of the 21- to 30-year-old males. In this age group approximately three times more potential study subjects were screened than survived the selection process (see Table 3-1, Chapter 3). The socially unstable, migratory character of the male 21–30-year age group accounts for the fact that approximately one out of three individuals screened were finally selected as study subjects. The same problems were encountered in recruiting uncommitted heterosexual male study subjects in this 21–30-year age group (see Table 3-11, Chapter 3). In the male homosexuals volunteering for this project who were beyond 30 years of age, a significant increase in the social stability and in the security of an existing committed relationship was obvious.

Of interest is the fact that a male couple with one partner in his midsixties and the other in his early seventies was screened and interviewed. Regretfully, at the intake interview, active participation by this couple in the research laboratory had to be denied because one partner had a pattern of erective insecurity that had not been elicited during the initial screening procedures.

When recruiting female subjects for the homosexual (and heterosexual) groups, 18–20-year-old study subjects were accepted who had established interpersonal sexual behavior patterns, since in Missouri 18 is the legal age of consent for women. Of course, there was investigative interest in an opportunity to evaluate young women who at this early age stated that they were fully committed to homosexuality (Kinsey *et al.*, 1953).

An older couple with one partner in her midsixties and the other in her early seventies was screened and then interviewed. They were not selected as study subjects because it was believed that their extreme concern with the possibility of identification (they lived in the local area) would have placed them under unacceptable pressure in the laboratory (Table 3-6, Chapter 3).

There were 2 men and 2 women who were eliminated from consideration on the basis of their medical histories. The 2 men were rejected because of severe hypertension, and 1 woman was not included due to an established diagnosis of diabetes. All 3 were in the over-51 age group and were members of committed couples. One 31-year-old woman was eliminated when it was learned during history-taking that she was under treatment for a venereal disease.

RECRUITMENT OF HETEROSEXUAL
STUDY GROUP A

Heterosexual study group A was recruited during the final two years (1967 to 1968) of the research program in homosexuality. Following prior successful patterning exemplified by the original heterosexual study group and the homosexual study group, recruitment was accomplished initially by approaching the teaching staffs and student bodies of local educational institutions, then by word of mouth through the community, and occasionally through friends in other geographic areas. There was no real problem finding committed couples in the local metropolitan community, although a significant percentage (22 percent) of the men and women in study group A were recruited on a national level. Procedures for recruiting heterosexual assigned partners were identical to those described earlier for recruiting homosexual assigned partners.

ELIMINATION OF SUBJECTS

Since no study subjects were included in heterosexual study group A who had a Kinsey rating over 1, an unacceptable sexual preference rating accounted for the rejection of 21 volunteers.

Twelve of the 114 male (Table 3-11, Chapter 3) and 9 of the 121 female heterosexual volunteers (Table 3-14, Chapter 3) were rejected because they reported a degree of homosexual experience either beyond Kinsey 1 or, more frequently, described homosexual experience within the year prior to organization of the research group.

Of the total 57 male and 57 female study subjects finally selected for study group A, 2 men and 1 woman were in the 51–60-year age group. Actually, 4 men and 4 women in this age range were interviewed, but 2 of the men and 3 of the women were rejected. One man was rejected for medical reasons (diabetes) and 1 because he had a continuing history of rapid ejaculation. Two of the 3 women rejected in this age group were simply not free to meet the time commitments necessary for the laboratory scheduling, and 1 woman was contemplating a marriage which, if established, would have terminated her cooperation with the research program.

The age categories of 21 to 30 and 51 to 60 provided the highest percentage of rejections for men (Table 3-11, Chapter 3), and the older age groups (41 to 50 and 51 to 60) had the highest rejection rates for women (Table 3-14, Chapter 3). In the male study group ages 21 to 30 there was frequent evidence of social instability once in-depth interviews were initiated during the selection process. The research team may have been overly cautious, but the same general criteria were applied to men in this age group as was true for the selection process involving male volunteers for the homosexual study group. The medical reasons for the high percentage of rejection in the small number of older men who volunteered as study subjects have been stated above.

For older heterosexual women, who had the highest rejection rate, there was a different problem. Social instability was not a primary concern; the problem was just the opposite. The heterosexual women expressed real concern with the possibility of public identification as study subjects. They frequently described a fear of general social opprobrium. Once such fears were vocalized, it was the research team's position that these women should not be invited to become study subjects. It was felt that fear of identification might distract from the effectiveness of sexual interaction in the laboratory.

Of real interest to the research team was the fact that the older women in study group A reflected the same high incidence of fears of identification if they cooperated as study subjects in the laboratory that were expressed by the same age group of women volunteers in the original heterosexual study group a decade previously. Of further import was the fact that such fears of social opprobrium were rarely expressed by the older female volunteers in the homosexual recruitment program. An outstanding exception to this statement has been described earlier in this chapter for an older homosexual couple.

Medical causes for rejection of volunteers were minimal. As described earlier, 1 older man was rejected because he had diabetes and 1 younger woman because she had hypertension. The only other medical rejection was in a single woman in the 21–30-year age group who was found to be in early pregnancy during the routine physical examination.

F O R M A T I O N   O F   H E T E R O S E X U A L
S T U D Y   G R O U P   B
(R E D U C T I O N   P R O C E S S)

As described in Chapter 1, study group B was comprised of selected members of the original heterosexual study-subject population reported in *Human Sexual Response* (1966). The reduction process by which study group B was established should be discussed in detail. The reduction process consisted of purposeful selection of those study subjects from the original project whose participation in the earlier laboratory studies could be fairly compared to the participation requested in heterosexual study group A. Relevant comparisons between existing data collected from the original heterosexual study-subject population during the first investigation and newly collected data from heterosexual study group A and the homosexual study group could then be made.

During the nine-year original heterosexual investigation, 276 married couples, 106 single women, and 36 single men had cooperated as study subjects in a multiplicity of research programs related to the physiologic aspects of heterosexual function. Thus, a total of 382 women and 312 men had been active as study subjects in the research laboratory during this phase of the overall research program.

Of the 276 married couples who had cooperated with the program, 19 did not participate in each of the observed techniques of masturbation, partner manipulation, and coitus. Fellatio and cunnilingus had not been investigated. There were a number of reasons for reluctance to participate in the full range of studies, but if either partner in a marriage expressed reservation to any form of sexual activity, no effort had been made to seek compliance. Since full·cooperation had not been obtained, these 19 couples were removed from statistical consideration.

There were 6 married couples who had cooperated to record sexual response patterns during pregnancy. Five of the couples had participated in research programs before pregnancy, and all continued to cooperate with other research programs after pregnancy. The statistics returned during the states of pregnancy were removed from consideration, but material developed before or after pregnancy was included in the overall statistics.

There remained 257 married couples who had engaged in the stimulative techniques of masturbation, partner manipulation, and coital activity in these programs. Most of the married couples, once committed to the research programs, had continued their participation over periods of one to six years.

Most of the 106 unmarried women who were possible subjects for selection into study group B had not been asked to respond in the laboratory to each of the stimulative techniques. There were 7 women with artificially created vaginas who constituted a special study group in vaginal agenesis that arbitrarily was removed from statistical consideration (Masters and Johnson, 1961). Forty-eight single women had cooperated only with the artificial coital experiments (Masters and Johnson, 1966; Johnson et al., 1970). Since male partner interaction was excluded as a part of their laboratory experience, the orgasmic facility of these women will not be presented for comparative consideration.

Finally, there were 27 single women who had volunteered early in the female sexual physiology studies to participate only in masturbational activity and who had not wished to accept assigned male partners in any form of sexual interaction. These women obviously could not be considered in comparison with the other study groups. Thus, of the 106 heterosexual single women who had participated over the years in various investigative programs, there were 24 who had been partners in assigned couples for studies of sexual function among uncommitted men and women.

Of the 36 single men who had been active in the primary heterosexual investigation, 7 had agreed to participate for masturbational evaluation only and thus could not be included in the overall statistics.

Therefore, in the primary research program, a total of 24 single women and 29 single men, all of heterosexual orientation, had participated without reservation in the laboratory in response to masturbation, partner manipulation, and coitus. One woman had interacted with a total of 3 assigned male partners over a four-year period, and 3 other women had interacted with 2 assigned male partners, thus establishing the total of 29 assigned couples who had participated in the original study.

There were 11 black married couples who were possible subjects for selection into study group B. One couple was among the 19 pairs eliminated from statistical consideration, leaving 10 black couples in the final 257 committed partnerships. There were 2 committed couples with a Spanish-American background. None of the assigned 29 male or 24 female partners was black or of Spanish-American descent. Two single black women, part of the original research population, were eliminated because they were in the group of volunteers who had cooperated only with the artificial coital experiments.

RESULTS OF THE REDUCTION PROCESS

The results of the reduction process are recorded in Tables 2-1 and 2-2. The first column in each table reports by age decade the number of both men and women who volunteered to form the original heterosexual research population. The second column indicates the number of study subjects in each age group who did not engage in all the modes of stimulative activity and could not be considered statistically. The third column represents the selective total of men and women used to form study group B which, in turn, was used to amplify reports of heterosexual functional effi-

TABLE 2-1

Study Group B (Reduction Table): Male Study Subjects

Age	Original Population *	No. Reduced	Study Group B (Reduction Population)	Percent of Sample
21–30	120	6	114	39.9
31–40	111	2	109	38.1
41–50	42	4	38	13.3
51–60	19	5	14	4.9
61–70	14	3	11	3.8
71–80	4	4	0	0
81–90	2	2	0	0
Total	312	26	286	100
				(1957–1965)

* Reported in Masters and Johnson (1966), p. 13.

TABLE 2-2

Study Group B (Reduction Table): Female Study Subjects

Age	Original Population *	No. Reduced	Study Group B (Reduction Population)	Percent of Sample
18–20	2	1	1	0.4
21–30	182	41	141	50.2
31–40	137	32	105	37.4
41–50	27	12	15	5.3
51–60	23	8	15	5.3
61–70	8	4	4	1.4
71–80	3	3	0	0
Total	382	101	281	100
				(1957–1965)

* Reported in Masters and Johnson (1966), p. 13.

ciency returned by heterosexual study group A. The final column
indicates the percentages of study subjects in each decade of age
grouping that made up the final total of 286 men and 281 women
who comprise the adjusted heterosexual study group (study
group B).

Since the standards for selection of the homosexual group and
heterosexual study group A were the same as those used for the
selection of the original heterosexual research population, study
group B, the reduced group, derived from the original heterosexual research population, should be comparable to the homosexual group and study group A in terms of age and educational
standards despite the reduction process described above. Statistical
comparisons between the three major study groups will be presented in Chapter 10.

The formal education levels for the men in study group B are
reported in Table 2-3. The 83.6 percent total of college or post-

TABLE 2-3

*Study Group B: Formal Education in
Male Study Subjects. (N = 286)*

Age	No.	High School *	College *	Postgraduate *
21–30	114	22	47	45
31–40	109	19	40	50
41–50	38	5	16	17
51–60	14	0	6	8
61–70	11	1	8	2
Total	286	47 (16.4%)	117 (40.9%)	122 (42.7%)
				(1957–1965)

* Listing dependent only upon matriculation (highest level).

graduate matriculation for male study subjects in study group B is
the highest of the three study groups, but the other two study
populations are quite comparable (82.0 percent for the male homosexual subjects and 79.0 percent for men in heterosexual study
group A) (see Tables 3-4 and 3-12, Chapter 3).

The levels of formal education for the heterosexual women

selected in the reduced female population (study group B) are reported in Table 2-4. There was a 61.9 percent level of college and postgraduate matriculation. These statistics are parallel to those of women in the homosexual group (67.1 percent) and study group A (70.2 percent) (Tables 3-9 and 3-15, Chapter 3), and they are essentially within the research team's original recruitment stan-

TABLE 2-4

Study Group B: Formal Education in
Female Study Subjects $(N = 281)$

Age	No.	High School *	College *	Postgraduate *
18–20	1	1	0	0
21–30	141	45	69	27
31–40	105	42	43	20
41–50	15	6	7	2
51–60	15	11	3	1
61–70	4	2	2	0
Total	281	107 (38.1%)	124 (44.1%)	50 (17.8%)
				(1957–1965)

* Listing dependent only upon matriculation (highest level).

dards of 60 to 70 percent college matriculation set for female study subjects. Obviously, the women in study group B had the lowest percentage of college matriculation among the three female research populations despite every effort of the research team to recruit women with advanced educational backgrounds. But these women volunteered to cooperate with the research from 1957 to 1965, while the other two groups were organized between 1964 and 1968. This gap of almost a decade in the recruiting of the first as compared to the last two study-subject populations might explain the increase in availability of female college matriculators for the last two groups.

SUMMARY

In this chapter there has been a discussion of the problems and screening techniques involved with establishing the homosexual research population. In addition, background material required to evaluate the comparability of the two heterosexual research populations, not only with each other, but also with the homosexual study group, has been reported. By following standards established in the ultimate composition of heterosexual study group B, the two study groups form comparable populations. Statistical analysis of group composition is reported in Chapter 10. There is an obvious bias in the level of formal education established for all the research groups. The reasons this bias was established in the original heterosexual research population have been given; the rationale for maintaining the bias so that significant statistical comparisons ultimately might be drawn between all subsequently recruited groups is apparent. Other variables, such as religion, socioeconomic status, occupation, and regional differences, were not fully investigated and are thus precluded from the analyses.

3

SELECTED STUDY GROUPS

Data regarding the homosexual study group and heterosexual study group A will be presented in table form and discussed in this chapter. The criteria for selection described in Chapter 2, the age distribution, Kinsey preference ratings, and formal educational levels will be reported, along with medical data and marriage and conception histories. A description of background material from the ambisexual study group is reported in Chapter 8.

THE HOMOSEXUAL STUDY GROUP

There were a total of 176 study subjects in the homosexual study group. The majority of the homosexual subjects were recruited from large metropolitan centers or smaller academic communities outside the St. Louis area.

Ninety-four male homosexual study subjects were evaluated in the research project (Table 3-1). Eighty-four of the men were involved in committed relationships composing 42 couples. Eleven of the committed relationships were over 10 years in duration, and an additional 14 couples had been together more than five years.

The 10 uncommitted male subjects were chosen because they reported lifestyles that evidenced no significant current emotional involvement with a sexual partner. Five of these men cruised the local gay bars, public toilets, or other known public meeting places in search of casual sexual partners. None of the 10 homosexual men reported a homosexual or heterosexual relationship that lasted more than three months, nor did they express interest in any long-term

TABLE 3-1

Homosexual Study: Selection of
Male Study Subjects $(N = 94)$

Age	No. of Subjects			Percent of Sample
	Screened	Interviewed	Selected	
21–30	104	62	33	35.1
31–40	81	61	48	51.0
41–50	18	14	12	12.8
51–60	5	3	1	1.1
61–70	1	1	0	0
71–80	1	1	0	0
Total	210	142	94	100

(1964–1968)

commitment. According to their description, they interacted with partners primarily for sexual satisfaction.

Three of the uncommitted study subjects agreed to be tested with more than one partner in the laboratory. One man was separately assigned to three partners on different occasions, and 2 men were assigned two partners each. The seven assigned couples formed by these 10 study subjects were added to the 42 committed couples for a total of 49 male homosexual couples interacting in the laboratory (Table 3-2).

TABLE 3-2

Homosexual Study: Couples Among Male Study Subjects
$(N = 94;$ *Male Couples,* $N = 49)$

84 study subjects as *committed* partners	42 couples
1 study subject (A) with 3 *assigned* partners	3 couples
1 study subject (B) with 2 *assigned* partners	2 couples
1 study subject (C) with 2 *assigned* partners	2 couples
Total	49 couples

(1964–1968)

The age distribution for the male subjects was from 21 to 54 years, with the highest concentration in the 31–40-year age bracket (see Table 3-1). Kinsey ratings from 1 to 6 were represented, as planned, with the greatest concentration in the 3, 5, and 6 categories (Table 3-3). The study subjects represented a matriculation dis-

TABLE 3-3

Homosexual Study: Kinsey Classification of Sexual Preference in Male Study Subjects (N = 94)

Age	\multicolumn{8}{c}{Kinsey Scale}						
	0	1	2	3	4	5	6	Total
21–30	0	0	6	9	5	5	8	33
31–40	0	2	5	8	8	15	10	48
41–50	0	2	0	3	0	4	3	12
51–60	0	0	0	0	0	0	1	1
Total	0	4	11	20	13	24	22	94
	(0%)		(11.7%)		(13.8%)		(23.4%)	
		(4.3%)		(21.3%)		(25.5%)		(100%)

(1964–1968)

tribution of 18.0 percent high-school, 41.5 percent college, and 40.5 percent postgraduate levels (Table 3-4).

TABLE 3-4

Homosexual Study: Formal Education in Male Study Subjects (N = 94)

Age	No.	High School *	College *	Postgraduate *
21–30	35	6	14	15
31–40	47	8	20	19
41–50	11	3	4	4
51–60	1	0	1	0
Total	94	17 (18.0%)	39 (41.5%)	38 (40.5%)

(1964–1968)

* Listing dependent only upon matriculation (highest level).

There was little genitourinary pathology identified in the male homosexual population (Table 3-5). Two volunteers had benign

TABLE 3-5

Homosexual Study: Genitourinary Pathology in Male Study Subjects ($N = 94$)

Findings	Age Group Distribution			
	21–30	31–40	41–50	51–60
Pathology				
Benign prostatic hypertrophy	0	0	1	1
Inguinal hernia (symptomatic)	0	1	0	0
History of gonorrhea	7	4	1	0
Additional data				
Uncircumcised penis	3	3	1	1
				(1964–1968)

prostatic hypertrophy, and 1 other study subject had a symptomatic inguinal hernia. Eight men were uncircumcised.

Twelve cases of gonorrhea had been previously diagnosed and apparently treated effectively in 10 of the 94 men in the homosexual population. Each of 2 men treated twice for gonorrhea reported being infected once in homosexual and once in heterosexual activity.

Eighty-two female study subjects were accepted for laboratory evaluation, including 76 women who were involved in committed relationships forming 38 committed couples. The age range was from 20 to 54, with the highest concentration being in the 21–30-year age bracket (Table 3-6).

There were 6 uncommitted women who, like the uncommitted males, were not currently interested in long-term relationships. One study subject had been involved in a lesbian relationship of six months' duration that had ended more than two years before the homosexual research program began. Three uncommitted female study subjects sought casual sexual partners through frequenting gay bars and joining activist groups. They described their sexual interactions as being primarily for tension release. There was a his-

TABLE 3-6

Homosexual Study: Selection of
Female Study Subjects $(N = 82)$

Age	No. of Subjects			Percent of Sample
	Screened	Interviewed	Selected	
18–20	5	4	1	1.2
21–30	72	54	37	45.1
31–40	68	41	31	37.8
41–50	17	14	10	12.2
51–60	3	3	3	3.7
61–70	1	1	0	0
71–80	1	1	0	0
Total	167	118	82	100
				(1964–1968)

tory of only one episode of heterosexual interaction for 1 study subject in the six months prior to the recruitment period.

Two of the uncommitted women interacted with 2 different assigned partners, forming 4 assigned couples. These, combined with the 38 committed pairs, totaled 42 homosexual female couples evaluated in the laboratory (Table 3-7).

All Kinsey ratings were represented, with highest concentrations being in the 3, 4, and 6 categories (Table 3-8). The female study

TABLE 3-7

Homosexual Study: Couples Among Female Study Subjects
$(N = 82; $ *Female Couples,* $N = 42)$

76 study subjects as *committed* partners	38 couples
1 study subject (D) with 2 *assigned* partners	2 couples
1 study subject (E) with 2 *assigned* partners	2 couples
Total	42 couples
	(1964–1968)

subjects represented a matriculation distribution of 32.9 percent high-school, 51.2 percent college, and 15.9 percent postgraduate levels (Table 3-9).

TABLE 3-8

Homosexual Study: Kinsey Classification of Sexual Preference in Female Study Subjects (N = 82)

Age	Kinsey Scale							Total
	0	1	2	3	4	5	6	
18–20	0	0	0	0	1	0	0	1
21–30	0	0	5	12	10	4	6	37
31–40	0	2	5	6	6	5	6	30
41–50	0	1	1	2	1	2	4	11
51–60	0	0	0	0	0	1	2	3
Total	0	3	11	20	18	12	18	82
	(0%)	(3.6%)	(13.4%)	(24.4%)	(22.0%)	(14.6%)	(22.0%)	(100%)

(1964–1968)

TABLE 3-9

Homosexual Study: Formal Education in Female Study Subjects (N = 82)

Age	No.	High School *	College *	Postgraduate *
18–20	1	1	0	0
21–30	38	11	20	7
31–40	30	8	17	5
41–50	10	5	4	1
51–60	3	2	1	0
Total	82	27 (32.9%)	42 (51.2%)	13 (15.9%)

(1964–1968)

* Listing dependent only upon matriculation (highest level).

The recorded pelvic pathology in the female population was minimal (Table 3-10). The cystoceles, urethroceles, and rectoceles were apparent at routine physical examination. The women with these findings of poor pelvic support had conceived and delivered full-term pregnancies. In 1 woman, the cystourethrocele and rectocele were symptomatic. Four women had undergone hysterec-

TABLE 3-10

Homosexual Study: Pelvic Pathology in
Female Study Subjects $(N = 82)$

Findings	Age Group Distribution				
	18–20	21–30	31–40	41–50	51–60
Cystocele	0	2	3	1	0
Urethrocele	0	2	2	1	0
Rectocele	0	1	2	1	0
Hysterectomy	0	0	1	2	1
Myomatous uterus	0	0	1	1	0
Pelvic and labial varicosities	0	0	1	0	0
Pelvic endometriosis	0	0	1	0	0
History of gonorrhea	0	2	2	0	0
				(1964–1968)	

tomies; in 1 of these women the ovaries were removed. Two women were found to have myomatous uteri at the time of physical examination prior to acceptance as study subjects.

One woman had pelvic and labial varicosities that became markedly engorged during sexual activity. There was also one case of asymptomatic endometriosis that was an incidental finding. Gonorrhea had been previously diagnosed and treated in 4 of the women. Three of these women described being infected during heterosexual activity. The fourth woman, classified a Kinsey 6, had had numerous female sexual partners and was not sure of the source of her infection, although she specifically denied having had any sexual activity with a man.

HETEROSEXUAL STUDY GROUP A

The heterosexual study group A was formed by 50 married and 7 assigned couples. Eleven of the 50 married couples were from outside the local area. All of the uncommitted heterosexual study subjects were from St. Louis.

The age range of the male study subjects was from 21 to 57 years, with the highest concentration being in the 31–40-year age group (Table 3-11). Except for 1 man rated as a Kinsey 1, no heterosexual study subjects of either sex were rated higher than Kinsey 0. The Kinsey 1 man reported no homosexual experience in the two years previous to the research project. The study subjects represented a matriculation distribution of 21.0 percent high-school, 35.1 percent college, and 43.9 percent postgraduate levels (Table 3-12).

TABLE 3-1 1

Heterosexual Study Group A: Selection of Male Study Subjects
(N = 57; Married, N = 50; Assigned, N = 7)

| Age | No. of Subjects | | | Percent of Sample |
	Screened	Interviewed	Selected	
21–30	44	29	17	29.8
31–40	49	37	30	52.6
41–50	15	11	8	14.0
51–60	6	4	2	3.5
Total	114	81	57	100

(1967–1968)

TABLE 3-1 2

Heterosexual Study Group A: Formal Education in
Male Study Subjects (N = 57)

Age	No.	High School *	College *	Postgraduate *
21–30	17	3	6	8
31–40	30	6	9	15
41–50	8	2	4	2
51–60	2	1	1	0
Total	57	12 (21.0%)	20 (35.1%)	25 (43.9%)

(1967–1968)

* Listing dependent only upon matriculation (highest level).

There was little male genitourinary pathology in study group A (Table 3-13). One instance of prostatic hypertrophy without

TABLE 3-13

Heterosexual Study Group A: Genitourinary Pathology in Male Study Subjects (N = 57)

Findings	Age Group Distribution			
	21–30	31–40	41–50	51–60
Pathology				
Benign prostatic hypertrophy	0	0	0	1
Inguinal hernia	0	1	1	0
History of gonorrhea	2	2	3	0
History of syphilis	1	0	0	0
Additional data				
Uncircumcised penis	0	1	1	0

(1967–1968)

symptoms was identified at physical examination, and there were two asymptomatic inguinal hernias. Seven cases of gonorrhea and one of syphilis (all previously treated with apparent success) were identified in the male study subjects at history-taking. Only 2 of the men, both married, were uncircumcised.

The youngest female volunteer selected was 21 years old, and the oldest, 56 years (Table 3-14). As would be expected, there was

TABLE 3-14

Heterosexual Study Group A: Selection of Female Study Subjects (N = 57; Married, N = 50; Assigned, N = 7)

Age	No. of Subjects			Percent of Sample
	Screened	Interviewed	Selected	
21–30	46	32	27	47.4
31–40	52	39	23	40.3
41–50	17	13	6	10.5
51–60	6	4	1	1.8
Total	121	88	57	100

(1967–1968)

an increased concentration of women in their twenties when compared to the age range in the male population. The study subjects represented a matriculation distribution of 29.8 percent high-school, 45.6 percent college, and 24.6 percent postgraduate levels (Table 3-15).

TABLE 3-15

Heterosexual Study Group A: Formal Education in Female Study Subjects (N = 57)

Age	No.	High School *	College *	Postgraduate *
21–30	27	7	12	8
31–40	23	7	11	5
41–50	6	3	2	1
51–60	1	0	1	0
Total	57	17 (29.8%)	26 (45.6%)	14 (24.6%)
				(1967–1968)

* Listing dependent only upon matriculation (highest level).

As was true for their male counterparts, there were very few instances of pelvic pathology identified at physical examination for the 57 women in heterosexual study group A (Table 3-16). There

TABLE 3-16

Heterosexual Study Group A: Pelvic Pathology in Female Study Subjects (N = 57)

Findings	Age Group Distribution			
	21–30	31–40	41–50	51–60
Pathology				
Urethrocele	1	1	0	0
Cystocele	1	2	1	0
Rectocele	1	1	1	0
Hysterectomy	0	0	1	1
Pelvic labial varicosities	0	2	2	1
Cervical lacerations	1	1	0	0
History of gonorrhea	2	2	0	0
				(1967–1968)

were two urethroceles, four cystoceles, and three rectoceles noted. One woman with all three pelvic hernias was symptomatic but not significantly distressed. Two women had undergone hysterectomies. In both instances the ovaries were retained. There were five instances of pelvic or labial varicosities. Two women evidenced badly lacerated cervices from childbirth injury. There were four reported cases of gonorrhea, apparently successfully treated.

MINORITY GROUP REPRESENTATION

Attempts to recruit black male homosexual couples as study subjects were unsuccessful. There was, however, 1 committed black lesbian couple in the female homosexual population. Both women were Kinsey 6 in sexual preference, 1 in the 21–30-year age group and 1 in the 31–40-year age group.

Efforts to recruit committed black heterosexual couples were only partially successful. Three of the committed couples in study group A were black. In 2 of the black couples, both partners had high school educations, while the third black couple had a postgraduate level of formal education for the husband and full college training for the wife. There was 1 Spanish-American married couple. Both partners had matriculated to high school.

Although there were only a few minority group committed couples, none of the homosexual or heterosexual men or women in the assigned study-subject populations were from a minority group.

MARRIAGE AND CONCEPTION
HISTORIES

The most significant contrast between the homosexual group and heterosexual study group A is in the pregnancy and presumed impregnation histories for female and male study subjects. As expected, the marriage and conception rates were significantly higher for study group A than for the homosexual group. There were 26 marriages and 33 conceptions for the 82 homosexual women (Table 3-17) as compared to the 66 marriages and 81 conceptions for the 57 heterosexual women (Table 3-18). The 94 homosexual men re-

---

TABLE 3-17

Homosexual Study: Combined Marital and Pregnancy History in Female Study Subjects (N = 82)

	Age Group Distribution					
	18–20	21–30	31–40	41–50	51–60	Total
Number of study subjects	1	37	31	10	3	82
Number of marriages	0	11	9	5	1	26
Conception history						
Conception	1	13	14	5	0	33
Full-term or premature delivery	0	8	10	3	0	21
Miscarriage	0	1	0	0	0	1
Abortion	1	4	4	2	0	11

(1964–1968)

TABLE 3-18

Heterosexual Study Group A: Combined Marital and Pregnancy History in Female Study Subjects (N = 57)

	Age Group Distribution				
	21–30	31–40	41–50	51–60	Total
Number of study subjects	27	23	6	1	57
Number of marriages	30	28	7	1	66
Conception history					
Conception	26	46	9	0	81
Full-term or premature delivery	17	40	8	0	65
Miscarriage	1	2	0	0	3
Abortion	8	4	1	0	13

(1967–1968)

ported 15 marriages and 11 presumed conceptions (Table 3-19) as compared to 72 marriages and 93 presumed conceptions for the 57 heterosexual men (Table 3-20).

It is important to emphasize that, despite widespread public assumption that individuals with homosexual orientation are not in-

TABLE 3-19
Homosexual Study: Combined Marital and Presumed Impregnation
History in Male Study Subjects (N = 94)

	Age Group Distribution				
	21–30	31–40	41–50	51–60	Total
Number of study subjects	33	48	12	1	94
Number of marriages	4	9	2	0	15
Conception history					
Presumed conception	4	6	1	0	11
Full-term delivery	2	4	1	0	7
Miscarriage	0	0	0	0	0
Abortion	2	2	0	0	4
					(1964–1968)

TABLE 3-20

Heterosexual Study Group A: Combined Marital and Presumed
Impregnation History in Male Study Subjects (N = 57)

	Age Group Distribution				
	21–30	31–40	41–50	51–60	Total
Number of study subjects	17	30	8	2	57
Number of marriages	19	38	12	3	72
Conception history					
Presumed conception	16	59	13	5	93
Full-term or premature delivery	14	50	9	4	77
Miscarriage	0	1	0	0	1
Abortion	2	8	4	1	15
					(1967–1968)

volved with such matters, marriage and reproduction were important factors in the lives of the homosexual study subject population. In order to emphasize this, the marriage and conception histories of the homosexual study subjects will be reported in greater detail than those of the heterosexual population.

HOMOSEXUAL STUDY GROUP: MARRIAGE
AND CONCEPTION HISTORIES

The one female study subject in the 18–20-year age group classification conceived at 17 and voluntarily aborted at approximately three months' gestation. Of the 37 study subjects in the 21–30-year age group category, 11 had been married (see Table 3-17). Nine of the women in this age category achieved 13 known conceptions that terminated in eight full-term or premature deliveries, one miscarriage, and four abortions (three voluntary, one involuntary). No woman in this age group described more than two conceptions.

The most interesting history was that of a study subject who reported that she had been married, achieved one full-term pregnancy, had one miscarriage at five months and yet insisted that she had had intercourse only five times in her life and, as a result, was classified as a Kinsey 5. She had the frequently encountered history of having a husband "not interested in sex" and gravitated to homosexuality originally as a means of sexual release. In time, she divorced and established a committed homosexual relationship; the child, a girl, was welcomed into the lesbian couple's stable social community.

There were 31 study subjects in the 31–40-year age group, of whom 9 had been married. Ten of the women in this group reported 14 pregnancy histories, from which there were eight full-term deliveries, two premature deliveries, and four voluntary abortions. It is interesting to note that of the 9 married women in this group, 1 had three children and another had two children and one abortion; yet both of these women had been so involved in homosexual activity before, during, and after their marriages that their sexual preference was classified as high as Kinsey 2 and Kinsey 3, respectively. The remaining eight pregnancies were described as single conceptions. One Kinsey 4 unmarried woman in this 31–40-year age group conceived, carried to term, delivered, and placed the baby for adoption.

Of the 10 individuals in the 41–50-year age group, 5 had married and 3 had conception histories that totaled three full-term deliveries and two voluntary abortions. Finally, of the 3 women in the 51–60-year age group, 1 woman (Kinsey 5) had married (the marriage lasted only three days), but there was no history of conception.

It is interesting that following the 21 full-term or premature deliveries among the 82 women in the homosexual population, there was only one attempt to breastfeed. This nursing effort was discontinued after approximately two weeks because, as the woman reported, she "didn't like it." Apparently there was no difficulty in milk production.

Although the number of marriages seems high for subjects of a homosexual research program, seven of the 26 marital commitments were brief, lasting six months or less. The longest marriage was recorded at 13 years (Kinsey 1). Two marriages were common-law in character (five years in duration) and were listed as marriages for statistical purposes; 1 of these women was classified as Kinsey 2 and 1 as Kinsey 3 in sexual preference.

In the male homosexual population there were 15 reported marriages among the 94 study subjects (Table 3-19). Three subjects who had been married were rated as Kinsey 1, 6 as Kinsey 2, 4 as Kinsey 3, and one each as Kinsey 4 and Kinsey 5. The most long-lived marriage, that of a 46-year-old Kinsey 1, lasted for 17 years, and the shortest, that of a Kinsey 5, lasted one week.

There were 11 presumed impregnations for the entire male study-subject group. Seven ended as full-term deliveries, and four ended in abortions. Five of the term pregnancies occurred within marriages, as did two involuntary abortions. Two voluntary abortions and the other two full-term pregnancies were reported by study subjects who had never married, but who were convinced that they had been responsible for the pregnancies.

The marriage and reported impregnation statistics of the male homosexual population may have some interesting implications, but the material must be evaluated with caution because records of reported marriages, conceptions, deliveries, and abortions do not provide all the pertinent facts necessary to suggest more than tentative conclusions. Of particular interest, however, is the strong suggestion of lower than normal fertility in the male homosexual study subject population. As stated above, there were eleven reported conceptions for the entire homosexual male study-subject group, seven ending as full-term deliveries and four as abortions. Two of the marriages, one of a Kinsey 1 subject and the other of a Kinsey 2, accounted for four of the full-term pregnancies and one involuntary abortion. Thus, only three full-term pregnancies, two voluntary abortions, and one involuntary abortion were reported from the remaining 92 members of the male homosexual study population.

From the viewpoint of fertility, this material stimulates one's curiosity. In order to reduce the possibly confounding influence of the male homosexual study-subjects' low incidence of heterosexual coitus, the total of 46 Kinsey 5 and Kinsey 6 male study subjects (see Table 3-3) whose heterosexual experience was minimal or absent was arbitrarily eliminated from conceptive consideration. There remained a total of eleven conceptions reported by 48 men with ratings of Kinsey 1 through 4. Two study subjects accounted for five of these eleven reported conceptions, leaving only six presumed conceptions among the remaining 46 homosexual male study subjects.

There are many relevant factors not accounted for in these simple marriage and conception figures. Use of contraceptive techniques, female partners' fertility status, conceptions of which male subjects were unaware, and conceptions for which they received false credit are but a few of the factors that would prevent any firm conclusions being drawn about the homosexual male subjects' fertility levels. Perhaps most important of all would be a means of assessing the rate of fertility in those homosexual men who genuinely desired to father a child; regrettably, data on this topic were not collected systematically. But the overall impression remains that a possibility exists that there may be a relatively low level of fertility in the male homosexual population.

Only implications can be drawn from the low conceptive incidence in the small reported sample. A detailed fertility study was not done on either the male or female homosexual study-subject population. Research attention was directed elsewhere, so suggestions of reduced male fertility have been drawn retrospectively. Probably the only contention that could be supported from the statistics available is that there is enough clinical evidence to make a well-planned investigation of this subject of homosexual male infertility worthwhile. In a small subgroup of homosexual men studied at the Institute several years after this work was completed, it was noted that lowered sperm counts were seen in a significant fraction of the group (Kolodny et al., 1971).

HETEROSEXUAL STUDY GROUP: MARRIAGE AND CONCEPTION HISTORIES

The 57 heterosexual women reported 66 marriages and 81 conceptions (see Table 3-18). The 57 heterosexual men reported 72 marriages and 93 conceptions (see Table 3-20). When impregnation histories provided by the 50 married men and the 7 uncommitted men are compared to the pregnancy histories of their female counterparts, it is interesting that the 57 men reported a presumed conception number of 93 while the 57 women identified 81 conceptions. This discrepancy is explained to some extent by the total of 72 marriages for the men as compared to 66 for the women. Also to be taken into account is the somewhat older age of the male population, allowing more opportunity for impregnation in other relationships. Also, 8 of the 57 women had no positive conception histories, compared to 5 of 57 men.

Of interest is the group of 7 heterosexual men and 7 heterosexual women who cooperated as assigned couples in study group A. None of these men and women were married at the time of their laboratory participation, but there were histories of six prior marriages for the men (1 man had been divorced twice) and four prior marriages for the women. Although they were without acknowledged commitment at the time of their participation in the research program, only 2 men and 1 woman took the position that as of the present they were ruling out any interest in a permanent relationship. Each of the 7 men and 7 women stated that they previously had been fully responsive sexually to the various types of sexual stimulation that were to be employed during their period of laboratory interaction. Their only expressed concerns were for their own physical attractiveness or for that of their assigned partner-to-be.

SUMMARY

The compositions of the homosexual study group and heterosexual study group A have been discussed and charted in some depth in this chapter. With the addition of the discussion of the reduction process by which the original heterosexual research group became study group B (see Chapter 2), three of the Institute's four basic research populations have been described. These study groups will be used to illustrate homosexual men and women's facility of sexual response in a laboratory setting in comparison to that of statistically comparable heterosexual research populations. Further, these study groups provide a unique opportunity for immediate comparison of the sexual physiology and sexual behavior of men and women of homosexual and heterosexual orientations. Finally, from these homosexual and heterosexual study groups, comparisons can be drawn to the ambisexual study population—the fourth basic research population—reported in Chapter 8.

4

STUDY SUBJECTS IN THE LABORATORY

There are many technical problems involved in conducting a research program dealing with the basic physiologic and psychosexual aspects of human sexuality. In part the success of the project depended upon meeting the emotional needs of the men and women participating in such a controversial research program. For example, meticulous scheduling arrangements led to effective security, which in turn provided the individual study subject with the psychosocial support so necessary to the success of the project.

Anxious homosexual couples and older men and women of each of the alternative lifestyles usually needed a great deal of reassurance about confidentiality, but once the security measures proved effective, the concerned parties cooperated with the research program without restraint. It is of inestimable importance for the research staff to maintain a consistently professional atmosphere in all interaction with study subjects so that these men and women may feel free to express themselves in as spontaneous a way as possible both in response to sexual stimuli and to questioning during interviews. Perhaps most important to research productivity was the decade of prior experience, which enabled the research team to contribute more effectively to the study subjects' general sense of comfort in the laboratory environment. Such a sense of comfort was not only a vital factor in effective recording of physiologic processes, it also improved the facility and frequently the integrity of study-subject interrogation.

An attempt has been made to describe procedural problems that arose during the research programs. The anxieties and concerns of both researchers and study subjects are emphasized. The laboratory

45

setting is described and concerns for privacy discussed along with details of the acclimation process requested by many members of the study groups. Finally, brief histories are presented of those homosexuals requesting exemption from standard laboratory procedures.

S C H E D U L I N G

A problem that persisted despite many efforts at resolution was that of scheduling homosexual partners for sexual interaction in the laboratory. Appointments for heterosexual subjects were far more easily arranged, since most of them lived in the local geographical area, but there were many complicating factors for the homosexual study subjects, particularly committed couples, most of whom lived far from St. Louis. Transitory illness, unforeseen business or professional demands, menstrual periods, important social engagements, children, and air-travel mix-ups were but a few of the problems faced in scheduling laboratory commitments for homosexual study subjects.

Without the almost unlimited cooperation of the large number of men and women who volunteered as study subjects in all categories of sexual orientation, the investigation could not have been conducted. The study subjects' willingness to make last-minute scheduling changes, patience with scheduling errors, and consistently high degrees of cooperation were constant sources of encouragement for the research team.

During the evaluation of the homosexual study subjects, observations usually were conducted on Friday nights, Saturday afternoons and evenings, and Sunday mornings. This concentration on weekend investigative sessions was designed for the convenience of both the study subjects and the researchers. Weekend scheduling provided both travel time and adequate opportunity for full cooperation by the study subjects without interfering with their normal work demands. Weekend timing also made Monday through Friday of each week available to the researchers for other professional commitments. For example, during the last two years of the homosexual investigation (1967 and 1968), weekdays and evenings were devoted to evaluating heterosexual study group A.

STUDY-SUBJECT POPULATION

Over the 14-year period from 1957 through 1970, a combined total of 1,076 men and women appeared at least once as a study subject in the laboratory. The vast majority of study subjects participated in laboratory evaluation on a number of occasions within the same project. There were 415 committed couples who participated in one or another of the various Institute projects. Assigned couples have not been totaled, since a number of men and women worked with more than one assigned partner within a project. The remainder of the study subjects were committed to research projects that did not require couple participation. These projects included such diverse interests as evaluation of intravaginal chemical contraceptives (Johnson and Masters, 1962; Johnson *et al.*, 1970) and the physiology of the artificial vagina (Masters and Johnson, 1961).

For the reader's convenience, Table 4-1 lists the number of men and women who functioned in the various study groups and the years the groups were activated. No man or woman ever was recruited to become a member of more than one study population. In addition, it is important to realize that patients of the Institute have never been observed in the physiology laboratory during any phase of their evaluation or care.

STUDY-SUBJECT CONCERNS

Problems inevitably have arisen during the volunteers' episodes of cooperation in the laboratory. It is difficult to assign a priority to the problems because the multiple psychosocial implications of a controversial research program inevitably magnify minor concerns into major crises, at least in the eyes of the research subject.

The two most frequently expressed concerns have been those of fears for sexual performance and fears of identification as a study subject. Other fears, such as concern for personal attractiveness to the partner, occurred on a less frequent basis. Obviously the presence of these inhibiting factors was also cause for research team anxiety.

TABLE 4-1

Study Subjects in the Laboratory, 1957–1970

Study Group	Male	Female	Committed Couples
I. Original heterosexual study group * (1957–1965)	312	382	276
II. Heterosexual study group A (1967–1968)	57	57	50
III. Homosexual study group (1964–1968)	94	82	42 (male) 38 (female)
IV. Ambisexual study group (1968–1970)	6	6	0
Assigned partners (heterosexual) †	8	14	...
Assigned partners (homosexual) †	11	13	...
Rectal intercourse group ‡			
Heterosexual	7	7	4
Homosexual	10	0	2
Dildo usage group ‡			
Heterosexual	1	3	1
Homosexual	0	6	2
Total	506	570	415

NOTE: No study subject ever participated in more than one study group.

* This population was reduced to form study group B in order to compare the originally collected data with that of study group A and the homosexual study group (see Chapter 2).

† Assigned to ambisexual partners only.

‡ Small groups assembled for the purposes of these limited investigations.

Protection from personal identification as a research subject was a constant source of anxiety. This concern was most frequently expressed by the homosexual couples, specifically by older men or women, but almost as frequently by heterosexual and ambisexual study subjects.

Security measures for protection of the cooperating personnel and for the research records have been of paramount importance since the initial investigations of heterosexual physiology were conducted during the decade of the 1950s. Even though the homosexual investigative programs originated in the 1960s, the security problems were more severe; in fact, security concerns were significantly in-

creased, not only for the homosexual and ambisexual study subjects involved in the research project, but for Institute personnel as well.

As was explained to every potential study subject, there is no such thing as guaranteed protection from identification. Each individual, however, was assured that every effort would be made to protect his or her anonymity not only while they cooperated with the Institute's research programs, but for the future as well.

As a routine security measure, research records have always been carefully isolated. Episodes of sexual interaction in the laboratory usually were reserved for the late evening or early morning hours or for weekends, and laboratory personnel were severely restricted in number. In short, many security techniques were utilized, most of which will not be discussed in order to preserve their effectiveness for the future. To the research team's knowledge, of the hundreds of men and women involved as study subjects in the research projects, only 6 have been openly identified as having participated in Institute programs, and in each instance, the decision to be identified as a study subject was made by the individuals themselves. Of course, many others living at long distances may have discussed participation in the research programs with friends or relatives without the research team being aware of these breaks in security; but it is also true that persons have claimed participation in Institute programs that never took place, further complicating the issue.

Fears of performance have been expressed by study subjects in dozens of different ways during the years of laboratory investigation. Such anxieties were expressed by both committed and assigned pairs. One note of interest is that during the late 1950s by far the largest number of vocalized performance concerns came from the male study subjects, but during the investigations of the mid-1960s, the female participants were beginning to become as concerned about effectiveness of performance as the men. The population without apparent concern in this area was the ambisexual study group, none of whom ever verbalized any concern for performance.

This anxiety over study subjects' sexual performance was shared by the research team. It was anticipated that there might be problems of satisfactory function in private arising from failure to function effectively in the laboratory, but, in fact, such problems never materialized. Despite anxieties that may have been initially expressed, the few men and women who failed to function effectively on a specific occasion in the laboratory, with one exception (Chapters 6 and 11) never evidenced serious concern during or after the failure episodes, nor did they report any functional repercussions in their private lives. They simply explained their ineffective performance by saying, "I was tired," "I just couldn't get involved," or "It wasn't my day," and moved into the next opportunity with confidence and success.

Successful sexual experience does breed confidence. It would indeed be rare for a sexually active man or woman to reach 60 years of age with a perfect score in sexual performance. The rare episode of failure to function effectively did not seem to bother sexually experienced individuals significantly. The men and women who cooperated with the Institute's research projects had significant sexual experience and seemed reasonably comfortable with their rare episodes of failure.

Usually it is relatively inexperienced men and women who allow a single episode of functional failure to build into crippling fears of sexual performance. If ever there was reason to support the concept that only sexually experienced men and women should be invited to participate in evaluation of sexual function in a laboratory setting, it is the fact that a depth of experience tends to lend comfort and objectivity to a failure episode. The functional efficiency of the study subject is discussed in detail in Chapter 6.

Concern over one's personal attractiveness as viewed by the partner was expressed frequently by male and female study subjects in both homosexual and heterosexual assigned relationships. These individuals with expressed concern for personal attractiveness frequently needed reassurance from their partners. Men and women in committed relationships rarely expressed such fears.

Occasionally concerns were expressed on the opposite side of the coin: Would the assigned partner be attractive? Would there be time to become comfortable personally with the previously unknown partner before sexual interaction? Would the partner be too demanding or too restrained or not cooperative enough sexually? These fears, like those for personal attractiveness, were verbalized primarily by assigned partners and seemed to be at least partially neutralized by the act of communicating them to the research team.

An anticipated complication of the research program was the possibility of study-subject exhibitionism. Although there is an undeniable element of exhibitionism inherent in volunteering for such studies, there has been no overt display of exhibitionism in any Institute research program. Dressing and toilet privacy were routinely maintained without incident, and there simply was no advantage taken of the occasions of nudity that were the inevitable by-products of any investigation of human sexual physiology. Every courtesy always was extended to the assigned partner, and married couples inevitably conducted themselves in a circumspect manner.

Assigned subjects voiced occasional concern about the risk of contracting venereal disease via their laboratory exposure, but this concern was minimized by use of appropriate screening procedures.

Finally, the anticipated problem of study subjects attempting social interchange with members of the research team should be mentioned. Again research-team anxieties proved unwarranted. No sense of real or implied intimacy was ever acted out or even suggested in verbal or nonverbal communication between study subjects and members of the research team. The chaperonage inherent in the composition of a male-female research team was ideal in preventing any such complications and in creating a sense of comfort and confidence on the part of the study subjects.

As an integral part of the dual-sex research-team function, psychosexual histories were taken by each member of the research team. Physical examinations of potential male and female study subjects were always chaperoned. But most important, no form of sexual activity was requested of a study subject in the laboratory, with or without a partner, unless both members of the research team were present. The exception to this statement was when an individual study subject or a couple was given the opportunity to respond sexually in the laboratory in private during their requested acclimation opportunity. Without this protective umbrella of a combination of chaperonage and professional support, many study subjects might have been handicapped in their freedom and confidence to express themselves sexually in a laboratory environment.

THE LABORATORY

The laboratory in which the homosexual study group, heterosexual study group A, and the ambisexual study group were evaluated was essentially the same in equipment and furnishings as that
established almost a decade earlier for the investigation of the original heterosexual study group. Before the newer research groups were
evaluated, the decision was made to use the same type of recording
equipment for the investigation of physiologic response that was
used a decade previously. It was anticipated that existing data from
the original heterosexual study group * would be compared with
data from the newly constituted study groups; therefore maintenance of reasonable equality in recording capacity seemed indicated
in the interest of research objectivity.

The temperature in the laboratory was maintained at approximately 78 degrees Fahrenheit. Lighting was controlled so that there
was no bright glare, but full visibility was maintained. Sound was
deadened but not totally controlled. Some study subjects requested
background music. When such requests were made, they were
granted.

Over 90 percent of the study subjects had never been observed in
sexual activity before cooperating with the Institute's research programs. There was no desire to put excessive pressure on any man or
woman by subjecting an individual to any possible source of anxiety
in the laboratory that could be avoided. Therefore, observers were
limited to the two principal investigators and occasional laboratory
personnel.

ACCLIMATION PROCESS

For many study subjects, acclimation to the laboratory procedure
and environment was a vital precursor to sexual interaction in the
laboratory. During the acclimation process, there was a brief discussion of the overall research concepts and goals of the investigative

* The original heterosexual study population was reduced to form study group B
(see Chapter 2).

program. Of course, before any laboratory episode, the specifics of the particular experiment in which the study subjects were to participate were presented in detail. The technical problems at hand, the information sought, the considered clinical risks, if known, and the reasons for employing particular investigative procedures were discussed with each volunteer at the outset of every investigative session. These precautions were taken not only to improve study-subject cooperation, but also to support the ethical standards that should apply to any investigative program involving human subjects.

All of the volunteers were cooperative in their laboratory appearances, and many became sincerely interested in the program's goals, the homosexual study subjects especially so. Many procedural suggestions were made by the study subjects that proved to be of real value, for there was a free flow of information between these men and women and research team personnel.

LABORATORY ACCLIMATION

The study subjects were introduced to the laboratory environment as another step in the orientation process. Equipment devoted to recording physiologic activity and the other laboratory facilities were demonstrated for potential research participants in order to engender in them a sense of comfort with their surroundings.

The study subjects were encouraged to set their own pace in reaching a state of comfort within the laboratory environment before sexual interaction was observed. For example, if to instill confidence there was a need for partners to interact sexually in the laboratory before observation techniques were initiated by research personnel, the opportunity was made available. Such opportunity seemed particularly indicated (1) when requested by a study subject, (2) when indicated by his or her general behavior during the preacceptance interview, or (3) when suggested by the content of the psychosexual histories obtained during the interview.

The acclimation process was further facilitated for the study subjects by prior exposure to the experiences of history-taking and physical examinations, during which the volunteers had become acquainted with the research team. Exposure of the potential research participants to these screening techniques helped to establish an aura of professionalism for the research team members that has been of inestimable importance in conducting investigative programs in an extremely controversial area.

It was observed that homosexual study subjects usually required considerably less acclimation opportunity compared to heterosexuals of similar age groups and educational backgrounds. For example, of the 16 assigned homosexual partners, only 6 requested time spent in laboratory acclimation. Of the 14 assigned heterosexual subjects (study group A), 9 required orientation procedures. This discrepancy between the sexual confidence and personal comfort of interacting homosexual and heterosexual assigned subjects occurred despite the fact that each study subject had a long history of effective sexual function. There is further discussion of this subject in Chapter 11.

When committed couples were compared, it was obvious that the homosexual study subjects responding in the laboratory felt less performance pressure than did the heterosexual study subjects. It was even more evident from both physical action and verbal comment, however, that the individual act of masturbation under observation was far less comfortable for the homosexual group than for their heterosexual counterparts. These variations in psychosexual behavior between individuals committed to alternative lifestyles will be discussed briefly in Chapter 11.

The ambisexual study subjects evidenced no need for acclimation opportunity before interacting sexually in the laboratory.

COMMUNICATION BETWEEN HOMOSEXUAL SUBJECTS

Regardless of sexual preference, study subjects were always encouraged to set their own pace when sexual activity developed in the laboratory. They were directed to take whatever time they required, to move into sexual approach as they saw fit, and to respond freely, both verbally and nonverbally, as they felt need. Consideration was given to standardizing instructions for procedures during sexual activity by regulation of time intervals, assigning which partner should initiate, and so on, but was discarded to allow fullest assessment of spontaneous behaviors and responses.

For committed male homosexual couples, sexual interaction followed patterns obviously familiar and fully acceptable to both partners. While the responding partners enacted many variations on the standardized techniques of sexual stimulation, rarely was there need for a discussion between the sexual partners as to procedural activities. Regardless of the stimulative approaches employed or of the decision of who approached whom first, the study subject being evaluated almost always had erections and ejaculated before the experimental session was terminated (Chapter 6).

Assigned male homosexual study subjects A, B, and C (Chapter 3), interacting in the laboratory with previously unknown male partners, did discuss procedural matters with these partners, but quite briefly. Usually, the discussion consisted of just a question or a suggestion, but often it was limited to nonverbal communicative expressions such as eye contact or hand movement, any of which usually proved sufficient to establish the protocol of partner interaction. No coaching or suggestions were made by the research team.

The committed lesbian couples also had well-established, individualized patterns of sexual interaction. Who was to stimulate whom and in what order, and whether there was to be mutual stimulation or a combination of "my turn-your turn" techniques, were rarely discussed in the laboratory. The stimulative approaches were free-flowing, seemed essentially unreserved, and quite obviously were not staged. The study subject being observed rarely failed to attain orgasmic release at least once before termination of the particular experimental opportunity. Actually more than 50 percent of all women responded at multiorgasmic levels at one time or another during sexual opportunities in the laboratory (Chapter 6).

When female study subjects interacted in the laboratory with their assigned partners, different patterns of interaction were evident when compared to the committed female pairs. While initial stimulative activity tended to be on a mutual basis, in short order control of the specific sexual experience usually was assumed by one partner. This assumption of control was established without verbal communication and frequently with no obvious nonverbal direction, although on one occasion discussion as to procedural strategy continued even as the couple was interacting physically.

The only other direction given specifically to the assigned individuals or committed couples by the research team prior to sexual interaction was the request that on any particular occasion they limit their sexual behavior to the stimulative approach designated, whether masturbation, partner manipulation, or fellatio/cunnilingus, or, for heterosexual subjects, coitus. For couples having coitus, any desired preliminary stimulation was accepted.

PRIVILEGE OF PRIVACY

When masturbational response was requested, the responding heterosexual and homosexual men and women were given the "privilege of privacy" if desired. Defined solely for this investigative program, privilege of privacy meant the exclusion from the laboratory of one's sexual partner and any other individuals aside from the research team. For many homosexual male and female study subjects, evaluation of masturbational response was conducted without partner presence. Fifty-seven of 94 males and 49 of 82 females requested privacy from their committed partner's observation during masturbational activity. Interestingly, each of the subjects who was willing to interact in the laboratory with multiple assigned sexual partners (Chapter 5) requested privacy for his or her own masturbational activity. In comparison, for heterosexual study groups A and B, privacy for individual masturbational activity was requested by less than one-third of the male and female study subjects evaluated. We have no secure explanation for this apparent discrepancy in psychosexual behavior.

EXCEPTIONS TO FULL PARTICIPATION

There were five exceptions to full participation in the laboratory requested and granted to members of the homosexual study group. Two men and 3 women requested restricted sexual interaction. One man requested playing purely a stimulator role; the other man insisted on only the role of stimulatee. Of the 3 women (X, Y, and Z), woman X refused to masturbate in the laboratory, and women Y and Z insisted on playing only stimulator roles. With the exception of 1 man, all of the homosexual study subjects who preferred playing a restricted role in sexual interaction were beyond 30 years of age and were members of committed couples. When the desire to interact sexually in a restricted manner that did not prejudice the investigative program was so strong, the request was honored.

Heterosexual study subjects in group A did not request limited sexual participation in the laboratory, and those in study group B that were restricted in activity by investigative demand were eliminated from statistical consideration.

Brief consideration should be given to the histories of those homosexual men and women who requested exemptions from the full cooperation expected from study subjects in the laboratory.

Woman X was a Kinsey 2 in the 31–40-year age group who did not want to masturbate in the laboratory environment. In explanation of her request, she reported a traumatic experience that occurred during her adolescence. She had been surprised while masturbating by her mother, punished severely (a physical whipping by her father; social privileges removed for a long period by her mother), and thereafter had taken great care to lock doors, hide in closets, and to otherwise secure her privacy in order to continue her masturbational practices. Her guilt centered upon getting caught rather than in response to the act itself.

Woman X initially had had a heterosexual orientation, starting with intercourse at 18 years, and she continued to be quite active sexually in a multiplicity of casual relationships until shortly after her thirtieth birthday. She was occasionally orgasmic, but usually she had to resort to masturbation in private to obtain release of tension after her sexual experiences with men.

She met and in short order became fully committed to a woman who was in her late thirties and a Kinsey 6. They had been living together for approximately two and one-half years when the couple was seen in the laboratory. Even in this fully satisfactory sociosexual arrangement, woman X had been unable to masturbate in front of her partner, although the partner frequently masturbated in front of her and encouraged her to similar openness. There was full freedom of cooperation in partner manipulation or cunnilingus on woman X's part, but she had been unable to reverse her early conditioning and masturbate openly.

Woman Y was a Kinsey 5 in the 41–50-year age group who had been gang-raped as a virginal woman 20 years old. There had been a good deal of physical trauma, necessitating some surgical repair of the vaginal barrel and the perineum. The story of the rape was common knowledge in the small town in which she lived, and her male contemporaries had not only been vicious in their comments, but demanding sexually. There had been no psychotherapeutic support provided by her family, and her inability to cope with the situation had led to total rejection of the male sex.

Rejecting all social and sexual experience with males, woman Y assumed a male role herself within 18 months after the rape episode. She moved to a bigger community, began supporting herself, dressed in a masculine fashion, cultivated a low voice, and deliberately selected a lesbian life. When seen in the laboratory, she had ruled in complete double-standard fashion a committed lesbian relationship of over four years' duration. This specific relationship had been deliberately sought by woman Y, who seduced her best friend into a lesbian relationship.

Woman Y regularly initiated sexual interaction, relieving her partner either by manipulation or cunnilingus or both, but she always refused physical approach or sexual release from the partner. As the partner was aware, woman Y masturbated at night to relieve tension. She maintained both dressing and toilet privacy for herself, but insisted upon freedom to observe her partner in both situations. She did not object to masturbating in the laboratory, but she was one of the women who requested that her partner not be present during the episodes. She cooperated twice with masturbational activity and was multiorgasmic on both occasions.

Woman Z, 29 years of age with a Kinsey 4 preference rating, had turned to lesbianism after a history of forced incestuous activity. Her mother had died when she was 12; her father had not remarried. There was one sibling, a brother three years older. Her father, apparently drinking heavily at that time, had initially forced intercourse when she was 19 years old. After a number of sexual experiences with her father, the brother, aware of his sister's new role, had demanded equal sexual opportunity to keep from spreading the word among her friends. For almost two years she received both men on demand. There was no reported sexual pleasure; frequently an artificial lubricant was necessary.

Woman Z left home at 21, refused further social interaction with any man, drifted into the gay bar society, and had multiple casual homosexual experiences during which she still was not responsive at orgasmic levels. Finally she established a long-term (over three years' duration) relationship with her current partner.

Woman Z also had insisted on full control of the couple's sexual activity. She initiated opportunity, satiated her partner with manipulation or cunnilingus, but always refused to allow the partner to approach her physically. The partner suspected, correctly, that woman Z used a vibrator frequently, since this activity was always conducted in private. There was no history of dressing or toilet privacy for this committed couple.

Woman Z cooperated fully with masturbational activity in the laboratory, but she requested that her partner not be present. She stimulated her partner with both manipulative and cunnilingal approaches, but she rejected any physical approach herself.

Each of the two homosexual men who refused full cooperation requested permission to play a specific role in sexual interaction in the laboratory. One man insisted on reacting sexually only in the role of stimulator, the other in that of stimulatee.

The stimulator was in the 41–50-year age group, a Kinsey 4 by sexual preference. He stated that he couldn't remember when he started masturbating, maintaining a frequency of at least five to seven times a week. He found that no male partner—and he had had many—could provide the degree of sexual pleasure that he could for himself. A number of female partners had also proved relatively unsatisfying sexually in any physical approach they made. He had finally stopped allowing his partners to approach him sexually almost 10 years before he was seen in the laboratory. He made his sexual interest quite clear before he was accepted as a study subject.

With his current relationship, the arrangement from the beginning had been that this man was pleased to satisfy his partner with manipulation and fellatio, but would always reserve his own release activity to self-manipulation, usually with his partner observing. The arrangement had proved satisfactory to both partners through two years of a committed relationship.

The stimulatee, a man in the 21–30-year age group and a Kinsey 6 in sexual preference, had been introduced to homosexuality by two older brothers who took turns manipulating the younger brother, but who reserved release opportunity to each other. The initiation occurred during the boy's fifteenth year. He continued as a willing responder to his brothers' frequent sexual approaches until age 19 without ever being allowed the stimulator role. He then moved into gay society, but always as the ejaculatee. As would be expected, his casual relationships were almost always with older men. At times he accepted money for his cooperation, but he never became a full-time prostitute.

He was totally committed to a homosexual orientation, but his cooperation in the laboratory was conditional upon not being required to assume the manipulator role. He participated as an assigned study subject.

SUMMARY

In this chapter, frustrations with scheduling, security problems, privacy concerns, anxieties over self-image and partner attractiveness, and communicative ploys have been described with relation to the study subjects cooperating with the Institute's research programs. Particular attention has been paid to the homosexual research population in this discussion, although comparisons with the hetero-sexual study groups have been drawn when indicated. Brief histories have been provided for 2 homosexual men and 3 homosexual women who made specific requests for restricted sexual interaction in the laboratory.

5

COMPARATIVE SEXUAL
BEHAVIOR PATTERNS

Descriptions of study subjects' sexual behavior patterns as observed in the laboratory are offered with four cautions: First, there is no assurance that a homosexual or heterosexual couple's overt patterns of sexual behavior as observed and recorded in the laboratory are identical to those that would develop for the same couple responding in the privacy of their own bedroom. The possible existence of discrepancy in physiologic response between sexual behavior in a more conventional setting and that encountered in a laboratory environment must always be kept in mind. The additional element of observation adds a further confounding variable. The same caution in interpreting laboratory results was voiced in 1966 when results were published from the original investigation of heterosexual physiology.

Second, descriptions of sexual behavior represent only the predominant variations in observed sexual response patterning. Unless a repetitively recurring behavior pattern emerged during any form of sexual interaction, no description of sexual behavior has been provided. The research team was far more interested in usual rather than extraordinary sexual behavior.

Third, over the years all of the study subjects, whether homosexually or heterosexually oriented, or whether in committed or assigned relationships, have been sexually experienced men and women. Historically, they have had no difficulty in sexual performance. In fact, one of the important reasons these study subjects were selected by the research team was because they were specifically facile in sexual response. In order to acquire secure information about the basic patterns of human sexual interaction, inevitably one must work with men and women who respond effectively. The carefully selected homosexual and heterosexual study subjects employed in the Institute's research programs must not be considered representative of a cross-section of sexually adult men and women in our culture.

Fourth, qualified investigators with similar opportunities to observe and evaluate hundreds of male and female sexual response cycles might occasionally have presented differing opinions of behavioral patterning in homosexual or heterosexual response. Regardless of the degree of observer experience, the reported opinion of human sexual interaction is at best suspect, and at worst, may simply be in error.

These four reservations always should be kept in mind when evaluating the comparisons that have been drawn by the research team of sexual behavior patterns created by homosexual and heterosexual men and women responding sexually in a laboratory environment.

COMPARATIVE PATTERNS:

MASTURBATION

Over the years, hundreds of masturbational cycles have been observed in the research laboratory. It has been of real interest that the minimal differences observed in masturbational behavior were primarily gender-linked rather than related to sexual orientation. Of course, many variations in technique were exhibited, but these variations were as frequently present in homosexual as in heterosexual study groups. Men and women were completely free to select whatever position and whatever technique of masturbation they desired within the confines of the laboratory.

Men moved immediately to the penis at the onset of self-stimulative activity. Usually one hand (the dominant hand) was employed. Until obvious penile engorgement was attained, the play was usually nondirective, almost aimless in character. Approximately three of five men masturbated while supine in bed, one of five standing, and the remainder sitting or lying face down. In the early stages, play was freely distributed between shaft and glans. Rarely was the scrotum manipulated.

When a relatively full erection developed, the force and rapidity of the stroking pattern increased. Manipulative concentration generally focused on the penile shaft with only secondary inclusion of the glans. When men tired, hands were alternated, but both hands were simultaneously employed infrequently. With onset of the second stage of the male's orgasmic experience (ejaculation), most men slowed or even stopped forceful stroking and simply held the penis as the ejaculatory process continued. Only a few men continued manipulative activity during the entire ejaculatory phase.

A few men of both homosexual and heterosexual orientation masturbated successfully lying face down and using the bedding to thrust against. There was minimal manipulation in these cases, and observation was severely hampered. There also were two heterosexual men who masturbated by pressuring the erect penis between the thighs. This technique of pressuring the thighs together was far more frequently employed by women to stimulate the clitoral area.

There was no incidence of ejaculation with a flaccid penis during observation of masturbational procedures in the laboratory.

There were no specific masturbational patterns that would identify women as heterosexually or homosexually oriented. Approximately four of five women masturbated in the supine position, with the remainder standing or lying face down and rubbing the mons area against the bedding. At the onset of self-stimulation, women generally were less direct in their approach to the clitoris than were men in approaching the penis. Some women briefly touched their breasts; others casually stroked the lower abdomen, the inner aspects of the thighs, and/or manipulated the labia before palpating the clitoris. However, once the clitoris was approached, contact usually was maintained.

Most women tended to manipulate the clitoral glans directly at the onset of stimulation. But as sexual tensions elevated and resultant increases developed in rapidity of manipulation and/or stroking pressure, women consistently moved from the glans to stimulation of the clitoral shaft or to the general mons area. As with the men, manipulation was typically conducted with the dominant hand, but when women tired they usually slowed the pace rather than changing hands. Far more than men, women deliberately varied the rate and pressure of genital stroking, at times even stopping and starting clitoral manipulation in a self-teasing manner. During orgasm most women, as opposed to most men, continued their manipulative activity, although at a somewhat slowed, irregular pace, throughout most of the episode.

Women of both homosexual and heterosexual orientation occasionally employed intrathigh pressure as a masturbational technique rather than any form of manual stimulation. The thighs were pressed close together, bringing pressure to the clitoral area. Some women maintained constant pressure, while others alternately squeezed their thighs together and then relaxed in a rhythmic manner. These pressure techniques were generally applied with the woman on her back or lying face down, although two women preferred the sitting position.

Although facilities were not available in the laboratory, a number of both homosexual and heterosexual women described using running water under pressure (usually in the bathtub) directed to the clitoral area as the preferred method of masturbational release. Vibrators were not used in the laboratory, although there were histories of such usage from all the female study groups.

COMMITTED COUPLES' INTERACTION

When either partner manipulation or fellatio/cunnilingus was the stimulative approach requested, the decision of who was to approach whom sexually, and in what order, was made by the couple before sexual interaction was initiated.

There was one dominant pattern of sexual behavior consistently observed in the sexual interaction of committed male or female homosexual couples that was infrequently present in the sexual activity of committed heterosexual couples. Usually, the committed homosexual couples *took their time* in sexual interaction in the laboratory. Generally there was a deliberately slowed approach to the entire stimulative process. The slowed approach was obvious to the observers and was confirmed later during subject interrogation. The interacting homosexual couples appeared to be more relaxed and gave the impression of more complete subjective involvement in the sexual activity than did their heterosexual counterparts.

The homosexual couples tended to move slowly through excitement and to linger at plateau stages of stimulative response, making each step in tension increment something to be appreciated. Stimulative approaches were usually free-flowing rather than forceful or directive in character, and rarely was there overt evidence of goal orientation. The exchange of pleasure at all levels of sexual excitation appeared to be of greatest importance, with the orgasmic experience merely one more step in the pleasure sequence.

In contrast, the sexual behavior of the married couples was far more performance-oriented. An apparent pressure to "get the job done" was usually evident during partner manipulation and fellatio/cunnilingus and was consistently present during coition.

The predominant heterosexual behavioral pattern was one of purposeful stimulation with obvious goal direction, regardless of which stimulative technique was employed. Most married couples, as they moved through their excitement and plateau phases toward end-point release, spent less time than committed homosexual couples at each phase of sex-tension increment. At times they created the impression that the objective experience of goal attainment was valued almost as much as the subjective experience of orgasmic release.

Interestingly, this sense of goal orientation, of trying to get something done over and beyond a mutual exchange of pleasurable stimuli, was exhibited almost as frequently by the heterosexual women as by their male partners. Preoccupation with orgasmic attainment was expressed time and again by heterosexual men and women during interrogation after each testing session. Apparently, the cultural pressures for goal attainment consistently imposed upon coital performance also affect other modes of heterosexual interaction, such as partner manipulation and fellatio/cunnilingus.

Obviously, there were exceptions to these generalized descriptions of sexual behavior. There were committed homosexual couples who were completely goal-oriented, and there were married couples who obviously enjoyed the pleasures of sex-tension increment regardless of end-point release. Still, the predominant sexual behavior of the committed homosexual and heterosexual couples followed the described behavior patterns closely.

COMPARATIVE PATTERNS:

PARTNER STIMULATION (FEMALE)

Sexual interaction within committed lesbian couples usually began with full body contact. There was holding, kissing, and caressing of the total body area before any specific approach was made to breasts or genitals. Only 6 of 76 homosexual female study subjects who were members of committed couples moved directly to breast stimulation, and there was only 1 woman who approached her partner's genitals at the onset of sex play.

In contrast, in committed heterosexual couples' interaction, the male's sexual approach to the female did include some close body contact and kissing, but rarely more than 30 seconds to a minute were spent holding close or caressing the total body area before the breasts and/or genitals were directly stimulated. This was considerably shorter than the corresponding time interval observed in homosexual couples. Actually, the most frequently observed behavior pattern involved the man's direct stimulation of his partner's breasts or genitals at onset of sexual interaction.

When the committed lesbian couple did turn to breast play, it was significantly prolonged compared to similar activity during heterosexual interaction. The full breast always was stimulated manually and orally with particular concentration focused on the nipples. Interestingly, almost scrupulous care was taken by the stimulator to spend an equal amount of time with each breast. As much as 10 minutes were sometimes spent in intermittent breast stimulation before genital play was introduced. The stimulatee always evidenced copious vaginal lubrication during these protracted periods of breast stimulation, and, on many occasions, the stimulator also was well lubricated (see Chapter 7). On two separate occasions a woman member of a committed couple was orgasmic during breast play alone before her genitals had been approached directly.

The focus of lesbian breast play was directed toward the subjective pleasure of the recipient. During the lengthy "play periods," the stimulator usually responded to the stimulatee's nonverbal communication of pleasure and expended specific effort to enhance the recipient's experience of the moment rather than forcing her rapidly toward higher levels of sexual excitation. Such nondemanding approaches served to elevate sexual tensions slowly, but most effectively.

In the sexual play of married couples, female breast stimulation was far more casual. Husbands apparently spent time in stimulating their wives' breasts as much, if not more, for their own immediate arousal as specifically to enhance the female partner's sexual pleasure. In most cases the man became so involved in his own sexual tensions that he seemed relatively unaware of the degree of his female partner's sexual involvement. There were only a few instances when the husband seemed fully aware of his wife's levels of sexual excitation and helped her to expand her pleasure quotient rather than attempting to force her rapidly to higher levels of sexual involvement. It was no surprise, then, that in contrast to lesbian interaction, the heterosexual women lubricated moderately at most during breast play, and there was no instance of orgasmic attainment during female breast stimulation by a male partner.

With four exceptions, the committed lesbian study subjects reported that subjectively they thoroughly enjoyed and were aroused by breast stimulation. This degree of involvement was not described by heterosexual married women. Almost one-third of the women queried in heterosexual study group A and in the original heterosexual investigation (from which study group B was derived) reported that their breasts were not a particularly important erogenous zone to them. However, all of the women thought that breast play was very important in their husbands' sexual arousal. Many committed women stated that the greatest sexual arousal they derived from breast play was from subjective appreciation of their husbands' evidences of pleasure in the exercise.

Whether or not this marked difference in sensitivity to breast stimulation between homosexually and heterosexually oriented women is the result of operant conditioning has not been established. There is, of course, the strong possibility that the higher levels of subjective appreciation of stimulative return from breast play inherent in intragender eroticism would tend to make lesbian breast play a more effective source of sensual pleasure. Particular support is given to this contention by the observation that frequently during breast play for one lesbian partner, both partners in a committed couple lubricated extensively.

There was another important behavioral difference between committed lesbian partners interacting and husbands approaching their wives in stimulation of the female breast. The lesbian women were well aware that at times in the menstrual cycle a woman's breasts and/or the nipples may be tender—even painful—to touch. A number of times early in breast play, lesbian stimulators asked their partners if their approach to the breasts caused discomfort. On several occasions the instructions from the stimulatee were to be gentle, and on two occasions the stimulatee requested that the breast stimulation be discontinued.

Throughout the years in the laboratory with both heterosexual research populations, no husband ever raised the question with his wife as to whether his approach to the breasts distressed her in any way. On three occasions wives asked for more gentle breast play, but no heterosexual woman ever requested cessation of play.

Close observation has suggested that there were many times when women were made physically uncomfortable by their husbands' approaches to the breast. Although frequently admitting later in private that the observer's impression of cyclic breast tenderness had been correct, the women simply did not inform their husbands at the time. The usual stated reason was because "he likes to play with my breasts so much I didn't want to distract him." When the husbands were queried separately, they expressed surprise at their wives' cyclic distress, and the unanimous reaction was, "Why didn't she tell me?"

During the committed lesbian couples' genital play, the labia, mons, inner aspects of the thighs, and vaginal outlet were almost always approached before the clitoris was stimulated directly. When clitoral contact was initially established, the contact was casual. After initial contact with the glans, the clitoral shaft usually became the primary focus of stimulative activity.

There were two predominant types of genital play evidenced by committed lesbian couples. First, there was the time-consuming, nondemanding approach, during which a responding partner was brought to highly elevated levels of sexual excitation, allowed to regress, and then returned to her previously elevated tension levels.

This "teasing cycle" might be repeated several times before orgasmic release was allowed.

During the second type of lesbian genital play, the responding woman was stimulated with more continuity and with rapidly increasing intensity until she was orgasmic. Shortly thereafter, the clitoris was again directly approached and the responding woman was provided opportunity for further orgasmic experience or experiences. As would be expected, a combination of the two behavior patterns was also observed rather frequently, but most couples seemed to prefer one of these two patterns of stimulative behavior.

When husbands moved to stimulate their wives' genitals, the labia, vaginal outlet, and internal vaginal barrel were manipulated on perhaps half of the occasions before the clitoris was approached directly. Again, there were consistent differences between lesbian partner and husband approaches to the female genital area. Rarely did lesbians attempt vaginal barrel stimulation with their fingers other than at the vaginal outlet. If penetration occurred, it was usually restricted to the outer third of the vagina. Husbands, however, did not reserve manual stimulation to the vaginal introitus; frequently they inserted a finger or fingers deeply into the vagina.

Many heterosexual women evidenced little pleasure from digital insertion and were obviously distracted by deep vaginal penetration, particularly if it occurred early in genital play. Again, there was sparse, if any, communication between husbands and wives. Only twice did wives ask their husbands to desist from deep manual penetration of the vaginal barrel. Yet when questioned about this presumed stimulative practice, the wives responded as they had when questioned about breast play. Approximately one-third of the wives questioned said that they felt that deep manual penetration of the vaginal barrel was more exciting to their husbands than stimulating for them, and they willingly tolerated the approach for this reason. The remaining two-thirds of the women questioned varied in response from ambivalence to stated pleasure in manual vaginal penetration, particularly if the penetration occurred late in genital play.

There was also a consistent difference observed in homosexual and heterosexual manipulative approach to the clitoris. The lesbian approach to full cycle stimulation has already been discussed. After a husband made the initial contact with his partner's clitoris, he generally attempted to maintain continuing contact with the glans. He rarely moved to the clitoral shaft or the mons area until after he lost contact with the glans during the clitoral retraction phenomenon that is associated with the plateau phase of the female sexual response cycle.

There was yet another difference between husbands and lesbian partners in the approach to clitoral stimulation—a difference that was based upon essentially parallel sexual behavioral patterning. When approaching the clitoris, whether the stimulator was female or male, the approach typically was a duplication of the stimulator's own previously observed masturbational patterns. In other words, the husband tended to approach his wife's clitoris in the same manner and with essentially the same techniques that he had demonstrated when masturbating under observation. The same was true for the lesbian approaching her partner's clitoris with manual manipulative techniques. She manipulated her partner's clitoris with the same physical approach that she had demonstrated when masturbating.

Since rapid, forceful stroking was the pattern of choice during male masturbation, it was also a consistent pattern during the male's manipulation of his female partner's clitoris. Apparently, the lesbian's less forceful approach to masturbation and therefore to her partner's clitoris was generally the more acceptable or at least the less distracting.

On the few occasions when less demanding clitoral play was evidenced by male partners, the husbands were questioned as to the reason for this particular variation in behavioral approach. Most indicated that either their wives or some other woman had suggested that a less forceful approach to the clitoris was usually preferred. Random questioning of some of the forcefully manipulating men also returned the information that either they had never had any direction from a female partner relative to clitoral approach or that requests for a less forceful approach had been brought up on other occasions but had been forgotten.

COMPARATIVE PATTERNS:
PARTNER STIMULATION (MALE)

Homosexual interaction within committed male couples tended to follow the same response patterns described for lesbian activity. A significant amount of time usually was spent in an initial approach involving the entire body. Direct genital stimulation was rarely employed at the onset of sexual interaction.

After general body contact, holding close, kissing, or caressing, frequently the first specific anatomic approach was to the nipples. Only 11 of the 42 committed male couples (Chapter 3) failed to include some form of nipple stimulation at an early stage of sexual interaction. As with the lesbian behavioral patterns, both manual and oral stimulative techniques were employed, but the committed females' seeming compulsion to spend relatively equal time at each breast was not observed during the interaction of male homosexual partners. If penile engorgement was not present before the stimulatee's nipples were approached, it invariably developed during this activity. At times a partially established erection reached an advanced expansive stage, and occasionally even nonrhythmic pelvic thrusting occurred. The naturally occurring waxing and waning of full penile erection (Chapter 7) was observed as the stimulative periods were prolonged. Although the usual preejaculatory mucoid emission from the urethral meatus was observed on numerous occasions, no man ejaculated in direct response to nipple stimulation. Less than one in four of the homosexual men also achieved erection while stimulating their partners' nipples.

The techniques of nipple stimulation varied significantly between committed male homosexual couples and married heterosexuals. Rarely did a woman approach her husband's nipples, either manually or orally. On the few occasions when nipple stimulation did occur, it was always of brief duration and, with one exception, did not create an erective response similar to that elicited by homosexual males.

Obviously, nipple eroticism was of far more significance to committed homosexual men than to married heterosexual men. Not only the homosexual stimulatees, but also their sexual partners were apparently influenced by prior conditioning. Regardless of partner role-playing, almost three-quarters of the committed homosexual male couples included some form of nipple stimulation in their sexual interchange, while no more than three or four in 100 married men were so stimulated by their wives.

Genital play techniques also differed between the male homosexual and heterosexual study populations. More time was taken in low-key, nondemanding genital play in male-male interaction than in female-male genital stimulation. The homosexual male partner's initial approach to the genital area tended to encompass the anus, thighs, perineal area, scrotum, and lower abdomen more frequently than when a wife stimulated her husband's genitals. She usually confined her stimulative approaches to the penis and the scrotum.

As previously described for the committed lesbian couples' sexual interaction, teasing techniques were employed frequently during committed male homosexual interaction. Once the responding homosexual male reached plateau levels of sexual excitation, his partner tended to observe him closely for nonverbal communication of sexual tension levels. He then altered the rate of the stimulative activity in an obvious effort to prolong the stimulatee's high levels of sexual excitation without moving him to orgasmic release. Characteristic of intragender empathy, many homosexual men frequently made selective approaches to the frenulum of the penis, a most sensitive area on the dorsal surface just beneath the coronal ridge. Time and again men were brought within obvious proximity of their orgasmic experience and allowed to regress to low plateau or high excitement levels before being cyclically restimulated.

On a number of occasions, stimulatees actually asked for release well before their committed partners provided ejaculatory opportunity. Obviously, this teasing technique represented a behavioral patterning established and accepted between the committed homosexual participants well before their research project participation. Regardless of which homosexual partner was the stimulator or the stimulatee, teasing techniques were employed consistently in the laboratory and usually occasioned extremely high levels of sexual pleasure.

When randomly queried about behavioral patterns, the committed male homosexual study subjects usually stated in essence that they stimulated their partners the way that they (the stimulators) would like to be stimulated. Alternatively, the men said that they and their partners had discussed the subject on a number of occasions and had exchanged information about their personal pleasure preferences.

When a wife moved to stimulate her husband's genital area, there was minimal stimulative attention paid to the lower abdomen, thighs, and perineal area, although scrotal exploration was observed consistently. Women usually concentrated their stimulative approach on the shaft of the penis rather than the glans. The frenulum was rarely stimulated electively. And once penile manipulation began, stroking usually was conducted at a steady pace until the male partner evidenced elevated sexual tension levels. Then there was increased rapidity and vigor of stroking until the man ejaculated.

Rarely did a wife identify her husband's preorgasmic stage of sexual involvement and suspend him at this high level of sexual excitation in a cyclic manner by slowing or even temporarily discontinuing the penile manipulative pattern for appreciable lengths of time before reconstituting full erection and stimulating ejaculation. On the few occasions when this pattern of sexual behavior was initiated by the wife, the man's overt expression of sexual pleasure was quite equal to that of the similarly treated male homosexual.

Wives were interrogated privately as to the sources from which they developed their penile manipulative techniques. Only three women reported that their husbands had suggested specific techniques for penile stimulation, such as identifying the sensitivity of the frenulum, the preferred rate of manipulation, or desired application of manual pressure. The principal expressed concern of most wives was not to stroke the penis too vigorously and hurt the male; beyond this fear, their technical approach to penile stimulation was totally the result of whatever personal experience they had acquired. Frequently, ejaculation was viewed as proof of a completely satisfactory manipulative technique.

Those women who had developed a pattern of teasing the male

at some length before providing ejaculatory opportunity typically stated that the technique had developed because they had applied to their partner the pattern of stimulation they would have enjoyed themselves.

When husbands were interviewed, their most frequent complaint was that their wives did not grasp the shaft of the penis tightly enough. Yet not one man with this complaint had ever taken the initiative and suggested this specific technical improvement to his wife.

COMPARATIVE PATTERNS:
FELLATIO / CUNNILINGUS

When fellatio/cunnilingus were the sexually stimulative techniques employed by committed homosexual and heterosexual couples at the research team's direction, the patterns of preliminary stimulative approach such as general body contact, breast play, and genital manipulation were identified as essentially interchangeable with the stimulative techniques employed by the same men and women during the partner manipulation observations. Therefore, description of the specifics of early stimulative approach will not be repeated.

In general terms, it can be stated that once again committed male and female homosexual pairs tended to adopt a slower, less demanding sexual approach. More time was taken in the sexual preliminaries, and there was far less expression of a subjective sense of urgency for goal attainment. During fellatio/cunnilingus, expressions of concern for performance were primarily restricted to the husband and wife group.

There were specific differences in sexual behavior patterning once the committed homosexual and heterosexual partners moved from the preliminaries of sexual interchange to the specifics of fellative or cunnilingal activity. The differences that existed were not essentially limited to those associated with sexual preference roles, as has been described for the partner manipulation interactions. Significant variations in actual fellative/cunnilingal behavior as observed in both homosexual and heterosexual study-group interactions were confined to cunnilingal activity. Thus, with these techniques the differences were both gender and preference oriented.

FELLATIO

There was minimal difference evidenced in the technique of fellatio between committed homosexual and heterosexual couples. From a functional point of view, there was little observable technical variation between sexually experienced homosexual males practicing fellatio upon their partners and sexually experienced wives similarly stimulating their husbands. The homosexual males did follow the general pattern of proceeding without any sense of haste, slowing and speeding up the fellative activity in a teasing technique. Other than this sexual preference-oriented approach to fellatio, there was little observed difference between the two groups. Both the homosexual males and the wives were obviously interested in creating as effective a stimulative opportunity for their partners as possible, and they succeeded about equally. Same-sex empathy did not seem to be of significant importance in effectiveness of fellative stimulation.

The only appreciable difference between homosexual and heterosexual fellatio was in the practice of swallowing the ejaculate. The uniform practice of both groups was for the male to ejaculate intraorally. Most homosexual males in fellating their partners to orgasm did swallow the ejaculate, while most women, whether wives or assigned partners, did not. There was no absolute pattern, however; at times there was swallowing, at times not, by the same individual, so only a general statement can be made. It may reasonably be presumed that unless sexual experience dominates, there is little to choose between the sexual effectiveness of committed male or female partners employing fellative techniques.

CUNNILINGUS

With cunnilingus, it was an entirely different matter. There simply was no comparison between the skillfullness of men and women when cunnilingus was employed as a stimulative technique. Not only were committed lesbians more effective in satisfying their partners, they usually involved themselves without restraint in the cunnilingal activity far more than husbands approaching their wives. They demonstrated much more inventiveness in cunnilingal stimulative approaches and, above all, had the advantage of gender empathy. They inherently knew what pleased and used this knowledge to specific advantage.

The lesbian approach to cunnilingus started with the breasts, moved to the lower abdomen and thighs, and, in turn, the labia and frequently the vaginal outlet before concentrating on the clitoris. Once focused on the clitoris, the approach varied greatly from forceful stroking to a slow, gentle stimulative technique. And the stimulators varied their approaches significantly from episode to episode with the committed partner. The more variation on the theme exhibited by the stimulators, the higher the levels of subjective involvement evidenced by the stimulatees.

The lesbian stimulators usually became quite involved subjectively during the cunnilingal activity. Most stimulators lubricated copiously, and there were two instances of orgasmic experience recorded by stimulators while subjectively involved in a stimulatee's multiorgasmic response pattern.

The husbands, despite experience and lack of restraint, usually were not as effective with cunnilingal stimulation as the lesbian stimulators. The husbands' approaches tended to be stylized with repetitive episodes of cunnilingus rarely demonstrating innovation in stimulative technique. The husbands, once focused on the clitoris, tended to stimulate forcibly until orgasm occurred. There was less evidence of subjective involvement by the wives than demonstrated by the lesbian stimulatees.

Husbands had erections during cunnilingus and obviously were sexually excited, but no husband ejaculated during cunnilingal approach to his wife, regardless of her level of sexual excitation or whether she evidenced multiorgasmic response patterning.

When interviewed in private, the consensus opinion returned from husbands was that they had usually viewed cunnilingus as a means to an end (coitus) and simply had not devoted as much concentration on effective stimulative techniques as they might have if they had viewed cunnilingus specifically as an end-point in itself.

On the other hand, the wives in private discussion stated that they considered fellatio to be a challenge; they saw it as a technique that they should become expert at if they were to conduct themselves (compete) as sexually effective women. Apparently the husbands had not felt so challenged, for they described no competitive social demand to be experts with the technique of cunnilingus. Their cultural challenge to sexual effectiveness had been and continued to be confined to their role in intercourse. Such is the cultural influence on man's sexual function; even the most sexually experienced heterosexual men understandably internalize the cultural dogma that coitus is the be-all and end-all of end-point release. There is also the possibility that some of the lack of male effectiveness in cunnilingus may well be a response to some unconscious, culturally determined inhibition on the part of either heterosexual partner.

ASSIGNED PARTNERS' INTERACTION

From this overview of sexual interaction in the laboratory, it is obvious that there are clearly marked differences in the behavioral patterns commonly practiced by committed homosexual and married heterosexual couples. When observing the behavioral characteristics of assigned homosexual and heterosexual partners interacting in response to partner manipulation and to fellatio or cunnilingus, however, the previously clearly established variations in sexual behavior patterns are indeed blurred. Assigned male and female homosexual partners spent far less time in total-body stimulation than did the committed homosexual couples. Regardless of whether the directed technique was to be partner manipulation or fellatio/cunnilingus, the assigned lesbian couples moved immediately toward breasts and genitals, while the assigned male couples rarely used nipple stimulation at any time. Direct approaches to the genitals at the onset of sex play was the procedure of choice.

The teasing techniques of controlled slowing and speeding up of manipulative effort so frequently observed in the interaction pattern of committed male and female homosexual couples, both during partner manipulation and during fellatio/cunnilingus, were much less in evidence and, when present, usually of shorter duration for assigned male and female homosexual couples. Only one long-continued, teasing approach was observed during interactive episodes of homosexual male assigned couples, and this teasing technique was specifically requested of the partner by the male homosexual who only wished to play the role of stimulatee (Chapter 4).

The assigned homosexual female couples at times did slow the stimulative process, and teasing techniques were more in evidence than during the assigned homosexual males' interaction. But the time spent and the variations in stimulative techniques employed by the assigned homosexual couples did not compare to those employed by the committed homosexual couples.

In brief, assigned homosexual pairs were essentially performance-oriented, providing little of the partner "care" evidenced by committed homosexual couples. Orgasm was the end-point goal, and the presumed quickest path toward orgasmic release of the partner was taken with alacrity by the stimulator so that it would soon be "my turn."

The sexual behavior patterns of the assigned heterosexual couples responding to partner manipulation and fellatio/cunnilingus were essentially indistinguishable from those of the assigned homosexual couples, except for the complete absence of teasing techniques. All assigned heterosexual partners were indeed goal-oriented. In fact, the only situation in which the goal of end-point release was even more evident than that of assigned homosexual couples was in the sexual interaction of assigned heterosexual couples.

Regardless of the stimulative technique requested of assigned heterosexual couples, the immediate approach was to the genital areas. The female breasts were stimulated manually and orally, but in a most perfunctory manner, by the male partners. When the assigned heterosexual female partners became aroused, it was almost entirely due to pelvic play. Although the assigned heterosexual female study subjects were experienced women, and in a high percentage of cases attained orgasmic levels of sexual excitation (Chapter 6), they did not appear to be deeply involved subjectively in their experience. Similarly, there also was no obvious return for the assigned heterosexual male partners from the techniques of partner manipulation and fellatio other than the immediacy of sexual tension release.

COMMITTED PARTNERS' COITION

The entire process of coital interaction provides far more opportunity for distraction than is true for any other method of sexual interchange. As previously stated, manual and/or oral stimulative approaches, when employed as precursors to coitus, were usually cursory in nature, brief in duration, or even forceful in character when compared to the usual pattern of slowed, tension-accumulative, overtly teasing techniques observed in homosexual behavior. For that matter, the precoital stimulative approaches were much more superficial and engendered far lower levels of subjective involvement than had been true for the same men and women when they were directed to employ partner manipulation and fellatio/cunnilingus to end-point release. This "eye-on-the-goal" precept of precoital interaction consistently reduced the subjective input from, and therefore the stimulative quality of, manual or oral sexual activity. Since there usually were significantly lower levels of subjective involvement with precoital stimulative techniques, there was far more opportunity for personal distraction during this phase of the entire coital process, and the observed incidence of distraction did elevate markedly.

With onset of the actual mounting process, there was further opportunity for distraction from sexual involvement for either one or both coital partners. In all but two of the observed coital opportunities among married couples and in every one among the assigned couples, the male partner initiated the mounting process when he was sufficiently aroused sexually. He arbitrarily decided when his female partner was ready to be mounted, hunted for the vaginal outlet, and inserted or attempted to insert the penis. Rarely did the man question his partner as to her level of sexual excitation. On the other hand, rarely did the woman offer her partner such important information, either verbally or nonverbally. Thus, through false presumption or poor communication or both, the actual mounting process was frequently observed to be a source of distraction for either the man or the woman or both.

When these sexually experienced men were questioned about

their concept of when their partners were ready to be mounted, the most frequent answer provided was, "I knew she was ready when she lubricated." While an obvious level of vaginal lubrication can be safely interpreted by the male partner as evidence of a state of physiologic penile receptivity, it must never be interpreted as an indication of the individual woman's psychological demand for immediate penetration.

Further distractive behavior developed for female partners as soon as coital connection was established. In more than 90 percent of the observed coital experiences, once the penis was encased in the vagina, the man not only initiated but controlled the thrusting pattern. This male domination of the thrusting pattern left to the female partner not only the immediate but also the continuing task of accommodating to the depth, the frequency, and the force of the male's thrusting action. This continuing requirement for accommodation distracted many women, at least temporarily, from whatever levels of sexual excitation they previously had attained during the period of precoital stimulation.

If there is full male dominance, and particularly if there is a relatively short period of time between vaginal penetration and ejaculation, the distractions of physical adjustment to coital mechanics may prove too high a barrier for the female partner to negotiate successfully. And although she may be orgasmic, her levels of subjective involvement in the coital act may remain at low levels.

Actually, the distractions of the mounting process (the timing, the hunting for the vaginal outlet, and the act of penile insertion) and of the woman's accommodation to the thrusting pattern were, at times, converted into and relished as teasing techniques when conducted with finesse by experienced coital partners. It was interesting to observe the manner in which some of the significantly experienced heterosexual study subjects converted these mounting and thrusting distractions into teasing techniques that resulted in exceptionally high levels of subjective involvement in the coital process for both partners. But such conversion did not occur frequently.

There also were specific teasing techniques inherent in coital thrusting patterns that were most effectively employed by responding husbands and wives. These variations were deliberate alterations in the rapidity of thrusting, the depth of thrusting, and even in the temporary cessation of thrusting as the man or woman observed his or her partner's levels of sexual involvement and deliberately teased the partner toward higher levels of sexual excitation. The potential for sex-tension increment with these techniques is, of course, unlimited. In the observed couples, the greatest detriment to effective female response was male control of the thrusting pattern. Had the factor of mutual cooperation generally been present, as it was on a number of observed occasions, the subjective return in intensity and duration of the female orgasmic experience would have been far higher than that usually observed. Obviously, the described variations in thrusting technique could only be successfully established if the male partner had sufficient ejaculatory control.

Coital positioning was left to the decision of the sexually reacting couple. There was evidence of male sexual dominance in that the male partner controlled coital position selection in by far the majority of cases. Again the female partner rarely assumed a parity role by suggesting a coital position. She simply waited for and then followed the male's lead. Over 80 percent of the coital episodes were conducted in the male superior position. The remaining coital episodes were experienced in the female superior position, with the exception of perhaps 1 or 2 percent of the coital episodes that were carried out with the female partner in the knee-chest position. None of these three coital positions interfered with adequate clinical observation.

ASSIGNED PARTNERS' COITION

When coitus was the directed sexual behavior, the assigned heterosexual partners still approached the female breasts and the genitals of both sexes directly, with little or no other anatomic preamble. The assigned partners tended to initiate the mounting process as soon as there was obvious lubrication and penile erection. There was total male dominance, not only of the mounting experience (timing and penile insertion), but of the thrusting pattern as well. The assigned female partners adjusted to male domination of the coital act on the basis of their extensive prior sexual experience. Coital activity simply became a mutual masturbational exercise, with each partner concentrating predominantly on his or her own needs. Because the sexually experienced male partners generally had good ejaculatory control, the assigned female partners usually had time to respond orgasmically. There were episodes of coital teasing techniques evidenced by members of the assigned partner group, but they occurred rarely. Levels of subjective involvement by either member of an assigned couple in the coital process were generally reported to be lower than those of members of committed couples.

POSTORGASMIC BEHAVIOR PATTERNS

Regardless of whether the study subjects were homosexually or heterosexually oriented, the behavior patterns during the resolution phases of the sexual response cycles experienced in the laboratory were more gender-linked than related to sexual preference. Although no sense of time limitation was interjected by the professional staff, the male study-subject population provided an interesting post-orgasmic behavioral pattern that was quite opposite to resolution-phase female behavior.

After men were orgasmic in the laboratory, whether through masturbation, partner manipulation, fellatio, or intercourse, they tended to rest only briefly. Although obviously involved in the sensuous experience, they quickly recovered and were soon ready to leave the bed. The majority of the women reacting to masturbation, partner manipulation, cunnilingus, or intercourse, were also deeply involved in the sensuous experience. But after completion of their orgasmic experience, they usually rested quietly, evidencing no immediate interest in leaving the bed.

When the opportunity presented itself, the postorgasmic woman tended to move toward or curl up against her sexual partner, whether male or female, and relax quietly, usually with her eyes closed. If not disturbed by her partner's sexual restlessness or departure, and particularly if her experience was multiorgasmic in nature, the woman usually became drowsy and frequently fell asleep. Rarely did postejaculatory men fall asleep in the laboratory.

Brief mention should be made of the men and particularly of

the women who after the initial orgasmic experience expressed interest in a repeat of such experience in the immediacy of the particular sexual episode. While the usual male postorgasmic pattern was that of a brief refractory period, during which he was impervious to further sexual stimulation, the experienced female frequently moved with continuity from one orgasmic experience to the next. There was no obvious period of time during which she was unresponsive to reapplication of the previously successful stimulative techniques.

Regardless of the gender-linked differences in facility for immediate postorgasmic response, the approach to reapplied stimulative activity was always the same. Whether male or female, homosexually or heterosexually oriented, or committed or assigned partners, there were no nongenital preliminaries when responding to a multiorgasmic interest. Study subjects always moved immediately to their partners' genital organs to restimulate sexual interest. The obvious goal of end-point attainment was omnipresent, and the direct genital approach was usually successful with sexually experienced study subjects unless satiation had intervened.

OTHER TYPES OF SEXUAL ACTIVITY

The only other sexual practices evaluated by Institute personnel were rectal intercourse and dildo usage. Both research projects were initiated and completed in 1970. Investigation of these two additional varieties of human sexual interaction were considered necessary to the Institute's basic commitment to provide perspectives for homosexual function within the framework of the physiologic and psychological aspects of human sexual interaction. Again, perspectives were to be drawn by comparing homosexual with heterosexual response patterns. Since vibrator usage offered no potential for increasing perspectives on homosexuality, an investigation of this stimulative technique was not conducted.

RECTAL INTERCOURSE

The physiology of rectal intercourse has not been presented in prior publications dealing with human sexual physiology. There has not been a complete investigation of rectal coition in that there were a limited number of study subjects and a restricted number of observed coital episodes by both preference groups. Five homosexual men and their partners (2 committed, 3 assigned couples), and 7 heterosexual women and their partners (4 married, 3 assigned couples) cooperated with the Institute's investigation of rectal intercourse. Each couple was involved in rectal coitus on two separate occasions in the laboratory. Following prior research patterning, none of the study subjects who were involved in the evaluation of rectal intercourse or of dildo usage had been members of other study groups.

Within the stated investigative restrictions, there have been no significant differences identified in physiologic response during rectal coitus, regardless of whether the participants were of the same or opposite gender. Therefore, the following brief descriptions of both the basic physiology and the behavioral patterns of rectal intercourse apply generally to both sexual orientations. Minor gender variations have been identified in context. The physiology of erection and of ejaculation have been discussed extensively in previous publications, so investigative focus was primarily restricted to observations of the penetratee, not the penetrator.

With one exception, no lubricative effect has been identified for the rectal area that can be described as a physiologic response to sex-tension increment. One woman with a history of years of frequent rectal penetration routinely evidenced a minimal degree of a mucoid moisture at the anal outlet just prior to a mounting episode. When questioned, the woman stated that she was aware of the lubricative effect. This effect had only been present for the preceding three years, although she described over ten years of frequent rectal intercourse. She also stated that she always controlled the penetrative sequence in that she did not allow a mounting attempt until she "felt wet." Although her vaginal outlet also was well lubricated, indicating significant sexual excitation, there was no direct extension of this lubricating material to the anal area. The source of this material remains unidentified. With this one exception, some type of artificial lubrication was used routinely in all other rectal penetrative episodes. Approximately half of the penetrations were lubricated by saliva.

Positioning in anal intercourse tended to vary with gender. Each of the 7 women voluntarily assumed variations of the knee-chest position, while only 2 of the 5 men assumed similar positions. The remaining 3 men simply lay face-down in a fully prone position.

In the immediacy of anticipated anal penetration, all the coital partners evidenced elevated levels of sexual excitation but, in addition, the male and female penetratees demonstrated weak, irregularly recurring contractions of the rectal sphincter. These anticipatory contractions were evident once the anal outlet was exposed. The contractions terminated as the sphincter was slowly dilated with the penetrative effort.

The response of the rectal sphincter to penetrative effort apparently depends upon the number and frequency of prior mounting episodes. Regardless of a history of frequent rectal coitus, the anal sphincter responds to the initial penetrative effort with a strong spastic contraction as an involuntary protective mechanism. When prior penetrative episodes have been infrequent, this involuntary spasm of the sphincter may be maintained for a minute or even longer. If a regular pattern of rectal penetration has been previously established, the initial protective spasm of the sphincter usually is short-lived, and involuntary relaxation of the muscle begins within 15 to 30 seconds. The more frequent the prior penetrative episodes, the more rapid and complete the rectal sphincter relaxation. Once the involuntary spasm is lost, the anal sphincter usually accommodates the penis with relative ease, and full penetration of the lower bowel can be accomplished without incident.

A secondary physiologic response of the rectal sphincter develops after full penetration. With the onset of a maintained thrusting pattern, the sphincter usually reverses its relaxation reaction and constricts tightly around the penile shaft.

In 13 of a total of 24 rectal coital experiences, the penetratees evidenced varying levels of personal discomfort during the mounting episodes. But once full penetration was obtained, there was no further evidence of penetratee discomfort. While the thrusting pattern was always initiated by the penetrator, the female partner usually joined actively in the thrusting experience with well-timed counterthrusting movements, exactly as she might have been expected to do with vaginal penetration. Only one male penetratee actively cooperated with his partner by initiating counterthrusting behavior. Generally, the male penetratees acted in a passive service role, while the female penetratees reacted as active sexual partners.

The female penetratees reached orgasmic levels of sexual excitation on 11 of 14 occasions during rectal intercourse. There were three instances of multiorgasmic experience. But male penetratees did not respond in similar fashion. There were only two male penetratee orgasmic experiences in a total of 10 opportunities, and in both instances the men masturbated while they were mounted rectally.

During the females' orgasmic experiences, the distended rectal sphincters contracted in simultaneous rhythm with the contractions of the orgasmic platform at the vaginal outlet (approximately 0.8-second intervals). Rectal sphincter contractions usually recurred three to five times before there was involuntary lengthening of the intercontractile interval. The rectal sphincter did not contract during intercourse when the two male penetratees had single orgasmic episodes initiated by self-manipulation.

There were no observed behavioral differences in the orgasmic episodes of the penetrators, regardless of whether their partners were women or men.

DILDO USAGE

Dildo usage was demonstrated in the laboratory by 3 lesbian couples and 3 heterosexual women. Each homosexual couple (2 committed, 1 assigned) followed the pattern of one woman acting as insertee and her partner as insertor. Two of the heterosexual women (1 was married) used the dildos as masturbational agents, and the third heterosexual woman was joined by her husband, who used the dildo in an insertor role. Each woman cooperated for three separate episodes of sexual interaction in the laboratory. As in the evaluation of rectal intercourse, there were too few study subjects reacting through an inadequate number of orgasmic cycles to establish investigative security. As with rectal intercourse, the subject matter was not deemed of sufficient importance to move investigationally beyond the collection of general information.

There was little to comment on during the early stages of sexual interaction between partners when dildos were employed. Once interacting sexually, each of the three lesbian couples and the one married couple moved first to mutual general body stimulation and then quickly to the breasts and genitals of the insertee before attempting dildo insertion. The sex play was apparently enjoyed by both partners with no evidence of a dominant role. The two heterosexual women using dildos as masturbational agents either manipulated the genital area manually or used the dildo in direct stimulation of the clitoral area before initiating vaginal insertion. It was only with onset of vaginal insertion of the dildos that significant differences in behavioral patterning were observed.

Each of the three homosexual couples used the dildo differently, evidencing variations in prior behavioral conditioning. After an initial period of genital play, lesbian couple A moved to a self-selected position that had the insertor sitting with legs spread wide apart and the insertee lying on her back with her pelvis positioned between her partner's legs. After careful initial insertion, the insertor continually varied the depth and rapidity of stroking. This teasing technique was continued until the insertee was in an advanced stage of sexual excitation. At this time the insertor, sensing the insertee's elevated level of sexual tension, increased the speed of the stroking and carried each thrust firmly into the depth of the vagina. With onset of orgasm, the stroking was continued forcefully until the experience was completed and the insertee signaled her partner to stop. After less than a minute's respite, the insertor reconstituted the stroking pattern in a nondemanding, teasing fashion until high levels of sexual excitation were reexperienced. Then the forceful thrusting pattern described above was reintroduced until orgasm again intervened. In each of the three episodes the insertee was multiorgasmic. Termination of the individual episode was indicated by the insertee when she reached satiation.

Lesbian couple B's pseudocoital positioning during interaction with the dildo was different from couple A's. The insertee assumed a knee-chest position with the insertor sitting to her left and beside her on the bed. Initially, the dildo was forcefully inserted into the depth of the vagina, and a rapid thrusting pattern was constituted from the start. The insertee immediately responded with counter-thrusting activity, and orgasmic release was quickly attained. On two occasions, one orgasmic experience was all that the insertee required. During the third episode, the insertee was multiorgasmic.

The insertee indicated to her partner whether to continue with further stimulation after the original orgasmic experience, or whether it was her desire to terminate the episode.

Lesbian couple C used the dildo in an attempt to simulate intercourse. The insertor strapped the dildo to her own pelvis just over the symphysis pubis, thus positioning the dildo in reasonable simulation of an erect penis. Dildo positioning was accomplished by a harnesslike belting arrangement that this couple provided for evaluation. After preliminary breast and genital stimulation of the insertee, the insertor penetrated her partner carefully and carried on the pseudocoital connection in a male thrusting pattern. Again the insertee responded with counterthrusting movements. Once full vaginal penetration had been obtained, wide variation was employed in the depth and rapidity of the dildo thrusting pattern until the insertee was orgasmic. In two of the interactive episodes the insertee was multiorgasmic, and on the remaining occasion she experienced a single orgasm and was satisfied. She controlled the pseudocoital experiences, signaling her partner to continue or to terminate the episode.

Of special note was the fact that, apparently highly excited by a combination of the pseudocoital thrusting pattern, by mons area stimulation from the strapped-on dildo, and by subjective appreciation of her partner's obvious sexual excitation, the insertor also was orgasmic on one occasion.

The two heterosexual women who used the dildo as a masturbational device did so in the usual supine position. After vaginal insertion, there was obvious variation in depth and rapidity of stroking until orgasm was experienced. One woman was orgasmic during each of her three episodes and was multiorgasmic on one occasion. The other woman was orgasmic on two occasions, but during one episode could not achieve orgasmic release. She stated that occasionally full sexual involvement did not develop when using the dildo in private.

The married couple had a history of using a dildo as a necessary adjunct to full coital activity. It was their established pattern of sexual interaction to use a dildo for the wife's orgasmic release before instituting penile insertion and completing male partner release with intercourse. They followed this behavior pattern during their cooperation in the laboratory. They agreed that the wife usually wanted multiorgasmic opportunity. After more than four years of marriage, the dildo had been introduced before intercourse as a means of satisfying the wife because the husband tended to ejaculate quickly and usually became quite sleepy after his orgasmic experience.

Following the pattern of their previously reported behavior, this couple initiated dildo insertion with the wife in a number of different positions and also practiced variations in depth of penetration and rapidity of stroking until the wife reached orgasm and, after a multiplicity of such experiences, indicated that she was sexually satiated. The husband then mounted and, having only himself to satisfy, initiated a rapid thrusting pattern and quickly ejaculated.

The dildos employed by the homosexual couples and the heterosexual women varied in length and width. In each case, the insertee supplied her own dildo for the laboratory evaluation.

There actually was little difference in general patterns of dildo usage, regardless of whether the insertees were homosexually or heterosexually oriented. In every episode the pseudocoital behavioral techniques of dildo usage varied, depending primarily upon the insertee for direction. Although in a service role, the insertors were obviously involved in the sexual experience and were primarily intrigued by the insertees' exhibition of sexual pleasure.

VOCALIZATION OF SEXUAL TENSIONS

Vocalizations developed during elevated sex-tension levels and with orgasmic experience in the laboratory and varied not only between individuals, but even with the same individual from time to time. In general, the more involved the man or woman became with his or her elevated sexual tensions and the more comfortable he or she was with the environment, the more vocalization occurred. Most study subjects vocalized the onset of the orgasmic experience in a relatively uncontrolled manner, but, in addition, many men and women indicated high levels of excitation (plateau phase) by a more controlled vocalization. There were no significant differences in patterns of vocalization identified in the responses of members of committed as opposed to assigned couples. Certainly there were no dominant patterns of vocalization that could be identified as homosexually or heterosexually oriented.

The ambisexual study group (Chapter 8) was certainly the most vocal research group in identifying elevated levels of sexual pleasure.

In brief, men and women tended to vocalize their elevated sexual tensions while reacting in a laboratory environment. Generally, the more sexually responsive the individual, the more socially secure he or she was in vocally signifying elevated levels of sexual tension.

SUMMARY

When differences in sexual behavior patterns between homosexual and heterosexual interaction were established, they were primarily in evidence in the committed couple population. The usual approach of the assigned couples, both heterosexual and homosexual, was essentially one of moving toward end-point release as quickly and efficiently as possible.

It is undeniable that the laboratory environment with its implied interest in orgasmic attainment was a factor in the performance orientation of the male and female study subjects. But the same environment was usually reacted to in a different manner by committed heterosexual and homosexual couples as opposed to the mating patterns of the assigned couples.

A review of laboratory observations of the sexual response patterns of homosexual and heterosexual study subjects in both committed and assigned relationships has been presented. As described, there are significant differences in response patterning between committed homosexual and heterosexual couples. But there are even more marked differences between committed and assigned couples, whether homosexual or heterosexual in orientation. These issues will be discussed further in Chapter 11.

Various sexually stimulative techniques have been discussed in relation to both homosexually and heterosexually oriented interaction in an effort to provide further dimensions to the Institute's investigation of perspectives of homosexuality. Variations in standard stimulative techniques have also been considered. In short, this chapter reports sexual behavior patterns developed in the laboratory by cooperating homosexual and heterosexual study subjects at research team direction.

6

COMPARATIVE
FUNCTIONAL
EFFICIENCY

Sexual functional efficiency is a subject that has had essentially no systematic investigative attention. What is the incidence of failure to function at orgasmic levels for sexually experienced men and women of either homosexual or heterosexual orientation? Do homosexuals or heterosexuals have the greater incidence of failure to function effectively in sexual encounters? Do sexually experienced men achieve orgasmic release more frequently than similarly experienced women? Are committed men and women more likely to achieve orgasmic levels of sexual tension than assigned sexual partners? Such comparative information has not been published, nor will the material in this chapter provide unequivocal answers to these questions. But a start has been made.

As a point of departure, this report describes the failure incidence of selected men and women with homosexual and heterosexual orientations responding to sexual stimuli in a laboratory environment. It will be recalled that chief among the criteria for selection for the various study groups was the fact that these men and women did not have a history of sexual dysfunction.

Thus, this chapter is a report of the response patterns of sexually functional men and women of either sexual preference responding in committed or assigned relationships to the stimulative techniques of masturbation, partner manipulation, fellatio/cunnilingus, or intercourse. In no sense should the reported results be construed to represent a cross-section of men and women in our culture. But there is a picture drawn of how sexually functional men and women can and do respond in a pressure situation (the laboratory environment) to sexual stimuli of both homosexual and heterosexual orientation. While no general conclusions should be drawn, this material does represent one aspect of the functional effectiveness of human sexual interaction and by use of comparative data provides yet another perspective for homosexuality.

The incidence of failure to achieve orgasmic levels of excitation while employing the stimulative techniques of masturbation, partner manipulation, and fellatio/cunnilingus is reported for the homosexual study population and (with the addition of intercourse) for heterosexual study groups A and B. The homosexual group and heterosexual study group A are evaluated in masturbation, partner manipulation, and fellatio/cunnilingus. Data on masturbation and partner manipulation are reported for heterosexual study group B, and functional efficiency in coitus is considered for both study groups A and B. Sexual functional efficiency is evaluated both by gender and by sexual preference, and there is specific discussion of selected individual functional failures. Statistical considerations of these experimental results are presented in Chapter 10.

HOMOSEXUAL STUDY GROUP

Female Study Subjects. There were 709 lesbian sexual response cycles observed in the laboratory; these were observed in 82 study subjects who participated in the research program (Table 6-1). The women were members of 38 committed and 4 assigned couples (see Table 3-7, Chapter 3). One woman requested that she not be required to masturbate in the laboratory, and 2 women stated a role preference, wanting to be the stimulator rather than the stimulatee during sexual interaction in the laboratory (see Chapter 4). Thus, the 211 cycles of masturbational origin were based on the responses of 81 study subjects, and the remaining response cycles, 306 partner manipulation and 192 cunnilingus, were developed by 80 of the 82 lesbians who participated fully and by 2 lesbian study subjects who participated partially in the investigative program (Table 6-1).

The women who constituted the 38 committed lesbian couples were observed in a total of 669 sexual response cycles, and members

TABLE 6-1

Homosexual Study: Functional Efficiency in
Female Study Subjects (N = 82 *), 709 *Observed Cycles*

Type of Stimulation	Observed Cycles	Functional Failures	Failure Incidence	Failure Percentage
Masturbation	211	2	1 : 105.5	0.95
Partner manipulation	306	2	1 : 153.0	0.65
Cunnilingus	192	1	1 : 192.0	0.52
Total	709	5	1 : 141.8	0.71
				(1964–1968)

* Three study subjects offered incomplete cooperation with this study.

of the 4 assigned couples completed 40 sexual response cycles
(Table 6-2). There were five failures to reach orgasmic release in the
sexual response cycles experienced by the committed couples. Two
occurred during the individuals' masturbational attempts; 2 women

TABLE 6-2

Homosexual Study: Functional Efficiency in Female Committed
(N = 38) *and Assigned Couples* (N = 4 *), 709 *Observed Cycles*

Couple Status	No. of Couples	Observed Cycles	Functional Failures	Failure Incidence	Failure Percentage
Committed	38	669	5	1 : 133.8	0.74
Assigned	4	40	0	0	0
Total	42	709	5	1 : 141.8	0.71
					(1964–1968)

* Four assigned couples formed by 6 lesbian volunteers.

failed to achieve release during manipulation by their partners, and
1 was unsuccessful in responding to cunnilingal stimulation (see
Tables 6-1, 6-5). There was no more than one episode of failure to
reach orgasm for any individual study subject and the failure episode
was not repeated during further sexual interaction in the laboratory.

These five failures were of minor moment. On one occasion there had been a respiratory infection during the few days immediately before cooperation in the laboratory. On another, there was onset of a menstrual period with severe cramping a few hours prior to the laboratory commitment. None of the women expressed the slightest concern over the failure episodes.

In the 40 cycles experienced by the 4 assigned couples, there were no failures to achieve orgasm (Table 6-2).

Male Study Subjects. There were 538 sexual response cycles developed by 94 homosexual male study subjects who cooperated fully or partially with the research program (Table 6-3). These men were

TABLE 6-3

Homosexual Study: Functional Efficiency in Male Study Subjects (N = 94*), 538 Observed Cycles

Type of Stimulation	Observed Cycles	Functional Failures	Failure Incidence	Failure Percentage
Masturbation	126	1	1 : 126.0	0.79
Partner manipulation	195	2	1 : 97.5	1.02
Fellatio	217	1	1 : 217.0	0.46
Total	538	4	1 : 134.5	0.75
				(1964–1968)

* Two study subjects offered incomplete cooperation with this study.

members of 41 committed and 7 assigned couples (see Table 3-2, Chapter 3). Each of the 94 study subjects responded to masturbational opportunity. There were 126 masturbational response cycles experienced with one episode of failure to either achieve an erection or to ejaculate (Table 6-3).

One hundred ninety-five cycles were instituted with partner manipulation. One man, a member of a committed couple, requested permission to play only the role of stimulator, and 1 assigned study subject requested only the role of stimulatee (see Chapter 4). Among the 93 study subjects cooperating both as stimulators and as stimulatees, there were two failures to respond at orgasmic levels. The same 93 stimulators cooperated to develop 217 response cycles using fellatio as the requested means of excitation for the 93 stimulatees. There was one failure to attain a full erection and to respond to orgasm during fellative activity (Tables 6-3, 6-5).

The four failures to function effectively were among members of the 41 committed couples during the 471 response cycles experienced by this group (Table 6-4). Three of the 4 men could not

TABLE 6-4

Homosexual Study: Functional Efficiency in Male Committed (N = 41) and Assigned Couples (N = 7 *), 538 Observed Cycles

Couple Status	No. of Couples	Observed Cycles	Functional Failures	Failure Incidence	Failure Percentage
Committed	41	471	4	1 : 117.8	0.85
Assigned	7	67	0	0	0
Total	48	538	4	1 : 134.5	0.74
					(1964–1968)

* Seven assigned couples formed by 10 male homosexual volunteers.

achieve or maintain erections during a specific episode of sexual stimulation and did not reach sufficiently high levels of excitation to ejaculate. The erective failures occurred once in each of the three types of stimulative approach under observation. One man could not ejaculate during partner manipulation despite maintaining a full erection for an extended period of stimulation. This transitory episode of ejaculatory incompetence has been seen at other times in the laboratory and will be discussed later in the chapter. There were no repeat failures to function for any of the 4 men.

Members of the 7 assigned male homosexual couples experienced 67 of the observed 538 cycles with no functional failures (Table 6-4).

Comparison by Gender. When evaluating sexual functional efficiency by gender, it is obvious that there is little difference in the facility of the sexually experienced male and female to respond to sexual stimulation in a laboratory environment. Of course, the stimulative approaches of masturbation, partner manipulation, and fellatio/cunnilingus are those with the least risk of failure (Table 6-5).

There were 171 more female response cycles than those of male reaction in the homosexual study group. Most of the extra female

TABLE 6-5

Homosexual Study: Comparison of Functional Failure Rates by Gender (Male Study Subjects, N = 94 *; Female Study Subjects, N = 82 †)

Gender and Type of Stimulation	Observed Cycles	Functional Failures	Failure Incidence	Failure Percentage
Male				
Masturbation	126	1	1 : 126.0	0.79
Partner manipulation	195	2	1 : 97.5	1.02
Fellatio	217	1	1 : 217.0	0.46
Total	538	4	1 : 134.5	0.75
Female				
Masturbation	211	2	1 : 105.5	0.95
Partner manipulation	306	2	1 : 153.0	0.65
Cunnilingus	192	1	1 : 192.0	0.52
Total	709	5	1 : 141.8	0.71
				(1964–1968)

* Two study subjects offered incomplete cooperation with this study.
† Three study subjects offered incomplete cooperation with this study.

cycles, however, occurred during lesbian study-subjects' multiorgasmic experience, a capacity rarely exhibited by men in general and not demonstrated in the laboratory by any of the 94 homosexual male study subjects. This is but further support of the Institute's prior contention that women but not men have the natural capacity to be multiorgasmic when responding to effective sexual stimulation.

The failure percentage of homosexual men was 0.75 and that of homosexual women, 0.71 (Table 6-5). These variations in the gender failure rates are not statistically significant (see Chapter 10). There was one more response failure for the lesbian population, but there were 171 more sexual response cycles in the female group than were developed by the male group. Using orgasmic attainment as a means of measuring functional efficiency, homosexual men do not function sexually with more efficiency than women, and women, though frequently multiorgasmic when given the opportunity, are not more effective sexual performers than men.

HETEROSEXUAL STUDY GROUPS

Data reflecting effectiveness of response to stimulative techniques identical to those evaluated for the male and female homosexual populations will be presented for both heterosexual study groups A and B. Study group A was evaluated in all three of the techniques described for the homosexual group: masturbation, partner manipulation, and fellatio or cunnilingus. Group B, for reasons previously described (see Chapter 1), was evaluated only in masturbation and partner manipulation, not in fellatio/cunnilingus. In addition, both heterosexual groups were observed in coition. The functional effectiveness of the male and female members of the heterosexual groups during coition will be considered later in this chapter.

It should be kept in mind that the material reported from study group B was collected as much as 10 years before the data returned from some members of the homosexual group and from heterosexual study group A.

HETEROSEXUAL STUDY GROUP A

Female Study Subjects. As described in Chapter 3, there were 50 married and 7 assigned couples who cooperated with the investigation. Among the 57 women there were a total of 462 observed cycles with four functional failures. Of the 462 total observed cycles, 142 were masturbational episodes without failure at orgasmic attainment. There were 161 partner manipulative experiences with two failures to reach orgasmic release, and 159 cunnilingal encounters, also with two failures to reach orgasm (Table 6-6).

TABLE 6-6

Heterosexual Study Group A: Functional Efficiency in Female Study Subjects (N = 57), 462 Observed Cycles

Type of Stimulation	Observed Cycles	Functional Failure	Failure Incidence	Failure Percentage
Masturbation	142	0	0	0
Partner manipulation	161	2	1 : 80.5	1.24
Cunnilingus	159	2	1 : 79.5	1.26
Total	462	4	1 : 115.5	0.87

(1967–1968)

One failure to reach orgasm with cunnilingus was with a female member of an assigned couple (Table 6-7). In this instance the male partner, his original history to the contrary, was obviously not effective with cunnilingal stimulation. Following suggestions, the male partner improved markedly in subsequent opportunity, so

TABLE 6-7

Heterosexual Study Group A: Functional Efficiency in Female Married (N = 50) and Assigned Study Subjects (N = 7), 462 Observed Cycles *

Couple Status	No. of Couples	Observed Cycles	Functional Failures	Failure Incidence	Failure Percentage
Married	50	418	3	1 : 139.3	0.72
Assigned	7	44	1	1 : 44.0	2.27
Total	57	462	4	1 : 115.5	0.87

(1967–1968)

* Observed cycles refers to masturbation, partner manipulation, and cunnilingus.

much so in fact that the female partner's failure was not repeated in further encounters. The remaining three failures, one with cunnilingus and two during partner manipulation, developed among the 50 married couples.

There were no untoward circumstances associated with these failures to function effectively. The women simply were not highly aroused during the three sexual opportunities. There was no recorded physical distress, nor was there an acute social problem. None of the 4 female study subjects failed to function effectively a second time in the laboratory.

Male Study Subjects. As noted in Table 6-8, there were a total

TABLE 6-8

Heterosexual Study Group A: Functional Efficiency in Male Study Subjects (N = 57), 384 Observed Cycles

Type of Stimulation	Observed Cycles	Functional Failures	Failure Incidence	Failure Percentage
Masturbation	115	1	1 : 115.0	0.87
Partner manipulation	123	1	1 : 123.0	0.81
Fellatio	146	1	1 : 146.0	0.68
Total	384	3	1 : 128.0	0.78

(1967–1968)

of 384 observed male cycles among the 57 study subjects. Masturbation was observed 115 times with one failure. There were 123 episodes of partner manipulation with one instance of failure to maintain an erection or to ejaculate. The 57 men responded to fellatio 146 times, again with one functional failure. Each of the three functional failures developed during the sexual interaction of married couples (Table 6-9).

There were no specific difficulties encountered during the failure episodes. In each instance the man simply failed to become sufficiently involved in the sexual encounter to respond with full erection. There was some penile engorgement evident, but it was not of functional adequacy. None of the 3 men ejaculated. There were no repeat failures to function effectively in further sexual encounters by any of the 3 men.

The assigned couples responded without failure during 52 sexual encounters in the laboratory (Table 6-9).

Comparison by Gender. A comparison of functional failure

TABLE 6-9

Heterosexual Study Group A: Functional Efficiency Male Married (N = 57) and Assigned Study Subjects (N = 7), 384 Observed Cycles *

Couple Status	No. of Couples	Observed Cycles *	Functional Failures	Failure Incidence	Failure Percentage
Married	50	332	3	1 : 110.7	0.90
Assigned	7	52	0	0	0
Total	57	384	3	1 : 128.0	0.78
					(1967–1968)

* Observed cycles refers to masturbation, partner manipulation, and fellatio.

rates by study-subject gender in heterosexual group A shows that there is no significant clinical difference in failure rates of men or women to respond to similar forms of sexual stimulation in the laboratory environment (Table 6-10). The failure percentage of the

TABLE 6-10

Heterosexual Study Group A: Comparison of Functional Failure Rates by Gender (Male Study Subjects, N = 57; Female Study Subjects, N = 57)

Gender and Type of Stimulation	Observed Cycles	Functional Failures	Failure Incidence	Failure Percentage
Male				
Masturbation	115	1	1 : 115.0	0.87
Partner manipulation	123	1	1 : 123.0	0.81
Fellatio	146	1	1 : 146.0	0.68
Total	384	3	1 : 128.0	0.78
Female				
Masturbation	142	0	0	0
Partner manipulation	161	2	1 : 80.5	1.24
Cunnilingus	159	2	1 : 79.5	1.26
Total	462	4	1 : 115.5	0.87
				(1967–1968)

men in study group A was 0.78, and that of the women, 0.87. There were 78 more observed cycles reported from the female research population as well as one more functional failure. Again, the 78 additional cycles are evidence of woman's innate capacity for multi-orgasmic response. Gender equality in sexual functional efficiency will be considered in detail in Chapters 10 and 11.

HETEROSEXUAL STUDY GROUP B

Female Study Subjects.   The sexual response cycles of hetero-sexual women were evaluated with the cooperation of 257 married women and 24 single women who formed assigned couples. This total of 281 women were observed in masturbation and partner ma-nipulation. As previously stated, cunnilingus was not evaluated in this study group. The 1,513 response cycles that are reported for this group consisted of a combination of masturbational and part-ner manipulative activity. There were four failures to reach orgasm during masturbation in 670 opportunities and an additional six fail-ures in 843 episodes of partner manipulation (Table 6-11).

The 10 failures to attain orgasmic release in the laboratory were recorded by the 257 married couples, who provided 1,437 observed sexual response cycles. There were no functional failures recorded for the 24 women who constituted the female component of the

TABLE 6-11

Heterosexual Study Group B: Functional Efficiency in Female Study Subjects (N = 281), 1513 Observed Cycles

Type of Stimulation	Observed Cycles	Functional Failures	Failure Incidence	Failure Percentage
Masturbation	670	4	1 : 167.5	0.57
Partner manipulation	843	6	1 : 140.5	0.72
Cunnilingus *	0	0	0	0
Total	1513	10	1 : 151.3	0.66
				(1957–1965)

* Cunnilingal stimulation was not evaluated during the original heterosexual study.

29 assigned couples, who interacted through 76 complete response cycles (Table 6-12).

Male Study Subjects. A total of 257 married and 29 single men responded to masturbational techniques and to partner manipula-

TABLE 6-12

Heterosexual Study Group B: Functional Efficiency in Female Married (N = 257) and Assigned Study Subjects (N = 24), 1513 Observed Cycles *

Couple Status	No. of Couples	Observed Cycles	Functional Failures	Failure Incidence	Failure Percentage
Married	257	1437	10	1 : 143.7	0.69
Assigned	29 †	76	0	0	0
Total	286	1513	10	1 : 151.3	0.66
					(1957–1965)

* Observed cycles refers to masturbation and partner manipulation; cunnilingus was not evaluated.
† The 29 assigned couples were formed with the cooperation of 24 single women.

tion through 826 response cycles (Table 6-13). Seven functional failures occurred among the male study subjects. Three times during 387 opportunities men were unable to masturbate to ejaculation. In two of these episodes the men did not achieve full erections

TABLE 6-13

Heterosexual Study Group B: Functional Efficiency in Male Study Subjects (N = 286), 826 Observed Cycles

Type of Stimulation	Observed Cycles	Functional Failures	Failure Incidence	Failure Percentage
Masturbation	387	3	1 : 129.0	0.77
Partner manipulation	439	4	1 : 109.8	0.91
Fellatio *	0	0	0	0
Total	826	7	1 : 118.0	0.85
				(1957–1965)

* Fellatio was not evaluated.

or ejaculate, and once, despite a full, long-maintained erection, the man could not ejaculate. There was no previous history of ejaculatory incompetence, nor was the episode repeated by this study subject during subsequent opportunities.

Four times in 439 cycles the male study subject did not ejaculate in response to manipulative stimulation from his female partner. In three of these opportunities there was insufficient erection for effective response, and again, 1 man was unable to ejaculate despite long-continued stimulation and a fully maintained erection with no history of ejaculatory incompetence.

The seven failures of male study subjects to function effectively occurred during the 739 cycles experienced by married couples who cooperated with the program. The 29 assigned couples completed 87 cycles of male masturbation and partner manipulation without a functional failure (Table 6-14).

Comparison by Gender. A comparison of functional failure rates by gender in heterosexual study group B indicates that there is no clinically significant difference in the failure rates of men or women to respond to similar forms of sexual stimulation in a laboratory environment (Table 6-15). The overall failure percentage of men in study group B was 0.85, and that of women, 0.66. There were 687 more observed cycles reported for the female research population, and there were three more functional failures to obtain

TABLE 6-14

Heterosexual Study Group B: Functional Efficiency in Male Married (N = 257) and Assigned Study Subjects (N = 29), 826 Observed Cycles *

Couple Status	No. of Couples	Observed Cycles	Functional Failures	Failure Incidence	Failure Percentage
Married	257	739	7	1 : 105.6	0.95
Assigned	29	87	0	0	0
Total	286	826	7	1 : 118.0	0.85
					(1957–1965)

* Observed cycles refers to masturbation and partner manipulation; fellatio was not evaluated.

TABLE 6-15

Heterosexual Study Group B: Comparison of Failure Rates by Gender (Male Study Subjects, N = 286; Female Study Subjects, N = 281)

Gender and Type of Stimulation	Observed Cycles	Functional Failures	Failure Incidence	Failure Percentage
Male				
Masturbation	387	3	1 : 129.0	0.77
Partner manipulation	439	4	1 : 109.8	0.91
Fellatio *	0	0	0	0
Total	826	7	1 : 118.0	0.85
Female				
Masturbation	670	4	1 : 167.5	0.57
Partner manipulation	843	6	1 : 140.5	0.72
Cunnilingus *	0	0	0	0
Total	1513	10	1 : 151.3	0.66
				(1957–1965)

* Fellatio and cunnilingus were not evaluated in heterosexual study group B.

orgasmic release. Again this presents evidence of woman's innate multiorgasmic capacity. Gender equality in sexual functional efficiency will be considered in Chapter 10 and discussed in detail in Chapter 11.

COMBINED HETEROSEXUAL
STUDY GROUPS A AND B

Table 6-16 shows the combined total of the response statistics for heterosexual study groups A and B. For all practical purposes, there was no significant difference in the functional efficiency of heterosexual men and women responding to effective sexual stimuli in a laboratory environment. Obviously there were many more female orgasmic cycles (765) developed during masturbation, partner ma-

TABLE 6-16

Heterosexual Study Groups A and B: Comparison of Failure Rates by Gender (Male Study Subjects, N = 343; Female Study Subjects, N = 338)

Gender and Type of Stimulation	Observed Cycles	Functional Failures	Failure Incidence	Failure Percentage
Male				
Masturbation	502	4	1 : 125.5	0.80
Partner manipulation	562	5	1 : 112.4	0.89
Fellatio *	146	1	1 : 146.0	0.68
Total	1210	10	1 : 121.0	0.83
Female				
Masturbation	812	4	1 : 203.0	0.49
Partner manipulation	1004	8	1 : 125.5	0.80
Cunnilingus *	159	2	1 : 79.5	1.26
Total	1975	14	1 : 141.1	0.76

(1957–1965, Group B)
(1967–1968, Group A)

* Fellatio and cunnilingus were evaluated with heterosexual study group A only.

nipulation, and fellatio/cunnilingus than were experienced by the male study subjects, and there were four more failures to complete the orgasmic cycle. But the difference in failure rates (0.83 percent male and 0.76 percent female) is obviously not clinically significant.

These statistical results will be considered in more detail in Chapter 10. Suffice it to say that just as was true for the homosexual study group, there was no significant gender-oriented difference in facility to respond to effective sexual stimuli demonstrated by the combined (A and B) heterosexual study groups.

COITAL FUNCTION

The functional effectiveness of male and female study subjects responding during coital interaction will be considered for both study groups A and B. These men and women have previously provided material representing response to masturbation, partner manipulation, and fellatio/cunnilingus (study group A) and masturbation and partner manipulation (study group B). There remain to be considered the returns from the same heterosexual study subjects responding to coital opportunity.

HETEROSEXUAL STUDY GROUP A

Female Study Subjects.   The coital experiences of the 57 couples in study group A totaled 189 observed cycles. After making allowance for the fact that there were seven male failures to function effectively, there remained 182 cycles during which there was full opportunity for female orgasmic response. Six female functional failures developed during the 182 cycles (Table 6-17). Five of these

TABLE 6-17

Heterosexual Study Group A: Functional Efficiency in Coition, Female Study Subjects (N = 57), 189 Observed Cycles *

Couple Status	No. of Couples	Observed Cycles	Functional Failures	Failure Incidence	Failure Percentage
Married	50	157	5	1 : 31.4	3.18
Assigned	7	25	1	1 : 25.0	4.00
Total	57	182 *	6	1 : 30.3	3.30
					(1967–1968)

* The 189 observed cycles was corrected to 182 observed cycles to allow for handicap of male partner failures (7).

incidences of lack of orgasmic attainment were in the married couple population, and there was one functional failure in the assigned couple group.

There was no unusual etiology in the five failures to achieve orgasmic release in the married couple group. Four women reported that they simply were not involved sufficiently to experience orgasm. One woman complained that during coition she was disturbed by vaginal irritation, and examination revealed evidence of a trichomonal vaginal infection. The orgasmic failure in the assigned cou-

ple group was experienced by a woman who was not feeling well
and had just recovered from an upper respiratory infection.

Male Study Subjects. Among the male members of heterosexual
study group A there were four instances of erective failure and
three of premature ejaculation for a total of seven male functional
failures during 189 attempted coital response cycles. One episode
of erective failure and one of premature ejaculation occurred during the interaction of the assigned couples. The remaining two episodes of rapid ejaculation and the three instances of erective failure
developed within the married couple group (Table 6-18).

TABLE 6-18

*Heterosexual Study Group A: Functional Efficiency in Coition,
Male Study Subjects (N = 57), 189 Observed Cycles*

Couple Status	No. of Couples	Ob- served Cycles	Impo- tence	P.E.	(Total)	Failure Incidence	Failure Percent- age
Married	50	161	3	2	(5)	1 : 32.2	3.11
Assigned	7	28	1	1	(2)	1 : 14.0	7.01
Total	57	189	4	3	(7)	1 : 27.0	3.70

(1967–1968)

P.E. = premature ejaculation.

The four incidences of erective failure occurred during anticipated coital connection. One failure was during a first episode of
coital interaction in the laboratory for an assigned partner. The
man was simply too distracted by his surroundings and did not
achieve an erection. The three failures of married men to function
effectively developed at different times in the coital interaction.
One man was not sufficiently involved from the onset of stimulative activity to achieve an erection. A second man lost his erection
during the mounting phase, and the third man was distracted during coition and lost his erection. Neither of the last two men could
regain full erection during the particular sexual episode. The rapid
ejaculatory response occurred once with an assigned partner with

no previous history of similar response patterning and twice in a married couple with an unreported tendency toward rapid ejaculation.

Both the male and female functional failures during coition were handled well by the study subjects in group A. There were no repeat coital functional failures for any of the men or women with the exception of the man who was responsible for the two episodes of too-rapid ejaculation. Adequate counseling and use of the "squeeze technique" * resolved the problem for this unit not only during further cooperation in the laboratory, but in private as well.

Comparison by Gender. Heterosexual study group A had very similar functional failure rates when coital activity in the laboratory was evaluated by gender alone. The functional failure incidence for the 57 women responding coitally in a combination of committed and assigned partnerships was 1 : 30.3, and the functional failure rate was 3.30 percent (Table 6-17). For the 57 men the functional failure incidence was 1 : 27.0 and the functional failure rate was 3.70 percent (Table 6-18).

There was no clinical significance in the 0.40 percent higher functional failure rate for men in intercourse. This subject will be considered in Chapters 10 and 11.

HETEROSEXUAL STUDY GROUP B

Explanation of Data (Female). A brief contributory discussion is in order relative to the rationale for selectivity and in explanation of previously published data. When the original heterosexual research program was reported in 1966, there was brief statistical consideration of a total of 7,500 sexual response cycles developed during the female-oriented phase of the program. The study group B under consideration here was reduced from this original heterosexual study population as described in Chapter 2. In terms of the female sexual response cycles, the records indicate that of the total of 7,500 cycles in the original data, there were 1,513 that were a combination of both masturbational and partner-manipulative activity. This material has been presented previously in this chapter.

As a point of information, there also were 613 cycles developed

---

* Masters and Johnson (1970), pp. 102–106.

by artificial coital equipment and 1,259 response cycles in other research programs during which female orgasmic release was either not indicated or was of no importance to the particular investigation being conducted. These cycles were removed from statistical consideration. Finally, there were nine instances in which adequate research notations of the woman's sexual response pattern were lacking when the research charts were reviewed. These records also were removed from consideration.

Thus there remain 4,106 female sexual response cycles developed through coition and available for statistical evaluation as return from heterosexual study group B's participation in the Institute's research programs.

As men and women responded to coital stimulation during the initial investigation of the heterosexual response patterns, it was decided to focus on the sexual physiology of each gender separately in order to concentrate the effectiveness of observation. Therefore, in study group B there were 4,106 observed coital cycles during which the female partner was the investigative subject (see Table 6-19). Obviously, the male partners also had to function effectively in these sexual episodes, for without the man's erective capacity and adequate ejaculatory control, woman's physiologic response during coital interaction could not have been evaluated fairly. Once observation directed exclusively to the female sexual response patterning was terminated by the woman's orgasmic attainment (or obvious failure), the cooperating men were encouraged to ejaculate if they wished. When given such permission, the men invariably sought orgasmic release.

The same ground rules did not apply to women during the 1,674 cycles (discussed later in this chapter) when only men were evaluated during coitus. It obviously was necessary for the female partner to cooperate with the responding male, but woman's orgasmic attainment was not vital to a study of male sexual physiology and therefore was not directly observed or recorded for statistical incidence. If the female partner had not been sexually satisfied during an investigative episode directed toward the male's sexual response patterns and needed sexual release, however, she was encouraged to express her needs and her partner was encouraged to respond in kind.

There was yet another important reason why the female partner's orgasmic function was not evaluated objectively during the extensive investigation of male sexual physiology. Except for special projects (intravaginal contraceptive physiology, for example) (Johnson and Masters, 1962 and 1970), the investigation of various aspects of woman's sexual physiology had already been essentially concluded before specific attention was devoted to the physiology of the male sexual response cycle.

There still remain for statistical consideration 4,106 coital cycles during which observation of a complete sexual experience for the female partner was anticipated at onset of stimulative activity. Many diverse female response patterns were under inspection during these thousands of coital opportunities. They included breast reactions, sex-flush color distribution, labial color changes, waxing and waning of vaginal lubrication production, orgasmic platform formation, onset and duration of contractions during orgasmic experience, cardiorespiratory response patterns, and many other physiologic reactions. The more effective the female's response in terms of sex-tension increment, the more information was obtained. Therefore, complete records were kept as to the effectiveness of the woman's sexual performance during the 4,106 observed response cycles.

Distractions.   It is also important to emphasize that many times specific observations were made during intercourse that theoretically could have been distracting to the sexually responding female partner. But many similar observations already had been made of the women during masturbation or partner manipulation, so there was some degree of conditioning to the laboratory environment when investigations of coitus were conducted. This direct interference with responding sex partners by the research team was much more of a factor during the original heterosexual investigation than during the homosexual group and study group A evaluations, where a minimal number of physiologic patterns were recorded (see Chapter 7).

Also pertinent to present discussion is the fact that there were 133 male failures to function effectively during intercourse while female coital response was under direct observation and the male partner, although necessary, was playing a secondary role. Therefore, the total of 4,106 coital cycles devoted to evaluation of female orgasmic attainment must be reduced by 133, the number of times when male functional failure made female coital orgasmic attainment impossible.

Female Study Subjects. As previously described in this chapter, study group B consisted of 257 married couples and 29 assigned couples formed by 24 cooperating women (Tables 6-12, 6-14). These 281 women responded in coital activity many times in the laboratory. There were 108 failures of female study subjects to achieve orgasmic release during coitus, with married women accounting for 94 functional failures in 3,494 opportunities. The remaining 14 failures to function effectively were recorded in 479 opportunities during sexual interaction between assigned couples (Table 6-19).

TABLE 6-19

Heterosexual Study Group B: Functional Efficiency in Coition, Female Study Subjects (N = 281 *), 4106 Observed Cycles †

Couple Status	No. of Couples	Observed Cycles	Functional Failures	Failure Incidence	Failure Percentage
Married	257	3494	94	1 : 37.2	2.69
Assigned	29 *	479	14	1 : 34.2	2.92
Total	286	3973 †	108	1 : 36.8	2.72
					(1957–1965)

* Four of the 24 single women cooperated to accept 5 extra single male partners to form 29 assigned couples for the laboratory investigation.

† The 4106 observed cycles was corrected to 3973 observed cycles to allow for the handicap of male partner functional failures (133) during coition.

Failure incidence and failure percentage of female orgasmic attainment during coition has been computed on the basis of 3,973 actual opportunities. The overall failure incidence in orgasmic attainment was 1 : 36.8 coital episodes, and the failure percentage was 2.72. There was no significant difference in the failure incidence of female partners in married couples compared to women in assigned couples. This is in marked variation to the results of the male study-subject evaluation (see Table 6-20).

Among the married couples there were 9 women who failed to function effectively on two occasions and 4 women who failed three times to reach orgasm during periods of laboratory observation. None of these 13 women stated that she always reached orgasm in private with her husband. Distraction was by far the most frequent explanation given when the women were not orgasmic during coition in the laboratory.

Each of 2 assigned female partners failed to achieve orgasmic release on two occasions. The remainder of the failures were single-episode experiences. Again, all of the women had reported previous instances of lack of orgasmic release during intercourse in private with partners of their choice.

Explanation of Data (Male). Of the 2,500 cycles specifically devoted to an investigation of male sexual physiology in study group B, 826 cycles were restricted to masturbational or partner-manipulative activity. The male's functional effectiveness in response to these two stimulative activities both as an individual and as a member of a married or an assigned couple has been reported earlier in this chapter (see Table 6-15).

Each of the 1,674 remaining response cycles was devoted to investigation of many facets of male coital behavior. There was specific interest in such diverse physiologic responses as variations in penile thrusting patterns, gross testicular physiology, urethral bulb reactions, prostatic physiology, and male behavioral response during the ejaculatory process.

When male functional efficiency during coitus in the research laboratory is considered statistically, the 1,674 male coital response cycles must be added to the 4,106 coital cycles developed by study group B participants during investigation of female coital physiology. As previously stated, the male role was obviously one of secondary importance to the unidimensional female investigative program; however, notes were made as to the effectiveness of the male partner's sexual function, for without successful male functioning, female cycles could not have been completed and evaluated. Therefore, there were a total of 5,780 coital response cycles during which male sexual function, even when it was of secondary importance to the research interests, was observed and reported as to effectiveness of coital performance.

Male Study Subjects. There were 80 incidences of male functional failure during the 1,674 cycles when the male was the primary investigative target as opposed to 133 failures during the 4,106 cycles when his functional role, although acknowledgedly vital, was still not under direct investigation. This failure percentage of 4.78 percent while under direct investigation as opposed to a 3.24 percent failure rate while functioning in a less performance-oriented capacity indicates that expressed performance demand may involuntarily generate some measure of functional anxiety even for sexually experienced men.

There were a total of 213 male functional failures in 5,780 coital opportunities (Table 6-20). These statistics are reported for the

TABLE 6-20

Heterosexual Study Group B: Functional Efficiency in Coition, Male Study Subjects (N = 286), 5780 Observed Cycles *

Couple Status	No. of Couples	Observed Cycles	Functional Failures			Failure Incidence	Failure Percentage
			Impotence	P.E.	(Total)		
Married	257	5179	156	18	(174)	1 : 29.8	3.36
Assigned	29	601	33	6	(39)	1 : 15.4	6.49
Total	286	5780	189	24	(213)	1 : 27.2	3.69

(1957–1965)

* Total accrued from 1674 response cycles in which male sexual physiology was the subject of investigation plus 4106 response cycles developed by male study subjects during the investigation of female coital physiology (reported in Table 6-19).
P.E. = premature ejaculation.

individual male and are also considered within the framework of his relationship as either a married man or a member of an assigned couple.

There were 257 married men responding to 5,179 coital opportunities. Married men were unable to establish or sustain erections satisfactory for coital function 156 times, and 18 times men ejaculated during or shortly after penetration. Both erective insufficiency and premature ejaculation were classified as coital failures. The 29 assigned couples interacted coitally 601 times. There were 33 occasions of erective failure and six instances of too-rapid ejaculation. When the functional failure statistics of married men and the men in assigned couples are combined, the overall incidence of male failure to function effectively was 1 : 27.2 coital episodes and the failure percentage was 3.69.

There were no incidences of ejaculatory incompetence as had been noticed during both homosexual and heterosexual response to partner manipulation or to heterosexual masturbation.

The percentage of failure to function effectively during coition for men in assigned couples was approximately twice that of the married men. We have no secure information that would explain this significant statistic. Interestingly, a similar functional failure discrepancy between married men and men in assigned couples did not occur when the same men were responding to the stimulative techniques of masturbation or partner manipulation (see Table 6-14).

Of the 156 failures to attain or sustain erections in the married couples group, there were 7 men who failed to function effectively on two occasions and 1 man who could not function during three different episodes. These failures occurred over several years of laboratory cooperation, with the shortest time between erective failures being approximately 18 months. The man with three failures to attain secure erections participated with his wife over a five-year period in different laboratory programs. There was a minimum of 20 months between erective failures. The remaining failure episodes developed singly for men cooperating with the various programs. Almost unanimously the men's complaint was one of distraction leading to erective dysfunction. This was true for men in married or assigned couples. None of the men who failed to achieve or maintain erections in the laboratory environment reported similar occurrences in their private lives.

There were 4 men functioning as assigned partners who had two episodes each of erective failure. Again, the failure episodes were separated by periods of time. In no instance were they recorded in sequential episodes. No assigned partner reported continued erective insecurity in his private life.

Comparison by Gender. Heterosexual study group B also had very similar functional failure rates when coital activity in the laboratory was evaluated by gender alone. The functional failure incidence of the 281 women responding coitally in a combination of committed and assigned partnerships was 1 : 36.8, and the functional failure rate was 2.72 percent (see Table 6-19).

For the 286 men the function failure incidence was 1 : 27.2 and the functional failure rate was 3.69 percent (see Table 6-20).

There was no clinical significance assigned to the 0.97 percent higher functional failure rate for men in intercourse. This subject will be discussed in Chapters 10 and 11.

EJACULATORY INCOMPETENCE

Three men experienced single episodes of ejaculatory incompetence during the laboratory study, 2 in heterosexual study group B, and 1 in the homosexual study group. None of the 3 men had ever experienced the dysfunction previously, nor was there a repeat of the functional disability during subsequent sexual encounters in the laboratory. The following is a more detailed description of these unusual episodes of functional failure.

One man, a member of heterosexual study group B, was unable to ejaculate during a masturbational episode. An erection was rapidly and fully established, but during the next half-hour, despite long-continued periods of self-manipulation, he could not ejaculate. Even during the interludes between masturbational activity, the erection was maintained at approximately one-half to three-quarters of full engorgement.

The ejaculatory incompetence developed during the man's first experience in the laboratory. He had not requested an opportunity for orientation to laboratory procedure and gave no history of functioning sexually under observation. He ejaculated within 3 minutes of onset of masturbational stimulation during his second visit. With masturbation, partner manipulation, and coitus he ejaculated a total of 11 times in the laboratory without further dysfunction. This was the only incidence of ejaculatory incompetence during 387 masturbational episodes developed in the laboratory by male members of heterosexual study group B.

A second man, also a member of heterosexual study group B, could not ejaculate during an episode of partner manipulation. He had been married for three years before cooperating with the laboratory study and had not reported prior sexual dysfunction. He had ejaculated without incident with masturbational stimulation. However, during the first partner-manipulative opportunity, he could not ejaculate. An erection was readily obtained and maintained over a 25-minute period through several episodes of forceful manual stimulation by his wife, but he could not ejaculate. Both husband and wife were distressed by this failure episode and apprehensive about further laboratory experience. They decided to continue in the research program, however, and subsequently this man ejaculated a total of eight times in the laboratory during masturbation, partner manipulation, and coition without further evidence of dysfunction. This was the only incidence of ejaculatory incompetence in 439 episodes of partner manipulation of male study subjects recorded by couples in heterosexual study group B.

Finally, there was a homosexual male who also could not ejaculate during partner manipulation. He gave no history of functional failure, and the dysfunction was not repeated during further laboratory experience. His committed partner (two years) also stated that he had not observed this difficulty in their previous sexual interchange. After the failure episode, the man ejaculated a total of five times without further functional inadequacy during episodes of stimulation by partner manipulation and fellatio. This was the only incidence of ejaculatory incompetence in 195 observed episodes of partner manipulation by homosexual male couples.

A month to six weeks after the episode of dysfunction, each of the 3 men was questioned about subjective attitudes and feelings experienced during and after the functional failure. There were several reasons for research team curiosity. First was the constantly present concern for research subject protection. What manner of residual trauma might become a factor of consequence in the future for these cooperative study subjects? What was the possibility that this unusual sexual dysfunction might develop in other members of the male study groups? Once these anxieties were alleviated, research interest was focused on any information that might lead to better understanding of and improved treatment for clinically established states of ejaculatory incompetence. Although interviewed independently, the 3 men gave almost identical accounts of their subjective impressions as the incompetence was experienced.

In each episode there had been initial sexual anticipation, followed by sensual pleasure occasioned by the physical stimulation whether by self or partner. Erection developed for the homosexual man during the anticipation phase and for the 2 heterosexual men during the early stages of penile manipulation either during masturbation or by the female partner. Increasingly elevated stages of sexual excitation were readily achieved until plateau phase levels of sexual involvement were experienced. As each man described his reactions, it was apparent that from a psychophysiologic point of view he had reached that level of sexual excitation when he subjectively felt ejaculation imminent, but had not moved far enough into the plateau phase to have reached the stage of ejaculatory inevitability.

The research team had noted that as plateau-phase levels of sexual involvement continued without ejaculatory release, each man developed a somewhat anxious facial expression and requested or applied increased manual pressure or a more rapid penile stroking pattern. At this point in time, the 3 men were obviously trying to force the ejaculatory experience, but despite their every effort, it simply did not happen.

In describing the failure experience, all 3 men stated that shortly after they had sensed that ejaculation was imminent, the feeling developed that they could continue indefinitely at current excitation levels without ejaculating. They further stated that initially they did not lose the feeling that ejaculation was imminent, but they had lost any real sense of ejaculatory demand. The subjective description was one of being suspended in sexual pleasure and able to go on indefinitely. When the sense of lack of interest in ejaculating turned to that of inability to ejaculate, the men tried to force the issue, and when unsuccessful, they became anxious and lost most of their prior sense of sexual pleasure.

When the 3 men verbally expressed the feeling that they did not think they were going to ejaculate, stimulative activity was temporarily discontinued. After resting briefly, each man independently requested a return or returned to sexual stimulation. In no instance did the men reach as high levels of subjective sexual involvement during subsequent stimulative activity as that accomplished during the initial episode. The stimulative approaches, always confined to the penis, continued alternating with rest periods from 20 minutes to half an hour and were finally terminated at research team suggestion.

The 3 men also stated that although some level of sexual pleasure was maintained throughout the encounter, their sexual excitement was certainly blunted after the first break in stimulative activity. They attributed this lowered level of sexual involvement to performance anxiety.

COMMITTED VERSUS ASSIGNED COUPLES

The issue of the sexual functional facility of committed as opposed to assigned partners should be discussed briefly. The basic question is, of course, do men and women in a committed relationship tend to function sexually as well as, better than, or less effectively than men and women who have no emotional bond? As a secondary issue, the question also might be raised as to whether there is a significant difference between the sexual functional efficiency of committed versus assigned couples, if the factor of sexual preference is added. Both questions can be reasonably resolved by perusal of Tables 6-21 and 6-22.

If the stimulative approaches of masturbation, partner manipulation, and fellatio/cunnilingus are accepted as basically manipulative opportunities, the factor of sexual preference can easily be added to the primary question of the relative functional efficiency of committed versus assigned couples.

It can be determined from Table 6-21 that although there is a minimal statistical difference between assigned and committed couples in functional efficiency in orgasmic attainment, the difference is of no clinical consequence. There were obviously fewer functional

TABLE 6-21

*Homosexual and Heterosexual Study Groups A and B:
Functional Efficiency in Manipulative Stimulation*

Study Group, Type of Stimulation, and Couple Status	Female			Male		
	No. of Couples	Ob- served Cycles	Failure Percent- age	No. of Couples	Ob- served Cycles	Failure Percent- age
Homosexual study group: masturbation, partner manipulation, fellatio/ cunnilingus *						
Committed	38	669	0.74	41	471	0.85
Assigned	4	40	0	7	67	0
Heterosexual study group A: masturbation, partner manipulation, fellatio/ cunnilingus †						
Committed	50	418	0.72	50	332	0.90
Assigned	7	44	2.27	7	52	0
Heterosexual study group B: masturbation and partner manipulation ‡						
Committed	257	1437	0.69	257	739	0.95
Assigned	29	76	0	29	87	0

* Refer to Tables 6-2 and 6-4.
† Refer to Tables 6-7 and 6-9.
‡ Refer to Tables 6-12 and 6-14.

failures in assigned couples than in committed couples, both for the homosexual study group and for heterosexual study groups A and B. But the number of sexual response cycles for the committed couples outstrips those of assigned couples by literally hundreds of opportunities.

The clinical position can safely be taken that when men or women respond to the sexually stimulative techniques of masturbation, partner manipulation, and fellatio/cunnilingus in the laboratory, the gender of the study subjects, their sexual preference, or

TABLE 6-22

Heterosexual Study Groups A and B:
Functional Efficiency in Coition

Study Group and Couple Status	Female			Male		
	No. of Couples	Ob-served Cycles	Failure Percent-age	No. of Couples	Ob-served Cycles	Failure Percent-age
Heterosexual study group A *						
Committed	50	157	3.18	50	161	3.11
Assigned	7	25	4.00	7	28	7.01
Heterosexual study group B †						
Committed	257	3494	2.69	257	5179	3.36
Assigned	29	479	2.92	29	601	6.49

* Refer to Tables 6-17 and 6-18.
† Refer to Tables 6-19 and 6-20.

whether they are members of committed or assigned couples makes not the slightest bit of difference in their overall sexual functional facility as measured by orgasmic attainment. Gender, sexual preference, or relationship commitment did not influence the sexual functional efficiency statistics significantly.

Turning to Table 6-22, the additional response of committed and assigned couples in heterosexual study groups A and B to coital stimulation is portrayed. Here there is a different picture. Regardless of whether the number of observed cycles was between 100 and 200 (study group A) or 3,000 and 5,000 (study group B), the committed couples, despite an overwhelmingly greater number of observed cycles, consistently evidenced a lower functional failure rate than was true for the assigned couples. While there is lack of statistical security in comparing the large and small numbers of observed response cycles, the committed couples did function more effectively in intercourse than did the assigned couples.

When considering intercourse from a gender point of view, the picture is not so clear. There simply was not any clinically significant difference in sexual functional efficiency between men and women in committed couples, but the men in the assigned couples

certainly had a higher failure percentage than their women partners. Aside from the possibility of increased social pressures to perform, which lack of knowledge of the assigned female partner may
have placed on the male, the research team has no ready explanation for this clinical discrepancy.

When evaluating this material, the reservation must always be
kept in mind that the research team was dealing with sexually experienced men and women. Yet the clinical implications that may
be drawn from these statistics are relatively unlimited. The cultural
concepts that men are the sex experts or that they function more
effectively sexually than women may be seriously questioned on the
basis of these data.

The frequently stated preference concept that insists, "My way
is better than your way" also may go by the boards. Barring levels
of subjective involvement, there is no difference in functional efficiency between homosexual and heterosexual men and women in
response to similar sexual stimuli.

It is also apparent that men and women who move to coital activity are at greater risk of sexual functional failure than the same
men and women who confine their sexually stimulative activity to
masturbation, partner manipulation, or fellatio/cunnilingus. There
will be additional discussion of this material in Chapter 11.

S U M M A R Y

A significant amount of clinically and statistically comparable
material has been presented relative to the functional facility of
homosexual and heterosexual men and women to respond effectively in the laboratory to various types of sexual stimulation both as
individuals and as active members of committed or assigned couples.
Background material necessary to appreciate the dimensions of the
heterosexual aspects of the Institute's investigation of human sexual
function (study groups A and B) has been presented as well as
similar material for the homosexual group.

Further perspectives for homosexuality have been created by presenting comparable statistics relative to homosexual and heterosexual men and women's facility to respond at orgasmic levels to

similar sexual stimuli. For the first time, sexual functional efficiency in terms of failure of orgasmic attainment has been reported so that comparisons may be made relative to gender, to sexual preference, and to the roles of committed and assigned partnerships for the sexually experienced study subjects. Finally, selected individual failures to function effectively in the laboratory have been discussed briefly, and the unusual male functional failure of ejaculatory incompetence has been considered in more detail.

The statistics returned from the 14-year laboratory investigation of alternative styles of human sexual interaction will be considered in Chapter 10. Implications that may be drawn from these statistics will be discussed in Chapter 11.

7

HOMOSEXUAL
PHYSIOLOGY

Information about human sexual physiology has been reasonably established in the last quarter century through the cooperation of hundreds of men and women responding to heterosexually oriented sexual stimuli in a laboratory environment. Analysis of the physiologic patterns of homosexual men and women has been made far simpler by prior experience with heterosexual research programs. The four phases of the human sexual response cycle have been established; sexual anatomy not only reidentified but specific function in response to effective sexual stimuli established as target organ responses; general body reactions to effective sexual stimuli confirmed; and the astonishing number of similarities between male and female sexual physiology underscored.

A number of investigators have made fundamental contributions to our knowledge of this subject, but they have evaluated and discussed only the heterosexual man's and woman's physiologic capacity to respond to effective sexual stimuli, not that of the homosexual male or female. Is there a fundamental difference in sexual physiology if the respondents are homosexually rather than heterosexually oriented? Based upon more than four years of intensive observation of hundreds of completed sexual response cycles in homosexual men and women in response to a multiplicity of sexual stimulative techniques, the answer is an unequivocal *no*.

All of the physiologic response patterns originally identified in heterosexual study subjects were present in homosexual study subjects as well. No additional response patterns unique to homosexual interaction were identified. The physiologic reactions that develop in men and women in response to effective sexual stimuli follow gender-linked patterns from the onset of the excitement phase through the resolution phase, regardless of whether the stimuli are homosexually or heterosexually oriented. The only identifiable difference between homosexual and heterosexual reactions to similar sexual stimuli was in the wide range of subjective appreciation of these stimuli (see Chapter 5).

In homosexual functioning there are, of course, variations on the generally established theme of the heterosexual man or woman's physiologic response to effective sexual stimulation; this is particularly true with respect to advanced degrees of deep vasocongestion in the primary and secondary organs of reproduction (the target organs). But there are similar variations that have been identified during heterosexual and ambisexual encounters (see Chapter 8).

Since the fundamental patterns of physiologic response to effective sexual stimulation have been identified and described, there is no value in detailed repetition. This abstracted report of the physiologic responses of homosexual men and women in a laboratory environment is presented for casual reference. For a more detailed, anatomically oriented discussion of human sexual physiology as developed in a laboratory environment by heterosexual study subjects, reference should be made to *Human Sexual Response*.

SEXUAL RESPONSE PATTERNS:
SCHEMATIC DIAGRAMS

Schematic representation of the sexual response patterns previously published for heterosexual men and women have been reproduced here for reference convenience. These representative response patterns are equally applicable to men and women responding to homosexual stimuli. Every phase of the established heterosexual response cycle is duplicated in homosexual interaction.

Homosexual male and female sexual response cycles were recorded only at the beginning of the research program. Since it was immediately obvious that there was to be no identification of significant differences from the physiologic patterns previously established in heterosexually oriented response cycles, recording was discontinued as a nonproductive distraction to the study subjects.

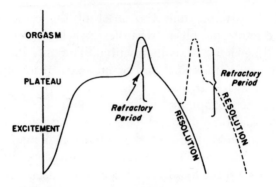

FIGURE 7-1

The male sexual response cycle. (From Masters and Johnson, 1966.)

It should always be kept in mind that these schematic diagrams of intensity of response to effective sexual stimuli are indeed just schematic diagrams. Figure 7-1, which schematically illustrates a single male sexual response cycle, obviously could have had a number of other variations in plotted patterns of response, but the illustration still represents the most frequently experienced male response cycle regardless of whether the sexual stimuli are hetero-sexually or homosexually oriented.

The three sexual response cycles illustrated for the female (Figure 7-2) are the most frequently observed patterns of sexual reaction. Obviously, there are any number of variations on the three main themes. Pattern A represents the most consistently identified complete response cycle for women. The dual orgasmic peaks are drawn to represent woman's natural physiologic potential for multi-orgasmic experience; they do not represent an established consistency in her sexual response cycle.

Pattern B schematically outlines woman's most frequently occurring sexual frustration—that of attaining relatively high levels of sexual stimulation without developing subsequent orgasmic release of these sexual tensions. When denied orgasmic release, women usually experience a slow, drawn-out resolution phase with subjective feelings of pelvic engorgement or aching that develop from continuing pelvic venous congestion.

Pattern C illustrates the explosive potential of woman's sexual

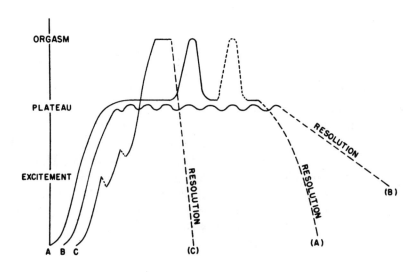

FIGURE 7-2

The female sexual response cycle. (From Masters and Johnson, 1966.)

capacity as she responds to a "teasing technique" of repeated initiation and withdrawal of or reduction in an effective stimulative approach. The resultant lengthened duration and increased intensity of her orgasmic experience is illustrated by the flattened peak of the curve, and the resolution phase not only is of short duration, but usually is accompanied by excessive lethargy, rapid onset of drowsiness, and even sleep. As in the male cycle, it matters not in the plotting of a female sexual response pattern whether the stimuli that initiate the reactions are homosexually or heterosexually oriented.

When orgasmic release is experienced, the major difference in the sexual response cycle between men and women is the male refractory period present in both homosexual and heterosexual response cycles. The duration of this refractory period generally increases in direct parallel to the man's age. It represents that period of time during which the male cannot repeat his orgasmic experience, regardless of the availability of previously effective stimulative techniques, a cooperative partner, or even a continuing erection.

In essence, the plotted response patterns indicate that the human female is innately multiorgasmic and the male is not. The heterosexual or homosexual woman may move from orgasmic experience to orgasmic experience without lowering her sexual excitation level below that of a low plateau-phase or high excitement-phase reaction.

If the homosexual or heterosexual man is to return to orgasmic experience, his sexual tensions must drop to low excitement-phase levels before his response cycle can be reactivated. Most men need a matter of at least several minutes' respite before they are capable of restimulation to achieve a second ejaculatory response. The minutes may turn into hours or even days as aging progresses.

Since the four phases of the sexual response cycle, excitement, plateau, orgasm, and resolution, apply to sexually stimulated homosexual as well as sexually excited heterosexual men and women, they will be used to facilitate the reportorial process.

HOMOSEXUAL PHYSIOLOGY:
TOTAL-BODY RESPONSE

Homosexual men's and women's physiologic responses to effective sexual stimuli are not confined to the reproductive organs. As with heterosexual subjects, the total body responds to the influence of elevated sexual tension. This generalized total body response is best exemplified by a widespread increase in myotonia (muscle tension) and in superficial and deep vasocongestion.

There are, of course, specific as well as generalized physiologic responses to sex-tension increment. As sexual interest elevates, so does the respiratory rate, the heart rate, and the blood pressure. Bowel tone may be increased, kidney function amplified, the neuro-endocrine system stimulated, and even the special senses of hearing, sight, and smell modified by sex-tension increment.

There are no consistent differences in electrocardiographic recordings of homosexual men and women responding to various levels of sexual stimulation when these tracings are compared to those of heterosexual men and women at similar levels of sexual excitation. Also, respiratory rates, blood pressure elevations, and circulating blood volumes only vary with the intensity and duration of the individual man's or woman's sexual excitation, not with his or her sexual preference. Since electrocardiographic material has been published previously in *Human Sexual Response* and by a number of other investigators (Fletcher and Cantwell, 1977; Littler *et al.*, 1974; Stein, 1977), the publication of a sample cardiogram will not be repeated in this text.

Throughout the body both a generalized increase in muscle tone and spasticity of specific muscles are apparent in both sexes. Examples of generalized increase in muscle tone were provided by homosexual men and women during sexual interaction under direct observation. The fingers clinch, the toes curl, the abdominal muscles contract, and muscles of the face and neck evidence tension. There may be tightening of the entire muscle complex of the perineal body as well as of the musculature that supports the female pelvic organs. This generalized increase in muscle tone rarely becomes apparent until late in the excitement phase, and it increases through the plateau phase.

An example of increased tension in a specific muscle is the involuntary constriction of the rectal sphincter that frequently occurs late in the plateau phase in sexually responsive homosexuals of both sexes (see Chapter 5). This same pattern was also seen in heterosexual study subjects.

Muscle tensions, whether generalized or specific, reach their peak during orgasmic experience, and fairly rapid dissipation of these tensions is an integral part of the resolution phase. If orgasm is not experienced, however, recognizable levels of generalized muscle tension may linger for hours in various muscle groups.

There also are a number of examples of both superficial and deep concentration of blood (vasocongestion) that are an integral part of each homosexual man's or woman's physiologic response to subjectively appreciated sexual tension, just as they are part of the heterosexual's physiologic response. An example of superficial vasocongestion would be that of the sex flush that develops over the diaphragm and may spread to the abdomen, chest, neck, face, forehead, as well as to the arms, back, and buttocks. This flush rarely appears until late in the excitement phase, increases and spreads widely during plateau, and vanishes immediately after orgasmic experience. If orgasm is not experienced, the sex flush involutes more slowly and in reverse order from its onset: first from the back and the arms; then from the face, neck, chest, and abdomen; and finally from the diaphragm.

Deep vascular engorgement is usually confined to the primary and secondary organs of reproduction (target organs) and to other auxiliary pelvic structures. Some examples of the concentration of venous blood in the target organs are increase in female breast size, onset of penile erection, or development of the orgasmic platform in the outer third of the vagina. Existing varicosities in the pelvis and legs may become severely engorged as sexual tensions elevate. These specific anatomic reactions to elevated sexual tensions will be discussed in context.

It may be of psychological as well as physiologic significance that severe degrees of deep vasocongestion in the target organs were established by homosexual women far more frequently in committed as opposed to assigned relationships. As described in Chapter 5, committed homosexual women usually spent an extraordinary amount of time in sexual play. On an average, they took far more time in sexual interaction than homosexual women in assigned relationships, than ambisexual women in their homosexual phases, or than heterosexual women responding to their husbands' sexual approaches.

It was apparent that advanced degrees of deep vasocongestion resulted from more time spent with such teasing techniques as starting and then slowing or even temporarily suspending sex play, or varying both the intensity and ingenuity of sexual approaches. When assigned female homosexual partners moved through sexual response cycles with relative rapidity, or for that matter, during the infrequent occasions when committed homosexual women also moved rapidly through their sexual response cycles, an appreciable reduction was identified in the venous congestion of the target organs. It also should be mentioned that on the few occasions during heterosexual partner manipulation and cunnilingus when husbands took long periods of time to stimulate their wives and teasingly varied the intensity and even the ingenuity of their stimulative approaches, an advanced degree of venous engorgement was present in the breasts and pelvic organs of these heterosexually oriented women.

The same increases in vasocongestion of the target organs were evident during the interaction of committed male homosexual couples. These men usually spent significant periods of time during partner manipulation and fellatio in teasing their partners by altering the intensity and the rapidity of the sexually stimulative process before encouraging ejaculation. Again, the longer the time spent in stimulative play, the more advanced the venous stasis of the penis and testes (target organs). Similarly, on the relatively rare occasions when wives spent long periods of time with deliberately controlled teasing techniques during partner manipulation or fellatio, their husbands evidenced similarly advanced degrees of deep vasocongestion of the target organs. There also were occasional incidences of advanced vasocongestion of the target organs identified in assigned male homosexual couples and in ambisexual men in their homosexual phase. But these incidences were the exceptions, not the general rules.

Thus, the slowed venous flow in the target organs that was so frequently observed during the sexual interaction of committed male and female homosexual couples is not a specific effect of homosexuality. It was observed on infrequent occasions in ambisexual, assigned homosexual, and heterosexual interaction. Instead of being related to sexual preference, the physiologic response of advanced deep vasocongestion is usually a secondary result of spending long periods of time in effective sexual stimulation before experiencing sexual release.

REPRODUCTIVE ORGANS

The physiologic changes in the primary and secondary organs of reproduction that develop in response to effective sexual stimulation should be restated briefly.

FEMALE TARGET ORGANS

The homosexual female's breasts are indeed target organs when sexual stimulation is initiated. As described in Chapter 5, a significant amount of time usually is spent by committed female homosexual couples in breast stimulation. The nipples erect early in the excitement phase unless they are partially or completely inverted, in which case no overt reaction has been recorded.

The areolae begin tumescence during late excitement and early plateau phases. When the breasts have not been nursed, the entire breast increases in size as sexual excitation progresses. Since only one homosexual study subject nursed a baby and then only for two weeks (Chapter 3), breast engorgement was pronounced in all observed female response cycles when the interaction between stimulator and stimulatee continued at a leisurely pace. When there was long-continued breast play, the stimulatee's breasts usually increased in size from one-quarter to an estimated one-third over sexually unstimulated baseline measurements.

A pattern of female breast reaction to sexual stimuli unique to the lesbian study group was identified. The stimulator's breast size also was observed to increase measurably during long-continued periods of sexual interaction. Though lesbian couples were almost always in a "my turn-your turn" interaction pattern, with one giving and one receiving physically stimulative approaches to the breasts, the woman giving (manipulating or suckling her partner's breasts) frequently reached that level of sexual excitation necessary to achieve obvious increase in her own breast size. In most instances there was minimal breast engorgement for the stimulators, but occasionally the engorgement was estimated at as much as a one-quarter increase over the sexually unstimulated baseline size. This pattern of breast engorgement for the stimulators was particularly obvious for the two women who insisted on manipulating their committed partners and did not allow their partners to approach them physically at any time (Chapter 5).

The stimulator was not only responding to her sexual arousal that developed from the physical approach to her partner's breasts. but she was also subjectively appreciating and being sexually stimulated by her partner's verbally and nonverbally communicated high levels of sexual excitation. As a matter of sequential timing, it was noted that once the stimulatee's breast engorgement was obvious, the stimulator's breast distention, if it was to occur, followed within 2 to 5 minutes. Only one stimulator developed breast engorgement more than 5 minutes after the stimulatee had responded, and there were no instances when the stimulator evidenced breast engorgement before the stimulatee.

There was no obvious breast reaction to orgasmic experience. During the resolution phase, breasts lost their deep vascular engorgement far more rapidly when the responding lesbian was orgasmic than in the very few instances when she was unable to achieve release (Chapter 6).

Deep vasocongestion was also easy to identify in the female genital organs during lesbian interaction. When stimulative approaches are confined to masturbation, partner manipulation, and cunnilingus, effective observation of the external genitalia is far simpler than when intercourse is a factor. Again, obvious physiologic responses to elevating sexual tensions were identified for both the stimulator and the stimulatee.

When the genitals were approached in partner manipulation or cunnilingus, almost all committed lesbian partners had moved into stimulator-stimulatee roles. Both partners usually had experienced some degree of overt sexual stimulation varying from general body stroking to breast suckling, and both partners, regardless of their role of giving or receiving sexual pleasure, usually had developed an obvious amount of vaginal lubrication.

Vaginal lubrication appears early in response to any form of effective sexual stimulation experienced by the human female. It is but a matter of a few seconds from onset of stimulation to obvious lubrication production. However, once initiated, lubrication is not produced at a steady pace by either homosexually or heterosexually oriented women. In general, lubrication flow increases or diminishes in direct proportion to the elevation or regression of sexual tension. In other words, the production rate of lubrication is tied to the degree of involvement with or distraction from the sexual opportunity at hand.

Homosexual or heterosexual women rarely respond from the onset of the excitement phase through plateau to orgasm in a direct, continuing line of constantly elevating sexual tension. Usually there are distractions that at least momentarily lower the degree of sexual involvement. Most distractions, such as reduction in effectiveness of a particular stimulative technique, sounds or sights foreign to the specific sexual interchange, or introduction of irritating or unacceptable stimulative approaches, slow the production of vaginal lubrication. Of course, if the distractive element is of sufficient influence, there may be complete cessation in the flow of lubrication. And responding women, regardless of their sexual preference, are easily distractable until late in the plateau phase of the sexual response cycle.

As has been noted, by the time an approach was made to the genitals of one partner, both lesbians in a committed relationship were usually well lubricated. Once genital play was instituted, however, the stimulatee usually far outproduced the stimulator. There were exceptions to this observation. The two women who insisted on playing only the stimulator role (see Chapter 5) were as well lubricated while manipulating their partner's genitals as were the highly aroused partners themselves. One lesbian member of a committed couple, a very heavy lubricator, did indeed produce more lubrication than her partner, regardless of whether she was in a stimulatee or stimulator role.

There was no obvious difference in lubrication production between homosexual or heterosexual women as long as the stimulative techniques of masturbation, partner manipulation, or cunnilingus were used exclusively throughout the entire sexual response cycle. When the techniques of partner manipulation or cunnilingus were employed by husbands as a preamble to anticipated coital connection, however, lubrication frequently developed irregularly and was estimated to be in less copious amounts than that produced by the same women when they were anticipating end-point release from a stimulative technique other than intercourse. Women anticipating intercourse may involuntarily put a different value on the stimulative techniques of manipulation and cunnilingus when considering them as a means to an end rather than an end in themselves. Certainly women anticipating intercourse were more easily distracted while responding to precoital manipulative or cunnilingal stimulation than during episodes employing these standard stimulative techniques when coitus was not allowed.

The clitoris responds in identical fashion to effective stimulation regardless of whether the stimulators are heterosexually or homosexually oriented. The retraction reaction that elevates and flattens the shaft of the clitoris on the inferior surface of the symphysis pubis occurs late in the plateau phase, regardless of the source of stimulation. It has not been established whether there is a preorgasmic expansion of the clitoral glans to parallel the immediate preejaculatory penile glans expansion described in the section on male target organs later in this chapter. This lack of information results from the fact that as the clitoris retracts, it withdraws beneath the minor labial hood and the glans cannot be observed readily during the woman's orgasmic experience.

The orgasmic platform develops as a deep vasocongestive response that encompasses the outer one-third of the vagina and extends to the minor labia. It results from engorgement of the vestibular bulbs that lie in the lateral walls in the outer third of the vagina and join in the midline just below the clitoris through the clitoral veins. The vestibular bulbs are a plexus of thin-walled veins quite similar to the erective tissue of the penis. The degree of venous engorgement that forms the orgasmic platform varies with the intensity of sexual stimulation, regardless of the sexual preference of the responding woman. The orgasmic platform develops late in the excitement phase or even well into the plateau phase. But once established, the platform is not static in dimension. It increases modestly in dimension as sexual tensions elevate and decreases in size if the effective stimulative approach is withdrawn, a severe distraction is introduced, or orgasm is experienced.

Apparently there is no such entity as a fully formed orgasmic platform in the sense that the platform continues to evidence modest increases or decreases in venous engorgement as effective stimulative activity is prolonged or delayed. Slowly increasing engorgement is particularly noted during the late plateau phase, just before orgasm is experienced. This lack of a static dimension for the vasocongestion of the orgasmic platform parallels the plateau-phase cyclic vasodistention and vasoconstriction of erective tissue in the penis described later in this chapter.

In many instances of lesbian interaction, a grossly engorged orgasmic platform almost occluded the outlet of the vaginal barrel. These women were completely lost in sexual excitation. This degree of platform development was usually identified in lesbian women who had been exposed to long-continued sexual stimulation before the genital organs were approached directly, a pattern of sexual behavior typical of the interaction of committed lesbian couples (see Chapter 5).

Contractions of the orgasmic platform in the outer third of the vagina and of the uterus during the homosexual woman's orgasmic experience are physiologically identical to those of heterosexual women. There always are individual variations in the intensity of orgasmic contractions and duration of orgasmic experiences. But even these physiologic response patterns vary from woman to woman and within the same woman from one experience to the next, regardless of whether the sexual stimuli are homosexually or heterosexually oriented. The ambisexual research program provided further information to confirm these investigative findings (see Chapter 8).

When the orgasmic platform is well established, there also is an advanced degree of both superficial and deep venous congestion of the other genital viscera. The color change of the minor labia (sex skin) is a superficial vasocongestive reaction that is particularly evident in responding lesbians. This onset of labial color change approximates in timing sequence the development of the orgasmic platform. Since there were only two lesbian study subjects who had experienced more than one full-term delivery (see Chapter 2), the usual burgundy-wine, sex-skin coloration characteristic of multiparous women was rarely observed. The labial coloration observed ranged from a bright pink to a cardinal red. When a labial color change takes place, the woman will be orgasmic if the stimulative approach that has brought about the color change is maintained and no major distraction is experienced.

The vagina involuntarily lengthens and then expands in diameter, particularly at the transcervical level, in response to elevated sexual tensions, but these alterations in vaginal physiology are coital precursors and of little importance in lesbian interaction unless a dildo is employed. There are other physiologic alterations in the pelvic viscera, however, that are of some consequence in lesbian response.

With long-continued sexual stimulation, the uterus, particularly that of a multiparous woman, usually increases in size; and the broad ligaments that support the uterus also may be palpably engorged with venous blood. Uterine enlargement is particularly apparent in women who have had children, with approximately a 50 percent increase in size identifiable with some frequency just before orgasmic-phase experience being identified with some frequency. The nulliparous uterus also evidences passing engorgement, but on a much smaller scale; its engorgement is identified as a transitory deep vasocongestive reaction that may only provide one-fifth to one-quarter enlargement. If there is no orgasmic release of the sexual tensions that have created this advanced degree of deep venous congestion, lesbians may experience clinical symptoms of lower abdominal or pelvic aching, or even significant pain.

Four lesbian members of committed couples demonstrated advanced degrees of pelvic congestion during sexual interaction with their partners and complained of a sense of fullness and mild aching in the pelvis, but no pain. These four women were examined just before the onset of sexual stimulation and were examined again when the pelvic vasocongestive reaction was at its maximum, just before they could have anticipated orgasmic release. Finally, the four women were examined a third time, immediately after their orgasmic experiences. For each of these women, orgasms developed during partner manipulation and were quite intense, with the orgasmic platforms contracting a minimum of 10 and a maximum of 13 times. Each of the four women cooperated with the research team to allow the three sequential pelvic examinations to be done on two separate occasions when they were responding successfully to partner manipulation. While there is the factor of potential stimulation from the pelvic examination techniques, at least it was present in all cases.

As the result of the sequential pelvic examinations, the examiner had the distinct impression that the ovaries had enlarged to an estimated 30 to 40 percent over their initial baseline size during the period of sex-tension increment, and then had lost this transitory venous engorgement in the immediate postorgasmic period.

This clinical observation merely represents the examiner's subjective impression and not only has not been confirmed, but may be no more than an example of wishful thinking. Although the ovarian stroma is more concentrated than that encountered in the testicle, the ovarian blood supply certainly is profuse. It is theoretically possible that there could be transitory deep venous engorgement of the ovaries concomitant with venous congestion of the vagina and the uterus. A more detailed investigation of the possibility of transitory ovarian venous congestion resulting from advanced degrees of sexual tension certainly is in order. The theoretical influence of such a physiologic response pattern on the ovary as a possible etiologic agent in multiple ovulation warrants continued research.

One lesbian regularly developed aching and occasions of pain in both lower quadrants of the abdomen when she was delayed from attaining orgasm for long periods by her partner's deliberate "teasing" or holding back of release opportunity. The woman had delivered two children, had had one abortion (see Chapter 3), and had obvious varicosities of the legs and in the pelvis. She stated that for the previous three years when there was long-continued sex play without orgasmic release, she would begin to ache in the lower abdomen.

A baseline pelvic examination was done before the initiation of sexual stimulation. A second pelvic examination was conducted shortly after the onset of bilateral lower quadrant aching and demonstrated palpable venous engorgement of the broad ligaments and an obvious increase in uterine size. Ovarian palpation was equivocal in that the examiner could not be sure whether there was definitive enlargement. Presumably the engorged varicosities in the broad ligaments or even the transitory enlargement of the uterus could have caused the pelvic aching.

When the ovaries were palpated during the pelvic examination, the complaint of aching in the lower quadrant intensified to an acute pain level. This was a relatively stoic woman, and the pain response was far beyond that which might be normally anticipated from ovarian palpation during a pelvic examination. The pelvic aching disappeared soon after the woman was provided with opportunity for orgasmic release by her partner. When a postorgasmic pelvic examination was done, the vasoconcentration in the broad ligament had dispersed, the uterus had returned to baseline size, and selective ovarian palpation did not produce anything resembling the level of physical distress that had been present when there was an advanced degree of venous congestion in the pelvis.

Whether this is an example of female gonadal congestion that corresponds to the testicular engorgement men experience in late plateau-phase sexual excitation is, of course, questionable, but it is not beyond the realm of possibility. Three women have been identified in a gynecologic practice with similar histories of severe aching that develops in the lower abdomen during long-continued sex play and is relieved by orgasmic experience. No pelvic pathology was evident during routine pelvic examination of these three women.

MALE TARGET ORGANS

Both superficial and deep vasocongestive reactions to sex-tension increment are evident in the penis and the testes.

An example of a superficial vasocongestive reaction is the transitory color change that develops in approximately 20 to 25 percent of males responding to late plateau-phase levels of sexual tension. The coloration, which varies in intensity, appears on the coronal ridge of the penis at the separation of the glans and shaft and, when present, is as pathognomonic of impending orgasm for the male as is the minor labial color change for the female. The committed homosexual males demonstrated a penile coronal color change of greater intensity and with greater frequency than did the assigned male homosexual couples.

The phenomenon of erection results from the slowing of venous drainage from the two corpora cavernosa and from the corpus spongiosum, which are cylinders of erectile tissue that make up the body or shaft of the penis. In addition, the corpus spongiosum, which contains the urethra, expands distally to form the glans or head of the penis and proximally to form the urethral bulb.

We have tended to believe that once penile erection has been accomplished, it becomes a static entity that usually continues without alteration until after ejaculation. But such is not the case. Sexual interchange between committed homosexual males particularly emphasized this point: There are many degrees of penile engorgement. Incomplete penile engorgement is obvious, but what represents a state of complete penile engorgement? There is no secure answer to the question of when an erect penis is fully erect.

When committed male couples, either in partner manipulation or fellatio, took long periods of time to tease the stimulatee, speeding or slowing stimulation repetitively, apparently well-established erections continued to expand. Many times the research team felt certain that the particular erection had peaked in engorgement, only to observe minimal further expansion. Late continuing expansion of the erective process usually is confined to increases in the diameter of the penile shaft or to overall engorgement of the penile

glans or both. Routinely, men responding to long-continued stimulative techniques of partner manipulation or fellatio had a more
pronounced degree of penile erection immediately before ejaculation
than did the same men when they masturbated. They usually took
less time in masturbation because they were much more goal-
oriented.

In contrast, the assigned male homosexual couples usually spent
significantly less time during partner manipulation and fellatio, and
these men only evidenced approximately the same degree of penile
engorgement immediately prior to orgasmic release as that developed when the men masturbated individually.

Heterosexual husbands responding to their wives' manual and
oral stimulation generally had more penile engorgement when these
techniques were used to obtain end-point release than when responding to the same stimulative techniques employed by the same
women but as stimulative precursors to directed intercourse. On
the infrequent occasions during partner manipulation or fellatio
when wives spent a great deal of time in teasing play with the erect
penis before providing their husbands with ejaculatory opportunity,
there was slow, continuing expansion in penile diameter that continued in such an inevitable manner up to the orgasmic sequence
that the inference was created that there always was the anatomic
possibility of minimal further shaft or glans expansion. This continuing slow expansion in shaft or glans diameter of the established
erection until orgasm intervenes parallels in physiologic potential
the continuing modest expansion of the established female orgasmic
platform described earlier in this chapter.

When intercourse occurred, there was usually less penile engorgement evident during the mounting process than was present for the
same man late in plateau phase when responding to masturbation,
partner manipulation, or fellatio.

To date, there is no mechanism for evaluating the possibility of
late-continuing expansion in penile diameter during coital connection. But it would be a surprise if the deep vasocongestive reaction
of the penis did not continue as a slowly progressive, expansive
process during coital connection, presuming, of course, that the
mental or physical distractions that so frequently accompany intercourse were held to a minimum and that the male partner did not
ejaculate rapidly.

One other minor variation on the basic theme of the male's physiologic response to effective homosexual stimulation was the immediate preejaculatory expansion of the penile glans. This deep vasocongestive reaction was not identified during the original investigation of the heterosexual male's physiologic response to sextension increment, but probably it was present, for it has occasionally been identified in heterosexual study group A males. This further expansion of the already grossly engorged glans does not occur with established regularity, but when it does develop, it parallels the man's subjective appreciation of unusually high levels of sexual excitation.

The terminal glans expansion phenomenon was most in evidence when committed male homosexual partners interacted in the laboratory. It also was seen on a few occasions in heterosexual group A males when married couples spent a good deal of time in partner manipulation and fellatio before releasing the highly excited male to his ejaculatory experience. Terminal glans expansion rarely was seen during masturbational experience. To date, its occurrence as an immediate preejaculatory reaction during coital connection has not been determined, but it would be surprising if terminal glans expansion did not occur with some regularity during intercourse. In essence, terminal glans expansion is physiologic evidence of a high degree of sexual excitation, and it only develops in the male's immediate preorgasmic phase.

Man's two-stage orgasmic experience occurs in physiologically identical fashion, regardless of whether the stimuli are heterosexually or homosexually oriented. Just as is evidenced by the lesbian study subjects, there are individual variations in intensity and duration of the homosexual male's orgasmic experience, but these are variations between individuals or within the same individual from time to time and not significant physiologic variations that can be attributed to sexual orientation alone. Additional information to support this position came from the ambisexual investigation (see Chapter 8).

Penile erection also occurred regularly for the homosexual stimulator while manipulating his partner either manually or orally. Usually the stimulator's penis achieved reasonably full engorgement from 5 to 10 minutes after the stimulatee's erection was fully established. No stimulator ejaculated while manipulating his partner.

Engorgement of the testes is a consistent deep vasocongestive response to effective sexual stimulation. The testes begin to expand in diameter late in the excitement phase or in the early plateau phase. It was rare to have no observable testicular engorgement by the time responding homosexual males ejaculated in the laboratory. The only times when testicular engorgement could not be demonstrated was when men ejaculated very rapidly after onset of masturbation, partner manipulation, or fellatio.

Testicular engorgement was occasionally observed in men in stimulator roles who became so involved in their male partners' reactions that their own sexual excitation reached plateau-phase levels while they were satisfying their partners either with manipulation or fellatio.

Testicular Aching.   Widely known clinically is the development of aching, even severe pain, that can occur in the scrotum when long-maintained sexual excitation without subsequent ejaculation keeps the testes engorged with blood for significant periods of time. This pain syndrome also has been noted when a male loses an erection or fails to ejaculate for any reason after experiencing high levels of sexual excitation for long periods of time. The testicular aching or pain is relieved promptly by an ejaculatory experience. The clinical syndrome of testicular pain during episodes of long-continued sexual excitation parallels that experienced by the few female study subjects who developed lower abdominal aching under similar circumstances. The testicular and lower abdominal distress were both relieved immediately by orgasmic experience.

SUMMARY

The physiologic material returned from the laboratory phase of the Institute's overall investigation of human sexual function supports the contention that evidences of deep vasocongestion and increased muscle tension are specific indicators of advanced degrees of sexual excitation in men and women whether of homosexual or heterosexual orientation. Penile erection and vaginal lubrication are parallel phenomena. Continuing engorgement of the female's orgasmic platform during high levels of sexual tension parallels continuing expansion in penile diameter as the male also reaches high levels of sexual excitation. The color changes of the minor labia sex skin and penile coronal ridge are also parallel phenomena and are pathognomonic of impending orgasm. And testicular pain from localized, deep vasocongestion may have a parallel reaction in the ovarian pain that also develops as a localized, deep pelvic vasocongestive response to long-continued sexual stimulation.

8

AMBISEXUAL STUDY GROUP

By mid-1968 the Institute's investigation of homosexual response patterns was terminating and there was an end in sight for the work with the heterosexual study subjects in group A. The functional efficiency of homosexual and heterosexual study subjects in the laboratory had been assessed, and restricted subjective and objective comparisons were being drawn between persons with homosexual and heterosexual orientations. There remained the need to broaden the dimensions of recently acquired information on alternative patterns of sexual behavior.

While recruiting the homosexual study-subject population, the research team encountered many men and women who had reported a considerable degree of sexual experience involving partners of both sexes. Subjects describing a history of sexual experience in which male and female partners were involved in approximately equal numbers had been encountered frequently. These men and women were given a Kinsey preference rating of 3.

From 1964 to 1968 the recruitment of Kinsey 3 men and women who were living as homosexuals was not particularly difficult. In fact, during the four-year period, 20 female and 20 male Kinsey 3 subjects were selected as members of the homosexual study-subject population. Most of these recruits had been living in committed homosexual relationships of at least one year's duration, while 1 man and 2 women volunteered to participate in the assigned homosexual groups. They also had been living as homosexuals for at least one year when recruited.

On the other hand, 5 Kinsey 3 individuals were encountered who, when contacted, were living as heterosexual partners in committed relationships. Since the decision had been made to include as heterosexual subjects only individuals with a Kinsey preference rating of 1 or 0, these men and women were not recruited for heterosexual study group A (see Chapter 1).

During the active recruiting period, research team members became aware that occasionally they were being confronted by another type of potential study subject with an atypical history. These men and women reported frequent sexual interaction with members of both sexes and also described the additional exceptional characteristic of an apparent complete neutrality in partner preference between the two genders. These individuals were living lifestyles in which commitment to a dyadic relationship had never played a part. Sexual experience was viewed as purely a matter of physical release, and gender was of no importance in acquiring a partner for any sexual episode. These individuals were clearly not sociopaths: They had no histories of trouble with the law or with authority figures; no patterns of poor performance at work, school, or in the military; and no difficulty in functioning responsibly in most facets of their lives. Furthermore, none of these persons had histories of psychologic pathology.

The research team believed that it would be valuable to assemble, interview, and evaluate a number of such people, both male and female, in a manner similar to that used with the homosexual and heterosexual research groups. It was thought that this group of subjects with no subjectively identifiable or outwardly expressed sexual preference might serve as a valuable reference group in interpreting the significance of patterns of physical response, sexual behavior, or fantasy material reported from study groups of homosexually and heterosexually oriented subjects.

A decade later, in evaluating and analyzing the data from this project, it appeared that a new term must be employed to designate the specific characteristics identified in this unusual group of men and women. Although others (Richard Green, 1974) have sparingly used the term synonymously with *bisexual*, the Institute, following the suggestion of Mark Schwartz, has taken the option of creating its own definition for the term *ambisexual*. According to Institute parlance, an ambisexual is a man or woman who unreservedly enjoys, solicits, or responds to overt sexual opportunity with equal ease and interest regardless of the sex of the partners, and who, as a sexually mature individual, has never evidenced interest in a continuing relationship.

There is clearly a different (and larger) group of individuals who are bisexual, in the sense of having significant sexual experience with partners of both genders, who do not meet the above criteria that define ambisexuality. It is also fair to say that the term *bisexual* has been widely abused and distorted in both public and professional usage. Current public usage of the bisexual label has been so misused that today any man or woman who previously has lived a totally committed heterosexual or homosexual lifestyle and experiences a single episode of sexual interaction with a partner of the opposite sexual preference may immediately consider himself or herself bisexual. As a result of this current pattern of indiscriminate application, the label of bisexuality often means whatever the user wishes to imply.

Thus, from early in 1968 through most of 1970, a multidimensional investigative program was conducted to recruit and evaluate a group of study subjects who could be identified by the Institute's definition of ambisexuality. The criteria for identification and selection of a subject as ambisexual were (1) that the individual express no preference in terms of sexual partner selection either through personal history or by subjective description, (2) that he or she was currently living an uncommitted ambisexual lifestyle and had never as an adult evidenced any interest in a continuing relationship, and (3) that the man or woman could be rated close to Kinsey 3 in sexual experience. It was decided that fantasy patterns, while they were expected to have a unique composition, would not be included as a primary selection criterion.

Fantasy patterns collected from men and women in homosexual or heterosexual study populations usually reflected evidence of transitory individual or group fixation (see Chapter 9). But any composition of fantasy patterning that is individual- or group-directed is not considered as representative of the ambisexual individual, for such is not his or her orientation. The ambisexual is primarily concerned in fantasy with past or anticipated sexual opportunities or experiences. He or she rarely individualizes a partner in fantasy.

RECRUITMENT

It was difficult to find men and women who met the criteria of ambisexuality not only in their overt sexual behavior but in their lifestyles as well. Obviously, no study subjects used in previous studies could be included in the ambisexual group.

Although the first tentative recruiting steps were taken on a national level in January, 1968, it was late summer of that year before a total of 12 men and women could be assembled who were truly ambisexual both in psychosocial orientation and in overt sexual experience. Admittedly the numbers are small, too small for objective comparison with the other study groups, but 11 years ago this represented a significant recruiting success. The size of this group should not be taken as indicative of the prevalence of ambisexuality in the general population; no such figures are available.

During careful history-taking, no expression of sexual preference, present or past, could be elicited from these men and women. After early or midadolescence, they had always thought of themselves as completely free to express their sexual needs with a partner of choice, regardless of the sexual orientation of that prospective partner. In short, their mature sexual preference was, and apparently always had been, that of the partner of the moment.

The 6 ambisexual men recruited for this project were primarily classified as Kinsey 3 in sexual preference rating. The Kinsey 2 and Kinsey 4 study subjects were close to a Kinsey 3 preference classification when histories of sexual experience were taken. The 6 ambisexual women also were either Kinsey 3 or near 3 in sexual preference when recruited. A Kinsey 2 rating was assigned to 1 woman, and 2 women were determined to be Kinsey 4 when their histories were taken (Table 8-1).

The male ambisexuals ranged in age from 26 to 41 years and the females from 27 to 43 years (Table 8-2). A minimum formal educational level of college matriculation was required for each of the 12 ambisexual subjects (Table 8-3).

The marital, pregnancy, and presumed impregnation histories of

TABLE 8-1

Ambisexual Study Interchange Experiment:
Sexual Preference Classification *

Age Group	Sexual Preference Classification	
	Male Ambisexual	Female Ambisexual
21–30	2-3-3	4-3-3
31–40	3-3	3-4
41–50	4	2
Total	6	6

(1968–1970)

* Kinsey classification of sexual preference.

TABLE 8-2

Ambisexual Study Interchange Experiment: Age Distribution

Age Group	Ambisexual Study Subjects		Assigned Study Subjects			
			Homosexual		Heterosexual	
	Male	Female	Male	Female	Male	Female
21–30	3	3	4	5	3	6
31–40	2	2	5	5	3	5
41–50	1	1	2	3	2	3
Total	6	6	11	13	8	14

(1968–1970)

the 6 men and 6 women are so brief that charting is not warranted. One woman (Kinsey 2) had been married for four months and divorced at her instigation. According to her history, the marriage was contracted purely for the convenience of her partner: She had no investment in the personal relationship. She maintained an open lesbian relationship during the brief marriage. None of the other 11 ambisexual men or women had ever married. Two women (Kinsey 3 and Kinsey 4) described conceptions that resulted in one full-term pregnancy and one voluntary abortion. In both cases the pregnancies were designated by the women as contraception failures.

TABLE 8-3

Ambisexual Study Interchange Experiment: Formal Education *

Study Subjects	High School (Percent)	College (Percent)	Postgraduate (Percent)	Total
AMBISEXUAL				
Male	0	3 (50.0)	3 (50.0)	6
Female	0	5 (83.3)	1 (16.7)	6
Total	0	8 (66.7)	4 (33.3)	12
ASSIGNED PARTNERS				
Male				
Heterosexual	2 (25.0)	3 (37.5)	3 (37.5)	8
Homosexual	4 (36.4)	5 (45.4)	2 (18.2)	11
Subtotal	6 (31.6)	8 (42.1)	5 (26.3)	19
Female				
Heterosexual	3 (21.4)	7 (50.0)	4 (28.6)	14
Homosexual	4 (30.8)	6 (46.2)	3 (23.0)	13
Subtotal	7 (25.9)	13 (48.2)	7 (25.9)	27
Total	13 (28.3)	21 (45.7)	12 (26.0)	46
				(1968–1970)

* Listing dependent only upon matriculation (highest level).

The woman who had the full-term pregnancy (Kinsey 4) did not nurse and placed the baby for adoption immediately after birth.

Two ambisexual men (Kinsey 3 and 2) reported three presumed conceptions that terminated in two full-term pregnancies and a voluntary abortion. The Kinsey 3 man claimed responsibility for two of the conceptions—a term pregnancy and the abortion. They developed from two different relationships.

All 6 women practiced contraception. Four were using oral contraceptives, 1 an intrauterine device, and 1 a vaginal diaphragm when they participated in the Institute's research program. Two of the 6 men had vasectomies.

No physical or metabolic defects were identified among the ambisexual research group or the heterosexual or homosexual assigned partners when routine physical and clinical laboratory examinations were conducted prior to final selection as study subjects.

A S S I G N E D   P A R T N E R S

The recruitment of assigned partners to interact with the ambisexual study group was also an unusual experience for the research team because of the multidimensional sexual orientation inherent in ambisexuality. In order to provide adequate research breadth, assigned partners were assembled to represent four different sexual orientations: male homosexual, male heterosexual, female homosexual, and female heterosexual.

The assigned partners were recruited by the same techniques that had been established for the three prior research populations. The assigned partners were recruited specifically so that their ages were reasonably close to those of the ambisexual study subjects with whom they were to interact sexually (see Table 8-2). With the exception of 1 homosexual man who described a single, overt heterosexual experience some six years before laboratory cooperation, all of the 46 assigned partners were either totally homosexual (Kinsey 6) or totally heterosexual (Kinsey 0) in reported sexual experience. Formal education ranged from high-school to postgraduate levels of matriculation (see Table 8-3). There were no black or Spanish-American volunteers among the ambisexual study subjects or their assigned partners.

The assigned partner population comprised a total of 19 men, of whom 11 were homosexual and 8 heterosexual, and 27 women, of whom 13 were homosexual and 14 heterosexual. This relatively large number of assigned partners was necessary for two reasons. First, extra numbers of assigned female partners were necessary in order to work around their menstrual periods. Second, the relatively large number of assigned partners made scheduling less difficult, particularly a scheduling that always had to revolve around the availability of the ambisexual study subjects, 9 of whom did not reside in the St. Louis area.

S C H E D U L I N G

The assigned partners were active in the research program on at least one occasion and frequently interacted with more than one ambisexual subject when substitution was required. Generally, when an assigned partner and an ambisexual man or woman were paired, they continued as sexual partners throughout the required pattern of stimulative techniques, whether homosexually or heterosexually oriented. Exceptions to this ideal investigative pattern were created by scheduling difficulties, illness, menstrual periods, or assigned partner withdrawal from the program. Different assigned partners were substituted freely as required to maintain scheduling continuity.

The episodes of sexual interaction in the laboratory were separated by at least a week and, in some instances, by several months. This time gap was created by two factors. First, it was the research team's intent that personal familiarity or a comfortable, confident sexual relationship between responding ambisexuals and their assigned partners be minimized. Second, the actual scheduling difficulties previously described made continuity impossible. Laboratory observations of the sexual interaction were conducted primarily on weekday evenings and over weekends to facilitate study-subject cooperation.

O R I E N T A T I O N   P R O C E D U R E S

Before the observed sexual response episodes were scheduled, there was opportunity offered for those who wished to be oriented to laboratory procedures and the laboratory environment. Repeating the pattern set by study subjects in the homosexual and the heterosexual research populations (see Chapter 4), the heterosexual assigned partners requested more orientation opportunity than did the homosexual assigned partners.

Eight of the 22 heterosexual assigned partners required orientation procedures, while only 6 of the 24 homosexual assigned partners expressed such a need. None of the 12 ambisexual subjects requested an opportunity for laboratory orientation or expressed need for privacy during their masturbational episodes (see Chapter 4). There was no concern for sexual performance evidenced by the ambisexual men and women in either their homosexual or heterosexual phases.

For the purposes of this research project, the assigned partners were deliberately not informed that they were interacting sexually with an ambisexual man or woman. The assigned partners were encouraged to interact with the available (ambisexual) partner, setting their own pace and responding without reservation at whatever levels of sexual tension developed in response to sexual stimuli. In every instance of sexual interaction in the laboratory, the assigned partners simply presumed that the ambisexual partners were of the same sexual orientation as themselves, and reacted accordingly.

Since homosexual and heterosexual physiology had been investigated in detail before the onset of the ambisexual study, only the ambisexual study subjects were evaluated physiologically. All participants in this research program were involved in the psychosexual aspects of the investigation.

The assigned partners were informed that the research team was interested primarily in sexual behavior; that they would not be involved in an investigation of sexual physiology; that they were perfectly free to interact sexually and to respond both verbally and nonverbally as they saw fit; and that the research team's only condition during any sexual episode was that subjects were to employ the specific technique requested as the primary form of sexual interaction.

The ambisexual men and women were requested not to reveal the duality of their sexual preference to the assigned partners; as far as is known, they complied with this request. They were directed to react to their assigned partners' sexual approaches and to strive for an equal exchange of stimulative opportunity rather than attempting to dominate the sexual interaction. They were not to play passive sexual roles; they were simply to refrain from imposing any particular sexual behavior pattern. The purpose of these instructions was to enable the research team to observe the ambisexuals' reaction to both homosexual and heterosexual approaches rather than to encourage them either to set the pace of the interaction or to be in conflict for dominance with the assigned partners. In short, ambisexual men and women were specifically encouraged to allow their assigned partners freedom of sexual expression whenever possible. The ambisexuals were to react rather than to initiate. Only if the assigned partner's sexual interest appeared to lag was the ambisexual to assume a role of initiating rather than reacting to sexual stimuli.

PROJECT DESIGN

The 12 ambisexual study subjects cooperated in the laboratory investigation over approximately a two-year period. Each of the 6 ambisexual men reacted sexually with 3 men of homosexual orientation and with 3 women who reported only heterosexual experience. Each of the 6 ambisexual women responded sexually to 3 women who were entirely homosexual in orientation and to 3 men who were totally heterosexual in experience.

Masturbation was evaluated in the laboratory for the 12 ambisexuals, but not for their assigned partners. The ambisexual subjects were observed only to determine the physical pattern of their masturbational activity. They each were asked to provide one episode of masturbation to orgasm while under observation. Each of the men had one masturbational ejaculation. Four women were multiorgasmic and 2 women had single orgasms for a combined total of 13 female orgasmic experiences.

It was planned that each ambisexual would interact with 3 assigned heterosexual partners in response to the stimulative techniques of partner manipulation, fellatio/cunnilingus, and coition. Thus, each ambisexual experienced a total of nine episodes that were heterosexually oriented.

Each ambisexual man and woman responded to two different stimulative techniques with each assigned homosexual partner (partner manipulation and cunnilingus/fellatio). There were 3 assigned homosexual partners, so a total of six homosexually oriented episodes were experienced by each ambisexual.

Counting the single masturbational episode, each of the 12 ambisexual study subjects participated in 16 different episodes of sexual interaction during the research project (nine heterosexual, six homosexual, and one masturbational episode). Frequently, more than one orgasm was experienced by either the ambisexual or the assigned study subject during any specific episode, for both partners were given full freedom to enjoy orgasmic expression on every occasion of sexual interaction in the laboratory.

Observation of rectal intercourse was not requested by the research team, nor was it suggested by the interacting partners. Two of the 6 ambisexual men described experience with rectal intercourse, 1 who had interacted with several different female partners and 1 as the penetrator in a homosexual relationship. One of the 11 male homosexual assigned subjects described frequent experience with rectal intercourse, preferring the role of penetrator. Four other members of the group reported occasional experiences in penetrator and/or penatratee roles while the remaining 6 men gave histories of rare or no experience with rectal intercourse.

FUNCTIONAL EFFICIENCY

The orgasmic cycles that developed in free sexual interchange between the ambisexual study subjects and their assigned partners have been charted, and failures to function effectively have been identified. A brief review of this material is in order.

AMBISEXUAL MALE FUNCTIONAL EFFICIENCY

Homosexual Phase. The homosexual phase of the ambisexual male interchange experiments is presented in Table 8-4. Each ambisexual male responded to 3 homosexual assigned partners. He experienced episodes of partner manipulation and fellatio with each assigned partner. Each assigned partner also had full opportunity for sexual involvement and orgasmic release using the same stimulative techniques.

The 6 ambisexual males and the 11 homosexual male assigned partners combined to produce a total of 36 orgasmic cycles in response to partner manipulation and 41 cycles with fellatio (Table 8-4). During the 77 complete orgasmic cycles that developed for both ambisexual and assigned male partners in response to partner manipulation and fellatio, there was one functional failure. A male ambisexual in the 41–50-year age group failed to maintain an erection during manipulation by his partner and did not ejaculate.

TABLE 8-4

Ambisexual Study Interchange Experiment: Male Homosexual Phase

Age Group	No. of Ambi-sexual Study Subjects	No. of Homo-sexual Assigned Partners	No. of Orgasmic Cycles			
			Partner Manipulation		Fellatio	
			Ambi-sexual Male	Assigned Male	Ambi-sexual Male	Assigned Male
21–30	3	4	10	9	9	11
31–40	2	5	6	6	7	7
41–50	1	2	2 *	3	3	4
Total	6	11	18	18	19	22
			(Total = 36)		(Total = 41)	
						(1968–1970)

* One ambisexual male failed to maintain an erection or to ejaculate during one episode of partner manipulation.

When queried, he stated that he had repeatedly distracted himself and just had not felt involved sexually during that particular experience. This man had no recurrent episodes of dysfunction during further opportunities for sexual interaction in the laboratory.

From the viewpoint of functional efficiency, there were no appreciable differences between the ambisexual males in their homosexual phase and their homosexual assigned partners in ability to respond at orgasmic levels. There also were no obvious differences in the levels of subjective involvement experienced in their sexual interaction.

Heterosexual Phase. Table 8-5 represents the same 6 ambisexual males reported in Table 8-4. In this instance, however, the men were in their heterosexual phases. The sexual interaction between the ambisexual men and their 3 assigned female heterosexual partners consisted of partner manipulation, cunnilingus/fellatio, and coition. The results reported are typical of those usually encountered when sexually experienced heterosexual men and women interact freely in the laboratory. Consistently, more female orgasmic cycles were recorded than those developed by males with each of the different stimulative techniques.

A heterosexual female assigned partner in the 41–50-year age

TABLE 8-5

Ambisexual Study Interchange Experiment:
Male Heterosexual Phase

Age Group	No. of Ambi-sexual Males	No. of Hetero-sexual Female Assigned Partners	No. of Orgasmic Cycles					
			Partner Manipulation		Fellatio/ Cunnilingus		Coition	
			Male	Female	Male	Female	Male	Female
21–30	3	6	9	12	10	14	9	12
31–40	2	5	7	7	6	9	6	7
41–50	1	3	3	3	4	4	3	2 *
Total	6	14	19	22	20	27	18	21

(1968–1970)

* One female assigned partner failed to obtain orgasmic release during one coital episode.

group failed to obtain orgasmic release during one coital episode. She stated that she did not know why she was not orgasmic. She felt well, was involved sexually, had not noticed any distraction, but "it just hadn't happened." There was no repetition of the dysfunction during her other sexual episodes in the laboratory.

AMBISEXUAL FEMALE FUNCTIONAL EFFICIENCY

Homosexual Phase. The 6 female ambisexuals' performance statistics in their homosexual phase are charted in Table 8-6. Again, during partner manipulation and cunnilingus there is repeated evidence of the physiologic capacity of sexually active women to be multiorgasmic. The female ambisexuals in their homosexual phase combined with their lesbian partners to provide a total of 49 partner manipulation and 56 cunnilingal orgasmic cycles.

One failure to achieve orgasmic release was recorded by a female ambisexual study subject during cunnilingus. This was the woman's only experience with the particular assigned partner. Early in their sexual interaction the ambisexual subject approached the assigned partner first, at the assigned partner's request. The assigned partner was multiorgasmic with cunnilingus. When it was the ambisexual's

TABLE 8-6

Ambisexual Study Interchange Experiment:
Female Homosexual Phase

| | | | No. of Orgasmic Cycles | | | |
| | No. of Ambi- sexual Study Subjects | No. of Homo- sexual Assigned Partners | Partner Manipulation | | Cunnilingus | |
Age Group			Ambi- sexual Female	Assigned Female	Ambi- sexual Female	Assigned Female
21–30	3	5	12	14	16	13
31–40	2	5	8	7	10	8
41–50	1	3	4	4	3 *	6
Total	6	13	24	25	29	27
			(Total = 49)		(Total = 56)	
					(1968–1970)	

* One ambisexual female failed to obtain orgasmic release during one episode of cunnilingus.

turn to be stimulated, an argument developed over an extraneous matter, and thereafter the ambisexual woman could not become sufficiently involved to be orgasmic. There was no other failure of functional efficiency by this woman with other lesbian partners in the laboratory.

It is interesting to compare the functional facility in orgasmic attainment of the female ambisexuals in their homosexual phase with that of their assigned lesbian partners. As was true for the male ambisexuals in their homosexual phase (see Table 8-4), there is no significant difference between the ambisexual women and their lesbian assigned partners in effectiveness of sexual performance as measured by orgasmic attainment. There also were no obvious differences in expressed levels of subjective involvement in their sexual interaction.

Heterosexual Phase. In Table 8-7 the ambisexual females' heterosexual phase is charted. As expected, when the heterosexual male assigned partners reacted with the ambisexual women through partner manipulation, fellatio/cunnilingus, and coition, there was

TABLE 8-7

*Ambisexual Study Interchange Experiment:
Female Heterosexual Phase*

| Age Group | No. of Ambi- sexual Females | No. of Hetero- sexual Male Assigned Partners | No. of Orgasmic Cycles | | | | | |
| | | | Partner Manipulation | | Fellatio/ Cunnilingus | | Coition | |
			Male	Female	Male	Female	Male	Female
21–30	3	3	9	12	9	15	9 *	11
31–40	2	3	6	8	7 †	10	6	7
41–50	1	2	3	4	3	4	3	4
Total	6	8	18	24	19	29	18	22

(1968–1970)

* One male assigned partner had premature ejaculation during one coital episode.
† One male assigned partner failed to maintain an erection or to ejaculate during one episode of fellatio.

female dominance in frequency of orgasmic attainment. A comparison of Tables 8-6 and 8-7 demonstrates that it made no difference whether the assigned partner was male or female insofar as the ambisexual female's capacity to attain orgasm was concerned.

There were two sexual functional failures of male assigned partners. One man had an episode of premature ejaculation during intercourse, and another man failed to achieve erection or to ejaculate while responding to fellatio. The man who experienced the rapid ejaculation stated that he had not had any sexual activity for approximately 10 days and "got too excited." The assigned partner with erective failure offered no explanation, stating quietly, "This has never happened to me before." He laughed with his partner about his failure and was apparently quite comfortable with the situation. Neither incident was repeated in other opportunities.

SUMMARY OF FUNCTIONAL EFFICIENCY EXPERIMENTS

In order to provide statistics that can be evaluated with reference to those of the homosexual study group and heterosexual study groups A and B, the combined responses of the ambisexual study subjects and their assigned partners have been summarized in Table 8-8.

The summary table lists 36 homosexual and 37 heterosexual male orgasmic cycles, all accumulated in response to partner manipulation. The 36 homosexual orgasmic cycles were developed during the ambisexual males' homosexual phase while interacting with homosexual male assigned partners. (The 36 orgasmic cycles

TABLE 8-8

Ambisexual Study Interchange Experiment: Summary of Orgasmic Cycles in Ambisexuals and Assigned Partners *

Orientation of Stimulation	Masturbation		Partner Manipulation		Fellatio/ Cunnilingus		Coition	
	Male	Female	Male	Female	Male	Female	Male	Female
Ambisexual (self)	6	13	...	...	...	...	...	...
Homosexual	...	...	36	49	41	56	...	...
Heterosexual	...	...	37	46	39	56	36	43
Total	6	13	73	95	80	112	36	43
							(1968–1970)	

* Summation of Tables 8-4, 8-5, 8-6, and 8-7.

were developed mutually between ambisexual and homosexual males [see Table 8-4].)

The 37 heterosexual male orgasmic cycles experienced during partner manipulation were developed from two sources. First, the male ambisexuals responded 19 times in their heterosexual phase to partner manipulation provided by heterosexual female partners (see Table 8-5); second, the heterosexual male assigned partners responded 18 times to partner manipulation provided by ambisexual women in their heterosexual phase (see Table 8-7).

From the same sources and accumulated in the same manner, there were a total of 41 fellatio-stimulated male orgasmic cycles developed by ambisexual males in their homosexual phase in cooperation with their assigned homosexual male partners (see Table 8-4). Also, there were a total of 39 fellatio-stimulated male orgasmic cycles developed by the combined stimulative approaches of assigned heterosexual female partners during the ambisexual males' heterosexual phase (see Table 8-5) and by ambisexual females approaching their assigned heterosexual male partners (see Table 8-7).

There were 49 partner manipulation orgasmic cycles developed conjointly by ambisexual women and their assigned lesbian partners during the ambisexual women's homosexual phase (see Table 8-6). There were an additional 46 partner manipulation orgasmic cycles developed from the two remaining sources: First, there were 22 orgasmic cycles experienced by the assigned female study subjects when stimulated by ambisexual males in their heterosexual phase (see Table 8-5); second, the ambisexual women experienced 24 orgasmic cycles when stimulated by the assigned male heterosexual partners during the ambisexual women's heterosexual phase (see Table 8-7).

The total of 80 fellatio-stimulated orgasmic cycles (41 homosexual and 39 heterosexual) experienced by the ambisexual men and the assigned male study subjects was accumulated in a manner similar to that described for the partner manipulation statistics. Reference is suggested to Tables 8-4, 8-5, and 8-7 as statistical sources.

Similarly, the total of 112 cunnilingus-stimulated orgasmic cycles (56 homosexual and 56 heterosexual) experienced by the ambisexual women and the assigned female study subjects was accumulated using the same method as that described for the partner manipulation statistics. Reference is suggested to Tables 8-5, 8-6, and 8-7 as statistical sources.

The assigned partner statistics were included in the overall summary tables both as further support of and as clarification of the sexual response efficiency of the ambisexual study subjects. If the ambisexuals had not responded or involved themselves sexually with approximate equality in both their homosexual and heterosexual phases, a lack of equal commitment might have been reflected by some statistically demonstrable loss of sexual responsivity evidenced by either their homosexual or heterosexual assigned partners. There was no loss of physiologic responsivity that could be statistically determined, and there certainly was no loss of subjective involvement that could be observed for the assigned partners of either preference.

When the same stimulative techniques were employed, it did not make the slightest difference in facility of orgasmic attainment whether the ambisexual men or women were responding to homosexual or heterosexual stimulation from assigned partners. During partner manipulation, the number of orgasmic cycles developed was almost equal regardless of the heterosexual or homosexual orientation of the stimulative activity; the same was true in response to fellatio and cunnilingus (see Table 8-8).

The ambisexual statistics also reinforce the consistently observed fact that, given the same environment, the same number of sexual opportunities, and effective sexual stimulation, sexually functional women will respond at orgasmic levels more frequently than men. This dominance in orgasmic attainment can be seen in Table 8-8. The 6 female ambisexuals developed 13 masturbational orgasmic cycles, as compared to one each for the 6 male ambisexual subjects. During both homosexually and heterosexually originated partner manipulation, the combined male subjects (ambisexual males and assigned male homosexual and male heterosexual study subjects) developed 73 orgasmic cycles, while the combined female group (ambisexual females and assigned female homosexual and female heterosexual study subjects) developed 95 orgasmic cycles.

Fellatio (homosexually and heterosexually employed) resulted in 80 male orgasmic cycles and cunnilingus (homosexually and heterosexually employed) in 112 female response cycles. Finally, there were a total of 36 male and 43 female orgasmic cycles developed during intercourse by both male and female ambisexuals in combination with their assigned heterosexual male and female partners.

Yet another way to evaluate the ambisexual study subjects and the assigned homosexual and heterosexual partners is by evaluating functional efficiency in orgasmic attainment. The incidence of failure to achieve orgasm has been presented in failure percentages for the homosexual study group and for heterosexual study groups A and B (see Chapter 6). The statistics accumulated in the ambisexual study group will be presented in the same manner as those from these previous research groups. A measure of evaluating the functional efficiency of the ambisexuals in both their homosexual and heterosexual phases can be achieved by comparing the results reported in Tables 8-9 and 8-10 with those presented in Chapter 6 for the other study groups (see Tables 6-5, 6-10, and 6-15).

When the ambisexual males and their assigned homosexual and heterosexual partners were evaluated, there were 2 men who failed to complete an orgasmic cycle in 159 sexual opportunities during masturbation, partner manipulation, and fellatio for a failure percentage of 1.26 (see Table 8-9). When the ambisexual females and

TABLE 8-9

Ambisexual Study Interchange Experiment:
Functional Efficiency of Ambisexuals and Assigned
Partners in Manipulative Stimulation

Gender and Type of Stimulation	Observed Cycles	Functional Failures	Failure Incidence	Failure Percentage
Male *				
Masturbation	6	0	0	0
Partner manipulation	73	1	1 : 73	1.37
Fellatio	80	1	1 : 80	1.25
Total	159	2	1 : 79.5	1.26
Female †				
Masturbation	13	0	0	0
Partner manipulation	95	0	0	0
Cunnilingus	112	1	1 : 112	0.89
Total	220	1	1 : 220	0.45

(1968–1970)

* Male ambisexuals, N = 6; homosexual male assigned partners, N = 11; heterosexual female assigned partners, N = 14.
† Female ambisexuals, N = 6; heterosexual male assigned partners, N = 8; homosexual female assigned partners, N = 13.

their assigned homosexual and heterosexual partners were evaluated, there was one failure to achieve orgasmic release in 220 opportunities of masturbation, partner manipulation, and cunnilingus for a failure percentage of 0.45.

During coital opportunity (see Table 8-10), the male research population (ambisexual males in their heterosexual phase and as-

TABLE 8-10

Ambisexual Study Interchange Experiment:
Functional Efficiency of Ambisexuals and
Assigned Partners in Coition

Gender	Observed Cycles	Functional Failures	Failure Incidence	Failure Percentage
Male *	36	1	1 : 36	2.80
Female †	43	1	1 : 43	2.33
				(1968–1970)

* Male ambisexuals, N = 6; male assigned partners for female ambisexuals, N = 8.
† Female ambisexuals, N = 6; female assigned partners for male ambisexuals, N = 14.

signed heterosexual male study subjects) failed to function effectively once in a total of 36 coital opportunities for a failure percentage of 2.80, and the female group (ambisexual females in their heterosexual phase and assigned heterosexual female study subjects) failed to achieve orgasm once in 43 cycles for a failure percentage of 2.33. As was also true for both heterosexual study groups A and B, the failure to function effectively during intercourse exceeds that associated with any of the other frequently employed stimulative techniques.

Finally, the functional efficiency of the ambisexual men and women in both their heterosexual and homosexual phases should be considered apart from response statistics in conjunction with their assigned partners. These data describing the functional efficiency of ambisexual men and women as a separate group are presented in Tables 8-11 and 8-12.

Each of the 6 ambisexual men masturbated to orgasm once in the laboratory (see Table 8-11). Combining the ambisexual males' homosexual and heterosexual phases, there were 37 orgasmic cycles in response to partner manipulation with one failure to maintain an erection and ejaculate, and 40 full cycles in response to fellative stimulation without a functional failure. The 1 ambisexual male functional failure, which occurred during partner manipulation in a homosexual phase, created a failure percentage of 1.20 (see Table 8-12).

TABLE 8-11

Ambisexual Study: Summary of Orgasmic Cycles in
Ambisexuals (Male, N = 6; Female, N = 6)

Gender and Age Group	No. of Ambi- sexual Study Subjects	No. of Cycles			
		Mastur- bation	Partner Manipu- lation	Fellatio (Male)/ Cunnilingus (Female)	Coition
Male					
21–30	3	3	19	21	9
31–40	2	2	13	12	6
41–50	1	1	5 *	7	3
Total	6	6	37	40	18
Female					
21–30	3	7	24	28	11
31–40	2	5	16	20	7
41–50	1	1	7	8 †	4
Total	6	13	47	56	22

(1968–1970)

* Male ambisexual partner failed to maintain an erection or ejaculate in homo-sexual phase.
  † Female ambisexual partner failed to obtain orgasmic release in homosexual phase.

The 6 ambisexual women masturbated to orgasm 13 times in six laboratory episodes (see Table 8-11). Combining both heterosexual and homosexual experiences, there were 47 partner-manipulation orgasmic cycles without dysfunction and 56 cunnilingal cycles with one episode of orgasmic failure. The failure occurred during cunnilingus in a homosexual-phase encounter. The failure percentage was 0.86 (see Table 8-12).

When the ambisexual men and women experienced coition in the laboratory, they were paired with heterosexual female and heterosexual male assigned partners. The ambisexual study group responded with 18 male and 22 female orgasmic cycles without any recorded failure to function effectively (see Tables 8-11 and 8-12).

Obviously, the functional efficiency of the sexually experienced ambisexual men and women responding to sexual stimulation in a laboratory environment is fully comparable to that of the three

TABLE 8-12

*Ambisexual Study: Functional Efficiency of Ambisexuals in
Manipulative Stimulation and Coition
(Male, N = 6; Female, N = 6)*

Gender and Type of Stimulation	Observed Cycles	Functional Failures	Failure Incidence	Failure Percentage
Male				
Masturbation	6	0	0	0
Partner manipulation	37	1	1 : 37.0	2.70
Fellatio	40	0	0	0
Total	83	1	1 : 83.0	1.20
Female				
Masturbation	13	0	0	0
Partner manipulation	47	0	0	0
Cunnilingus	56	1	1 : 56.0	1.79
Total	116	1	1 : 116.0	0.86
Coition				
Male	18	0	0	0
Female	22	0	0	0
				(1968–1970)

other basic study-subject populations. When in their homosexual phase, ambisexual men and women responded approximately as effectively at orgasmic levels as the male or female homosexual study subjects (see Chapter 6). When in their heterosexual phase, the ambisexuals' functional efficiency is comparable to that reported for the men and women in heterosexual study groups A and B (see Chapter 6).

PSYCHOSEXUAL PATTERNS

The psychosexual response patterns of the ambisexual study-subject populations should be considered in context. How did ambisexual men and women interact in the laboratory with homosexual and heterosexual assigned partners? Was different behavioral patterning evident for the ambisexuals during their homosexual and heterosexual phases? Was there a gender-linked difference apparent in ambisexual responsivity? These legitimate questions and others in a similar vein can be dealt with through the descriptions of the behavior of the ambisexual study subjects and their assigned partners during the various combinations of sex preference interaction in the laboratory.

As a general observation, it can be stated that there were no apparent reservations in sexual approach between the interacting ambisexual and his or her assigned partners of either homosexual or heterosexual orientation. The ambisexual men and women not only were confident in their approach to any sexual opportunity, they obviously thoroughly enjoyed any sexual opportunity that was presented.

AMBISEXUAL MALES

When male ambisexuals interacted with assigned homosexual male partners during episodes of partner manipulation and fellatio, the sexual response patterns were almost exactly those reported in Chapter 5 for sexual interaction observed in assigned homosexual male couples. The sexually interacting ambisexual man and his homosexual partner were obviously performance-oriented. The approach to the genitals was immediate and direct. Early in the interaction, a "my turn-your turn" pattern was established, usually without obvious verbal or nonverbal communication. With one exception, neither the male ambisexuals nor their assigned homosexual partners evidenced much interest in more than one ejaculatory experience.

When the same ambisexual men responded in their heterosexual phase to assigned heterosexual female partners in partner manipulation and fellatio/cunnilingus, there was initially usually more mutuality in genital stimulative activity, but there was little general body contact before the couple turned to my turn-your turn patterning. Cultural influence did not appear to dominate; during most of these sexual opportunities, the ambisexual men were initially approached by the heterosexual women more frequently than the men had to approach the women.

Repeating the interaction pattern previously demonstrated by assigned heterosexual couples (see Chapter 5), during partner manipulation and fellatio/cunnilingus the ambisexual males usually moved directly to their female partners' breasts and genitals. When it was the women's turn to be the stimulator, they usually moved directly to penile manipulation. There was little demonstration of deliberately slowed or purposefully "teasing" stimulative techniques in genital stimulation by either sex. The approaches to the genitals, whether manipulative or fellative/cunnilingal, were not only direct, they were demanding.

The assigned heterosexual female partners were frequently multi-orgasmic, thereby elevating the ambisexual males' levels of involvement with their overtly expressed sexual responsivity. The men made no attempt to match the women in multiorgasmic attainment. Had it not been for the multiorgasmic demands of the female partners, the heterosexual episodes of the ambisexual men might have terminated more rapidly than the homosexual episodes, since the heterosexual interactions moved so quickly toward mutual conclusion.

Although the ambisexual males in their homosexual phase were certainly performance-oriented, there was much more striving for the goal of orgasm evident in their heterosexual phase. This expression of cultural influence was evidenced not only by the ambisexual study subjects but by their assigned heterosexual partners.

Of special interest was the behavior of the ambisexual men during intercourse. Despite the directions from the research team to not initiate but to react to the assigned partner if possible, directions that were usually followed during partner manipulation and fellatio/cunnilingus, the male ambisexuals deviated from these instructions during intercourse. The ambisexual men initiated and controlled the mounting process and set the thrusting patterns during every coital opportunity.

The assigned female partners never suggested any variation in the cultural pattern of male coital dominance. These sexually experienced women, who initiated activity and interacted freely and with a sense of equality during partner manipulation and fellatio/cunnilingus, moved immediately to the culturally established, restrictive role of only reacting to rather than initiating mounting procedures or thrusting patterns when coition was the required technique of sexual interchange.

AMBISEXUAL FEMALES

When the interactions of ambisexual women were evaluated, it was evident that less culturally derived restraint was expressed by the ambisexuals in their homosexual phase than in their hetero-sexual phase. The ambisexual women evidenced more initiative in performance programming, more comfort both in giving and re-ceiving pleasure, and more freedom in expressing themselves in orgasmic experience during their partner-manipulative and cun-nilingal interactions with female partners.

There seemed to be two dominant factors in the ambisexual women's homosexual-phase response patterns. First, when the as-signed lesbian partners initiated sexual interaction and the ambi-sexual women simply reacted (in compliance with the instructions from the research team), the breasts or genitals usually were not approached at first contact by either the assigned female partners or the ambisexual women.

Second, variation in stimulative approach and alteration of stimulative pace were regularly recurrent behavior patterns during the interaction of ambisexual women with their lesbian assigned partners. As a result of the absence of immediate approach to the target organs and the recurrent use of teasing techniques when there was genital approach, far more time was taken in partner manipulation and cunnilingal interaction than was consumed by the male ambisexuals with their assigned male homosexual partners during partner manipulation and episodes of fellatio.

Once the interaction between the ambisexual women and their female partners was in full sway, the ambisexual women did not play a passive role. A my turn-your turn pattern developed rapidly, usually without overt communication. Many times women were or-gasmic and then were provided with or requested opportunity for ad-ditional orgasms before the stimulator and the stimulatee roles were reversed. Frequently the ambisexual women played the role of the stimulator first, controlling the orgasmic episodes of their partners before enjoying release themselves. There was only one exception to this general pattern of equality in dominance of role-playing.

One assigned homosexual partner preferred to dominate the sexual episodes in their entirety. She did so on each of the occasions that she interacted with ambisexual women, whether through partner manipulation or cunnilingus. After initially establishing a mutually stimulative approach, she always insisted on giving before receiving pleasure.

Despite the partner mutuality demonstrated during homosexual-phase interactions, the same 6 ambisexual women reacting to partner manipulation and fellatio/cunnilingus in their heterosexual phase with assigned heterosexual male partners let the men set the pace throughout the entire sexual interaction. Adapting to the change in stimulative pace that inevitably occurred because the men routinely initiated the sexual behavior patterns, the women responded freely to immediate pelvic and breast play. With the heterosexual male assigned partners dominating the sexual interchange, the women routinely were satisfied first in the my turn-your turn pattern of partner manipulation and fellatio/cunnilingus before accepting the responsibility of providing their male partners with release.

COITUS

When coition was anticipated, the assigned heterosexual males approached the ambisexual women's breasts and genitals directly. The women moved quickly to male genital play, but only after the initial male approach. Thereafter, the stimulative techniques were employed mutually until the male partner decided that mounting was in order. In every instance the initiation of the mounting episode, the decision as to coital positioning, and the thrusting pattern were instigated and controlled by the male assigned partners. Despite this male dominance, ambisexual women responded without any evident reservation and were multiorgasmic as frequently as during their homosexual phase.

When the ambisexual men and their assigned heterosexual female partners were directed toward intercourse, the males again dominated: The ambisexual men did not wait for the female partners' approaches, but moved to the women (against specific research team direction) and reacted just as described above for the assigned heterosexual males during intercourse with the ambisexual women.

In short, whether the study subject was an assigned heterosexual male or an ambisexual male, there was usually reasonable equality evidenced in role-playing during partner manipulation and fellatio/cunnilingus opportunities with the female partners, but when intercourse was the directed form of interaction, the cultural influences were too strong for both the male and female partners. Dominance was immediately initiated by the men and cooperated with fully by the women, regardless of whether the man or woman was ambisexual or heterosexual in preference.

Both ambisexual men and ambisexual women verbalized more freely in homosexual episodes. But homosexual men and women also tended to verbalize more freely than their heterosexual counterparts. The ambisexuals did not identify any greater subjective pleasure from orgasmic return occasioned by homosexual stimulation as compared to their experiences with heterosexual stimulation. Rather, such factors as physical well-being, periods of continence, social pressures occasioned by demands of their jobs, or the menstrual cycle were identified as being responsible for differences in subjectively appreciated pleasure in orgasmic attainment. As a general observation, it should be repeated that it was apparent that the ambisexual men and women not only were confident in their approach to any sexual opportunity, but they thoroughly enjoyed whatever opportunity was presented.

PHYSIOLOGIC OBSERVATIONS

The ambisexual study subjects were observed carefully to determine possible physiologic variations from the responses previously identified in homosexuals and heterosexuals. There simply was no difference observed in the physiologic response patterns of ambisexual men or women, whether they were responding to homosexually or heterosexually oriented stimuli. Since the physiology of human sexual response has been described for heterosexual interaction (Masters and Johnson, 1966) and for homosexual encounter (see Chapter 7), there will be no restatement of this material as recorded from ambisexual interaction.

The only major physiologic difference between ambisexual men and women in their ability to respond to both heterosexual and homosexual stimulation in the laboratory was the repeatedly mentioned natural physiologic capacity for multiorgasmic response in women.

FANTASY PATTERNS

The fantasy patterns of the ambisexual men and women are reported and discussed in Chapter 9.

DISCUSSION

To suggest that definitive answers have been found to questions the research team raised about the subject of ambisexuality at the outset of this chapter would be to deny the complexity of the issue. It is hoped, however, that the material described has provided some insight. The Institute's concept of ambisexuality has been established and expanded through many interview opportunities as well as through laboratory observations of sexual behavior. This concept is summarized from a psychosexual viewpoint in the following paragraphs.

The true ambisexual is neither homosexual nor heterosexual: He or she is, quite simply, ambisexual. It is interesting to note that while the exclusive heterosexual (Kinsey 0) usually considers any form of bisexuality (Kinsey 1 to 5) to be a bastardized form of homosexuality, and that the equally exclusive homosexual (Kinsey 6) frequently describes the bisexual (Kinsey 1 to 5) as an individual with insufficient courage to commit himself or herself to a fully homosexual orientation, the ambisexual rarely if ever expresses such a value judgment concerning the sexual behavior of other people. He or she thinks, feels, and acts from both heterosexual and homosexual points of view and does not feel called upon to defend or reject either orientation.

From the ambisexual's point of view, heterosexuality and homosexuality are neither right nor wrong, good or bad, better or worse. In fact, the true ambisexual really has no frame of reference for evaluating either orientation. Human sexual function is seen as a reality, a birthright, an integral and important part of every man and woman's life, to be directed and controlled as he or she chooses. Sexual opportunity is accepted or rejected on the basis of physical need, and the attractant is the personality and physical attributes of the potential partner, certainly not the gender of that partner. In fact, the most important attractant is the sexual opportunity, and a distant second would be the personality or physical attractiveness of the potential partner. There simply is no thought given to the gender of the potential partner as a qualifying factor in sexual attraction.

An important insight into the nature of the ambisexual man or woman is the frequently expressed lack of interest in either a committed relationship or a family structure. Whether this attitude bespeaks a diminished capacity for love and affection, or whether it is a true matter of preference alone, is unknown at present. As a general pattern, ambisexual men and women reported little or no residual affection for their siblings and more a sense of nostalgia than any depth of affection for their parents. No sense of rejection was identified. By free admission, the lifestyle of the ambisexual is a lonely one. This loneliness may prove to be the Achilles' heel of the ambisexual, one that may prove more significant to each individual with the passage of time.

Only with longitudinal, prospective studies will it be possible to judge the permanence of the ambisexual's lifestyle. Companionship becomes vital to all individuals, particularly as they age. Mental deterioration associated with the aging process can be as much delayed by psychosexually stimulating companionship as advanced by arteriosclerosis. Whether the ambisexual can find sufficient resources within himself or herself to counteract the negative aspects of the inevitable social isolation that is concomitant with his or her chosen lifestyle will be the ultimate test of the ambisexual's permanence and prevalence in society.

Anthropologists have speculated on the existence of the ambisexual in our culture. This study is only an early step in the quantification of their presumptions. When considering ambisexuality within our social framework, two immediate possibilities come to mind. The ambisexual may represent a stage of psychosocial orientation from which we have moved to a state of relative sexual discrimination represented by full heterosexual or homosexual commitment. Alternatively, the ambisexual may represent a level of sexual, if not social, sophistication toward which heterosexual and homosexual societies are moving.

In brief, ambisexuality may represent either a prior point of departure or an anticipated end-point in our psychosocial structuring. The research team is currently more comfortable with the speculation that ambisexuality represents more a prior point of departure than a societal end-point.

In the meantime, it is best to take any self-proclamation of ambisexuality with a degree of skepticism. It is safe to presume that if a man or woman supports or attacks either a homosexual or a heterosexual lifestyle, he or she is probably not an ambisexual. The ambisexual is relatively atypical in our population. He and she are, however, most interesting persons from whom the health-care professions have a great deal to learn, particularly in the area of psychosexual adjustment.

9

INCIDENCE AND
COMPARISON OF
FANTASY PATTERNS

As material in this text attests, many currently held concepts of standardized sexual behavior and of homosexual and heterosexual role-playing have been based on cultural myths and misconceptions, some of which have been exploded by the research techniques of laboratory evaluation and in-depth interview. This brief discussion of the basic aspects of sexual fantasy is presented to underscore how little we know of the fantasy patterning of fully functional heterosexual, homosexual, and ambisexual men and women.

Since the emphasis of this book is on perspectives of homosexuality, equal attention has been given to the fantasy patterns of heterosexual study subjects. This has been done for two reasons: First, although collected from 1957 to 1970, the material has not been previously reported. Second, some knowledge of the incidence of fantasy patterns of sexually functional heterosexual men and women provides yet another facet in the ongoing process of placing homosexuality in perspective. One of the better means of acquiring perspectives of homosexual function is to establish fully comparable dimensions of heterosexual function.

Again, it should be emphasized that the sexually functional study subjects who cooperated with the Institute's laboratory investigation of human sexual response were a highly selected group of men and women (see Chapter 1). They must *not* be presumed to represent a cross-section of the general population, nor should this discussion of their reported fantasy patterning be considered out of context.

Before moving further, it is also important to emphasize clearly that this report of a portion of the Institute's fantasy material has been confined appropriately to the basic aspects of the subject. Attention will be devoted exclusively to attempts to categorize subjectively identified sexual fantasies and to establish the relative incidence of these fantasies in a comparative fashion by gender and by sexual preference. There will be no attempt at clinical interpretation of fantasy material in this text. This basic approach is used to provide yet another dimension to the perspective of homosexuality.

At this time, no attempt will be made to develop a clinically oriented discussion. Detailed descriptive material of individual fantasy patterns and clinical interpretations of the fantasy material will be presented in a separate monograph at a later date. There simply is not space available in this text for an adequate clinical discussion of the fantasy material.

The research team was interested in whether there were any general trends in reported fantasy patterns that could be identified in a highly selected, sexually functional study-subject population and whether, if present, these trends might vary significantly with the study-subjects' established sexual preference.

METHODS

The fantasy material was derived from homosexual, ambisexual, and heterosexual (A and B) study groups. Interviews including questions related to fantasy patterning have always been an integral part of every volunteer's intake interview. But the research team has never considered intake interviews to be a secure source of subjectively oriented information. After study subjects had had the opportunity to develop a sense of comfort and of accomplishment in the laboratory, men and women in the various study groups were randomly selected for further discussion of their fantasy patterning. Dream-sequence material was not elicited. Two interviews were conducted, one by each member of the research team. Both interviews were completed within one month. Over the years, 30 men and 30 women were recruited from each sexual preference study group for interviews directed toward fantasy material. The obvious exception in stated recruiting numbers was the ambisexual study group, which totaled only 6 men and 6 women; however, each of the 12 ambisexual volunteers was interviewed for fantasy content in the format described above.

It was presumed that after successful sexual interaction in the laboratory, the study subjects would have increased confidence not only in themselves, but in the professionalism of the research team and in its commitment to the protection of volunteers. In turn, it was anticipated that this unique climate of comfort with sexual material would produce a more candid and detailed disclosure of sexual fantasies than might otherwise have been expected. These presumptions proved correct, for there was far more communicative freedom demonstrated during the second set of interviews than had been evidenced during the intake interviews. Material obtained during the second set of interviews will be given primary consideration in this chapter.

It was also presumed possible that fantasy patterns identified during these in-depth interviews of sexually functional men and women might place a different perspective on fantasy content described by sexually dysfunctional homosexuals and heterosexuals while in treatment at the Institute. Sexual fantasies of dysfunctional homosexual men and women are considered briefly as an integral part of the case history material reported in Chapters 13 through 16 in the clinical section of this text.

C A T E G O R I E S :   F R E E - F L O A T I N G   A N D S H O R T - T E R M   F A N T A S I E S

When the interview material was reviewed, it was evident that study-subject sexual fantasy patterns usually could be separated into two categories. In the first category are free-floating fantasies spontaneously evolved by men and women in response to sexual feelings or needs without restraints of time or place. In the second category are fantasies employed as short-term, stimulative mechanisms, frequently in response to imminent sexual opportunity. These short-term fantasies usually can be identified as repetitively enjoyed "old friends" used to initiate or enhance a sexual experience or as a supportive mechanism when concern for sexual performance develops. Of course, there are instances when the two categories overlap, particularly before and during masturbational opportunity, but generally they are easily distinguishable.

By far the most frequently reported of the two categories were fantasies of the free-floating variety. Perhaps the lower incidence of short-term fantasy can be explained by the consistently high levels of sexual effectiveness of the chosen study-subject population. Little or no delay in arousal during sexual opportunity in the laboratory was evidenced, and expressed concern for performance was rare. In other words, little need developed for an "old friend." It appears that with unquestioned sexual confidence developed from a background of essentially positive sexual experience, the need for the crutch of short-term fantasy support is lessened immeasurably.

COMPARATIVE INCIDENCE
OF REPORTED FANTASIES

The collected fantasy material has been separated by category and listed by incidence in relation both to gender and to sexual orientation of the study subjects. Table 9-1 presents the five fantasy patterns most frequently reported by committed men and women of homosexual and heterosexual orientation. Material returned from interviewing ambisexual study subjects is not included in this table, since the number of men and women interviewed was too small to be considered a representative sample. There will be brief mention of frequently recurrent fantasy patterns of these ambisexual study subjects, however, during the discussion of the most common fantasies of the different preference groups.

In general, homosexual, heterosexual, and ambisexual women reported more active sexual fantasy patterning than the male study subjects of the same sexual orientations. Homosexual men and women described a more active and diverse fantasy patterning than their heterosexual counterparts. Ambisexual men and women were far behind both heterosexual and homosexual groups in reported frequency of sexual fantasizing.

TABLE 9-1

Comparative Content of Fantasy Material:
Frequency of Occurrence

Homosexual male (N = 30)
  1. Imagery of sexual anatomy
  2. Forced sexual encounters
  3. Cross-preference encounters
  4. Idyllic encounters with unknown men
  5. Group sex experiences
Homosexual female (N = 30)
  1. Forced sexual encounters
  2. Idyllic encounter with established partner
  3. Cross-preference encounters
  4. Recall of past sexual experience
  5. Sadistic imagery
Heterosexual male (N = 30)
  1. Replacement of established partner
  2. Forced sexual encounter
  3. Observation of sexual activity
  4. Cross-preference encounters
  5. Group sex experiences
Heterosexual female (N = 30)
  1. Replacement of established partner
  2. Forced sexual encounter
  3. Observation of sexual activity
  4. Idyllic encounters with unknown men
  5. Cross-preference encounters   (1957–1968)

HOMOSEXUAL MALES

The homosexual male study subjects reported a higher incidence of free-floating fantasy than the heterosexual men. Both groups infrequently used short-term fantasy with sexual encounters, except during masturbation. The most frequently described fantasy by homosexual males was in the free-floating category. It involved specific male body imagery. Fantasies concentrated primarily on the penis and buttocks, although shoulders and facial characteristics were mentioned. Usually when body imagery was the fantasy target, there was no identification of an individual male as a fantasy subject. Only one committed (and no assigned) homosexual study subject identified his current partner in his fantasies.

The homosexual males' fantasies contained more violence than did those of the male heterosexual study subjects. Free-floating fantasies of forced sexual encounters were the second most frequently reported fantasies by homosexual male study subjects. In the forced sexual encounters men were imagined as victims almost as frequently as women. In all but one instance, the homosexual male subject played the role of rapist. The rapes were consistently fantasized as particularly repellent to the rapee, who usually was pictured as restrained and forced into sexual service by physical abuse such as whippings or beatings.

Of particular interest was the high incidence of cross-preference fantasies in the homosexual study population. This was the third most frequently described fantasy among homosexual men. Usually the free-floating content was of forced sexual participation, although there was frequent switching between the roles of forcing and being forced. As opposed to the physical rapes described above, when force was present in cross-preference sexual encounters, it usually was psychosocial in origin. For example, the fantasy of being forced by a dominant older woman to service her sexually and that of seducing a resisting younger woman into unwanted sexual participation occurred with about equal frequency.

There were also a number of fantasized cross-preference relationships with identified women from the homosexual man's past experience. In these instances there was no suggestion of forced sexual participation. Instead, content ranged from simple sexual curiosity to expectations of pleasure. When coital activity was imagined, curiosity or anticipated pleasure was described with about the same frequency as psychosocially forced participation.

The fourth most frequently described fantasy pattern for homosexual men involved idealized sexual encounters. These fantasies were free-floating in category. The imagery was almost always directed toward partners unknown to the men personally but frequently identified as entertainers or men seen at a distance. In every instance, these idealized sexual encounters involved a daydream of a chance encounter on a specific occasion. No continuity in relationship or even a repeat performance was fantasized.

The fifth most common fantasy pattern was in the short-term category. The fantasy pattern usually was of observing rather than participating in group sexual activity. The groups involved in the imagery of free sexual interchange were always of mixed gender.

HOMOSEXUAL FEMALES

The lesbian population recorded the highest fantasy incidence of the four study groups. Although a wide range of content was reported, targets were divided almost equally into male and female subjects.

Forcing or being forced sexually was the most frequently reported fantasy pattern. These fantasies were almost entirely free-floating in category. Forced sexual encounter was more frequently initiated by psychosocial pressure than by physical means. Sexual dominance and sexual subservience were regularly recurrent fantasy content. There was no frequency correlation possible between forced compliance in a stimulatee role and forcing compliance in a stimulator role because the fantasizing lesbians reported frequently switching back and forth from the role of stimulatee to that of stimulator.

The committed lesbian population did report a far higher incidence of free-floating fantasy involving their established partners than any of the other study groups. These fantasies were second in frequency of occurrence. Relationships were idealized and the individual sexual encounters savored step by step to mutual sexual satiation. Forced sex was never an element when established partners were involved in the fantasy pattern. No partner identification was reported by members of assigned lesbian couples.

Cross-preference fantasies involving male partners and generally resulting in intercourse were reported third in frequency by the homosexual women. They were generally free-floating in character. In these cross-preference encounters, sexual activity forced by imagined social pressures or other psychologically threatening circumstances dominated the fantasy content. When an identified male was involved in the fantasy, psychosocially forced coital activity was usually imagined; however, pleasurable fantasies involving coital opportunity were frequently described. When the coital act was anticipated as a desired encounter, the imagined male partner usually was unidentified.

Lesbians used recall of past sexual experience (short-term fantasies) as sexually stimulative mechanisms in both masturbation and cunnilingus, as opposed to the heterosexual females' concentration of short-term fantasy on masturbational opportunity. The fantasy content varied considerably, but it consisted primarily of recall of some particularly gratifying sexual experience that became an "old friend" through constant replay. These varying short-term fantasies of past sexual experience were the fourth most often reported pattern.

Fantasy patterns with sadistic content were fifth in reported frequency. There were fantasies of physically destructive approaches to helpless victims, who were imagined as male and female with approximately equal frequency. The fantasy content usually went beyond physically forced rape to include sadistic specifics almost always directed to the reproductive organs. The female objects of these fantasy patterns usually were personally identified, while the men who were attacked generally remained faceless. These fantasies were usually free-floating in category, but an occasional short-term pattern was reported.

HETEROSEXUAL MALES

The committed heterosexual male's most frequently reported free-floating fantasy pattern was specific identification of another woman in place of his established partner. In most instances, the sexual object was well known to the fantasizing male, while in others the woman, though identified usually as a public personality, was not known personally. When a woman was idealized in fantasy, she always was more than willing to comply with the fantasizing male's sexual demands.

Forced sexual encounter was the second most frequent fantasy pattern reported by heterosexual men. Many heterosexual men introduced thoughts of rape during free-floating fantasies and even occasionally as a short-term performance stimulant. For heterosexual men the mental imagery of being forced sexually was of just slightly greater incidence than the imagery of using force in sexual assault. Usually when heterosexual men imagined themselves forced sexually, it was by a group of unidentified women rather than by a single female. When they were forcing the sexual encounter, the fantasy usually involved one woman who generally was identified.

When first cooperating in the laboratory, both married and assigned heterosexual male partners developed short-term fantasy patterns based on an awareness of the research team's observation of their sexual activity. The fantasy content was one of being observed during sexual activity, usually by a number of people. Occasionally, the fantasizing man imagined himself having intercourse in the laboratory with an unimportant partner while a specific woman he desired as a sexual partner looked on. These fantasies, specific to the laboratory situation, were the third most frequently reported patterns. The short-term stimulation of "awareness of observation" diminished in value and in frequency of recurrence, however, as the man had further experience in the laboratory. After the stimulative value of playing to an audience was lost, the men occasionally found it necessary to revert to a short-term "old friend" fantasy as a sexual stimulant. The "old friend" was usually one of rape content.

Some form of homosexual imagery was the fourth most frequently reported fantasy pattern. This cross-preference encounter almost always developed as a free-floating fantasy. The subject matter was generally limited to physical attributes, although personality identifications were made. Facial attractiveness, muscular development, penile erection, and shape of buttocks were the most frequently imagined physical features. Fellatio was the most frequently fantasized sexual activity. Although curiosity was expressed regarding rectal penetration, it was an infrequent fantasy element. Many aspects of homosexual interaction were imagined, some with curiosity, many with a suggestion of social rejection. The fantasy content ranged from physical anticipation and performance envy to impulses toward sadism.

Fifth in frequency were free-floating fantasies of group sex. The membership of the group was usually described as including both sexes, but women were far more frequently fantasized than men as sexual partners. At times there was personal identification of group members, but more frequently they were faceless. Women's breasts and buttocks were far more frequently fantasized than their faces.

The least frequently reported fantasy by the committed heterosexual men was that involving the currently established partner. The current partner was rarely identified in free-floating and never as a short-term stimulative fantasy, regardless of whether the hetero-sexual male was married or an assigned subject.

HETEROSEXUAL FEMALES

The heterosexual female study subjects were more deeply in-volved in fantasy than their male counterparts. Like the hetero-sexual men, the female study subjects rarely fantasized their married and never their assigned partners. The most frequently reported fantasy was free-floating in category and involved a specific male. The imagery ranged from entertainers to casual acquaintances to men seen at a distance. When the fantasized male was identified by but not known to the woman, her fantasies were frequently di-rected toward different parts of the anatomy, such as shoulders, hair, penis, legs, buttocks; intercourse was the constantly fantasized sexual activity.

Forced sexual encounter with an unidentified male or males was the second most commonly described fantasy. This type of fantasy was usually free-floating in category, although occasionally being forced sexually was a short-term, "old friend" fantasy pattern. Be-ing raped while helpless to resist was consistently fantasized, while the heterosexual women rarely reported assuming the role of rapist and attacking a helpless male. Although usually fantasizing them-selves as restrained from effective resistance to the rape episode, there was little sadism and no masochism reported as fantasy content.

Compared to the heterosexual males, there was greater use of short-term fantasies during the heterosexual women's first few visits to the laboratory. Observation fantasies ranked third in re-ported frequency. These women consistently imagined themselves having intercourse before a large group of men and women. As was true for the heterosexual men, fantasies stimulated by the laboratory experience tended to disappear as comfort with the environment and security in sexual performance were established. The lack of stimulative return from the observation process was usually replaced by the same short-term fantasy used with masturbation. This short-term fantasy most frequently was forced sexual encounter.

Fourth in frequency were free-floating fantasies of idyllic trysts. Occasionally there was identification of a specific male to share the tryst, but generally faceless men were the sexual partners. Escape to the perfect lover was usually the content of the married women's sexual daydreaming, rarely the assigned partners.

Daydreams of homosexual content were the fifth most frequently reported fantasy by the female heterosexual study subjects. They were almost entirely of the free-floating category. As stated above, when the heterosexual women's fantasy content involved a male partner, there was only an occasional instance of personal identification of a well-known partner. But in more than half of the heterosexual women's homosexual fantasy patterns, specific identification of the female partner was reported. Usually the identified female subject was an older woman who by strength of personality, by employing societal blackmail, or by threatening physical punishment had seduced the fantasizing woman and, after destroying her will to resist, forced her into sexual participation, either in the role of stimulatee or as stimulator. There were also a number of instances in which the seducer role was played in fantasy by the heterosexual female. Again, the woman to be seduced was usually identified. In these homosexual fantasies, heterosexual women were most aroused by thoughts of forced participation, regardless of whether they were being forced sexually or doing the forcing.

AMBISEXUAL MALES

The 6 ambisexual male study subjects described less frequent use of fantasy than any other study group. When fantasy was employed, it was always of the free-floating category. There was no reported use of short-term fantasy as a sexual stimulant, nor did the ambisexual men indicate unusual sexual stimulation arising from laboratory observation of their sexual activity. This may be explained by the fact that 5 of the 6 men reported prior group-sex experience.

When used, the free-floating fantasies were of a different vein than those described by heterosexual and homosexual men. The content rarely involved men or women as sexual objects. There also was very little imagery of sexual anatomy, such as breasts, buttocks, or penis. Instead, fantasy content usually was directed toward potential sexual opportunity or consisted of a detailed review of some particularly stimulating prior sexual experience. The ambisexual men's free-floating fantasy content usually involved reliving the physical aspects of a specific sexual episode, regardless of whether the partner was male or female. There also were reported patterns of fantasizing anticipated sexual events, with little attention paid to the gender of projected partner or partners.

There was no reported imagery of forced sexual encounter, nor were there recorded statements of need to dominate or to be dominated in sexual interaction.

AMBISEXUAL FEMALES

Although the ambisexual women were significantly more involved in sexual fantasy than the ambisexual men, there certainly was not the degree of fantasy involvement reported by homosexual and heterosexual female study subjects. Unlike ambisexual men, the ambisexual women concentrated on their peers as sexual objects, so there were personalized men and women in their fantasy content. Neither gender nor specific partner identification, however, seemed to be of great importance. The focus was primarily on specific details of sexual activity or a review of a successful sexual episode, even though the particular activity or episode was fantasized with a partner or partners. Like the ambisexual men, the ambisexual women tended to concentrate more on future sexual opportunity and the details of prior sexual experiences than on the actual men or women who had been or might become partners.

Again, there was no reported content of forced or violent sex, nor was there expressed need to dominate or be dominated sexually.

Four of the 6 ambisexual women described a moderately repressive childhood environment with free-floating fantasies, not necessarily of sexual content, employed as a major release mechanism. When there was specific personalization in the fantasy, the adolescent's daydreams involved both sexes without apparent dominance. This point of information on psychosexual development, although replicated in the history of only one ambisexual male, may be one of the keys to future investigation of the ambisexual man's or woman's psychosocial orientation.

THE HIGH-INCIDENCE FANTASIES

CROSS-PREFERENCE FANTASY

By far the most intriguing return from investigation of the fantasy patterning reported by homosexual and heterosexual men and women and most relevant to this particular investigation was the high incidence of cross-preference fantasies. In cross-preference fantasy, homosexual men and women imagined overt heterosexual interaction and, conversely, heterosexual men and women fantasized homosexual interchange.

Frequently, the content of the cross-preference fantasies returned from the in-depth interviews differed markedly from material reported by the same study subjects during intake interviews and from opinions expressed during their periods of laboratory participation. In handling sexual fantasy material, particularly that which runs counter to cultural mores, there must be a constant awareness of the great difference between what men and women publicly profess as acceptable sexual conduct, what they report as fantasy content during most interviews, and what they fantasize privately and reveal only in unusual circumstances.

Cross-preference sexual interaction had been described as "unthinkable," "revolting," "inconceivable," during discussions with small groups of fully committed heterosexual or homosexual men and women. Yet the very men and women whose public condemnation of variant sexual activity was most vitriolic evidenced a significant curiosity, a sense of sexual anticipation, or even fears for effectiveness of sexual performance when musing in private interviews on the subject of cross-preference sexual interaction.

The high incidence of cross-preference fantasy patterning was of particular relevance to the Institute's research programs. The pattern was reported frequently by members of each study group with the exception of the ambisexual study subjects, for whom—obviously—the concept of cross-preference is irrelevant. This was the third most frequently reported fantasy by both male and female homosexual study subjects, the fourth most common pattern described by heterosexual male study subjects, and fifth in popularity for heterosexual female study subjects (see Table 9-1).

Although content of the cross-preference fantasies covered a wide range, the most frequently expressed attitude by both homosexual and heterosexual study subjects was more of curiosity than of rejection. Some heterosexual men and women fantasized homosexual activity in a positive sense by expressing curiosity, obvious sexual excitation, and anticipation of sexual interaction in a freely interactive pattern. Homosexual men and women also frequently expressed a sense of curiosity and a pleasure perspective in their cross-preference daydreaming.

Of course, there was negative content in which forcing or being forced sexually into cross-preference activity was fantasized, particularly by heterosexual women. But the negative-content fantasies were in the minority for all other study groups.

It may be recalled that heterosexual male and female study subjects were overwhelmingly Kinsey 0, with no higher than a Kinsey 1 sexual preference rating (see Chapter 3). Thus, as a result of the Institute's controlled selection process, the heterosexual study groups represented a far greater concentration of unequivocal heterosexual orientation than would be true for a cross-section of this country's avowed heterosexual population.

The Institute's homosexual study group ranged in sexual preference ratings from Kinsey 1 to Kinsey 6 (see Chapter 3). Obviously, there was a far greater incidence of prior heterosexual experience among the male and female homosexual study subjects than previous homosexual experience in the heterosexual study groups.

Initially, the research team presumed that the high incidence of cross-preference fantasy by the homosexual male and female study subjects might be explained by the significant amount of their prior heterosexual experience. This concept proved false, however. When the material was reviewed, the recorded fantasy patterns of the Kinsey 5 and 6 male and female subjects were just as frequently directed toward cross-preference imagery as those reported by the remaining members of the homosexual group with sexual preference ratings from 1 through 4.

When coitus was the subject matter of homosexual fantasy, mental imagery expressing curiosity and anticipated pleasure was encountered with a slightly higher frequency than the incidence of imagined forced participation. When other sexual techniques were fantasized, the incidence of curiosity and anticipated pleasure was significantly higher, but there were rare occasions of fantasized forced sexual participation.

The content most frequently reported by members of the male heterosexual study group included identification of a specific woman (other than the current partner) as a desired sexual partner. The heterosexual women (also ignoring their current partners) tended to fantasize sexual activity with a man they could identify but did not know. The homosexual males continued in the pattern of ignoring their current partners in sexual fantasy. The fantasies of the lesbian group were somewhat different in content, however; they were the only study group to bring their current partners into the fantasy content with any significant frequency, but they did so primarily in idealized situations rather than in imagery related to daily-living backgrounds.

While the homosexual and heterosexual men and women frequently fantasized individual partners with or without personal identification in stimulative situations, the ambisexual men and women tended to fantasize sexually stimulative situations rather than individualizing their partners. Ambisexual men adhered to this content patterning more than did ambisexual women. In their daydreaming, ambisexual women identified individual sexual partners but with little apparent regard for their gender.

FORCED SEXUAL ACTIVITY FANTASY

The second most frequently reported fantasy content of heterosexual men and women and of homosexual men was that of forced sexual interaction. It was also an integral part of sadistic imagery, which was the fifth most frequently reported fantasy by homosexual women (see Table 9-1). In the fantasies of forced sexual interaction, the homosexual or heterosexual men or women imagined themselves as either being forced to respond sexually under physical or psychosocial duress or forcing a similarly handicapped target to respond to sexual approach against his or her will. Frequently, the fantasizing men or women played both the role of rapist and that of rapee interchangeably; this was particularly true for heterosexual men. Obviously, there is always an element of sadomasochism involved in rape or sexual coercion. This discussion arbitrarily labels as sadistic only those fantasy patterns in which overt physical sadomasochism occurred that was beyond the element of forced sexual activity.

Although minimally reported, the homosexual group fantasized a higher incidence of sexual violence (sadism) as a part of the forced sexual activity than did the heterosexual study groups. There was no fantasized violence reported by the ambisexual group.

When gang rape was fantasized, there was variation in reported role-playing both by sexual preference and by gender. In his fantasies, the homosexual male was consistently active in the gang rapes, but occasionally he reported playing an additional role of planner or organizer of the rape. His victims were as frequently men as women.

The heterosexual man employed gang-rape fantasies frequently, but, interestingly, he played the role of rapee a little more frequently than that of rapist. When in the rapee role, he was usually restrained and forced by a gang of women. When playing the role of rapist, the fantasy content more involved observation of the victim's distress from other men's sexual approaches than actual participation in the rape.

The homosexual woman switched back and forth between rapist and rapee roles in most gang-rape sequences; however, there was sadistic content in a number of her gang-rape scenes. In most cases, the sadistic gang-rape segments were fantasized in revenge against another woman. Her role was one of organizer of the rape, and her pleasure usually was derived from observation of the rapee's suffering rather than from her own active participation in debasing her chosen victim.

In the heterosexual woman's fantasies of gang rape, she was predominantly the victim. She usually fantasized herself as powerless to resist, whether physically restrained or socially dominated, and in her daydreaming she was forced sexually time after time. Heterosexual women repeatedly used gang-rape fantasies as a short-term stimulant when masturbating or when responding to cunnilingus.

The heterosexual and homosexual men and the homosexual

women usually employed gang-rape imagery as a free-floating, not a short-term fantasy.

GROUP-OBSERVATION FANTASY

Although the homosexual and heterosexual study groups were equally exposed to observation procedures in the laboratory, it was only the heterosexual study groups that incorporated the laboratory environment into frequently recurrent fantasy content. The heterosexual males and females each reported group observation of their sexual activity as the third most frequently recurrent fantasy, and both study goups also noted that as comfort with the laboratory environment and confidence in sexual activity increased, the incidence of the observation fantasies decreased. Neither the male nor the female homosexual study group reported a significant incidence of personal observation fantasies.

It may be recalled that with onset of sexual activity in the laboratory, it was far more important to the heterosexual than to the homosexual study groups to have orientation periods before actually being observed in sexual interaction. This suggestion of relatively greater psychosexual insecurity in heterosexual than in homosexual study subjects has no ready explanation, but it continues to intrigue the research team. This subject is discussed in Chapter 11.

CONCLUSION

As stated in the introduction to this chapter, only the basic aspects of the fantasy material collected by the research team have been released at this time. This material has been collected from a carefully selected group of sexually functional study subjects of both genders and varying sex preferences. Before any attempt is made to establish presumed clinical significance, consultation will be sought from multiple sources. However, categories of fantasy patterning and incidence of specific content has been considered in a reportorial context.

Every study subject, regardless of sexual preference, indicated that he or she had recurrent fantasies that the subject felt no desire or need to act upon in real life. Thus, the fact that homosexual

men and women had fantasies of heterosexual activity did not necessarily indicate the presence of a latent or unrealized commitment
to heterosexuality, nor did cross-preference fantasies enjoyed by heterosexual men and women necessarily indicate a latent demand for
overt homosexual experience. Similarly, forced sexual encounter
fantasy was frequently reported by both homosexual and heterosexual males and females, but again no desire to act out such fantasies was evidenced. Further research is required to distinguish the
occasional individuals who actually have a strong tendency to act
out their fantasy patterns from the vast majority who do not.

If interpreted correctly, fantasy patterns and dream sequences
may be important sources of information for psychotherapists. But
aside from disciplinary influence, interpretative guidelines usually
are based on the therapists' own concepts of culturally standardized
gender portrayal and sexual behavior. These concepts include presumed specifics of homosexual and heterosexual role-playing. Of
necessity, a gross lack of empirical research data has forced therapists into the position of relying heavily on cultural dictum when
dealing with problems of sexual preference.

As an aid to interpretation of fantasy material derived from sexually dysfunctional men or women, regardless of preference, psychotherapists might profit from familiarity with the categories and
frequencies of fantasy patterns developed by sexually functional
men and women. For example, since cross-preference sexual fantasies occurred so frequently among the sexually functional homosexual and heterosexual men and women who formed the Institute's
study-subject groups, currently popular psychotherapeutic interpretations of this type of fantasy patterning may profit from some re-
thinking.

This chapter reflecting categories and incidence of study-subject
sexual fantasy patterning has been presented in accordance with
the Institute's overall research concept of learning from those men
and women who function effectively in order to help those with
sexual difficulties. Future publication will include detailed coordination of the bulk of the fantasy material, together with provision of
sufficient background material to orient the reader to the individual
members of the study-subject groups that were the reportive sources
of this material. Such information must be at hand in order to sup-

port interpretive comment and to encourage objective evaluation of the material by interested health-care professionals.

It should be borne in mind that the general subject matter of fantasy patterning reported in this section represents material that in many instances was collected more than a decade ago. This material may or may not be representative of today's social structuring. As cultural mores change, so may fantasy content. For example, only male homosexual and heterosexual study subjects reported fantasies of group sex frequently enough to have this type of imagery listed in the five most frequently described fantasy patterns by any study group (see Table 9-1). Quite possibly female homosexual and heterosexual study subjects, if currently interviewed, might report this fantasy pattern as an increasingly popular sexual daydream.

Certainly it is incumbent upon the health-care professionals to avoid being locked into preconceived concepts of recurrent frequency, stylized content, or even established interpretation of fantasy patterns. Therefore, there may be real value in a repetition of this type of investigative scrutiny of sexually functional men and women at least every decade. For if fantasy patterns of sexually functional persons vary significantly in recurrence, so may the recurrent fantasy patterns of the sexually dysfunctional population alter significantly. If and when fantasy patterning alters, so must clinical interpretation.

I O

PRECLINICAL
STATISTICS

In order to develop legitimate comparisons between homosexual, heterosexual, and ambisexual men's and women's facility in responding to various types of sexual stimuli in the laboratory, there must be evidence that the separate study groups are indeed comparable research populations. Only if such evidence can be presented should comparisons of functional efficiency in sexual interaction be drawn between the two genders and the three sexual preferences.

Heterosexual study group B was selected from the men and women in the Institute's first research population (1957 to 1965). If comparisons were to be drawn between existing data from this first research population and data returned by study groups recruited later, reductions had to be made in the total population of the first study group because many of its members were recruited for special projects that did not include intercourse or the other common stimulative techniques (masturbation, partner manipulation, or fellatio/cunnilingus). This reduction process has been described in Chapter 2.

The homosexual study group, recruited from 1964 to 1968, and heterosexual study group A (1967 to 1968) were established nearly a decade after the first research population was originally constituted. Finally, the ambisexual study group was recruited and evaluated during a two-year period from 1968 to 1970. Thus, the total time span for study-subject recruitment and laboratory evaluation covered a 13-year period from 1957 to 1970. No members of any specific study group were members of any other study group.

Over the years, the research team's primary concern in recruiting was that the study groups constituted later should correspond as closely as possible in composition to the original heterosexual study group (from which group B was derived). The necessity of matching study subjects' ages and levels of formal education was constantly kept in mind during each recruiting process (see Chapter 2). The one specific criterion required for selection of all study subjects was that each man and woman give a history of effective sexual functioning. An individual who described any prior difficulty with sexual interaction was not accepted as a volunteer.

Unless criteria set for the original heterosexual study group had been matched successfully while recruiting heterosexual study group A and the homosexual study group, comparable research populations would not have been established. Hence, it remained the Institute's responsibility to establish the comparability of the research groups when presenting and comparing statistically the sexual functional efficiency of the study-group members both by gender and by sexual preference. The ambisexual study group (see Chapter 8) is composed of too few members (6 men and 6 women) to be statistically evaluated in comparison to the three major study groups described above; however, the average ages of the men and women and their formal educational levels were certainly comparable to those of the original heterosexual study group.

In order to compare the study-group membership as to age and levels of formal education, Tables 10-1 and 10-2 have been prepared. In these tables, the study-group members are listed in total numbers, by gender, and in their assigned or committed couple roles. In this chapter all statistical comparisons that are reported as significant met the $p < 0.05$ level of significance. Age comparisons were accomplished through the appropriate factorial analyses of variance. Comparisons of formal educational levels were computed with chi-square analyses.

It is quite evident (Table 10-1) that there are no statistically significant differences in the average age of male subjects in the three basic study groups (homosexual group and heterosexual groups A and B) or in the ages of female members of the same three groups. There is a significant difference in the mean age of the total male study population (34.19) and the mean age of the total female study population (31.90). This male-female age differential is expected in social relationships, however, and since the

TABLE 10-1

Age Distribution of Homosexual Study Group—
Heterosexual Study Groups A and B

	Total Number	Mean Age *	Standard Deviation
Homosexual study group			
Males	94	33.35	6.90
Assigned males	10	33.10	7.72
Committed males	84	33.38	6.85
Females	82	32.22	8.24
Assigned females	6	30.83	9.66
Committed females	76	32.32	8.15
			(1964–1968)
Heterosexual study group A			
Males	57	34.51	7.73
Assigned males	7	36.14	11.91
Committed males	50	34.28	7.10
Females	57	31.68	7.28
Assigned females	7	31.29	7.25
Committed females	50	31.74	7.36
			(1967–1968)
Heterosexual study group B			
Males	286	34.72	10.36
Assigned males	29	33.17	8.80
Committed males	257	34.90	10.52
Females	281	31.80	9.40
Assigned females	24	31.13	8.22
Committed females	257	31.86	9.52
			(1957–1965)

* Mean age of male study subjects, 34.19; mean age of female study subjects, 31.90.

disparity is consistently present in all three study groups, it would not appear important to this discussion.

In order to simplify comparisons, the homosexual study group and its recruitment contemporary, heterosexual group A, will be

evaluated briefly. In turn, the statistical comparability of heterosexual study groups A and B will be established.

There were no significant differences in the average ages of male
and female study subjects in the homosexual group as compared to
the heterosexual men and women in study group A (see Table
10-1). There also were no significant differences between the two
study groups in the mean ages of committed males and committed
females, nor were there any significant differences between the same
two groups in the average ages of the assigned males and assigned
females.

Direct statistical comparisons of mean ages between the assigned
and committed study subjects in any study group were not done
because of the disproportionate sample sizes. Comparisons of such
disproportionate sample sizes in an analysis of variance (the analysis employed in determining differences in mean age) would yield
incorrect statistical results.

When comparing the levels of formal education for the men and
women in the homosexual groups and those in heterosexual study
group A (Table 10-2), no statistically significant differences were
demonstrated. But there was a statistically significant difference between the levels of formal education of the men and women, regardless of study-group association. There was a disproportionately
larger number of males than females who had postgraduate levels
of formal education and, consequently, a disproportionately larger
number of females than males who had no more than high school
levels of formal education. But this gender discrepancy in levels of
formal education was present in both the homosexual group and
heterosexual study group A.

For evaluation of formal educational levels, in contrast to age
analyses, comparisons were made directly between assigned and
committed individuals even though there were large differences in
sample size. This was done because the statistical technique used
for evaluating formal education levels was chi-square (χ^2) analysis,
which is not affected by differences in sample size.

There were no significant differences in levels of formal education between assigned and committed males in heterosexual study
group A and the homosexual study group, and also no differences
in levels of formal education between the men forming the same

TABLE 10-2

Formal Education of Homosexual Study Group—
Heterosexual Study Groups A and B

Group and Level of Education	Assigned Couples				Committed Couples			
	Male		Female		Male		Female	
	No.	Per-cent	No.	Per-cent	No.	Per-cent	No.	Per-cent
Homosexual study group								
High school	2	20.00	3	50.00	15	17.86	24	31.58
College	5	50.00	2	33.33	34	40.48	40	52.63
Postgraduate	3	30.00	1	16.67	35	41.66	12	15.79
Total	10	100	6	100	84	100	76	100
								(1964–1968)
Heterosexual study group A								
High school	1	14.28	2	28.57	11	22.00	15	30.00
College	3	42.86	3	42.86	17	34.00	23	46.00
Postgraduate	3	42.86	2	28.57	22	44.00	12	24.00
Total	7	100	7	100	50	100	50	100
								(1967–1968)
Heterosexual study group B								
High school	5	17.24	9	37.50	42	16.34	98	38.13
College	12	41.38	10	41.67	105	40.86	114	44.36
Postgraduate	12	41.38	5	20.83	110	42.80	45	17.51
Total	29	100	24	100	257	100	257	100
								(1957–1965)

two preference groups. Similarly, there were no significant differences in formal education between assigned and committed females and no differences between female members of these two preference groups.

Finally, there were no statistically significant differences between heterosexual study groups A and B either in mean age or in formal education. There still remains a statistically significant difference between the amount of formal educational experience reported by the men as compared to the women, but, as stated previously, this difference was present within each study group.

Thus, the statistical comparability of the homosexual study group and heterosexual study groups A and B has been established.

A major dimension of homosexuality can be put in perspective by drawing comparisons in the functional efficiency of human sexual interaction. How effective is the sexual interchange of homosexual men and women as compared with that of heterosexuals? Are there significant differences in functional efficiency either between the genders or between sexual preference groups? How do ambisexuals fit into the overall picture of sexual functional efficiency—can any valid comparisons be made for ambisexuals? Answers to these questions are reflected by the data presented in Tables 10-3, 10-4, and 10-5.

The facility to achieve orgasm in response to various forms of sexual stimulation is one way to carry out a comparison both between genders and between sexual preference groups. However unidimensional this type of physical measurement may be, it at least allows generalized comparisons to be drawn between statistically comparable populations.

Tables 10-3 and 10-4 summarize the results of 12 years of laboratory observation of human sexual function. In addition, they provide comparative statistics reflecting the functional efficiency of study subjects involved in sexual interaction, both by gender and by sexual preference.

Sexual functional efficiency statistics have been reported from a negative point of view: namely, the incidence of failure to achieve orgasmic release in response to specific forms of sexual stimulation. Functional failure statistics are presented for masturbation, partner manipulation, and fellatio/cunnilingus (Table 10-3) and for coition (Table 10-4).

It is obvious from perusal of Table 10-3 that there were no quantitative differences between homosexual men and heterosexual men in facility to respond at orgasmic levels of sexual excitation when masturbating or in response to the stimulative techniques of partner manipulation or fellatio.

Exactly the same statement can be made when comparing the sexual functional efficiency of homosexual women to that of heterosexual women in response to masturbation, partner manipulation,

TABLE 10-3

Summary Comparison of Failure Rates in Manipulative Stimulation by Gender and Preference in Homosexual Study Group— Heterosexual Study Groups A and B *

	Sexual Preference							
	Homosexual				Heterosexual			
Gender and Type of Stimulation	Observed Cycles	Functional Failures	Failure Incidence	Failure Percentage	Observed Cycles	Functional Failures	Failure Incidence	Failure Percentage
Male †								
Masturbation	126	1	1 : 126.0	0.79	502	4	1 : 125.5	0.80
Partner manipulation	195	2	1 : 97.5	1.02	562	5	1 : 112.4	0.89
Fellatio	217	1	1 : 217.0	0.46	146 ‡	1	1 : 146.0	0.68
Total	538	4	1 : 134.5	0.75	1210	10	1 : 121.0	0.83
Female §								
Masturbation	211	2	1 : 105.5	0.95	812	4	1 : 203.0	0.49
Partner manipulation	306	2	1 : 153.0	0.65	1004	8	1 : 125.5	0.80
Cunnilingus	192	1	1 : 192.0	0.52	159‡	2	1 : 79.5	1.26
Total	709	5	1 : 141.8	0.71	1975	14	1 : 141.1	0.76

(1957–1968)

* Summary developed from combination of Tables 6-5 and 6-16 (see Chapter 6).
† Homosexual males, $N = 94$; heterosexual males, $N = 343$.
‡ Heterosexual fellatio and cunnilingus evaluated only with study group A, *not* study group B.
§ Homosexual females, $N = 82$; heterosexual females, $N = 338$.

or cunnilingus. There simply is no quantitative difference between homosexual and heterosexual female study subjects in facility to respond at orgasmic levels to these stimulative techniques in the laboratory.

Not only is there no quantitative difference in capacity for orgasmic attainment when comparing men and women of different sexual preferences, there also is no significant difference found when comparing the functional facility of the two genders. The failure percentages (Table 10-3) attest to no quantitative differences in the functional failure rates of sexually experienced men as

TABLE 10-4

Summary Comparison of Failure Rates in Coition by Gender—
Heterosexual Study Groups A and B *

Study Group and Years	Male Study Subjects							Female Study Subjects				
	No.	Ob-served Cycles	Functional Failures			Failure Inci-dence	Failure Per-centage	No.	Ob-served Cycles	Func-tional Failures	Failure Inci-dence	Failure Per-centage
			Impo-tence	P.E.	(Total)							
Study group A (1967–1968)	57	189	4	3	(7)	1 : 27.0	3.70	57	182	6	1 : 30.3	3.30
Study group B (1957–1965)	286	5780	189	24	(213)	1 : 27.2	3.69	281 †	3973	108	1 : 36.8	2.72
Total ‡	343	5969	193	27	(220)	1 : 27.1	3.69	338	4155	114	1 : 35.5	2.74
												(1957–1968)

* Summary combines information from Tables 6-17, 6-18, 6-19, and 6-20 (see Chapter 6).
† Reduction in female numbers explained in Table 6-18 (see Chapter 6).
‡ Combined study groups A and B.
P.E. = premature ejaculation.

compared to the functional failure rates of sexually experienced women responding to the same types of sexual stimulation. The total combined failure rates (the combined failure percentages for masturbation, partner manipulation, and fellatio/cunnilingus) are remarkably similar: 0.75 percent for homosexual males, 0.71 percent for homosexual females, 0.83 percent for heterosexual males, and 0.76 percent for heterosexual females.

In brief, it can be stated unequivocally that in the laboratory there is no significant quantitative difference in subjects' ability to respond at orgasmic levels to the stimulative techniques of masturbation, partner manipulation, and fellatio/cunnilingus, regardless of whether the gender is male or female or the sexual preference is homosexual or heterosexual. The implications of these statistics, the results of 12 years of laboratory evaluation of sexually functional heterosexual and homosexual couples, will be discussed in Chapter 11.

Table 10-4 provides a different perspective of sexual functional efficiency; it summarizes functional failure statistics when coition was evaluated as the primary source of sexual stimulation. It may be recalled that all the men and women in heterosexual study groups A and B were evaluated in coital interaction in addition to the other forms of sexual stimulation (see Chapter 4). In Table 10-4 comparisons are made between the functional effectiveness of these men and women in coital connection. The last horizontal column reports the statistics returned from the two combined heterosexual study groups (A and B). A total of 343 men responded through 5,969 coital opportunities with 220 functional failures, resulting in a failure rate of 3.69 percent; while 338 women responded through 4,155 coital opportunities with 114 failures to attain orgasm, yielding a failure rate of 2.74 percent.

These figures may be somewhat misleading. In view of the number of episodes of observed coital function (5,969 for men, 4,155 for women), there clearly is statistical significance in the 0.95 percent differential in facility of male and female study subjects to respond effectively during coital activity (Rao, 1952). From a practical point of view, however, there is little clinical significance in the minimal percentile difference in sexual functional effectiveness between heterosexual male and female study subjects.

As a matter of fact, if we were to consider orgasmic facility alone, the reported percentage of male failures during coitus would be slightly lower. This figure (3.69 percent) specifically represents men's failures to function effectively in intercourse—but criteria for male functional failure in coition must include the incidence of premature ejaculation as well as that of erective inadequacy. While premature ejaculation does indeed lead to coital functional failure, it does not represent orgasmic failure. If comparison is made solely between male and female orgasmic failures, the corrected male functional failure rate is 3.24 percent instead of 3.69 percent. Therefore, the final comparative statistics for failure to attain orgasmic release during intercourse are 3.24 percent for men and 2.74 percent for women, leaving a differential of only 0.50 percent. Although even this small percentile differential remains statistically significant, there certainly is no significant clinical difference between sexually experienced men and women in facility to attain orgasmic release when responding to coital opportunity in a laboratory environment.

But there is a marked difference between the ability to respond at orgasmic levels of sexual excitation during intercourse and facility for orgasmic expression in response to other forms of sexual stimulation (see Table 10-3). The significance of these differences between sexual functional efficiency in coition and in manipulative stimulation was presented in Chapter 6 and will be discussed in detail in Chapter 11.

Table 10-5 reports the facility of ambisexual men and women to respond effectively to sexual stimulation in the forms of masturba-

TABLE 10-5

Summary Comparison of Failure Rates by Gender: Ambisexual Study Group *,†

Gender and Type of Stimulation	Observed Cycles	Functional Failures	Failure Incidence	Failure Percentage
Male				
Masturbation	6	0	0	0
Partner manipulation	37	1 ‡	1 : 37.0	2.70
Fellatio	40	0	0	0
Total	83	1	1 : 83.0	1.20
Female				
Masturbation	13	0	0	0
Partner manipulation	47	0	0	0
Cunnilingus	56	1 §	1 : 56.0	1.79
Total	116	1	1 : 116.0	0.86
Coition				
Male	18	0	0	0
Female	22	0	0	0
				(1968–1970)

* Summary is a restatement of Table 8-12 (see Chapter 8), given here for reader convenience.

† Male ambisexual study subjects, N = 6; female ambisexual study subjects, N = 6.

‡ One male ambisexual failed to maintain an erection or ejaculate.

§ One female ambisexual failed to obtain orgasmic release.

tion, partner manipulation, fellatio/cunnilingus, and coition. Although the number of study subjects was too small and their laboratory experiences were too few to allow statistical comparisons with the returns from the homosexual and heterosexual study populations represented in Tables 10-3 and 10-4, an obvious trend in clinical response patterns has been established. The general pattern would indicate that there is no specific clinical difference evident between the response patterns of the ambisexual in his or her homosexual or heterosexual phase and the sexually responsive men and women in the homosexual or heterosexual study groups, respectively. The implications of these statistics will be discussed in Chapter 11.

SUMMARY

The dimensions of this chapter have been confined to the presentation of pertinent statistical material. At the outset, the statistical comparability of the three basic study groups (the homosexual study group and heterosexual study groups A and B) was established. It has been demonstrated that there is no quantitative difference in the functional efficiency of sexual interaction in the homosexual study group as compared with the heterosexual study groups. In addition, it has been pointed out that there is no quantitative difference between the functional efficiency of sexually experienced men and women, regardless of their sexual preference, when responding in a laboratory environment to the stimuli of masturbation, partner manipulation, and fellatio/cunnilingus. There is, however, a significant difference in functional failure percentage between heterosexual men and women in response to coital opportunity in the laboratory, but the difference is so small (0.50 percent) as to be of little if any clinical significance.

The functional efficiency of the ambisexual population is also presented. Although the small size of the ambisexual study population prohibits valid quantitative comparisons with the other study groups in sexual functional efficiency, the trend in response patterning is emphasized.

In brief, the statistical dimension of functional efficiency in sexual interaction is used to compare the male and female members of the homosexual and heterosexual study populations. This approach is yet another means of providing perspective for the homosexual population.

I I

PRECLINICAL

DISCUSSION

In 1964 the Institute initiated a long-term research program designed to broaden the dimensions of currently held perspectives on homosexuality. The dimensions to be expanded were those upon which Institute personnel traditionally have concentrated investigative interest: the physiologic and psychological aspects of human sexual function and dysfunction. For example, it was anticipated that if the physiologic patterns of homosexual study subjects' sexual interaction could be identified, comparisons might legitimately be drawn to the physiologic patterns previously described for men and women in heterosexual study groups. If such comparisons could be drawn effectively, a new dimension would be added to health-care professionals' perspectives on homosexuality.

PHYSIOLOGIC CONSIDERATIONS

SEXUAL FUNCTIONAL EFFICIENCY

Table 10-3 (see Chapter 10) is by far the most important table in the preclinical section of this text. Brief scrutiny of this table makes if abundantly clear that there is no statistically significant difference between sexually experienced male homosexual and male heterosexual study subjects in facility to respond at orgasmic levels to the stimulative techniques of masturbation, partner manipulation, and fellatio. Similarly, it is evident that there is no statistically significant difference in facility of orgasmic attainment between sexually experienced female homosexual and female heterosexual study subjects in response to masturbation, partner manipulation, and cunnilingus. How should health-care professionals interpret this information?

Results returned from research projects must be viewed with objectivity, for the statistics can easily be given undue importance and can just as easily be undervalued. For example, major pitfalls may be encountered if attempts are made to draw universally applicable conclusions from the ability of sexually experienced study subjects to respond successfully in the laboratory to various forms of sexual stimulation.

Pertinent questions must be raised to avoid unwarranted assumptions. For example, does this knowledge of equality in sexual effectiveness between homosexual and heterosexual males and females mean that these men and women would react in private with essentially the same levels of functional efficiency as were evidenced in the laboratory? The answer is that we have not the slightest idea. There might be a physiologic difference between sexual response patterns developed in private and those observed in the laboratory. To make the unfounded assumption that there could be no difference between sexual response in private and in the laboratory would be to give undue importance to the statistics presented in Table 10-3. But to give little credence to the laboratory findings because they cannot be directly compared to private sexual interaction would be to grossly undervalue the research returns. What must *not* be done under any circumstance is to bend the research results to satisfy personal need. Unsupported connotations that tend to give credence to personal beliefs about patterns of human sexual interaction or even about sexual orientation must not be read into these reported research results.

Few important conclusions, but some very interesting speculations, can be safely drawn from the material at hand. A secure base of indisputable fact should lead the inquiring researcher more toward speculation than to leave him or her resting in a safe scientific harbor, pontificating conclusions. It is a fact that under specifically controlled conditions, there is no inherent difference in physiologic facility to respond at orgasmic levels between homosexual and heterosexual men and between homosexual and heterosexual women. And it is interesting to speculate that if there were an inherent genetic differential between homosexual and heterosexual men and women, as has been frequently claimed by the general public, by members of the theological profession, and—at times—by health-care professionals, there might well be demonstrable differences in physiologic facility for sexual interaction and in capacity to respond to similar forms of sexual stimulation. *There were none.* Yet, the fact that homosexuals and heterosexuals function in an essentially identical manner in the laboratory certainly does not warrant a didactic statement that no genetic differences will be established by future research. To date, no such differences have been demonstrated. The Institute's current position is simply that the results of these controlled laboratory experiments suggest that it is unlikely that the identification of a genetic determinant for homosexuality or heterosexuality will be accomplished in the future.

But there is more to be gleaned from Table 10-3 (see Chapter 10). Vertical perusal of the Failure Percentage columns lends statistical support to another fact. There are no demonstrable physiologic differences between sexually experienced men and women in facility to respond at orgasmic levels to masturbation, partner manipulation, and fellatio/cunnilingus in a laboratory setting.

Time and again in this text and in *Human Sexual Response* (1966), evidence has been presented of woman's innate multiorgasmic capacity as opposed to man's usual restriction to single orgasmic experience. Now there is reliable evidence that in addition to a significantly increased orgasmic capacity, sexually experienced women have a facility to attain orgasm equal to that of sexually experienced men when responding to the same forms of sexual stimulation under controlled laboratory conditions.

Table 10-4 (see Chapter 10) adds yet another dimension to this presentation of facts, conclusions, and speculation. The new dimension has been created from the results of over a decade of evaluating male and female functional efficiency during intercourse. In simplified form, it can be stated that in just over three times in 100 episodes of intercourse in the laboratory men failed to reach orgasmic release, and that the incidence of female failure to achieve orgasmic release in similar circumstances was just under three times in 100 opportunities. Over the 12 years of observation of coital function in the laboratory, the research team has been amazed at the low incidence of sexually experienced men and women failing to achieve orgasmic release during episodes of coital interaction in the laboratory. Now the fact that there was such a minimal percentile difference (0.50 percent) between the two genders in failure of orgasmic attainment lends further credence to the Institute's oft-stated conclusion that men and women are incredibly similar, not different, in facility to respond to effective sexual stimuli.

The safe conclusion can be drawn that, from a purely functional point of view, woman has the physiologic potential to be a more responsive sexual entity than man. These laboratory returns also lead to the speculation that, in this country at least, man's culturally established role as the sex expert, as the more facile sexual responder, or as the more effective sexual performer will not be supported much longer.

In short, we now know that when selected heterosexual and homosexual study subjects interact sexually in the laboratory in response to masturbation, partner manipulation, or fellatio/cunnilingus, there are no significant statistical differences in facility of orgasmic attainment, regardless of the sexual preference or the gender of the interacting study subjects. We also know that with the same experienced heterosexual study subjects responding to coital stimulation in the laboratory, there is no clinical difference between men and women in facility to attain orgasmic release. It is impossible to assess how important this information will prove to be, particularly when considering its potential application to the understanding and treatment of clinical problems of sexual dysfunction. Since we simply have not had these facts at our disposal prior to completion of these research programs, it will take clinical trial to determine their true worth.

Yet another important fact can be gleaned from contemplation of the figures in Tables 10-3 and 10-4 (see Chapter 10). Functional failure rates for sexually experienced men and women during coition in the laboratory were approximately four times higher than the average functional failure rates experienced by the same men and women when responding to the stimuli of masturbation, partner manipulation, and fellatio/cunnilingus. This fact leads to the speculation that the coital functional failure rate may be higher because two people are simultaneously involved in sexual interaction during coitus, as opposed to the individual alone (masturbation) or two persons usually alternating in the stimulatee/stimulator roles (partner manipulation and fellatio/cunnilingus). It would seem inevitable that two people, however sexually experienced, would have greater difficulty in responding effectively to the mutual sexual stimulation of intercourse than would either individual when responding primarily to his or her own sexual interests (masturbation, partner manipulation, fellatio/cunnilingus).

Immediate clinical application might be made of this heretofore unpublished information. One might speculate that the additional risk of functional failure apparently inherent in coition as opposed to the other forms of sexual stimulation would make heterosexual partners all the more eager to communicate freely and to learn all that they can about the opposite gender's facility in coital interaction. For the more one knows of the opposite sex's sexual anatomy, sexual interests, sexual needs, and sexual facilities, the more effectively he or she can function in sexual intercourse.

As described in Chapter 6, there was no statistical difference in ability to respond at orgasmic levels between men and women in committed relationships and those in assigned partnerships when masturbation, partner manipulation, and fellatio/cunnilingus were the stimulative techniques (Table 6-21, Chapter 6). During intercourse, however, the men and women in assigned relationships had a slightly higher incidence of functional failure than those in committed relationships (Table 6-22, Chapter 6).

When considering the functional efficiency of sexually experienced individuals responding to sexual stimuli in the laboratory, it does not seem to make much difference whether the individual is male or female, homosexual or heterosexual, committed to a sexual partner or not. Although these facts may be hard to deal with from a psychosocial point of view—for they certainly run against the current of our cultural heritage—they are indeed facts. Again, to draw untoward conclusions from these facts would be just as unfortunate as to ignore them. The interpretation and application of this material will certainly involve a multiplicity of disciplines in the future.

Table 10-5 (see Chapter 10) reports the functional efficiency of a small group of ambisexual male and female study subjects. It is obvious from the recorded statistics that when ambisexuals were in their homosexual phases, they reacted to the same forms of sexual stimulation with the same levels of physiologic effectiveness and with the same types of subjective involvement as homosexual men and women, and when in their heterosexual phases, their sexual efficiency and subjective involvement paralleled that of heterosexual male and female study subjects.

This small group was not of sufficient numbers nor were enough laboratory episodes observed for the returns to be statistically comparable to the much larger homosexual and heterosexual research populations. Yet, careful examination of the material reported in Chapter 8 does add important clinical support to the concepts previously discussed in this chapter, namely, that sexual preference makes no difference in the sexual facility of experienced men and women and that gender alone carries with it neither an increased nor decreased potential for effective sexual response. Ambisexuality by its very existence lends strong support to the concept of equality in functional efficiency between the two sexual preference groups.

PSYCHOSEXUAL CONSIDERATIONS

In the laboratory specific psychosexual differences were identified between the sexual behavior of committed male and female homosexual couples and that of married men and women (see Chapter 5). There were even greater psychosexual differences identified between the sexual interaction patterns of committed and assigned couples, whether of homosexual or heterosexual orientation (see Chapters 4 and 5). But far more important than identification of these variations in sexual behavior is the development of plausible explanations for the etiology of the differences.

When members of the four research populations, the homosexual study group, the heterosexual study groups (A and B), and the ambisexual study group, were interacting in the laboratory, there was every opportunity to observe sexual behavior. In addition to unlimited opportunity for observation, there was equally extensive opportunity for discussion with and questioning of the cooperative male and female study subjects before or after any particular episode of sexual interaction. The material that follows in this chapter reflects the research team's selective filtration of information acquired from the study groups during extensive interview opportunity. Rather than presenting this material in outline form supported by a series of questions and answers or with a specific disciplinary orientation, a free-flowing, reportorial style has been selected. A separate publication is planned for the future to deal in far greater depth with the subjectively oriented material acquired from discussions held with representative members of the study-subject population during the years of laboratory investigation of human sexual function.

Before moving further, the Institute's use of the terms *committed* and *assigned* warrants further consideration. The Institute's *working* definition of a committed homosexual couple is a couple that has lived together for a year or more, and a committed heterosexual couple is indicated by the existence of a marriage license (see Chapter 1). Obviously, these criteria of commitment are completely inadequate, but they were the best available in 1957 when the research began and, unfortunately, may still be the best available today, for any word that presumes to describe a subjective state of mind inevitably is inadequate. To be "committed" to someone is, if possible, even more vague in delineation than to be "in love" with someone. Since there are hundreds of levels of subjective involvement that have been termed "love," there may be an even greater number of subjectively determined levels of interpersonal identification verbalized as commitment.

There is difficulty with interpretation particularly when the term "committed couple" is used in an attempt to define a subjectively derived relationship involving two people. Perhaps it may relieve the confusion a bit to state that beyond the working definition's basic criteria of a marriage license and a year's coresidency, the Institute's long-held concept of a committed couple is a unit of two people, whether of homosexual or heterosexual orientation, who are reasonably familiar with each other's individual personalities and who, for reasons that they usually cannot define, have chosen to share a life together in spite of such significant knowledge.

By Institute dictum, an "assigned couple" is composed of sexually responsive men and women formed into a transitory homosexual, heterosexual, or ambisexual partnership by a process of research-team selection. The men and women who functioned in the assigned-couple category in the Institute's research programs had never met before being introduced in the laboratory.

VARIATIONS IN SEXUAL BEHAVIOR

When considering variations in sexual behavior between committed homosexual couples and marital units, one can always fall back on the concept of intragender empathy, usually verbalized by the old cliché, "It takes one to know one." This aphorism leaves much to be desired as an explanation of the etiology of the variations in sexual behavior patterning reported in Chapter 5. There is even difficulty in assigning a specific role to the cliché, for it obviously serves both as a widely accepted explanation for homosexual preference and as a most effective homosexual recruiting slogan for the sexually timid. (As a successful recruiting slogan directed toward the sexually unsophisticated, "It takes one . . ." probably ranks third behind "If you loved me, you would . . . " and "How do you know, if you haven't tried?") If accepted at face value, this oft-employed recruiting slogan would discourage any attempt to understand subjectively appreciated variations in sexual behavior.

Does the fact that in the laboratory there were observable variations in sexual patterning between committed homosexual and married couples warrant in-depth consideration? Probably, for there are lessons to be learned through appreciation of the psychosexual aspects of both lifestyles. Why did committed homosexual couples generally become more involved subjectively in the sexual interaction than married heterosexual couples? If this be true—and it was—why was there no statistically significant difference in the facility of orgasmic attainment between the two research populations when responding to similar sexual stimuli (see Chapters 6 and 10)?

In order to provide acceptable answers to these questions, information from years of observation of sexual interaction and material from multiple study-subject interviews are blended with a significant degree of research-team speculation in the remainder of this chapter.

Homosexuals.   Perhaps the key to the clinically apparent higher level of subjective involvement of committed homosexual couples in sexual interaction compared to that evidenced by married couples was the observed tendency in homosexuals toward free flow of both verbal and nonverbal communication between stimulator and stimulatee (see Chapter 5). Information relative to sexual needs, levels of sexual involvement, what pleased or what distracted was usually exchanged openly during sexual activity or discussed without reservation after any specific sexual episode in anticipation of future sexual opportunity.

What occasioned such an unusually high level of communicative interchange between committed homosexual partners? Quite probably: *necessity*. For inherent in committed homosexual relationships are immediate sexual advantages and long-range disadvantages. An immediate advantage is the previously mentioned factor of intragender empathy. Men know quite specifically, merely by subjective anticipation, what usually pleases men, and women are indeed the only experts on the subjective appreciation of women's sexual feelings. Subjective involvement in the committed homosexual couple's sexual interaction is usually maintained at highly effective levels by this intragender empathy and by freedom to identify individual sexual needs, distractions, pleasures, or antipathies.

The committed homosexual also has the immediate advantage of security in sexual performance that is inherent in any sexual relationship in which there is no built-in functional dependency upon a partner. When totality of sexual interest can be focused almost exclusively on self, as is inherently true in any "my turn-your turn" pattern of sexual interaction, and when one's own sexual facility does not depend on more than a partner's voluntary cooperation (specifically not the partner's sexual facility), there is marked reduction in the incidence of fears of performance or indulgence in spectator roles during sexual interaction. In a committed homosexual relationship, each partner has the psychosexual freedom to enjoy the couple's overt sexual interplay for himself or herself alone. Therefore, he or she is far more free to appreciate the subjective aspects of the sexual interaction as an individual without the major distractions inherent in the heterosexual couple's culturally oriented assumption of responsibility for the partner's degree of sexual involvement. This cultural concept of responsibility for the partner is, of course, particularly apparent during coition.

But there are long-range disadvantages inherent in the basic stimulative techniques available to homosexual men and women—partner manipulation and fellatio/cunnilingus. Although there are also the two pseudocoital techniques of rectal intercourse and dildo usage, plus occasions of mutual masturbation, these were regularly employed by only a minority of the committed homosexuals who volunteered as study subjects. Therefore this brings the discussion back to the previously expressed point: *necessity*. Since there are only two widely popular stimulative approaches employed by interacting committed homosexuals, these techniques of *necessity* must be constantly varied and refined to the utmost to avoid the loss of stimulative effectiveness through long-continued familiarity.

The inherent disadvantage of these stimulative approaches is that they are fundamentally my turn-your turn interactions, as opposed to the "our turn" potential of coitus. While the my turn-your turn approach is obviously a satisfactory means of accomplishing sexual release, the partners' preorgasmic levels of sexual tension and their orgasmic episodes are usually experienced separately, not as an immediate return from mutual stimulation as supplied during coition.

When elevated levels of sexual stimulation are mutually experienced rather than individually enjoyed, there is potentially a broader dimension of sexual arousal than is available to individuals with a pattern of responding in the relatively restrictive stimulatee or stimulator roles. Of course, there are many sources of sex-tension increment, but when partners become mutually involved sexually, these sources tend to resolve into three major facets of sexual stimulation. First, it is sexually stimulating for individual A when he or she approaches the partner's body physically. When the partner simultaneously moves to stimulate A's body, A indeed has developed a second source of physical pleasure. Finally, if A's partner reaches high levels of sexual tension during their mutual sex play and effectively communicates this degree of sexual involvement to A, either verbally or nonverbally, there is a third source of sex-tension increment that is subjectively appreciated by A. A becomes increasingly involved sexually by identifying subjectively with his or her partner's elevated levels of sexual involvement.

When partner manipulation and fellatio or cunnilingus were employed as the selected methods of sexual release by homosexual and heterosexual couples reacting in the laboratory, opportunities for sexual arousal after preliminary erotic approaches usually were restricted to two of the three major facets of sex-tension increment, because the mutuality of simultaneously giving and receiving physical stimulation was generally held to a minimum. When an individual is acting essentially in a stimulator role in a my turn-your turn situation, the stimulator enjoys the sensual return from approaching his or her partner's total body and has the simultaneous opportunity of subjectively appreciating his or her partner's sexual arousal, if present. Lacking for the stimulator, however, is the third source of sex-tension increment, which would be present if his or her erogenous areas were simultaneously being manipulated by the stimulatee.

If sexual partners had consistently employed mutually stimulative approaches when using manual or oral techniques in the laboratory, the three major sources of sex-tension increment would have been present.

How does this discussion of the multiple aspects of stimulative involvement explain the fact that there generally was an even greater difference in subjective involvement evident in sexual interchange between committed and assigned homosexual couples than between committed homosexual and married couples? It does not, of course, for both committed and assigned homosexual couples have the same long-range handicap of inherent restriction in the variety of basic stimulative techniques, and both usually employed the my turn-your turn stimulative approaches in the laboratory.

But committed as opposed to assigned homosexual couples usually made every effort to get the most from their technically restrictive opportunities at sexual interchange. Originality of sexual approach and subjective appreciation of the partner's pleasure quotient, together with the highest level of verbal and nonverbal communication of any of the study groups, tended to enhance the sensuous aspects of the committed homosexual relationship and therefore to neutralize the long-range disadvantage of channelized stimulative opportunity.

Comparably, a number of the homosexual men and women who functioned as assigned partners took the easy-and-popular way out of this persistent dilemma of channelized stimulative techniques. The assigned subjects made little attempt to establish communication in order to enhance the sensuous aspects of their transitory sexual relationships. Instead, they consistently moved to neutralize the long-range disadvantage of the restrictive number of basic stimulative techniques by adding to their subjective appreciation of the sexual interaction the zestful "seasoning" of regularly recruited new partners. It was their position that, if need be, or if the mood struck, there could be a different seasoning for every sexual encounter. It seemed to them that little or no effort need be expended on the art of communication or in establishing and maintaining a relationship, as long as new recruits were in unlimited supply.

The concept of maintaining high levels of subjective sexual involvement by constantly changing partners works well, particularly when the man or woman devoted to this lifestyle is relatively young and acceptably attractive. But this circle of freedom constricts when one grows older, or unfortunately, is no longer physically or socially attractive enough to acquire new partners with satisfactory regularity. Then the casual homosexual devoted to a "cruising" lifestyle is in difficulty. He or she usually reacts to reduction in physical attractiveness in a self-protective manner by attempting to establish a committed relationship. If for any reason there is not a seemingly inexhaustible supply of new partners available, the uncommitted homosexual may be forced to make some restriction in his or her heretofore highly valued, independent lifestyle in order to establish and support a committed relationship, which—when there is adequate motivation—can provide sufficient variety to stimulate lagging sexual interest or facility.

Of course, the problem is not as simplistic as this limited discussion would suggest. But in the laboratory the basic differences between committed and assigned homosexual couples in subjective appreciation of sexual interchange existed as described, and as intelligent men and women they discussed openly the advantages of their sexual preference and its inherent disadvantages. They also discoursed at length on the importance of committed relationships or the lack of them. This discussion drew heavily for source material from these freely communicative interchanges.

From the aspect of facility in orgasmic attainment, there was little to choose between the committed and assigned homosexual groups as they interacted in the laboratory (see Chapters 6 and 10). But frequently during in-depth discussions with the study subjects, an assigned homosexual partner's fears for the future emerged. He or she usually openly admitted that the motivation behind his or her cruising propensities was the continuing requirement for new partners to serve as a vital aphrodisiac to his or her sexual satisfaction.

Of course, committed homosexual and married couples also reported "other partner" opportunities. The concept of supplementing the established partner by a transitory "new face" as a reliable source of maintaining sexual interest and sexual facility is hardly new for men or women of any sexual persuasion. There were major attitudinal differences verbalized for the role or value of the new face. For the members of committed heterosexual and homosexual couples, new faces usually were "sometime things" in their sexual value systems. For the men and women constituting assigned homosexual and heterosexual couples, the need for new faces was a way of life.

Heterosexuals. A discussion of the subjective aspects of committed heterosexual couples' sexual interaction should add comparative dimensions to perspectives of homosexuality. As was true for the homosexual study population, there are immediate technical advantages and long-range disadvantages to sexual interaction between heterosexual men and women. Heterosexual couples can use any combination of the popular techniques of partner manipulation, fellatio/cunnilingus, and intercourse as well as the less frequently experienced rectal intercourse, dildo usage, or mutual masturbation. Therefore variation in stimulative approaches is potentially greater than that available to homosexual couples, and in theory, at least, the heterosexually oriented man or woman has greater opportunity for subjective pleasure derived from the free, inventive interchange of sexual techniques. Of course, in order to achieve this freedom of sexual expression, he and she must deny both theological and cultural concepts that coitus is the only acceptable form of end-point release during sexual interaction. For example, as long as manipulation of partner or fellatio/cunnilingus are considered only as means to an end sexually rather than as potential ends in themselves, the heterosexual's inherent advantage in multiplicity of sexually stimulative techniques is severely reduced and the immediate technical advantage in committed heterosexual interaction as opposed to committed homosexual activity is neutralized.

Then the long-range disadvantages inherent in intergender interaction make themselves felt. Committed heterosexual partners inevitably encounter difficulties when they attempt intergender interpretation of sexual expression. There is an immediate sense of frustration that eventually may turn to trauma when men presume to understand the subjective aspects of female sexuality or when women become convinced that they are "experts on men's sexuality." Men simply have no frame of reference from which to appreciate the subjective aspects of women's orgasmic experience, any more than women have the slightest concept of what it feels like to ejaculate.

As previously suggested, this relatively inviolable barrier to subjective appreciation of the opposite gender's sexual feelings should inspire committed men and women to attempt to educate each other in the intricacies of intergender interpretation. Obviously, this process of mutual sex education can best be accomplished by identifying pleasurable or distracting sexual approaches or by occasionally discussing at some length after sexual encounters how each partner feels or has felt during the activity. In short, the abysmal lack of knowledge of men by women and of women by men should constantly stimulate communicative interchange, particularly if the men and women are partners in a committed relationship. Yet, this pattern of communicative interchange was notably present in committed homosexual, *not* heterosexual relationships, even though the homosexual partners already had the immediate advantage of intragender empathy.

Free communicative flow was only occasionally evidenced by committed heterosexual couples, even though these men and women repeatedly identified the necessity for such communicative interchange during casual discussions with the research team. For a few committed heterosexual couples this vital exchange of information did take place in the laboratory, but between the great majority of married partners there was little voluntary exchange of psychosexual material. As the direct result of this communicative vacuum in material of sexual content, the cliché "It takes one to know one" stands unchallenged, and the married couple's inherent sexual advantage over the committed homosexual couple in diversity of sexually stimulative approaches is more than neutralized in two ways: first, by the concept that intercourse is the only acceptable endpoint of sexual interchange, and second, by persistent neglect of the vital communicative exchange of letting one's partner know what pleases, what distracts, what might be enjoyable, and what is not acceptable.

In other words, the committed heterosexual couple is handicapped sexually, first by theological and cultural covenant, and—a far more important second—by a potentially self-destructive lack of intellectual curiosity about the partner.

There was full agreement in open discussion with committed heterosexual men and women that the third most frequent long-range sexual disadvantage married couples face arises from the cultural concept that man should function in the role of sex expert. In view of the material already presented in this chapter, it is indeed fortunate that this particular cultural influence is waning rapidly. It simply cannot be destroyed fast enough, for adherence to the concept of inherent male expertise in matters sexual is an anathema to effective heterosexual interaction.

Man in his culturally assigned expert's role is presumed to know or, more likely, presumes that he knows what pleases his partner sexually. He does not ask, listen, or anticipate suggestion or direction from her, he just acts. And woman, equally exposed to the same unfortunate cultural concept of man's sexual expertise, does not inform, direct, or suggest, she usually just endures. For, she reasons, "He should know; he's the expert," and if his approach leaves something to be desired, she simply assumes that he doesn't care. So neither heterosexual partner enjoys the subjectively experienced sexual pleasure that is his or her right, regardless of whether there is regularity of orgasmic attainment. But that is not all.

As a corollary to the "male-is-the-sex-expert" myth, the culture is also responsible for another long-range disadvantage that has consistently been evidenced by heterosexual couples interacting sexually in the laboratory. And this disadvantage has been aimed at the heart of heterosexual interchange: intercourse.

Intercourse becomes only a means of sexual service, or even just a sexual contest, instead of one of the better means of communication between committed heterosexual couples when, responding to cultural influence, the man exerts his "expert's role" by arbitrarily setting the pace during coital interaction.

As described in Chapter 5, the man initiates the mounting process when he is ready, presuming that if his partner is lubricated, she is ready. Usually he hunts for, finds the vaginal outlet, and inserts the penis; yet, the woman could have accomplished the insertion with greater facility, for she certainly would not have had to hunt and find. He selects coital positioning, usually without consultation as to his partner's preference, and she almost always defers to his decision. He predominantly sets the thrusting pattern and presumes that she will respond and will be pleased. And usually she makes every effort to cooperate with his thrusting pattern whether she is pleased or not.

One wonders by what divine gift of providence the human male is endowed with such infinite knowledge of woman's sexual anatomy and sexual needs. When reflecting on the degree of male dominance in coital interaction, we have a better understanding of the many pitfalls that the culture has placed in the way of an enduring heterosexual partnership for unsuspecting men and women. The research team has consistently been amazed at how little thought even the most experienced sexual performer gives to the subject of coital interaction and, as a result, how little heterosexual men and women know of the subject of sexual interaction. The major concern is not how much sexual pleasure committed heterosexual partners miss in their ignorance, but how severely they handicap and even destroy the potential of one of their better means of communication.

Having to contend with so many cultural pressures, it would seem that the average married couple would follow the behavioral pattern set by committed homosexual couples of neutralizing their inherent psychosexual disadvantages by improving communication of sexual information, laughing at mistakes, and educating each other by making pertinent suggestions—yet so few do. The few married couples who did communicate freely in the laboratory in order to enhance their sexual pleasure gave every evidence of being as fully involved subjectively in their mutually stimulative sexual interaction as any committed, freely communicative homosexual couple.

Members of assigned heterosexual couples, the least involved subjectively of the committed and assigned homosexual and heterosexual study groups in sexual interaction, routinely substituted the "grass is greener" concept of a multiplicity of new partners as an effective source of sexual stimulation—at least this was the tenor of their answers to interviews with the research team. The assigned heterosexual couples suffered in comparison with the assigned homosexual couples in two regards: (1) While the men and women in assigned homosexual couples usually freely communicated their immediate sexual needs and responses (predominantly in a nonverbal manner), there was little similar communicative exchange between the members of assigned heterosexual couples, and (2) the immediate advantage of intragender empathy was, of course, absent for the heterosexual couples.

The men and women who formed assigned heterosexual couples had the common ground of elevated sexual tensions amplified both by the stimulation of an unusual environment and of a new partner, and they responded with the expected surge of sexual tension and urge for orgasmic release. Theirs was essentially an exercise in mutual mechanical service. There simply was no verbal and little nonverbal communicative dimension to their sexual interaction. From the point of view of end-point release, they were most successful—yet, they missed so much, and most of the men and women were unaware of the loss.

Ambisexuals. The ambisexual study group should be considered briefly, although a more detailed report of the psychosexual aspects of ambisexuality is presented in Chapter 8. As previously discussed for homosexual and heterosexual orientations, there are also immediate sexual advantages and long-term disadvantages inherent in the ambisexual lifestyle.

The ambisexual has an immediate sexual advantage in that he

or she is totally without sexual preference. While this orientation has an unarguable advantage when it comes to partner availability, the theoretical advantage of having everybody as a potential sexual partner is actually of minor moment to the ambisexual. Of far more importance is the great advantage that accrues from his or her preferential nihilism. The ambisexual enjoys a unique vantage point in social interaction that homosexual or heterosexual men or women rarely if ever attain. For as an immediate corollary to the absence of sexual preference, the true ambisexual inevitably is without any significant level of sexual prejudice. And any individual who can live in today's society without the handicap of sexual prejudice is indeed privileged, for sexual prejudice is a cornerstone that supports any number of other social biases. Certainly the most bemusing return from interviews with the 12 ambisexuals (see Chapter 8) was the development of reasonably secure evidence of an almost complete absence of sexual prejudice and a startlingly low level of personal bias. It is no wonder that the true ambisexual is rarely encountered in today's society.

The immediate sexual advantage that the lack of sexual prejudice and accompanying low levels of personal bias provides the ambisexual is that it turns many potential partners into available partners. The ambisexual seems to embody a tremendous sexual appeal that springs not only from unrestricted confidence in sexual performance but also from freedom to express sexual interest without prejudice or bias that might neutralize the appeal.

The ambisexual has the immediate, short-term advantage of two major sources of sexual stimulation. First, merely because he or she is ambisexual, there is the potential of an almost infinite variety of sexually stimulative activity as compared with inherent preference limitations of men and women with restrictive homosexual or heterosexual orientation. Second, the ambisexual relies even more than the uncommitted heterosexual or homosexual man or woman on the constantly revolving door of new-partner rotation as a continuing source of sexual pleasure. As has been described, the unceasing parade of new faces and bodies is a well-established sexual stimulant, but only up to a point. Beyond that point, the ambisexual's long-range sexual disadvantage rears its head. For even with constant partner rotation, there can, in time, come sexual boredom, when a new face is just a new face.

The ambisexual's life is not without thorns. As a long-term psychosocial disadvantage, he or she is essentially alone in a crowd. Although the ambisexuals evaluated during the research program had relatively extrovertive personalities, they gave no history of interest in identifying with a partner. Ambisexuals apparently do not develop a common ground for continuing psychosocial interchange with any man or woman, for they either do not have the facility for it or do not feel the need to establish a continuing relationship. Their effectiveness in sexual performance as judged by facility in orgasmic attainment was fully equal to that of sexually effective homosexual and heterosexual study subjects (see Chapter 10). But without the aptitude for or interest in subjective identification with other personalities, the ambisexual man or woman is almost unidimensional in sexual behavior. He or she obtains satisfaction only from goal attainment and has little or no appreciation of the partner's involvement in the sexual interaction.

The ambisexual's firmly established pattern of sexual behavior is an initial identification of mutual sexual attraction with a potential partner; then a well-rehearsed move to sexual interaction resulting in an explosive experience of tension release; and then on to another partner. There is essentially no communicative dimension to the ambisexual's sexual experiences. The sexual experience is simply one of mutual service.

Obviously, the ambisexual's long-range disadvantage is the almost total lack of psychosexual identification with any partner. Ultimately this "man-is-an-island" philosophy creates a lifestyle of social isolation, which the older ambisexual study subjects described during interviews as "too much," "overwhelming," and "depressing."

As emphasized in Chapter 8, what the future holds for the ambisexual men and women as they age is unknown, for there has been no research. Whether they continue in the same vein of personal isolation or forsake their ambisexual orientation for a continuing relationship (following the frequently recurrent behavior pattern of unattached, aging homosexual males or females) remains to be seen. After in-depth interviews with ambisexual study subjects, the research team would be surprised if "aloneness" did not become an intolerable burden and in time the die was not cast for companionship.

COMFORT FACTOR IN THE LABORATORY

Significant variations in comfort levels were evidenced during sexual interaction in the laboratory when men and women with homosexual preference were compared to those with heterosexual orientation. There were a number of homosexuals who sought orientation opportunity and heterosexuals who requested masturbational privacy. However, there was a significantly higher percentage of homosexual study subjects who requested privacy * when masturbating in the laboratory than was true for members of the heterosexual study groups, and on the other hand, a much higher percentage of heterosexuals than homosexuals who requested opportunity to orient themselves to the laboratory environment before cooperating actively with the research programs.

There are no ready explanations for these observations of variant behavior in the laboratory reflecting study-subject privacy needs or area orientation requirements. Why should the homosexual be more concerned with privacy during masturbation and the heterosexual more anxious about facility to function effectively in a laboratory environment? Interrogation of the men and women who requested the special privileges of privacy or laboratory orientation was not particularly productive in determining the etiologic factors responsible for these variations of psychosexual behavior.

However, a leading suggestion was returned from interrogation of two homosexual men. Both stated that they enjoyed self-manipulation a great deal more when it was done in mutual accord with a partner. To masturbate individually seemed to them to be a questionably acceptable practice, even though they thoroughly enjoyed the act when there was simultaneous partner participation. A request to masturbate without the partner simultaneously engaging in similar action created a sense of discomfort. Feeling pressured by the research team's request that they masturbate on an individual basis and believing that their potential pleasure quotient was being reduced by the request or that the partner might feel "left out," they became somewhat anxious and asked for the privilege of masturbating in private.

* The privilege of privacy as defined solely for the Institute's investigative programs means the exclusion from the laboratory of one's sexual partner and any other individuals aside from research team members (see Chapters 4 and 5).

In contrast, heterosexual study subjects reported engaging in simultaneous masturbation with their partners far less frequently than the homosexual research population. Thus, when scheduling individual rather than mutual masturbational activity, the research team obviously requested more alteration in sexual behavior patterning for homosexual than for heterosexual study subjects. This alteration in behavior pattern may have been a factor in the increased anxiety on the part of some homosexual men masturbating as individuals rather than with their partners, but it certainly was not the complete explanation.

Any factor that increases levels of performance anxiety can be detrimental to effective sexual interaction, and no one would deny the fact that contemplating sexual interaction in the laboratory tends to increase performance pressures. Heterosexual study subjects demonstrated an increased need for orientation opportunity as compared with members of the homosexual study group. Regardless of degree of sexual experience, heterosexual men and women have consistently evidenced a far higher level of concern or even anxiety for effectiveness of sexual performance in the laboratory than have homosexuals (see Chapters 4 and 5). As will be described and discussed in the clinical section of this text (see Chapters 15 and 16), there have been a number of instances when multidimensional fears for sexual performance have moved men and women from anxious heterosexual into confident homosexual orientations. When the individual is immersed in pressures to perform sexually, interaction between the two genders obviously has higher possibility of functional failure than intragender sexual interchange.

Responding to interrogation, committed heterosexual men and women frequently admitted that they were anxious not only about their own performances but about those of their partners. Expressed concerns for the partner's sexual performance were uniquely heterosexual in origin. If present, this specific type of performance fear was never verbalized by a homosexual study subject. Thus, the more frequent requests by heterosexual study subjects for orientation opportunities before interacting sexually under observation became more comprehensible. Both heterosexual partners gained performance courage through quiet, unobserved opportunities at sexual interaction in the laboratory before participating actively in research programs. In short, being allowed to set their own pace in acclimatization to the laboratory environment greatly increased the comfort factor for many heterosexual study subjects, not only in relation to their own sexual function, but to that of their partners.

There was an additional advantage that the increased incidence of orientation opportunity provided the heterosexual study group. Those heterosexual men and women who requested orientation opportunity went through their acclimatization process before masturbating openly in a laboratory setting. Since the homosexual study subjects requested less orientation opportunity, they placed themselves in the bind of an immediate performance demand. Some of the homosexuals' increased incidence of requested masturbational privacy may have been in response to a need for orientation opportunity, which they had not recognized subjectively or refused to admit consciously.

As anticipated, the 12 ambisexual study subjects requested neither orientation opportunity nor masturbational privacy during their episodes of cooperation with the Institute's research programs; nor did they demonstrate clinically any need for such special handling.

In any event, the research team can only speculate as to the etiologic factors in the sexual behavior variance evidenced by members of the two major sexual preference study groups when first exposed to demand for sexual functioning in the laboratory.

CONCLUSIONS TO BE DRAWN

When speculating on possible clinical applications of the textual material, what reasonably secure conclusions can be drawn from the facts assembled? The central thesis developed from this research program is that no real difference exists between homosexual men and women and heterosexual men and women in their physiologic capacity to respond to similar sexual stimuli. In other words, there is no basis in physical fact for the oft-repeated dictum, "My way is better than your way." It is reasonable to speculate that, when absorbed, this finding should lead to significant modification in current cultural concepts.

Now that it has been established that homosexual men and women are not physiologically different, it is also reasonable to speculate that in the near future, a significant measure of the current onus of public opprobrium will be eased from the men and women with homosexual preference. Of course, there will continue to be adjustment problems for homosexuals as cultural concepts alter. Homosexual men and women must gather the social courage to move quietly away from the bulwarked position of "preference denial" to which they have been driven by cultural condemnation; at the same time, however, they must not make the mistake of overreacting to the newly developing opportunities for social acceptance. Psychosocial prejudice does not alter overnight.

Of equal importance to the foreseeable increased acceptance of homosexuality is the fact that the potential of woman's physiologic sexual capacity will have to be acknowledged, accepted, and adjusted to by both men and women in our culture. From a speculative point of view, this leaves the heterosexual male in the pressured circumstance of having to undergo a major cultural alteration from a psychosexual point of view. Whether he adjusts well or cannot withstand the ego shock of role alteration will be a fascinating scene to observe. If the heterosexual male accepts the basic physiologic fact that he does not have the physical potential to ejaculate as often as his female partner can be orgasmic, if he realizes that he need only establish ejaculatory control or, with required frequency, provide his partner with other means of sexual release, he will adjust well. If he clings to the male dominance role in sexual interchange, insisting on maintaining control of male-female sexual interaction by presuming he understands his female partner's sexual needs and goals, he probably will be in difficulty. The male in our culture has the most to gain both physiologically and psychosexually as a full sexual partner. He no longer has a future as the "sex expert."

Woman also has a major psychosexual adjustment to make. If she interprets her potential capacity for multiorgasmic attainment as a psychosocial advantage rather than as a simple physiologic fact, she may nullify any possibility of an effective psychosexual partnership with the man of her choice. Nor should her physiologic capacity become an effective recruiting argument for lesbianism. It is primarily the male population, in its refusal to assume a sexual partnership role and to acknowledge woman's inherently high level of sexual capacity, that will provide significant social argument for lesbian commitment.

There is one more important lesson to be learned from this report of laboratory observations of human sexual function. The teachers of this lesson are the men and women who had episodes of sexual failure in the laboratory. How did they handle these failures?

With one exception (the man and wife who became quite anxious when he had an episode of ejaculatory incompetence), the sexually experienced men and women who failed to function effectively did not become anxious or fearful. They reacted positively, offering an explanation if there was a legitimate one, or they simply smiled and said, "Let's try again another time." They did not automatically anticipate future sexual difficulty on the basis of a specific episode of functional failure. In short, the sexually experienced study subjects treated sexual function as a natural function that at times fails to respond in a fully satisfactory manner, as do all other natural functions. The study subjects treated their episodes of sexual failure without fanfare, and although several subjects experienced more than one episode of failure in the laboratory, none of these individuals ever reported any residual sexual dysfunction in their private lives.

The lesson is a basic one. Episodes of sexual dysfunction can and do occur at any time for anybody. If they could be treated casually, if they could be discussed quietly, and if the partners could smile and say, "Let's try again another time," the incidence of male and female sexual dysfunction in this culture would be markedly reduced.

REACTION TO PUBLIC OPPROBRIUM

Brief consideration must also be given to the ever-present problem faced by the homosexual community, namely, anticipating and responding to the varying levels of social opprobrium initiated by religious conviction and maintained by legislative dictum and the personal discomfort of the critics. Interestingly, the degree of publicly expressed social antipathy toward homosexuality probably varies in intensity on a reasonably well-delineated geographic basis. Multifaceted aspects of this subject were discussed in depth with most of the homosexual study subjects.

The majority of committed homosexual couples who participated in the research program came from major metropolitan areas outside the St. Louis area (see Chapter 2). When the homosexual research population was queried privately as individual men and women independent of their committed or assigned partners about the social pressures they had encountered or were facing, presumably as a result of the lifestyle they were living, the tenor of their answers was geographically oriented. As expected, there was generally less concern for social ostracism or job security expressed by homosexuals living in larger cities than by those from smaller communities.

A more important factor than population concentration must be taken into account, however. There was a much higher incidence of fear of identification reported by homosexual study subjects who lived in metropolitan areas in what might fairly be termed politically and religiously conservative sections of the country than was verbalized by the research subjects who lived in cities of comparable size located in currently more liberal areas of the country.

An example of this geographic influence on comfort with public expression of homosexual preference was provided by those study subjects living academically oriented lives. Regardless of size or prestige of the academic institution, if the college or university was located in a conservative area, not a single homosexual man or woman had publicly identified his or her sexual preference. When the academic institution was located in a more liberal section of the country, approximately half of the couples had publicly acknowledged their committed homosexual relationship. Most of these couples were, of course, from larger metropolitan areas. None of the couples in the academically oriented group were from a secondary school environment, where increased social and professional pressures inevitably would have been encountered if a homosexual relationship had been acknowledged.

From a psychosocial point of view, it is evident that pressures arising from threatened or real societal rejection frequently strengthen the bonds of a committed homosexual relationship when the individual members are relatively well-educated, intelligent men and women. Regardless of geographic placement or prior public statement of sexual preference, committed partners repeatedly described the strength of their relationship as their "port-in-the-storm" retreat from social pressures. When interviewed individually and in similar depth, no married man or woman ever expressed a similar level of need for personal security that he or she anticipated might be derived from their ongoing partnership.

One can speculate that the uniquely high levels of communicative interchange previously described in Chapter 5 as characteristic of the committed homosexual couple may be an inevitable result of the partners' mutual effort to build their relationship into a strong social bulwark. The research team has no other ready explanation for the consistently effective communicative interchange that was evidenced by committed homosexual partners and—with but a few outstanding exceptions—was comparatively absent in the married couples who cooperated with the Institute.

Thus, social opprobrium can even be a long-term sexual advantage to the committed homosexual in that it tends to make the partners place particular value upon the established relationship. When such value in a relationship is expressed by both partners, freedom of communication is inevitably enhanced. The couple usually reflects this high level of communicative interchange achieved outside the bedroom by elevated subjective involvement in sexual interaction in the bedroom. At least such was true for the committed homosexual study subjects, as they reported a mutual dependency on their relationship and reacted to their partners' sexual approaches subjectively as well as physiologically in the laboratory.

Obviously, the unattached homosexual, with his or her increased cruising tendency, has a higher chance of encountering social trauma and, of course, legal difficulty. Again, the incidence of public retribution depends primarily on the geographic area in which the homosexual lives and on whether the area is politically and religiously conservative. Since the unattached homosexual usually takes more chances with public identification than does the committed homosexual, and since the unattached homosexual's position not infrequently is one of defying rather than living with prejudice, his or her life usually runs a more stormy course.

The preclinical section of this text has been written in an effort to present the essence of the years of laboratory evaluation of human sexual function. Amplification of various aspects of this material will come from future publications. The baseline information has been presented for one overriding purpose: to provide comparative dimensions of human sexual function so that secure perspectives on homosexuality can be developed.

CLINICAL STUDY,
1968–1977

I 2

CLINICAL
INVESTIGATION

When the program for continuing investigation of human sexual response was established in 1954, the first step taken was adoption of a research protocol that called for basic science evaluation of male and female sexual function as exemplified by experienced heterosexual partners responding to effective sexual stimuli in a laboratory setting. It was anticipated that theretofore unknown data returned from that phase of the overall research program would be valuable in the development of more effective techniques for the clinical treatment of heterosexual dysfunctions.

A report of the basic science investigation of heterosexual function was made to the health-care professions in 1966 with the publication of *Human Sexual Response*. Once basic science research productivity had been generated, the second step in the investigative process was the creation of a 10-year clinical control period for evaluation of the Institute's newly developed techniques for treatment of heterosexual inadequacies. This control period terminated in 1968, and returns from the clinical treatment programs were reported in 1970 in *Human Sexual Inadequacy*.

The homosexual phase of the open-ended investigation of human sexual response began in 1964 with the Institute attempting to respond to the overwhelming cultural and scientific need for an objective investigation of homosexual function. The same protocol of basic science precedence to new clinical treatment constructs was employed. The research program was initiated with an evaluation of physiologic response patterns demonstrated by sexually experienced homosexual men and women responding to effective sexual stimuli in a laboratory setting. This evaluation of homosexual function was completed in 1968 after almost five years of laboratory involvement.

The 10-year period of clinical control for creating and evaluating treatment techniques for homosexual dysfunctions and dissatisfactions began in 1968 and was terminated in 1977. With this textual presentation, the Institute reports to the health-care professions both the basic science investigations of homosexual function and the new clinical programs designed to treat sexual inadequacies of homosexual orientation.

Although the original investigations of physiologic response to heterosexually and homosexually oriented sexual stimuli were completed over a decade ago, the new clinical treatment techniques, which were originated in 1959 (heterosexual) and 1968 (homosexual) and were directed toward relief of sexual dysfunctions and dissatisfactions, will be continued indefinitely.

In the future, as the Institute's therapy concepts alter, treatment techniques improve, and educational and training facilities expand, pertinent information gleaned from the experiential maturity of these clinical research programs will regularly be made available to the health-care professions.

DEFINITIONS

When the Institute's clinical therapy programs were expanded to include treatment of homosexual dysfunction, it was soon evident that the definitions of impotence and anorgasmic states previously established for the heterosexual phase of the clinical research program were not always applicable to dysfunctional homosexual men and women. As discussed later in this chapter, the ability to masturbate effectively has been employed in defining male potency or female orgasmic status in homosexuals as a replacement for definitions based upon coitus. The ability to masturbate effectively was not used as a criterion to define sexual dysfunction in heterosexuals. The rationale behind this specific difference is that both mutual masturbation and partner manipulation are frequently encountered—indeed, almost universal—patterns of male and female homosexual interaction. In contrast, these techniques are less frequently employed in heterosexual interaction for specifically directed end-point release.

The act of vaginal penetration so uniquely involved in the definitions of heterosexually oriented male impotence and female coital anorgasmia is clearly not an integral part of homosexual interaction. It is also apparent that since rectal intercourse is not a consistently utilized form of male homosexual interaction, facility in rectal penetration could not be considered a vital factor in arriving at a definition of homosexual impotence.

Thus, an important difference in sexual potency between heterosexually and homosexually oriented men is that the homosexual male has no absolute requirement for attaining or maintaining an erection of sufficient quality for accomplishing a penetrative act. (Though admittedly a penetrative act, fellatio creates only minor nomenclature confusion because the male does not need even a partial erection for oral penetration.)

Similarly, since it is also apparent that rectal and vaginal penetration are not regularly recurrent sexual techniques employed by lesbians, these penetrative acts have not been considered in defining lesbian anorgasmic states.

It was decided that the most commonly used forms of homosexual interaction would be used as a composite measuring device, just as was done when establishing definitions for heterosexually oriented dysfunctions a decade previously. Thus, male and female homosexual function would be measured by the individual's facility to respond to masturbation, partner manipulation, and fellatio/ cunnilingus. Further, once a male or female homosexual was found to be impotent or anorgasmic through his or her lack of effective response to these stimulative techniques, impotency was labeled as primary, secondary, or situational and anorgasmia as primary, situational, or random. It was anticipated that if these specific definitions could be established, the research team initially and, later, the health-care professions would have a common language with which to identify and discuss homosexual dysfunctions or dissatisfactions.

A primarily impotent homosexual male has been defined as a man who has never been able to respond by attaining and maintaining full erection with any of the techniques of masturbation, partner manipulation, or fellatio. A diagnosis of secondary impotence reflects a homosexual man who in the past has been able to respond effectively with all three stimulative techniques, but currently is losing or has completely lost his erective security. A situationally impotent homosexual has been defined as a man who has responded at least once by attaining and maintaining a full erection in response to one or two of the three stimulative techniques, but who has no history of full erective response to all three stimulative approaches.

The primarily anorgasmic lesbian has been defined as a woman who has never been orgasmic in response to any of the techniques of masturbation, partner manipulation, or cunnilingus. The situationally anorgasmic lesbian has been identified as a woman who has responded at orgasmic levels to one or two of the three stimulative techniques, but never to all three. The randomly anorgasmic lesbian reflects a woman who has been orgasmic at least once in response to each of the three stimulative approaches, but has rarely reached orgasmic levels of sexual excitation in response to any form of sexual stimulation.

The only real intergender difference in definition of sexual dysfunction is between the diagnoses of secondary impotence and random anorgasmia. A diagnosis of secondary impotence implies actual loss of physiologic or psychosexual capacity to achieve erection. A random anorgasmic state does not imply loss of facility to be orgasmic. It connotes a low level of stimulative interest or sexual involvement or both rather than a lack of capacity to respond to effective sexual stimuli.

The subtle difference in these definitions reflects the fact that different facilities are being measured. A diagnosis of impotence indicates a lack of facility to function effectively in the cultural male role of attaining and maintaining an erection, not the specific lack of orgasmic capacity. For example, occasionally men can and do ejaculate through a completely flaccid penis. Anorgasmic states reflect inability to achieve orgasmic release of sexual tensions, not lack of a facility to function in a culturally defined female role of involuntary preparation for vaginal penetration by developing lubrication (the female physiologic counterpart to male erection).

Any general discussion of male sexual dysfunctions should include the frequently encountered distress of premature ejaculation and the infrequently identified dysfunction of ejaculatory incompetence. But the Institute has not described premature ejaculation as a major homosexual dysfunction, because it rarely represents a serious problem to interacting male homosexuals. It is usually not considered a matter of major moment if one or both men ejaculate rapidly after onset of sexual interaction, because neither man is dependent upon the other's ejaculatory control to achieve sexual satisfaction. Over the 10-year control period, only two homosexual men have requested admission to therapy at the Institute for treatment of rapid ejaculation. Both men had originally become rapid ejaculators during heterosexual interaction as young men. Each man had a history of usually ejaculating in heterosexual interaction before he could completely undress.

Instead of being treated in the Institute's therapy program, these two men and their partners each received brief counseling on two occasions. The "squeeze technique" was explained,* and after working with their partners for a few days, the men reported "satisfactory" control. Since these couples were not admitted to the research program because their distress was easily reversible and did not warrant employing intensive sex-therapy techniques, these couples have not been included in the recorded treatment statistics.

The rapidly ejaculating homosexual is far easier to reverse than the prematurely ejaculating heterosexual, because the heterosexual man must learn ejaculatory control during cooperative intravaginal thrusting patterns with a responsive woman. The homosexual has no such requirement for security of ejaculatory control. The homosexual man's concern for control is primarily to extend his own personal pleasure factor, while the heterosexual man's need is primarily focused on providing for his companion's personal pleasure factor.

As a homosexual dysfunction, ejaculatory incompetence has been described as the consistent inability to ejaculate in response to the stimulative techniques of masturbation, partner manipulation, or fellatio without difficulty in attaining or maintaining an erection. Ejaculatory incompetence has not been described in this text as a problem in homosexual interaction, simply because no homosexual man has presented this complaint to the Institute. When such a complaint is encountered in an applicant from the homosexual population, it will be acknowledged and treated with essentially the

* Masters and Johnson (1970), pp. 102–106.

same techniques as those employed in treating the heterosexual with ejaculatory incompetence. This sexual dysfunction should be reversed when possible, because lack of effective treatment for ejaculatory incompetence can lead the homosexual male to fears of performance and to secondary impotence.

C L I N I C A L   R E S E A R C H   P O P U L A T I O N S

From 1968 through 1977, the Institute accepted for treatment 151 homosexually oriented men and women with complaints reflecting sexual inadequacy. For investigative purposes, the problems of homosexual inadequacy have been separated into two definitive categories: the sexually dysfunctional and the sexually dissatisfied. Homosexual men and women categorized as sexually dysfunctional were contending with such sexual distresses as impotence, anorgasmic states, or sexual aversions. They were leading overt or covert homosexual lives and had Kinsey ratings ranging from 3 through 6.

Homosexuals identified as sexually dissatisfied were men and women who expressed the desire to convert or revert to heterosexuality. As employed by the Institute, the terms *conversion* or *reversion* warrant further explanation. For a homosexual individual to be considered as a candidate for therapeutic conversion to heterosexuality, he or she would have had little or no prior heterosexual experience (Kinsey ratings of 5 or 6). Homosexuals listed as candidates for reversion to heterosexuality had Kinsey ratings that ranged from 2 through 4. These applicants represented three basically different lifestyles. The first was a group of men and women who had been living overt homosexual lives, with or without an established relationship. The second was a similar, socially oriented group of men and women who were living as covert homosexuals. The third group was composed of married men and women living openly as heterosexuals and involved in covert homosexual interchange.

THE SEXUALLY DYSFUNCTIONAL POPULATION

During the 10-year clinical control period for treatment of homosexual inadequacy (1968–1977), a total of 81 homosexual couples requested treatment for sexual dysfunction. This dysfunctional population was composed of 56 homosexual male couples and 25 lesbian couples. The 56 male couples are listed by diagnosis in Table 12-1.

TABLE 12-1

Dysfunctional Homosexual Male Couples
(N = 56; *Dysfunctional Homosexual Males; N = 57*)

Couple Involvement and Type of Impotence	No. of Patients *	No. of Couples	Functional Homosexual Partners	
			Committed	Casual
One partner dysfunctional				
Primary	3	3	3	0
Secondary	49	49	34	15
Situational	3	3	1	2
Both partners dysfunctional				
Primary	2	1	...	...
Total	57	56	38	17

* One primarily impotent, 2 secondarily impotent, and 1 situationally impotent homosexuals were secondarily diagnosed as sexually aversive.

There were 5 homosexual males who were primarily impotent, and 2 of these primarily impotent men formed 1 committed couple. The remaining 3 primarily impotent men were members of committed homosexual relationships with no homosexual dysfunction evidenced by the other partner.

There were 49 secondarily impotent men who requested treatment. Thirty-four men came with partners from currently committed relationships of six months to 23 years in duration. The remaining 15 men came to the Institute for treatment with casual partners. All of the partners, whether committed or casual, were sexually functional homosexuals.

Three men were diagnosed as situationally impotent. Two of these men sought treatment with casual partners, 1 with a committed partner. These 3 partners also were sexually functional homosexuals.

One man with primary impotence, 2 men with secondary impotence, and 1 man with situational impotence were additionally treated for sexual aversion.*

There were 25 sexually dysfunctional lesbian couples who sought treatment from the Institute (Table 12-2). Twenty-three of these

TABLE 12-2

Dysfunctional Homosexual Female Couples
(N = 25; Dysfunctional Homosexual Females; N = 27)

Couple Involvement and Type of Anorgasmia	No. of Patients *	No. of Couples	Functional Homosexual Partners	
			Committed	Casual
One partner dysfunctional				
Primary	7	7	5	2
Situational	13	13	8	5
Random	3	3	3	0
Both partners dysfunctional				
Primary	1 ⎫	1	. . .	. . .
Situational	2 ⎬			
Random	1 ⎭	1	. . .	. . .
Total	27	25	16	7

* Three primarily anorgasmic, 1 situationally anorgasmic, and 2 randomly anorgasmic lesbians were secondarily diagnosed as sexually aversive.

couples were formed by anorgasmic lesbians and their sexually functional partners. There were 2 couples in which both partners were sexually dysfunctional.

* The diagnostic category of sexual aversion was not described in *Human Sexual Inadequacy* and will be only briefly mentioned in this text, since a full discussion of this disorder will appear in the forthcoming book, *Textbook of Sexual Medicine* (Little, Brown, and Company, 1979). Succinctly stated, sexual aversion is a consistent negative reaction of phobic proportions to sexual activity or the thought of sexual activity. Sexual aversion occurs in both males and females, heterosexuals and homosexuals; it does not refer to a situation of esthetic preference or to dislike of a specific type of sexual activity, but rather to a pervasive negative reaction marked by high levels of anxiety.

The 25 couples were formed into four separate categories: (1) There were seven primarily anorgasmic women seen with their 5 committed and 2 casual partners. (2) Thirteen situationally anorgasmic women were treated with 8 committed and 5 casual partners. (3) Three women entered therapy with the complaint of random anorgasmia. These were seen with committed partners. (4) Two lesbian couples were seen in therapy with both partners distressed by states of sexual dysfunction. One couple was formed by a primarily anorgasmic lesbian with her committed partner who was situationally anorgasmic. The other couple was composed of a situationally anorgasmic lesbian with a committed partner who was randomly anorgasmic.

Additional complications were encountered during the treatment programs when interviews revealed that 3 of the primarily anorgasmic, 1 of the situationally anorgasmic, and 2 of the randomly anorgasmic lesbians were also sexually aversive.

THE SEXUALLY DISSATISFIED POPULATION

During the 10-year clinical control period, the Institute accepted a total of 67 clients and their opposite-sex partners in treatment of homosexual dissatisfaction (Table 12-3). This group of applicants

TABLE 12-3
Dissatisfied Homosexual Population (N = 67)

Patients in Therapy		No. of Married Patients	No. of Uncommitted Patients	Present Homosexual Dysfunction	Prior or Present Heterosexual Dysfunction	Prior Sexual Aversion (Heterosexual)	Sexually Aversive (Heterosexual and Homosexual)
Gender	No.						
Male	54	33	21	0	11 *	8	0
Female	13	7	6	1	9 †	5	2
Total	67	40	27	1	20	13	2

* Eleven men were sexually dysfunctional as heterosexuals (7 were impotent pretherapy, and 5 had premature ejaculation posttherapy); 1 of the 11 was sexually dysfunctional both pretherapy (impotent) and posttherapy (premature ejaculation).

† Nine women were sexually dysfunctional as heterosexuals (7 were anorgasmic pretherapy and 2 were anorgasmic pretherapy and posttherapy).

was composed of 54 men and 13 women. Thirty-one of the homosexual men were married and 2 men were living in long-term male-female relationships and were listed as married for reportorial ease. Twenty-one men were without committed relationships and were seen for reversion or conversion therapy with their female partners of choice.

Of the 13 lesbian women admitted to therapy, 7 were married and the remaining 6 women were seen in therapy with their male partners of choice.

None of the male applicants were sexually dysfunctional as homosexuals. One woman (Kinsey 6) was primarily anorgasmic during her homosexual commitment before requesting conversion treatment with a heterosexual male partner of choice.

The fact that the majority of the men (61.1 percent) and women (53.8 percent) accepted for sex-preference reversal were married warrants specific comment. The percentage of applicants who were living in married states or in long-term commitments was indeed a surprise to the research team, which had anticipated that the greater percentage of men and women requesting preference alteration would be uncommitted homosexuals. Of course, the general category of "married" does misdirect. For to live a married life does not in any sense indicate that the individual is living entirely a life of heterosexual orientation, nor does it indicate that the individual is even active in a heterosexual role.

Of the 33 committed men who applied for treatment, 14 were living apart from their wives and had been separated for periods of time varying from 10 months to 13 years. These 14 men were living almost entirely homosexually oriented lives and rarely had coital experience.

Five married men were identified as primarily or secondarily impotent in prior heterosexual experience and were leading lives of full homosexual orientation. Two of these men had separated from their wives, and 3 remained in the home. In all five instances their wives were fully aware of the husband's current sexual commitment.

In the remaining 14 men, 9 were identified by their wives as homosexuals only after they had fully withdrawn from all heterosexual interchange, in some instances for years. The remaining 5 men had been leading dual-preference lives. In these cases, either they had been surprised and identified as homosexuals by their wives or had admitted this orientation voluntarily to their wives in response to psychosocial pressures.

Three of the 7 married women were situationally anorgasmic as heterosexuals and, although living in the home, were not interacting heterosexually. They were functioning at orgasmic levels as homosexuals with their husbands' knowledge. Two other married women were living separately from their husbands and seemed entirely committed to homosexuality. In the 2 remaining married women applicants, the husbands had no prior knowledge of their wives' homosexual orientation until the wives told them that they needed the support of role-preference therapy.

Because a state of overt marital commitment exists, in no sense does this indicate a similar full heterosexual commitment for either men or women. Perhaps the existence of the legal commitment was a major influence in propelling the couples to seek professional support. In many cases the problems these couples brought to therapy were more severe than those encountered in direct treatment of unmarried conversion or reversion applicants, for not only were the usual problems of sex-preference alteration present, but frequently there was a history of severe heterosexual dysfunction.

Additional complications in the applicants' backgrounds added further intricacy to the treatment program for sex-preference reversal. Eight of the homosexual male applicants were secondarily diagnosed as sexually aversive in prior heterosexual interaction. Five of these men were married and were seen in therapy with their wives, and 3 were treated with female partners of their choice. Three of the 7 married women were also diagnosed as having been sexually aversive to heterosexual approach when originally applying to the Institute for reversion treatment. Two uncommitted lesbians seen in treatment for homosexual dissatisfaction were sexually aversive to heterosexual interaction (Table 12-3).

Two more of the 6 uncommitted women who applied for reversion treatment with male partners of choice were identified as sexually aversive to both homosexual and heterosexual interaction (see Table 12-3). Their heterosexual aversive reactions were treated at the same time they were in therapy with their casual male partners for homosexual dissatisfaction.

Of the 67 individuals who cooperated as partners in therapy, there were 33 committed heterosexual women and 7 committed heterosexual men. Six men were casual heterosexual partners, as were 21 women (Table 12-4). Some of the heterosexual partners

TABLE 12-4

Dissatisfied Homosexual Population
(*Partners in Therapy*, $N = 67$)

Partners in Therapy		No. Married Partners	No. Casual Partners	Heterosexually Dysfunctional Partners
Gender	No.			
Male	13	7	6	1 *
Female	54	33	21	4 †
Total	67	40	27	5

* One husband had premature ejaculation.
† Two wives were situationally anorgasmic, 1 female casual partner was situationally anorgasmic, and 1 female casual partner was primarily anorgasmic.

in therapy were also sexually dysfunctional. One husband was a premature ejaculator, and 2 wives were situationally anorgasmic. One casual female partner was primarily anorgasmic, and another casual female partner was situationally anorgasmic. All 5 dysfunctional partners in therapy were treated for their sexual dysfunctions simultaneously with the treatment of their homosexual partners for sexual dissatisfaction.

CLIENT COOPERATION

One of the important variables to be taken into account when treating homosexual dysfunction or dissatisfaction is the degree of cooperation offered by those men and women who come for treatment. When considering this problem, two generalizations can safely be made.

First is the observation that the homosexual men and women who were contending with the distresses of sexual dysfunction and who expressed the desire to become sexually effective as homosexuals were far more cooperative with the therapy program than those homosexuals complaining of sexual dissatisfactions and requesting conversion or reversion to heterosexuality. The second generalization would be anticipated by experienced psychotherapists. With two specific exceptions, committed or casual partners of the homosexual men and women who sought treatment from the Institute's staff were far more cooperative while in therapy than were the clients who sought specific therapeutic relief from their complaints of sexual dysfunction or dissatisfaction.

There is no all-encompassing explanation for the significantly reduced levels of cooperation in therapy evidenced by sexually distressed homosexual men and women when compared to the levels of cooperation offered by sexually distressed heterosexuals. Initially, it was presumed that pressures of social rejection had sensitized the sexually inadequate homosexual to such a degree that any manner of helping hand was viewed with suspicion, even though the helping hand had been specifically solicited by the suspicious individual. While the factor of public opprobrium cannot be ignored, it should not be given too much credence as the single cause of the homosexual patient's lessened cooperation. Experience has taught that the combination of the pressures of public rejection and the ego-deflating experience of contending with sexual dysfunction or dissatisfaction exerts a cumulative influence that usually is detrimental to the homosexual's emotional stability.

PRIOR REJECTION BY HEALTH-CARE PROFESSIONALS

Another detrimental factor that understandably elevated the distressed homosexuals' levels of anxiety in therapy, and to a significant degree could be held responsible for their relatively low level of cooperation in the treatment programs, was the widespread, well-founded fear that members of the health-care professions would be far from impartial in dealing with sexually distressed homosexual men and women. The available evidence certainly supports the homosexual population in their general contention that if they expected the worst from health-care professionals, they would be rarely disappointed. Many health-care professionals have refused treatment to sexually dysfunctional homosexual men and women. Of the 57 homosexual men who were treated by the Institute for sexual dysfunction, 26 reported that they previously had sought psychotherapeutic support from other health-care facilities, and 23 stated that they had been refused treatment for their specific sexual dysfunction (see Table 12-5). Eleven of these 23 men had been re-

TABLE 12-5

Male Homosexual Prior Treatment History
(Sexually Dysfunctional, N = 57; Sexually Dissatisfied, N = 54)

Chief Complaint	Total No.	Sought Treatment	Refused for Treatment	Refused for Treatment (More Than Once)	Referred to Another Therapy Source	Accepted In Treatment	Terminated Treatment (Unsatisfactory)	In Active Therapy at Admission
Dysfunction	57	26	23	11	0	3	3	0
Dissatisfaction	54	36	21	10	1	15	12	3
Total	111	62	44	21	1	18	15	3

fused treatment on more than one occasion. Not a single one of the 23 men refused treatment for sexual dysfunction had been referred to another treatment source. Three homosexuals had previously been accepted in therapy when they specifically requested treatment of sexual dysfunction. They terminated the therapy when it became apparent that the treatment program was directed toward conversion or reversion to heterosexuality rather than amelioration of their homosexually oriented dysfunction.

Of the 54 homosexual men who sought help in converting or reverting to heterosexuality, 36 had previously requested treatment for their sexual dissatisfaction (see Table 12-5). Twenty-one men stated they had been refused treatment for homosexual dissatisfaction by health-care professionals. Ten of these homosexuals reported more than one instance of refusal of treatment. Only 1 of the 21 men refused treatment for the complaint of sexual dissatisfaction was referred to another source of professional treatment by the health-care professional first consulted. Fifteen homosexual patients had been accepted in treatment for sexual dissatisfaction, and 12 of these had voluntarily terminated their therapy programs, deeming the results unsatisfactory. Three patients were still in active therapy when they requested admission to the Institute's programs. Permission to enter treatment was granted by the psychotherapists involved.

Nor were the homosexual men the only ones who were refused treatment for sexual dysfunction or dissatisfaction. Of the total of 27 lesbians who requested treatment by the Institute for sexual dysfunction, 14 had sought professional help from another health-care facility (see Table 12-6). Eleven of these women had been refused

TABLE 12-6

Female Homosexual Prior Treatment History
(Sexually Dysfunctional, N = 27; Sexually Dissatisfied, N = 13)

Chief Complaint	Total No.	Sought Treatment	Refused for Treatment	Refused for Treatment (More Than Once)	Referred to Another Therapy Source	Accepted In Treatment	Terminated Treatment (Unsatisfactory)	In Active Therapy at Admission
Dysfunction	27	14	11	8	0	3	3	0
Dissatisfaction	13	5	2	1	0	3	3	0
Total	40	19	13	9	0	6	6	0

psychotherapeutic support, 8 on more than one occasion. None of the 11 women refused therapy for sexual dysfunction had been referred to another treatment source. Three of the 14 lesbians who sought treatment for sexual dysfunction had been accepted in treatment, and each had voluntarily terminated her treatment program as unsatisfactory.

Thirteen lesbians requested support in their attempts to revert or convert to heterosexuality. Only 5 of these women had sought help from other professional sources, and 2 had been refused, 1 on several occasions. Neither of the 2 women refused treatment had been referred to another source of professional care. All 3 of the women who had been accepted in therapy had terminated the treatment programs when they became convinced sufficient progress had not been made.

OTHER FACTORS IN COOPERATION

A number of other factors tended to lower the degree of the homosexual clients cooperation with the therapists. Fears that successful treatment results could not be attained were frequently verbalized by homosexuals in both the dysfunctional and dissatisfied categories. There was also a resistance factor uniquely evidenced by the dissatisfied homosexuals. These clients frequently indicated and occasionally verbalized a deeply ingrained ambivalence as to whether they really wanted to convert or revert to heterosexuality. When there was a significant level of ambivalence, the clients, frustrated by their psychosexual insecurity, frequently projected their anxieties on the therapists.

Cooperation in treatment was at a particularly low ebb with the men and women who were living in overtly committed heterosexual relationships but were covertly engaged in homosexual encounters. Despite requesting treatment for some form of sexual inadequacy and despite having the courage during treatment to acknowledge an ongoing homosexual orientation, these men and women were still quite fearful of their spouses' reaction to the information. They were concerned initially whether the spouses would continue to accept them as sociosexual partners, and secondarily whether the spouses would break security and release their previously well-camouflaged identification with homosexual interests to members of the family, friends, or even to the general public. Faced with these understandable anxieties, they frequently relieved their tensions by attempting to force a break between themselves and their therapists. The covertly homosexual married men were particularly concerned with the presumed loss of face that might develop from a discussion of their homosexual activities with their female partners.

In short, fear of treatment failure, fear of spouse rejection, or fear of loss of public acceptance as information was leaked by a condemning spouse led to continuing high levels of client anxiety during the course of therapy. Such anxiety was occasionally relieved by open hostility, but far more frequently it was released by varying levels of foot-dragging or noncooperation with therapeutic suggestions or concepts. Once anticipated, such evidences of social or sexual insecurity can be neutralized with reasonable effectiveness by experienced therapists.

While there is no doubt that there was a multiplicity of factors leading to lowered levels of cooperation in treatment by sexually inadequate homosexual men and women, there is an even more important message contained in this section on client cooperation. The message is spelled out in the statistics reported in Tables 12-5 and 12-6 and discussed earlier in this chapter. No longer should the qualified psychotherapist avoid the responsibility of either accepting the homosexual client in treatment or, at the very least, referring him or her to an acceptable treatment source. The statistics tell a lamentable story of professional bias: If the applicants had been heterosexual men and women complaining to health-care professionals of the distress of sexual inadequacy, the statistics related to acceptance in treatment or referral to an acceptable authority would not have borne the slightest resemblance to those reported in Tables 12-5 and 12-6.

APPLICATION ACCEPTANCE

During the 10-year clinical control period of evaluation and treatment of homosexual inadequacy (1968 through 1977), the Institute accepted a total of 151 homosexual men and women who requested professional support in treating their sexual dysfunctions or reversing or converting their sexual orientations. Since there were different criteria exercised for acceptance into therapy for treatment of dysfunction as opposed to dissatisfaction, there should be passing mention of the process of client selection.

Before acceptance into therapy, homosexual applicants underwent a pretreatment interview. Some of the interviews were conducted in person with members of the research team. But most pretreatment interviews were conducted by telephone, because a predominant number of applicants lived far from St. Louis.

If a homosexual male or female applicant complained of a sexual dysfunction, such as impotence or an anorgasmic state, and expressed sincere interest in becoming a functional sexual partner in a homosexual milieu, the individual was freely accepted into treatment with but two areas of reservation. The first reservation centered upon therapeutic demand for an accompanying partner. The Institute insisted that sexually dysfunctional men and women have available a committed or casual partner of the *same* sex to share in the treatment program. The Institute also insisted that if there was to be a casual partner and he or she was not prepared to share sexual opportunity with the dysfunctional client after termination of the acute (two weeks) phase of the therapy program, there must be another homosexual companion available who was prepared to offer such cooperation.

A partner of choice is of markedly reduced value in the treatment of sexual dysfunction when his or her availability terminates with the acute phase of therapy. This is particularly true if there is no intimate companion available to substitute immediately after termination of therapy. This factor is so important in the outcome of treatment of both homosexual and heterosexual dysfunctions that the Institute historically has not accepted an individual into treatment with a casual partner unless there was some plan for continuity of a sexual partnership in the immediate future, either with the casual partner or with another acceptable companion.

The second reservation focused upon the client's psychological stability. It has always been the Institute's position that if symptoms of severe psychopathology are identified, the applicant will not be accepted in therapy. Had there been such identification, the homosexual man or woman would not have been accepted in therapy. Fortunately, there was no rejection of any homosexual applicant for treatment of sexual dysfunction resultant from a diagnosis of major psychopathology. In fact, no homosexual male or female applicant for treatment of sexual dysfunction was rejected by the research team.

When the homosexual applicant stated that he or she wished therapeutic support in his or her attempt to convert or revert to heterosexuality, such a request was very carefully screened. The individual and his or her committed or casual partner were accepted into the treatment program only if both members of the research team were fully convinced of the sincerity of the request. The homosexual applicant for treatment of sexual dissatisfaction underwent a far more detailed selection process than did the homosexual man or woman complaining of sexual dysfunction. Since men and women accepted for treatment of homosexual dissatisfaction were very carefully screened before the research team made a therapy commitment, they certainly do not represent an average cross-section of the applicant population.

Research team members were acutely aware that many homosexuals verbalize a desire to alter their sexual preference role both psychosocially and psychosexually. Although they may seek professional support with statements of unqualified sincerity in preference alteration, they are really quite ambivalent about desiring full conversion or reversion to heterosexuality.

On the other hand, when homosexuals sought treatment at the Institute stating that they wished to function effectively in both homosexual and heterosexual roles, and if their cooperating partners were fully aware of the applicant's admitted sexual ambivalence, such men and women were freely accepted into treatment. The Institute felt more secure in accepting homosexually dissatisfied men and women in treatment when the applicants for conversion or reversion to heterosexuality freely expressed their reservations about making the complete change in role preference or openly stated their desire to function in both roles.

Twelve homosexual men requesting reversion and 4 men applying for conversion therapy were refused treatment by the Institute's staff (see Table 15-1, Chapter 15). Three lesbian women also were refused treatment when they requested professional support in their considered attempt to revert to heterosexuality (see Table 16-1, Chapter 16).

Discussions of the rationale for refusal of treatment are presented in Chapters 15 and 16, which consider the treatment program for male and female sexual dissatisfaction. Every effort was made to see that those homosexuals who were refused treatment were directed to theoretically effective means of psychotherapeutic support; however, not all of the men and women applying for treatment took advantage of the referral suggestions.

There was one type of homosexually oriented client who escaped the Institute's screening techniques. This was the married man or woman who was accepted into treatment for some other form of stated sexual distress (a sexually dysfunctional partner, for example) and whose covert homosexual interest was not identified until during the course of therapy. Usually the client's homosexual orientation was either unknown to or was only partially surmised by the committed partner. When such an individual and his or her spouse had already been accepted in the therapy program under some other guise, he or she was treated for sexual reversion only if there was a specific request for such treatment, and if the partner was fully informed of the covert homosexual orientation.

If the individual did not desire reversion therapy, preferring instead to keep information relative to his or her covert homosexual interests from the partner, such a request was honored, and, when possible, treatment for the previously stated sexual or relationship distresses continued without interruption. If the covert homosexual influences precluded a successful treatment program, the therapy was terminated. This clinical situation occurred twice in the concomitantly conducted heterosexual dysfunction program during the 10-year clinical control period for treatment of homosexual dysfunction. When it was necessary to terminate treatment for heterosexual dysfunction because the covert homosexuality prevented successful treatment of the relationship distresses, the Institute always accepted full responsibility for treatment failure, thereby protecting the security of the information. When referral to another source of psychotherapeutic support for the uninformed partner was possible, such a procedure was followed assiduously.

FINANCIAL CONSIDERATIONS

When payment of fees for professional services was considered, the research team followed the precedent established a decade earlier when the new techniques for treatment of heterosexual inadequacies were first introduced. No homosexual applicant or his or her committed or casual partner was charged for treatment during the first five years of the clinical control period. In addition, during this five-year period, each couple was fully informed that the treatment techniques to be used were in experimental stages and that the therapists were inexperienced in the treatment of homosexual men and women for their sexual inadequacies. After the first five years, the charges for therapy have been exactly those requested for the heterosexual treatment program. A full fee has been charged when applicable. Since the Institute was established in 1964, approximately 30 percent of all applicants accepted for treatment of homosexual or heterosexual inadequacy have been treated on a sliding-scale basis or without charge.

TREATMENT FORMAT

The basic therapy format was essentially the same as that previously developed for the treatment of heterosexual dysfunctions and dissatisfactions (see *Human Sexual Inadequacy*). Until the investigation of the homosexual male and female's sexual physiology was established, there had been no effort to conceptualize therapeutic modalities for the treatment of problems of homosexual inadequacy. But once it was apparent that there were no basic physiologic differences in the sexual functioning of homosexual men and women when compared to heterosexual men and women, specific attention was devoted to the format of the therapy program.

It was decided to use the same techniques for the treatment of the sexually dysfunctional homosexual that had been developed 10 years previously to treat the sexually dysfunctional heterosexual. Since the same problems of impotence and anorgasmic states existed in both homosexual and heterosexual individuals, it seemed reasonable to assume that these dysfunctions would respond equally well to similar therapeutic approaches, regardless of whether the dysfunctional men or women were of homosexual or heterosexual orientation.

When first considering treatment for homosexual dissatisfactions, it was presumed that a different therapy format might be indicated, but this presumption soon proved to be without foundation. As experience was gained in evaluating homosexuals who expressed the desire to convert or revert to heterosexuality, it was apparent that there were two immediate requirements in order to achieve treatment success. First, there must be a high degree of client motivation for alteration of sexual preference, and second, there must be available an understanding *opposite*-sex partner who could be a major source of psychosexual support during the sexual-preference transition phase. Once the paramount need of the homosexual for partner support in therapy was recognized, the rapid-treatment techniques again seemed particularly indicated. Since partner support is a major requirement for success in treatment, the sooner the therapy program can be concluded, the better the chance of maintaining a high level of continuing partner cooperation.

Thus, the rapid-treatment techniques (two weeks' duration) for heterosexual inadequacies first introduced in 1959 were continued in the treatment of problems of homosexual dysfunction and dissatisfaction when these programs were first constituted in 1968.

No sexually dysfunctional homosexual man or woman has been treated without the presence and support in therapy of a committed or casual partner of the *same* sex, and no sexually dissatisfied homosexual man or woman has been treated for conversion or reversion to heterosexuality without the presence and support in therapy of a committed or casual partner of the *opposite* sex.

A brief review of the relatively standardized protocol of the first two days of rapid treatment is in order.

In the standard dual-sex team approach to treatment of homosexual dysfunction, both members of the dual-sex research team interview the members of the homosexual couple. When a homosexual man or woman presents with a *same*-sex partner for treatment of sexual dysfunction, the dysfunctional man or woman is first interviewed by the *same*-sex therapist and the accompanying partner by the *opposite*-sex therapist. The initial history is conducted in a most detailed fashion, with particular attention paid to the chronology not only of the sexual dysfunction, but also of the individual's personal history. Later in the first day, after the two therapists have had the opportunity to exchange information, second sex histories are taken, during which clients and therapists are interchanged so that the dysfunctional homosexual man or woman is interviewed by the *opposite*-sex therapist and the partner by the *same*-sex therapist.* During the second interviews, there routinely is more concentration by the therapists on attitudinal material and background information.

When homosexual dissatisfaction is the complaint, and the distressed homosexual is accompanied by a partner of the *opposite* sex, initial histories are taken in the same manner as those of sexually distressed heterosexual couples. The male therapist takes a first history from the male client, regardless of whether the male client is the sexually dissatisfied partner or the functional partner. There is similar initial interview linkage between female therapist and female client for first history-taking. The second histories are then taken in the usual cross-sex manner of switching therapists and clients. Again, the first histories are basically directed toward establishing the chronology of the developing homosexual dissatisfaction and an understanding of the applicant's lifestyle. The second or cross-sex histories are primarily concerned with attitudinal material and relationship status.

Physical examinations are also conducted on the first day of therapy for both the sexually inadequate homosexual and his or her committed or casual partner. General laboratory and basic metabolic studies are conducted on the morning of the second day of treatment. The physical examination and laboratory studies are instituted as clinical controls in an attempt to identify possibly detrimental physical and metabolic influences on the client's sexual functioning. It matters not whether a man or woman has a heterosexual or homosexual orientation when physical disabilities or metabolic disease are considered as etiologic factors in complaints of sexual inadequacy, for the influence of physical disability or metabolic dysfunction on sexual function is the same, regardless of the sexual-preference role of the involved person.

On the second day of therapy the couple in treatment and the therapy team meet to discuss the material gathered from the psychosexual and social histories taken and from the physical exami-

* The completion of both histories during the first day of the two-week period (rather than over the first two days, as described in *Human Sexual Inadequacy*) was begun for both homosexual and heterosexual clients during 1972. Prior to that time, the history-taking process was spread over two days. The actual time spent in obtaining histories has not been altered.

nations conducted on the first day. Every effort is made by the therapy team to mirror back to the distressed couple an unbiased reflection of the influences (when they can be identified) that played etiologic roles in the development of the homosexual dysfunction or dissatisfaction. Once identified and explained, these influences are attacked psychotherapeutically over the remaining course of the rapid-treatment program in an effort to at least neutralize their effects, if not to reverse their dominance.

Also during the second day of treatment, the client couple is given a beginning orientation to the fundamentals of both verbal and nonverbal communication as an important adjunct to the success of treatment.

Therapy on subsequent days varies with the severity of the complaint, the cooperation of the couple, the therapeutic progress at hand, and a myriad of other influences that alter from couple to couple. The therapeutic regime of the rapid-treatment technique for heterosexual dysfunction described in detail in *Human Sexual Inadequacy* is the treatment form employed for homosexual inadequacies and will not be repeated in this text, since the basic therapeutic techniques employed have been the same, regardless of whether homosexual or heterosexual inadequacies are under treatment. There will be a detailed discussion of the psychodynamics of the dual-sex team therapeutic format in future publications.

As in the treatment of heterosexual dysfunction, there was an important cumulative effect when the therapy was conducted on a daily basis. When treatment crises occurred (and they occurred regularly), the clients were never more than 24 hours away from active professional support. Therapy crises can be turned into important teaching opportunities rather than therapeutic setbacks if faced in the relative immediacy of their onset. The two-week rapid-treatment format with daily therapy sessions conducted on a seven-day-a-week basis inevitably provides an opportunity to approach treatment crises in the relative immediacy of onset that a once- or twice-a-week therapy format cannot provide. Even if the crisis cannot be resolved satisfactorily, immediacy of therapeutic effort usually eases the severity of the trauma experienced by the distressed couple, and, of course, lessens the hazards to the therapeutic regime. In addition, the importance of continuing therapeutic reinforcement and modeling is maximized in a daily treatment format, drawing upon the underlying principles of social learning theory in a most efficient manner.

Although the dual-sex team was routinely used as a basic component of treatment, alterations in professional personnel were made on an experimental basis. Four times a male therapist was substituted for the female member of the dual-sex team when dysfunctional homosexual male couples were at the end of the first week of therapy. In each instance, the return of the female therapist was requested by the clients. Variation in the established format of the dual-sex therapy team was interpreted by the homosexual male patients as meaning the therapists thought them "different" from sexually dysfunctional heterosexual men. Once drawn, such an implication was resented, and each of the four experimental attempts at therapist substitute was rejected.

A similar technique of substitution of a female therapist for the male member of a dual-sex team was attempted experimentally during treatment of two lesbian couples with complaints of sexual dysfunction. Again, the substitution effort resulted in a request for the return of the opposite-sex therapist, and again, the same rationale to support the clients' requests was presented.

FOLLOW-UP PROCEDURES

In order to provide an additional dimension for evaluating the treatment of homosexual males and females for sexual dysfunction or dissatisfaction, the research team attempted to follow for five years all men and women who were not overt treatment failures during the acute phase of the treatment program. The follow-up procedures consisted of regularly scheduled telephone calls and occasional revisits to the clinic if difficulties developed. The treated couple was also offered the opportunity to contact the Institute at any time when or if either partner felt that he or she was facing some manner of crisis.

Certainly this is not as secure a method of patient follow-up as that made possible by the opportunity to see the individuals for personal interviews on a regular basis. But since approximately 95 percent of the homosexual men and women who applied for treatment came from outside the St. Louis area, there were no viable alternatives to the techniques described above.

A brief statement should be made as to the reliability of information provided during the follow-up periods. Of course, there can never be real security in any information of this type. There is no doubt that some of the clients have purposefully misled the therapists with false reports. Others may have inadvertently accomplished the same result. As long as any clinical program is forced to rely upon data obtained by any form of verbal or written interrogation, the investigator can never be fully confident of the security of his information, regardless of the statistical evaluations made of the reported material.

PERFORMANCE PRESSURES

When cultural performance pressures, real or imagined, intrude upon the psyche of a sexually dysfunctional or dissatisfied man or woman, the immediate response ranges from dissimulation (sexual fakery) to severe anxiety (fears of performance and spectator roles). When he or she is faced with an immediate sexual opportunity and the overt physiologic responses of erection or lubrication are either delayed or absent, the elevated levels of psychosexual anxiety that develop in such a situation consistently force a retreat from reality for the involved man or woman. It matters not whether he or she is homosexually or heterosexually oriented.

This section will consider some of the dissimulation techniques and anxiety states that result from such cultural pressures together with clinical suggestions for reversal of these escape mechanisms.

SEXUAL FAKERY SYNDROME

Sexual fakery has probably always been a refuge for sexually inadequate men and women, regardless of sexual preference. Sexual fakery as practiced in a heterosexual milieu is discussed initially to provide perspective for the practice of sexual fakery as observed in the homosexual community.

Wives have fooled husbands for centuries by faking orgasm or by pretending to be sincerely involved in sexual interchange while mentally doing their culture's equivalent of the next day's marketing list. Unless the men were exceptionally experienced sexually, the wives' sexual fakery might be practiced successfully through many years of sexual interaction. But her thespian success put the wife in a dreadful bind, for she had painted herself into a corner. If she ever tired of mental marketing and opted for increased sexual involvement, she was forced to admit to years of sexual fakery in order to support her request for major alterations in the committed dyad's sexual practices. Failing the courage of full confession or fearful of her husband's reaction to the admitted sexual fakery, she usually continued indefinitely as a seemingly pleased, even anticipatory sexual partner. For her husband, having no reason to believe that his wife was not generally pleased with their mutual sexual experiences, rarely voluntarily changed his presumed "successful" sexual approaches.

As a result, the wife rarely became fully involved sexually. Instead, she frequently became a neurotic, sexually frustrated woman who ultimately rejected her husband on at least two counts: first, because he consistently evidenced no real concern for her sexual needs, for he certainly didn't fulfill them (obviating the fact that he had been deliberately kept unaware of them), and second, because he was a much duller man than she had realized since he had been so easily fooled on so many occasions for such a long period of time.

No one knows the extent of the sexual fakery indulged in by heterosexual women in our culture, but the women who at least on occasion have felt it necessary to fake their degree of sexual involvement certainly numbers into the millions.

Just the opposite is true for the married heterosexual male. As much as he might like to fake the levels of his sexual involvement on occasion, he cannot; either he has an erection of sufficient quality for penetration—or he does not. He can dissimulate with excuses like "tough day at the office," "have an important appointment tomorrow," or "don't feel well," but these excuses are at best short-term escape hatches. His wife is soon fully aware of the insecurity of his erective prowess and of the increasingly severe levels of anxiety that accompany the emergence of his symptoms of impotence. If he is in a committed relationship, a heterosexual male cannot indulge in any long-continued sexual fakery simply because, try as he might, he cannot successfully fake an erection.

The uncommitted heterosexual man can initiate sexual fakery with significant success by practicing various sociosexual withdrawal techniques. He may typically project the image of the perfect gentleman who never approaches sexually beyond a chaste "goodnight kiss," and in self-defense he withdraws socially from a female partner as soon as the frustrated woman begins to press for any form of overt sexual involvement. He also practices the time-honored excuses of a "busy day at the office," "don't feel well," and so on, when pressured to perform sexually by his casual female companion.

The single heterosexual male who consistently practices sexual fakery usually runs out of potential female companionship among his peer group rather quickly and either becomes progressively antisocial or drifts into an almost exclusively male social structure. In short, the impotent single heterosexual male frequently recruits himself into previously unconsidered homosexual opportunity as an escape mechanism from the threatening possibility that some female companion will have the opportunity to identify his impotent state and then spread that information throughout his social circle.

It is far easier for homosexual men than for heterosexual men to be successful sexual fakers. There is no reliable information on the extent to which the syndrome is practiced by homosexual men— just as there is no secure knowledge of the amount of sexual fakery among heterosexual women. But if detailed reports from the few sexually dysfunctional homosexual men treated by the Institute in the last 10 years are of any value, sexual fakery may be far more widespread among the male homosexual population than previously suspected.

The impotent homosexual male has at his disposal a most effective method of sexual fakery. He can easily assume a passive rather than an active role during sexual encounter. Once erective insecurity achieves dominance, the homosexual man tends to live a casual lifestyle, avoiding or dissolving committed relationships. If the impotent homosexual decides to pursue the path of sexual fakery, continuing relationships are quite threatening, for they place the dysfunctional male in jeopardy. In a committed homosexual relationship, just as in a marriage, erective insecurity is virtually impossible to hide.

With onset of erective insecurity, the ego-oriented fears of public disclosure surface immediately. Fear of identification as an impotent man is just as threatening to a homosexual as to a heterosexual man. It is just such fear that can place a committed homosexual relationship in jeopardy. A committed partner not only has a far greater opportunity to identify his partner's erective insecurity than a casual partner, but he also has every opportunity to disseminate the threatening information to the community of their mutual friends. By every evidence, the committed male homosexual relationships that were treated by Institute personnel for one partner's impotence were indeed secure social commitments. In addition to the usual stresses of homosexual partnerships, these relationships had withstood not only the trauma of the one partner's sexual dysfunction and his accompanying fears of disclosure, but, in most instances, also had weathered episodes of attempted sexual fakery by that partner.

With the exception of the couple composed of two primarily impotent men, every homosexual man treated for impotence admitted indulging in sexual fakery at least once, and most of the men described practicing sexual fakery many times. Typically, the man either insists that he has little or no sexual drive himself or that his sexual pleasure is derived principally from stimulating and relieving his partner. His sexual fakery can only succeed if he assumes control of the sexual interchange.

Homosexual men with different degrees of impotence usually practice different levels of sexual fakery. For example, men with occasional erections feign overwhelming sexual demand when the erections do occur, forcing the specific sexual episode to a rapid conclusion so that they can use the engorged penis as quickly as possible before losing the erection. This pattern of sexual behavior has a complete parallel in the reactions of increasingly impotent heterosexual men. When they do achieve an effective erection, they try to mount immediately, even if it is the middle of the night or on awakening in the morning. If they just can get the penis into the vagina and ejaculate before losing the erection, they can gain reassurance relative to their potency—at least for themselves—and at least for the moment.

If penile erection occurs irregularly or consistently has a short maintenance time, homosexual men move into a different form of sexual fakery by assuming a role of sexual service. When playing the service role, the impotent homosexual manipulates or fellates his partner, or serves as the penetratee in rectal intercourse. The relatively passive role in sexual interchange is well established in the homosexual community. It is frequently assumed by aging or physically unattractive homosexual males who have no established sexual partners. With the loss or absence of physical attractiveness, these men must concentrate on providing pleasure for their casual partners if they are to continue to attract sexual opportunities. Since this behavior pattern is widely practiced, the impotent homosexual is usually not suspect when he moves into a role of sexual service as a means of faking his sexual prowess.

But when impotence is fully established, when erections rarely if ever develop during sexual interchange, and when all performance confidence is lost, men of both sexual preferences have in common the safest of all sexual fakery techniques: that of negation of sexual interest. Many impotent men, homosexual and heterosexual alike, simply withdraw first from sexual and second from social interaction. If they are primarily or secondarily impotent at an early age, they tend to become almost exclusively antisocial. These men usually live alone without any continuing relationship or live with their families into their thirties or even forties. They tend to confine their social life to family events, interact with an ever-tightening circle of a few old friends, and lose themselves in their professions or their hobbies. They are constantly on guard to avoid any social interaction that conceivably could lead to sexual opportunity. To paraphrase: If nothing is ventured sexually, nothing is revealed.

The primarily impotent homosexual male is a man who rarely achieves an erection, and when he does, it usually is quickly lost. Therefore, his means of sexual fakery are severely limited. Besides sociosexual withdrawal from his peers, he can only play a full service role. His opportunities for sexual release are confined to nocturnal emissions, when they occur. In simple truth he rarely enters the sexual arena, for his only consistent return is sexual frustration.

The secondarily impotent homosexual lives with somewhat less restriction on sexual activity. As the security of his erections decreases, he loses confidence to interact in an active sexual role with other men. Therefore, if he is to fake sexually, it is generally in a service role. He usually retains the facility to masturbate and provides most of his own sexual release in this manner. Actually, his impotence may have become so severe that masturbation is his only outlet. The psychosexual trauma occasioned by loss of sexual function is frequently so serious that he carefully withdraws from sexual opportunity.

The situationally impotent male generally adjusts to his dysfunction far better than primarily or secondarily impotent men. He practices sexual fakery quite successfully by simply staying within the restrictions of his inadequacy. He tends to maintain an active but well-controlled sexual life. If only masturbation can be successfully completed, he will enter only mutual masturbational opportunities. If he can respond to partner manipulation and not to fellatio, he again arbitrarily limits sexual activity to manipulation. If fellatio is his basic outlet, only fellatio is given or received. At least he can move into homosexual interchange with some sense of security, although at times his casual sexual partners may be somewhat surprised when confronted by his seemingly autocratic limitations on acceptable sexual approaches.

Sexual fakery does not appear to be nearly as prevalent in the lesbian population as it is among heterosexual women. There are several reasons for the lesbians' comparative freedom in acknowledging sexual dysfunction when it occurs rather than attempting to deny the inadequacy.

First, it is obviously far more difficult for a woman to deceive another woman in a continuum of sexual encounters than it is to practice fakery successfully with an unsuspecting man. Inevitably the old cliché of "It takes one . . ." comes into play. Just as subjective appreciation of the partner's level of sexual involvement was used to their advantage by interacting homosexual women in the research laboratories (see Chapter 5), so the same levels of subjective appreciation would tend to make the interacting lesbian aware that her partner was not consistently reaching orgasmic release. Obviously, the lesbian with a succession of casual partners would have a far better chance of practicing successful sexual fakery than the homosexual woman with a committed partner.

Second, until the past few years there has not been the same level of cultural pressure placed upon lesbian women to reach orgasmic levels of sexual excitation as that experienced by heterosexual women. The heterosexual woman is faced with performance demands placed upon her by her male partners, who in turn are reacting to cultural pressures to service their female partners "successfully" to prove their masculinity. The pressures of having to be orgasmic to satisfy a partner's ego do exist in lesbian interaction, but not to the degree evidenced in heterosexual orientation.

Third, there also appears to be a pattern of freedom of open discussion and frank admission of sexual dysfunctions (when present) among committed lesbian couples. In the Institute's limited experience with sexually dysfunctional lesbian couples, a sense of failure as a woman or loss of face when anorgasmic were not expressed as frequently as was noted when working with anorgasmic wives.

These reasons may explain the lower incidence of reported sexual fakery among anorgasmic lesbian women when compared to similarly anorgasmic heterosexual women.

When sexual fakery is identified by the therapist, the practice usually is reversed with relative ease. The therapeutic mirror is employed to reflect to the client that even though he or she may be able to misdirect the sexual partner or partners indefinitely, the only one injured by the practice is the individual resorting to the fakery. This cover-up technique only delays the moment when the dysfunctional man or woman must face the reality of his or her sexual inadequacy. When a sexually distressed individual abandons fakery and openly admits the existence of a dysfunction, he or she has taken the first positive step toward reversal of the complaint. Once the individual realizes the practice of sexual fakery belittles the faker and, in continuing the dissimulation, makes reversal of the dysfunction extremely difficult, if not impossible, most men and women quickly move to a position of open honesty by admitting both the fakery and the sexual distress.

FEARS OF PERFORMANCE

Regardless of whether the sexually inadequate individual is a man or woman, homosexually or heterosexually oriented, 18 or 80 years old, fears for sexual performance, once firmly established, rarely if ever are permanently resolved *with* or *without* psychotherapeutic support. Occasionally sexual opportunities may be experienced without the incapacitating presence of performance fear, but if the sexual inadequacy is not reversed effectively soon after onset, the fears become too firmly implanted *to ever be completely erased.* The Institute's basic method of treating the homosexual's fears of performance is to initiate direct confrontation between the client and his or her fears. This therapeutic confrontation is conducted in a quiet, controlled, and positive manner by the *same*-sex member of the therapy team.

For generations cultural pressures have imposed the burden of sexual performance fears upon men, but in recent years, as a price they are paying for sexual equality, women have increasingly shared this cultural imposition. In discussing the techniques of homosexual client confrontation, male impotence will be used as an example of a sexual dysfunction that inevitably engenders fears of performance. The problem could have been illustrated equally well by discussing a lesbian's anorgasmic state.

The male therapist's insistence upon direct confrontation between the impotent man and his performance fears probably constitutes the most important step in the treatment of the homosexual male's sexual inadequacy. Not only is the impotent man made to face his Achilles' heel directly, but there is another most important therapeutic result. The confrontation procedures are also of vital educational value to the committed or casual sexual partner. It is the Institute's position that the simultaneous education of the sexual partner, whether committed or casual, is theoretically almost as important as the educational approach to the dysfunctional man himself.

The confrontation of the impotent man must be well directed and well organized, but it should be presented in a controlled manner and with a carefully projected sense of complete neutrality. The discussion is opened by the male therapist's quiet but commanding statement to the impotent man that his fears of performance will probably be with him for the rest of his life. A succinct explanation is given that the thought processes that engendered his paralyzing performance fears have become so deeply ingrained that they probably will not be completely erased, regardless of the psychotherapeutic technique employed. The basic confrontation and the accompanying explanation must be conducted with sufficient educational skills for the impotent man and his committed or casual partner to be made fully aware of the implications of such a disclosure; and yet there must be no panic or undue precipitation of anxiety.

Having so confronted the dysfunctional homosexual man and educated his partner, the vital next step in therapy is to suggest that there is a way out of the dilemma. The procedure of choice is to assure the impotent man that although he will never lose his fears of performance completely, therapeutic suggestions will be made by the therapy team, which, if followed by both partners, will enable him to go a long way toward neutralizing the influences of these fears.

Actually the specific suggestions presented by the therapists encompass a high level of dyadic cooperation. In most cases, the dysfunctional man is directed to select a word or brief phrase that will serve as a "catch phrase" to alert both parties in the dyad that immediate cooperation is imperative. The impotent man is then specifically directed to use the catch word or phrase to indicate to his partner that at that moment he is engulfed in his fears of performance. Of course, the fears can and do occur any time, anywhere, but he need only identify his performance anxieties when he is overtly involved in sexual encounter.

The mere fact that the dysfunctional man will acknowledge his performance fear when actively engaged in sexual interchange is of the utmost importance to both partners. For the impotent man, it not only means that he has found the courage to acknowledge openly his performance anxieties, but the taking of such action is concrete evidence that he is making a positive effort to help reverse his sexual distress. For the committed or casual partner, the sexually insecure man's acknowledgement of performance fears may have a possible twofold impact. First, it accentuates the trust placed in him by the dysfunctional man; and second, it provides an opportunity to make a contribution of significant value not only to the sexually inadequate man, but also to a mutually supported relationship, if one exists.

The two partners are instructed to follow a reasonably structured protocol after the catch word or phrase is uttered. When the signal phrase is verbalized, each partner should move to the other in a mutual exchange of sexually stimulative activity. Each man is urged to take advantage of the partner's immediate availability by using his (the partner's) body for his (the individual's) pleasure.

Generally, this open approach is a radical departure from the previously established pattern of sexual interchange within the relationship. The sexually functional partner has frequently made the mistake of allowing concern for his dysfunctional partner to influence or even control the frequency of the couple's sexual opportunities and/or the freedom of their sexual interaction. The dysfunctional individual usually controls the dyad's pattern of sexual interaction by default. The functional partner consistently expresses concern that the impotent man might feel pressured if he (the functional partner) were to openly admit his high level of sexual frustration. An unfortunate result of the functional partner's voluntary holdback is that he unwittingly increases the impotent man's performance pressures by leaving to him the responsibility for initiating most of the couple's sexual interaction.

There is another, somewhat obscured, hardship placed upon the relationship by the functional partner who has been reluctant to play a naturally responsive role in the couple's sexual interchange. As a result of his assumed pattern of sexual passivity, the functional partner frequently loses a sense of involvement in the dyad's sexual interaction. This course of passive compliability by the functional partner and its accompanying reduction of sexual involvement deprives the dysfunctional man of subjectively appreciated sexual stimulation that develops for any individual when his partner reaches high levels of sexual response. Thus, the impotent homosexual man who needs all the help he can get in sexual interplay has the additional disadvantage of losing the subjectively appreciated stimulus of interacting with a sexually involved partner.

When in response to use of the catch phrase the impotent man and his committed or casual partner move to each other physically and each uses the other's body for his own pleasure, the impotent man is immediately subjected to three different sources of sexual stimulation. When the impotent man uses his partner's body for his own (the impotent man's) pleasure, it is indeed sexually stimulating. Also sexually stimulating for the impotent man is the partner's sexual approach to his (the impotent man's) body. Finally, if the partner, as a result of the sensual interaction patterns, happens to reach obviously elevated levels of sexual involvement and communicates his high levels of sexual excitement both verbally and nonverbally, the impotent man has a third source of sexual stimulation, that of an inherent subjective appreciation of his partner's sexual arousal.

The functional homosexual partner must not make the mistake of approaching the dysfunctional man's body in an overt effort to stimulate him sexually by specifically trying to help him attain or maintain an erection. As previously stated, penile erection cannot be willed. It can only be experienced when it develops in response to subjectively appreciated physiologically or psychosexually initiated stimuli. The functional partner should always approach the dysfunctional man for his (the functional man's) pleasure, not with specific intent of providing the impotent man with an erection. If the functional partner approaches the dysfunctional man with the express intent of helping him achieve an erection rather than to enjoy his (the impotent man's) body for his own (the functional man's) self-centered pleasure, the motive of attempting to force an erection will be subjectively recognized by the impotent man and he will comply by trying to force an erection to accommodate the functional partner's presumed sexual demands. Again, no man can will an erection. Thus, sexual failure adds to sexual failure, the grave gets a little deeper, and the fears of performance become more firmly fixed.

There is one more advantage in having the functional partner please himself in self-centered sexual activity rather than act in a passively supportive manner. If the functional partner becomes involved sexually, his involvement then becomes an important factor in helping to neutralize the other great psychosexual problem of the impotent man, that of involuntarily playing a spectator role when he is engaged in overt sexual interaction.

SPECTATOR ROLES

As described in *Human Sexual Inadequacy*, the spectator role occurs when sexually dysfunctional men and women respond to the dominating influences of their fears of performance. For example, in addition to his role as participant, the impotent homosexual man becomes a spectator whenever overt sexual interaction develops. When sexual interaction is joined, he agonizes over whether he is to have an erection. If by chance he becomes erect, he can not believe his good fortune, so he anxiously watches to see if the erection will last. When the impotent man becomes a spectator, concentrating on the state of his own erection, he immediately distracts himself from the ongoing sexual interaction and negates or neutralizes most of the sexual stimuli that naturally develop from his partner's sexual approaches or his own sexual approaches to his partner.

If the impotent man is conditioned to be a spectator, he can be taught to direct his observational tendencies toward becoming subjectively involved with his partner, and not to continue self-distraction by observing his erective progress. When the functional partner is sexually involved, the impotent man receives a stimulative bonus by exposure to and subjective appreciation of the high levels of his partner's sexual excitation.

The essence of the therapeutic message given the impotent man is that he has been distracting himself by watching to see if there is to be an erection. Instead, it is suggested that he watch his partner for overt signs of sexual arousal, because appreciating a partner's sexual arousal is a sure source of increased sexual involvement for the observer. This partner observation technique is but one more therapeutic approach to increasing the dysfunctional homosexual's levels of sexual involvement.

PROGRAM CONCEPTS

When dealing with problems of sexual preference, it is vital that all health-care professionals bear in mind that the homosexual man or woman is basically a man or woman by genetic determination and is homosexually oriented by learned preference. In the same vein, a heterosexual man or woman is first a man or woman by genetic determinants and then is heterosexually oriented by learned preference.

Of course, it must be acknowledged that there always is the possibility of genetic influence that increases the potential predisposition of any man or woman to respond to homosexual rather than to heterosexual stimulation. While the possibility of such a factor is unarguable, there currently is not any convincing evidence to support this contention. Since there is no such evidence to date, it would be most unfortunate to continue support of current cultural concepts of the origins of behavioral patterning of homosexual commitment. There must no longer be blind support of cultural concepts that are obviously based on the vagaries of supposition, presumed potential, or scientifically unsupported contention.

For many decades, cultural bias and specific religious tenets have engendered public opposition to homosexual relationships. It is also obvious that these prejudices have existed in the health-care disciplines, where above all else professional neutrality should exist. As previously noted, Tables 12-5 and 12-6 fully support this contention. Thus, a major problem is raised for the practicing psychotherapist. What attitudes should he or she bring to the evaluation and treatment of homosexual men's and women's sexual inadequacies?

Primarily, the therapists must realize that homosexuality is not a *disease*. The therapists must also realize that homosexual dysfunction or dissatisfaction should only be treated if or when requested by the client. Any treatment conducted to support conversion or reversion to heterosexuality should only be initiated at the request of and with the full support of the client. Such therapy should only be undertaken after careful evaluation of the applicant's history to assure high levels of motivation for change, and after careful self-scrutiny on the therapists' part to be sure that a heterosexual bias does not exist.

In other words, the goal in therapy should always be stated by the client. A basic concept of the Institute's treatment method is that the therapy team does not have the right to impress its concepts or its principles upon the client. The client's social or sexual value systems are those that must be accepted and worked with in the therapeutic process, NOT those of the therapists.

Thus, the Institute's concepts for treatment of homosexual dysfunction or dissatisfaction are: Treat such dysfunctions or dissatisfactions with the same psychotherapeutic techniques, with the same professional personnel, and with the same psychosexual objectivity with which heterosexual dysfunctions are treated. In general, the results should approximate or improve on those returned from treating heterosexual dysfunctions. The Institute's only real reservation is that the sexually inadequate homosexual, particularly the man or woman who is sexually dissatisfied, must offer the therapist the same level of cooperation as that provided by the sexually distressed heterosexual if equally positive results are to be obtained. To date this level of open cooperation has not been fully accomplished.

I 3

MALE HOMOSEXUAL DYSFUNCTION

For the first time, impotent homosexual men have been treated for sexual dysfunction as an integral part of a 10-year controlled program of clinical evaluation. They have been accompanied in therapy by their *same*-sex committed or casual partners. Because such a long-range treatment program has not been described previously, discussions of investigative background, recruitment procedures, therapy principles, clinical syndromes, and presentations of relevant case reports are in order.

Fifty-seven homosexual men were treated for sexual dysfunction by the Institute during the 10-year clinical control period (1968 through 1977). Five of these men were primarily impotent, 49 secondarily impotent, and 3 situationally impotent (see Table 12-1, Chapter 12). Four of these 57 men were additionally diagnosed as sexually aversive. Actually, the 57 men constituted 56 couples, since 1 couple was formed by 2 primarily impotent men, 1 of whom was additionally sexually aversive. All of the committed or casual homosexual partners in the remaining 55 couples were sexually functional.

The laboratory investigation of homosexual men's and women's sexual physiology (see Chapter 7) was the first step leading toward a treatment program for dysfunctional homosexual males and females. As knowledge of the physiology of homosexual function accumulated, the concept of treating existent homosexual dysfunction seemed increasingly plausible, and satisfactory therapeutic results appeared attainable.

Sexually functional homosexual male and female couples were recruited from many metropolitan and/or academic centers throughout the United States to cooperate with the preclinical research programs (see Chapter 1). When these couples returned home, word spread quietly within the homosexual community, not only of the Institute's research interests in homosexual function, but of the treatment programs being developed in St. Louis for sexually inadequate male and female homosexuals.

The first request for treatment of male sexual dysfunction came from a situationally impotent male who was accompanied by a casual partner, and the second request came from a primarily impotent male who was treated with his committed partner. Both couples lived far from St. Louis. These 2 men represented the sum total of the sexually dysfunctional homosexual males treated by the research team in 1968, the first year of the 10-year period of clinical control. As knowledge of the treatment programs spread slowly through the homosexual community, 2 cases of impotence were treated the second year, 6 the third year, and 4 the fourth year. During the fifth year, 7 impotent men and their same-sex partners were treated by the research team. For the last five years of the clinical control period, 7 admissions per year has been the approximate level of case intake for treatment of homosexual impotency (Table 13-1).

TABLE 13-1

Homosexual Male Impotence $(N = 57)$:
Distribution by Year During the 10-Year Clinical Control Period

Type of Impotence	Year Treated										
	One	Two	Three	Four	Five	Six	Seven	Eight	Nine	Ten	Total
Primary	1	0	3	0	0	0	1	0	0	0	5
Secondary	0	2	3	4	6	7	8	6	7	6	49
Situational	1	0	0	0	1	0	0	1	0	0	3
Total	2	2	6	4	7	7	9	7	7	6	57

(1968–1977)

While the total number of impotent homosexual males treated over a 10-year period by the research team is not large, the fact that such a treatment program was in existence represented a major breakthrough in health care. For the first time, sexually dysfunctional homosexual men were requesting therapeutic support with firm anticipation of professional cooperation and with a reasonable chance of successful treatment. Why had it taken so many years for sexually dysfunctional homosexual men to seek health-care support with some degree of confidence? Of course, a variety of reasons were expressed by the client population in response to specific interrogation, but three fears, apparently widespread in the homosexual community, seemed to dominate the answers to this question. They were: (1) the homosexual male's fear of rejection by health-care professionals when requesting psychotherapeutic support, (2) his fear of treatment failure, regardless of the type of therapeutic approach, and (3) his fear of social exposure during or after the treatment process.

Even casual scrutiny of Table 12-5 (see Chapter 12) will clearly identify the validity of the first fear—the sexually dysfunctional man's fear that he would be denied treatment as soon as his homosexuality was identified. There is also further evidence of the health-care professional's refusal to accept sexually dysfunctional homosexual men in therapy. When the Institute's clinical treatment programs for homosexual dysfunction were initiated in 1968, no report was found in a search of the literature of any therapeutic attempt to reverse a homosexual man's basic complaint of impotence while allowing him to maintain the full integrity of his homosexual commitment.

The second fear, that of treatment failure, has been reflected by the dysfunctional homosexual males' extreme reluctance to seek professional aid for an established state of impotence. It is reasonably safe to assume that such attitudinal negativism with its accompanying therapeutic nihilism developed because clinical experience had convinced both the homosexual population and the health-care community that psychotherapy directed toward the homosexual male (and previously confined to attempts to convert or revert him to heterosexuality) would not be particularly productive.

Actually, the Institute's decision to differentiate between the widely differing clinical problems of homosexual dysfunction and those of homosexual dissatisfaction has no precedent in psychotherapy. Understandably, sexually dysfunctional homosexuals felt that they had the same relatively poor treatment prognosis as those who were sexually dissatisfied. In addition, remembering that in 1968 the general literature on the treatment of sexual dysfunction in heterosexuals was indicative of less than a high rate of success with therapeutic approaches that were time-consuming and expensive, it is little wonder that the impotent homosexual male had a real fear of treatment failure.

In order to provide perspective for the Institute's fledgling therapy program directed toward homosexual dysfunction, it might be recalled that 10 years earlier, when treatment programs for heterosexual inadequacy were originally constituted, the same fears of poor clinical results were widely prevalent among both the sexually dysfunctional heterosexual population and the health-care professions.

The third fear, that their sexual problems would become public knowledge, has been the overriding reason why so few dysfunctional homosexual males have sought treatment for impotence in the past. Male homosexuals have had little confidence that health-care professionals would provide them with the degree of security normally anticipated in a client-therapist relationship. In all probability, this protean fear of social exposure has a far higher incidence among dysfunctional men than the combined incidence of the two previously mentioned fears of treatment refusal and treatment failure.

Actually, the long-standing obsession of both men and women (homosexual and heterosexual alike) with possible identification of their sexual dysfunctions by the public or even by their sexual partner has been of such paramount importance that it has led not only to avoidance of therapy, but also to the widespread practice of a self-protective mechanism identified by Institute personnel under the all-inclusive term of *sexual fakery* (see Chapter 12).

PRIMARY IMPOTENCE

In a sense, primary impotence is the ultimate in male sexual dysfunctions, for a man so stricken, whether homosexually or heterosexually oriented, rarely develops a secure place in society. Unfortunately, he is so consumed with his psychosexual handicap that it assumes an all-pervasive control of his life. Since primary impotence of homosexual origin has not been considered previously, case reports will be presented in detail. No suggestion is made that these reports are generally typical of primarily impotent homosexual men. There have been so few cases to treat that the research team has no concept of what constitutes the general behavior pattern.

Five primarily impotent homosexual men were treated by the research team during the 10-year clinical control period. In each instance, the dysfunctional men were accompanied in therapy by committed partners. All 5 men responded positively during the acute phase of the treatment program, but there was one treatment failure. Approximately a year after the acute phase of treatment, 1 man experienced the return of erective insecurity. He lost confidence in his ability to interact sexually with his committed partner during episodes of partner manipulation and fellatio. Within a month's time, fears of performance so overwhelmed him that he ended his long-term relationship and reportedly withdrew from social or sexual encounter. Masturbational activity served as his only form of sexual release. The man refused to return for further treatment and also refused continuing cooperation with routine follow-up procedures.

On the basis of results obtained during the rapid-treatment phase and of five years of follow-up information, the other 4 primarily impotent homosexuals were not treatment failures. Statistical considerations of the treatment program are presented in Chapter 17.

CASE REPORT: COUPLE 1

Certainly the most psychosexually dysfunctional couple treated by the research team was a committed dyad of two men seen during the third year of the program. For identification purposes, the two men have been labeled Couple 1 and individually identified as Partner A, who was primarily impotent, and Partner B, who was also primarily impotent, and, in addition, sexually aversive. Because of the uniqueness of their plan of treatment, their case history will be presented in some detail.

Partner A, 34 years old, and Partner B, 29 years old, had been living in a committed relationship for approximately three and one-half years when they sought treatment as a sexually dysfunctional couple. Although from quite different backgrounds, the men had a unique commonality in the etiology of their sexual dysfunctions. As individuals, they unknowingly moved into what was to become an intensely committed homosexual relationship as an involuntary means of escape from years of psychosexual trauma that in both instances had been heterosexual in origin. For over three years, their relationship had been entirely asexual in character. It had become a satisfying psychosocial haven before the two men finally moved into attempted sexual interchange, an attempt that was completely unsuccessful.

A, a second sibling with a sister eight years older, grew up in an atmosphere of female dominance. His father left home when A was 4, and his mother worked to support the family, frequently holding two jobs. With the exception of weekends, this work schedule usually kept her out of the home during the majority of the children's waking hours. A's older sister was given the responsibility for her younger brother after she reached 15 years of age. After that time, there was essentially no supervision in the home. There also was no importance assigned to education, nor was there any attempt to establish a religious influence.

When A was 9 years old and his mother was at work, his 17-year-old sister began a series of attempts to masturbate the boy. When repeatedly unsuccessful, she frequently shamed him by telling him he would never grow up to be "a man." These episodes of attempted sexual interaction continued approximately twice a month for more than two years. Usually little or no erection occurred. There was no ejaculation. The boy never made a sexual approach to his sister. His reactions to her sexual approaches were described as ranging from strong resistance to passive acceptance. Finally, on one weekend when the mother was out of town, the sister had two female friends spend the night. The three girls apparently spent hours trying to masturbate the boy, now 11, two of them always holding him to keep him from running away. Their repeated assaults produced recurrent penile engorgement, but no ejaculation. He recalls crying and begging them to stop, for it was a very painful as well as frightening experience. The girls were apparently extremely vigorous in their manipulative attempts, as the penis was rubbed raw in a number of areas. When finally released by the girls, the boy couldn't void for hours and, when finally successful, noticed gross blood in the urine.

A was both mortified and terrified. The girls had threatened to tell his friends that "he wasn't a man" if he told his mother about their assault. Yet he was fearful of both the bloody urine and the fact that he had difficulty voiding, both of which lasted several days. In addition, his penis was very painful for many days after the episode. Even at 11 years of age, however, his fear of exposure to public ridicule won out over his concerns for the physical aftermaths of the attack, and he kept his own counsel. This was the last time his sister approached him sexually.

The symptoms of the physical trauma cleared, but not those of the psychosexual trauma. Fearful that word would be circulated of his inadequacy, the boy withdrew from friends at school and had many miserable nights as his anxieties and vengeful fantasies reigned unbridled. As he grew older, he became essentially antisocial. Stimulated by the onset of nocturnal emissions, his first attempt to masturbate at age 16 was an utter failure when he couldn't obtain an erection. The failure only reinforced the image created by his sister and her friends that he was sexually inadequate. As he grew older, his generalized sexual anxieties became specific apprehensions at the thought of "making out" with a girl, as was frequently discussed by his peers, for he was afraid that "making out" might be painful and was certain he would be a failure.

At age 23 A gathered his social courage and made his first attempt at intercourse by soliciting a prostitute. Following the usual pattern of many men contending with anxieties for sexual performance, A chose the prostitute knowing that if he failed, his friends wouldn't know. As would be expected, he was totally impotent. Again he was told he "wasn't much of a man," and having conclusively proved this fact to his own grim satisfaction, he never attempted to interact sexually with a woman until after meeting Partner B.

A sublimated his sexual needs. He lived alone, worked hard, and was advancing well in his profession. Masturbation was attempted on rare occasions, usually after he had been drinking, but it was always unsuccessful. He could not maintain erections and was never able to ejaculate. He had no overt homosexual interests, nor were there fantasies of specific homosexual content. His most frequent fantasies were of exacting revenge upon women in general and his sister in particular to make up for what had been done to him.

Partner A met Partner B as a staff member of the company for which he worked. B had been transferred from out of town and was apartment hunting. A offered B the use of his apartment until B "could find something of his own." At history-taking, A had no explanation for this quite uncharacteristic behavior, nor did B have any reason other than convenience for his acceptance. Yet, in a brief period of time and to the complete surprise of each, the two very lonely men came to like each other so much that they decided to continue living together.

B was an only child in a reasonably well-to-do family. The most vivid memories of his childhood revolved around sexual activity—that of his mother and father. He couldn't remember when he first heard his mother protesting loudly from behind the closed doors of the parents' bedroom. It seemed to him that she had always suffered from physical abuse by his father. By the time the growing boy was 10 years old, the mother probably was fully aware that he must be anxious—even frightened— by his parents' continuing bedroom conflict. She began privately describing to the boy the horrors suffered by women while sleeping with their husbands. Sex was portrayed as a wickedly sinful act, as something women should only be expected to tolerate to have children, and as men's vengeance upon unprotected women. The boy learned to hate weekends when his father, who traveled extensively on business, was at home, because that was when episodes of his mother's forced sexual participation and her accompanying cries of rage or pain (the boy was never sure which) usually occurred.

The boy grew up in a home that was devoid of warmth and was dominated by an angry, unhappy, possibly lonely wife who released her frustrations by vigorously supporting an extremely orthodox Catholic commitment for herself and her son.

At age 12, B was so upset during one particular episode when his mother's loud cries of protest seemed to go on much longer than usual that he rushed into his parents' bedroom and apparently saw them in intercourse. He was convinced that his father was seriously hurting or even killing his mother, and he tried to separate them physically. His enraged father jumped from the bed with a full erection, knocked the boy down, threw him out of the room, and locked the door. The boy was further traumatized when his mother's screaming soon redoubled in intensity. B vividly recalled the threatening sight of his naked mother trying to hide from him under the sheets and his first sight of a full erection when his father attacked him.

Shortly thereafter, the father left the home, and although he apparently continued to provide financially, he never returned. But the boy was still subjected to his mother's horror stories of sexual assault—she repeatedly described his father's bestiality and told him of the disgust all decent women felt for men's uncontrollable sexual appetites. As he moved through his teenage years, the boy dreaded the possibility that he might grow up to be an animal like his father.

B was horrified when he awoke one night with a full erection at age 17, and he was overcome with a sense of guilt and disgust when his first episode of nocturnal emission occurred at age 18. He showered for an hour to wash away the signs of his male sexual weakness. Whenever he overheard his peers talking, telling real or imagined stories or joking about sex, he always grew anxious, frequently was nauseated, felt faint, and quickly moved away from the storytellers. B was developing a general aversion to sexuality.

His mother had insisted upon a Catholic education for him. During his teens his every sexual thought was routinely repressed and just as routinely confessed. His psychosexual trauma was reinforced by religious dogma, and B never attempted to masturbate. His occasional nocturnal emissions caused him great anxiety, for he did not want to acknowledge any part of man's bestial nature. He was so threatened by any thought of sexual content that he never had a social date with a girl in his life. The thought of any manner of sexual interaction with a woman made him quite anxious.

After his mother's death when he was 20, B lived with an aunt, finished college, and went to work. At age 24 he was promoted and transferred to another city by his firm. He met a man (Partner A) who was also working with the firm and who offered to share his apartment while B looked for one of his own. As previously described, mutual compatibility was soon evidenced, and the two men decided jointly to continue living together to share expenses and enjoy each other's company.

The first six months A and B lived together were spent breaking down social defenses and establishing the first real friendship either man had ever known. One weekend and well into the next week they told each other every detail they could recall of the painful episodes of their past lives. Social fears and anxieties were first confessed, and finally sexual fears and anxieties were broached. Eventually, the catharsis of confession brought such a state of complete vulnerability that both men were encouraged to give a full exchange of the vividly remembered details of the psychosexual traumas in their lives.

Each man found it almost impossible to believe that the other partner had never successfully experienced any form of sexual activity. They both had thought themselves totally unique as severe sexual cripples. The relationship was strongly reinforced by the mutual vulnerability derived from the full confessions of their personal feelings of complete sexual inadequacy.

Over the following year, each man encouraged his partner to establish social relationships with selected women, but without success. After two such trials by A and one very abortive, anxiety-ridden attempt by B to talk with a girl in a bar, the men openly discussed their problems, realized that their sense of social inadequacy was strongly reinforced by their complete lack of sexual confidence, and following A's now somewhat time-worn suggestion, they decided to solicit help from a prostitute. Obviously neither A nor B had access to any other source of female sexual cooperation. A prostitute was solicited by A and brought to the apartment to spend the night. As might be expected, the experiment ended in disaster. The first sexual venture was in A's bedroom. During more than an hour's time with the prostitute, he failed to respond to any sexual approach. B was initially so anxious, continually so nauseated, and after an hour so terrified of even touching the woman that he refused to try when it was his turn.

During the next two years these two men grew even closer together. They worked well together professionally and were inseparable socially. There were no further attempts at heterosexual interaction. Actually, neither partner expressed interest in female companionship of any kind. A continued his attempts at masturbation once every month or so, consistently without success. Despite occasionally considering the possibility, B made no attempt to masturbate. Until the relationship had lasted more than three years there were no overt or covert homosexual overtones, although each man reported that a few times he fantasized some vague form of physical interaction with his friend. The fantasies were only of physical warmth or of general body contact. Neither A nor B reported daydreaming of specific sexual activity.

One night, after both men had spent several hours in a bar, A openly stated his masturbational need and retired to the privacy of his bedroom, where he again failed to masturbate successfully. B heard A sobbing and went to comfort him, only to be confronted by his naked friend with a full and threatening erection. B was immediately nauseated by seeing the erection, but he still moved to comfort his anguished and inebriated partner. A begged him to help, saying he would rather die than live this way. Despite his intense aversion to the erection, B clumsily attempted to release his partner, only to have the erection disappear soon after he approached. For both men the return from the episode was more in a positive than a negative vein. Despite A's functional failure, the experience broke down any barriers that still may have remained in the relationship.

Within the week the partners had agreed to try mutual masturbation. Although neither man ever approached the other physically, A tried to teach B by demonstration what little he knew about the subject. B still became quite anxious when observing the comings and goings of his partner's erections, but they persisted in their mutual masturbational attempts. Neither B nor A reported successful termination to their mutual masturbational experiences. Sometimes fleeting erections were achieved, sometimes not, but neither man ever ejaculated. Yet, each man described an increasingly strong sense of personal need to prove that he could function sexually as a man and the sincere hope that his partner would also be sexually successful. Careful questioning clearly established that neither man ever considered himself as being homosexual.

The couple came to the Institute for treatment neither as men committed to heterosexuality nor as men jointly or individually considering a homosexual commitment, but rather as two men deeply devoted to each other and in sincere need of psychotherapeutic support. Neither man even implied that he had a sexual role preference. Their mutually voiced demand was "to learn to *function* sexually." They looked to the Institute for support and direction and were accepted in treatment on these terms.

The men had a difficult decision to make. Their available alternatives in treatment were to become sexually effective homosexuals or sexually responsive heterosexuals or both. Exhaustively defined histories underscored the virtual impossibility of either man establishing an ongoing heterosexual relationship within the foreseeable future. The use of surrogate partners was considered, but since there was no hope of finding immediately available female sexual partners when the men finished the acute phase of treatment, the possible role of sexual surrogates was forfeited. Both partners' severe levels of social insecurity and B's state of overwhelming anxiety at the thought of even a social, let alone a sexual, relationship with a woman, were also contributing factors in their treatment decision.

Previous work has pointed up the possibility of reversing a man's homosexual orientation that has resulted from severe heterosexual trauma at an early age. While both A and B were subjected to severe sexual trauma of heterosexual origin at an early age, neither man had responded by openly embracing homosexuality, nor could either man function sexually in any manner. If either man could be considered homosexually oriented, it would be Partner A. He did offer to share his apartment for no reason he could or would declare. On one occasion, when a masturbational effort had failed and his defenses may have been lowered by alcohol ingestion, A did ask for sexual help from his partner some three and one-half years after they initially decided to live together. The two men did attempt mutual masturbation and, most important, they were obviously devoted to each other. B had a history of rejection of women in general, but he also became severely anxious at the sight of the male erection. Each man denied that he had ever thought of himself as homosexual. Although presuming that they were heterosexual, both men also stated that they had no interest in heterosexual interaction.

In the research team's clinical judgment, neither A nor B could be arbitrarily labeled homosexual, nor could they be considered heterosexual. They were evaluated as two men who, due to the pressure of circumstances, were currently living without an established sexual preference. Although admitting to continuing levels of sexual tension, neither man's physical need had been targeted.

In view of the investigative material presented in the preclinical section of this text, it should be underscored that the Institute does not utilize the diagnosis of latent homosexuality or, for that matter, that of latent heterosexuality. But, if the concept underlying such a diagnosis was applied to these two men, in truth one would have to say that their basic sexual orientation was latent or undifferentiated.

The basic concern expressed by both men was that they could not function sexually; they were mutually agreed that they wanted to alter this aspect of their lives. There was no question that they were primarily impotent, regardless of whether they were judged by heterosexually or homosexually defined criteria. Certainly, it was the psychosocial distress occasioned by their sexual inadequacies that brought the two men to therapy—not any concern for sexual preference.

The problem of how best to treat the individual sexual dysfunctions was discussed in all of its ramifications with both partners. For B, the potential influence of his Catholic background on his future comfort with any decision made was emphasized for both partners' consideration. Each man quietly made his own decision on the basis of the information at hand. They were decisions with which the research team was in full concurrence, but it should be emphasized that the decisions were *not* made for A or B by the research team. The partners decided that they had the best chance of functioning sexually by interacting with each other. Thus, this case is reported as a specific decision made jointly by two men to request professional assistance in orientation to full homosexual commitment. In addition, they requested continuing professional support during their transition phase. The research team responded positively to their requests.

The course of therapy was relatively uneventful. Initially, therapeutic attention was directed toward B's sexual aversion. Sensate-focus opportunities * were initiated while the genitals of both partners were off limits, and this anxiety-reducing approach was continued until B could touch his partner's body with comfort and even with a tentatively expressed sense of pleasure. A was fully co-

* Masters and Johnson (1970).

operative and made no attempt to push B to higher levels of involvement. B made rapid progress, due in no small part to the fact that he had taken giant strides to neutralize his sexual aversion to masculine sexual anatomy when he had participated in the couple's attempts at mutual masturbation.

When overt sexual involvement between the two men seemed indicated, B was again the research team's initial therapeutic target. It was felt that A's many failures at masturbation had created such elevated fears of performance that the best way to neutralize these anxieties was through B's demonstration of a successful masturbational experience. Technical suggestions were made, and B did respond successfully within 24 hours, ejaculating in A's presence much to the delight of both men. It was B's first ejaculatory experience other than during episodes of nocturnal emission. Attention was then focused on A, and with different suggestions for masturbational techniques based upon his own negative past experience, A also successfully reached orgasm as he followed B's example.

Taking therapeutic advantage of the euphoria created by their first individually successful sexual experiences and the significant degree of anxiety reduction that had already occurred, it was but a short step to successful mutual masturbational experiences.

It would be a serious clinical mistake to assume that therapeutic procedures only involved improving the impotent men's masturbational techniques. To avoid such an assumption, the technical suggestions have not been described. The mere mechanics of sexual function could never provide sufficient building materials to create and support an empathetic, secure relationship. Without the unqualified support provided each man by his partner, the most sophisticated of sexual gymnastics would probably have been of little value in altering either man's personally repugnant state of primary impotence.

At this point in therapy, the research team pointed out to the couple that they had the option of remaining at their present level of sexual interchange rather than moving further into overt homosexual interaction. For two days the men continued with successful mutual masturbational experiences while considering their options at great length. Apparently they were both concerned, because B was still apprehensive about approaching A's genitals and was even more concerned about having A approach him sexually. B resolved the problem by deciding not to let past traumatic experiences stand in the way of continuing expansion of mutual sexual interaction.

The sexual neophytes moved through partner manipulative experiences with little difficulty. A failed to maintain an erection during their first joint venture, but he responded successfully during a second opportunity. As expected with his aversive background, B had major difficulties with fellatio, both in approaching A's erect penis and in allowing A to approach him orally. Although he functioned effectively in both situations, he was not pleased with or even highly stimulated by fellatio. B's level of anxiety was at a higher level when his penis was in his partner's mouth than when he was fellating A. On the other hand, A enjoyed the experience of mutual fellatio more than that of partner manipulation.

This couple was followed for five years after the acute phase of therapy was terminated. They continued as a closely knit, most effective social partnership and as a fully responsive sexual dyad. B's continuing reluctance to participate in fellatio necessitated an alteration in their sexual behavior pattern. He compromised by learning to fellate A with some degree of comfort, but he requested manipulation rather than fellatio when A approached him. There was no description of attempting rectal intercourse.

Neither man ever expressed interest in establishing a continuing heterosexual relationship, nor for that matter did either partner make a move toward interacting sexually with another man. They continued to live essentially asocial lives, confining their public social activities, whether with men or women, to those required by their professional commitments.

Three other primarily impotent men were treated by the research team during the 10-year period of clinical control. These men had similar case histories typical of the environmental influences which apparently make a major contribution to the ultimate selection of a homosexual life. Each of the 3 men was accompanied in therapy by a committed partner. The committed partners' sociosexual backgrounds (although of significant importance to therapy) are not described in full detail due to space restrictions.

CASE REPORT: COUPLE 2

C, a primarily impotent homosexual, was 31 years old when he sought treatment from the Institute accompanied by his committed homosexual partner.

C could never remember when his mother and father were not polarized in their value systems or attitudes toward child care, yet he also recalled his parents' high level of mutual devotion. He was the younger of two brothers. His older brother (by four years) was an extrovert, well coordinated, an excellent athlete but at best a fair student. His father was openly delighted with the elder brother's athletic prowess, while his mother was sincerely distressed with his academic mediocrity.

C was apparently an introvert as a child and overweight during adolescence. He was poorly coordinated physically and could never play boys' competitive games with any success. In this area he was a disappointment to his father. But his excellent grades pleased his mother. As a boy there was required attendance at a Protestant Sunday school, but neither of his parents evidenced much religious conviction.

When his elder brother went to college, C was starting high school. As the only child in the home, he continued to receive mixed messages from his parents. His father was concerned with helping the boy improve his physical image and social attitude. His mother was oriented to academic and intellectual pursuit. Both parents felt that if he improved in their area of interest he would be far happier, for his was an essentially antisocial existence. C remembered his high-school years as a reasonably pleasurable existence while at home, but as a depressing experience in social interaction at school.

He had no friends. When he couldn't compete in games, he withdrew from his male peer group. There were no female peers as friends either. This lack of interest in girls originated more from a sense of rejection by them rather than from lack of interest on his part. For pleasure he read extensively, evidenced some real talent with the violin, and ate constantly.

Possibly resulting from envy of his older brother's physical coordination and outgoing personality, C could not remember when he wasn't intrigued with the male body. He admired the high-school athletes' muscles and always surreptitiously observed and compared genitals when he shared the shower room. H was delighted when, to his surprise, he found that in a flaccid state his penis was as large as or larger than theirs.

He had begun to play with his penis when he was 13 and was intrigued when it enlarged and disappointed when it lost engorgement. Since he had no male friends nor even a close relationship with his elder brother, there was no real source of sexual information. Neither parent ever talked to him about sex, but at 14 he was given a book to read on this subject.

As C moved through his early teens, he became more concerned about his appearance, lost a large amount of weight, and attempted to establish male relationships.

A major sexual trauma occurred during C's fifteenth year. Although he had tried a number of times, he had never masturbated successfully. By this time he had acquired his first friend, a boy from his class who also was struggling with social handicaps. One evening after both boys had been talking about sex, C showed the boy how he played with his penis. Although C reportedly only demonstrated penile manipulation with his own penis and never moved to or even thought of approaching his friend's genitals, the boy told his parents about the incident. These parents in turn not only told C's parents but many other parents and the high-school administrators as well. The friend's parents insisted that C was an active homosexual who had tried to seduce their son and that he was a threat to all the boys in his class. Of course, the word immediately spread through his peer group. He was ostracized socially, made the butt of jokes by both boys and girls, and was frequently attacked physically by his male peers. C's family, severely distressed by the trauma their son was experiencing, sent him away to school. (Whether C's story is the true version of the event with his friend is, of course, open to question. But when interviewed at length, and with nothing to gain or lose, C held staunchly to the theme.)

C never recovered from his public humiliation. He hated to come home for vacations, and when home, he rarely left the house. He finally accepted public opinion that he was homosexual; as a result, he was certain that he was considered unacceptable socially by his peers. His fantasies were of both homosexual and heterosexual content but were primarily focused on the penis. Thus, C was actually socially oriented to a homosexual preference role well before his first overt homosexual experience.

One night during his second year at boarding school, his roommate moved into C's bed. C was not only comfortable with this overt sexual approach, he welcomed the sexual opportunity. Both boys played freely with each other's genitals. When the roommate quickly erected and ejaculated, C was quite surprised, for he had never had this experience. He was both intrigued with his friend's ejaculatory experience and embarrassed that he could not do the same. He attempted to masturbate many times privately, always trying to force an erection and an ejaculation, but he rarely had a full erection and never an ejaculation. C became increasingly anxious about what he presumed was further evidence of physical weakness comparable to not being well coordinated enough to excel at competitive games.

The boys continued their sexual encounters, always with the friend ejaculating quickly. C became increasingly anxious when he couldn't ejaculate and, worrying about his sexual prowess, soon lost most of his ability to achieve or maintain an erection. However, he did learn to enjoy relieving his partner.

C visited the boy's home during a vacation and learned fellatio from one of the boy's friends. He spent the vacation fellating the two boys daily, thoroughly enjoying himself in the process although he rarely had penile engorgement. Even though the two boys tried to help several times, C could not respond to either manipulation or fellatio.

Thereafter, C's sexual interests and activities were homosexually oriented. He was quite active sexually when in college. He always serviced his partner and never allowed an approach to his genitals, since he was afraid his inability to achieve or maintain an erection would be discovered and discussed.

He rarely interacted with girls. At age 23 there was one abortive sexual episode when a girl moved to play with his genitals as he drove her home from a symphony concert. No erection occurred, and he never saw the girl again.

By the time he finished college and moved into the business world as an accountant, C was an active, cruising homosexual. He frequented gay bars and had a large number of casual sexual partners. He manipulated men freely, practiced fellatio routinely, was the penetratee in rectal intercourse occasionally, and enjoyed himself thoroughly.

Finally at 29 he met and became socially committed to a man who was five years older and who had been an active homosexual for six years. This man gave a history of a failed marriage based on sexual refusal by his wife and had moved into homosexual activity after a divorce.

C and his partner had lived together for almost two years when seen in therapy. They had approached two other professional sources in the hope that C could learn to interact sexually with his partner in other than a service role. In both instances they had been refused treatment and given no referral to another potential source of psychotherapeutic support.

When C and his partner entered therapy, C had never ejaculated in response to any form of sexual stimulation with the stated exception of nocturnal emissions. These reportedly occurred approximately once every seven to 10 nights and had continued at this level since onset when C was 15 years old.

What had not been appreciated by the partner or initially by the research team was the extent of C's fears of performance as a sexually dysfunctional man and his paralyzing fear that his sexual dysfunction would be revealed publicly. He had kept these fears well hidden. C had previously avoided any opportunity at a committed relationship, not because he didn't want or need the warmth and security of such companionship, but because he feared that his dysfunction, once revealed in the relationship, would become common knowledge among his peer group.

His sexual fakery had, of course, placed him in an almost inextricable position. His entire sexual experience, one of sexual service, had been portrayed to peers in his homosexual community as a role of his own choosing. Time and again he reiterated the position that he thoroughly enjoyed releasing a partner by manipulation or fellatio—and he did—but that he had no real need for the partner to provide him with release. This was hardly the truth, but it was good sexual fakery. What he did not admit to his peer group was that time and again during or after sexual encounters he had testicular aching, pain in his groin, and often had prayed for some means of release from his masked sexual tensions. When he tried to masturbate, and he often tried, he usually could not achieve, or maintain a full erection. He was always too fearful of erective failure and possible exposure to allow a casual partner to attempt manipulation or fellatio.

Only after several months in his committed relationship did C make a clean breast of the degree of his sexual dysfunction to his partner. The partner then tried diligently and with a surprising degree of originality to relieve C, but without success. As more than a year passed and the committed relationship remained one-sided sexually, evidences of strain developed in the two men's social interaction. C's partner had repeatedly suggested that C seek treatment for his dysfunction, and C just as steadfastly refused.

Finally, the partner took the position that C either seek aid or he (the partner) would regretfully terminate the relationship. The partner was only too aware of the destruction that can be wrought in a relationship when there is a persistent level of sexual dysfunction or dissatisfaction, since he believed he had lost a valued marriage for this reason. He did not want to see their relationship end in strife or bitterness, preferring a quietly agreed upon separation rather than to continue facing the usual consequences of continued tensions related to C's sexual dysfunction.

C finally accepted the fact that his partner was adamant in his demand that he seek help. As described, C did approach two other therapy sources that would not accept him in treatment before the couple requested and were accepted in treatment by the Institute.

Therapy problems centered almost exclusively around C's fears of performance. His fears of public identification with his dysfunction had been reasonably allayed by his sense of security in the relationship, his own voluntary admission of his sexual fakery, and the fullness of the commitment so frequently expressed by his partner. But by far the most important positive force in therapeutic progress was the free, open cooperation of C's committed partner.

C's fears of performance were as strongly entrenched as any that had been previously treated by the therapy team. The problems that arise in the treatment of fears of performance have been discussed in Chapter 12. Early stages of sensate-focus experiences provoked severe levels of anxiety for C, particularly when it was the partner's turn to approach C's body and even though the genital organs were off limits by direction of the therapists.

C repeatedly stated that he loved to touch his partner's body but that he was most anxious when the partner approached him. His established behavior pattern was severely resistant to alteration. But over a period of four days, confidence was gained and comfort expressed with general body touching. Then mutual genital approach was encouraged. At first C failed to achieve an erection when the genitals were placed on limits to manual exploration, but in 48 hours he was repeatedly experiencing though not maintaining full erections. C was by this time also suffering from testicular engorgement and was most uncomfortable with groin pain.

Early in the second week of therapy, during an episode of slow, nondemanding manipulation by his partner, C suddenly ejaculated through a partially erect penis. He had experienced no sense of ejaculatory inevitability. Within two more days erective security was reasonably established, although penile engorgement was not totally developed. Next, C responded orgasmically to the stimulation of fellatio, and finally, on the twelfth day of therapy, he was able to masturbate to orgasm. On both of these occasions he did experience the stage of ejaculatory inevitability. By this time his erections were full but were maintained for only a brief time span. When the therapy was terminated, C had met the criteria of a sexually functional homosexual male.

For the following months, C and his partner continued their effective social and sexual relationship, and C functioned sexually with increasing security. His fears of performance returned occasionally, but both C and his partner were able to contend comfortably with his occasional episodes of remission.

Approximately a year after the acute phase of treatment, C attempted to interact with another male homosexual in his peer group while his partner was out of town. The sexual experience followed an evening spent drinking together, and C failed to achieve an erection. The casual partner derided him when at the last minute C resorted to his sexual-fakery practice by attempting to return to his service role.

C was devastated by the experience. All of the fears of performance were reconstituted and were compounded by the return of fears of public identification. He feared his casual partner would describe his sexual inadequacy to their mutual friends. C lost all ability to function sexually with his committed partner, terminated the relationship, and followed this step by withdrawing from social interchange with any member of his established homosexual peer group. He did retain the facility to masturbate and used this technique frequently for sexual tension release. C refused an Institute offer of a revisit to confront the performance fears and shortly thereafter refused any further cooperation with follow-up procedures.

Although the complaint of primary impotence was reversed during the acute treatment phase and follow-up procedures revealed almost complete reversal of the dysfunctional status approximately one year later, this case is categorized as a treatment failure. Since C failed to function effectively during the first opportunity he made to interact sexually with a casual homosexual partner, the therapy could hardly be termed fully effective.

The depths of C's fears of performance as evidenced during therapy surprised the research team. Every effort was made to neutralize these anxieties. The committed partner was in large measure responsible for initial treatment progress, but neither partner cooperation nor therapeutic direction could counteract effectively the engulfing return of C's performance and public identification fears after his failure to function under the performance pressures that are inherent in a homosexual male's casual sexual encounters. Particularly unfortunate, of course, was the fact that he chose to try his wings after a long evening of drinking. Under such circumstances any man, homosexually or heterosexually oriented, regardless of his level of prior sexual experience, can and frequently does fail to attain or maintain an erection due to the pharmacologic properties of alcohol as a central nervous system depressant.

C's retreat from reality as evidenced by his course of action after the trauma of the casual sexual episode suggests not only that his fears of performance had been dealt with inadequately but that there remained a significant degree of underlying psychopathology which had not been identified during the acute phase of therapy. Professional concern, not only for the effectiveness of his sexual performance, but also for his emotional stability, was discussed with C by telephone, but he refused to return to therapy despite the assurance of full and continued cooperation from his partner.

Regretfully, textual requirements do not allow for detailed case reports of the remaining 2 primarily impotent homosexual men. This material will be presented in other publications. However, since there are no previous reports available reflecting this sexual dysfunction, pertinent elements in the case histories are summarized. Despite their entirely different backgrounds, there is a certain parallelism in the two men's lifestyles.

CASE REPORTS: PRIMARY IMPOTENCE

D and E were just as severely handicapped psychosexually as the three men whose backgrounds have been described. They had an additional disadvantage. Neither man had ever achieved sufficient personal security to hold down a regular job or support himself. One man, 28-year-old D, was fully supported by his family, while E, at 34 years of age had moved from minor job to minor job until he finally established a committed homosexual relationship with a partner who was able to support him. Both D and E had been severely traumatized sexually as teenagers. D reported an orthodox Jewish home with an implacably rigid but quiet father and a domineering mother. The subject of sex was totally unacceptable in his home. There was exposure to both heterosexual and homosexual opportunities within his peer group. Overcome with anxiety and guilt during these experimental episodes, D failed to function effectively. He presumed that his failure to respond sexually was just retribution for his sins of sexual pleasure.

E's mother had died when he was 10 years old. His education was routine. There was little interest expressed in academic accomplishment. The family was in the low-income group, and there was no religious input into the home. At age 14 he had been seduced into a role of sexual service by his stepfather and 22-year-old half-brother. The boy was taught to manipulate and fellate, and he was forced into the penetratee's role in rectal intercourse. He was never helped to function sexually by his seducers, and when at age 19 he sought personal relief in a casual homosexual opportunity, he could not function. Fearful of inadequate performance and subsequent public exposure, he returned to his service role.

The all-consuming levels of their sexual frustration led both D and E into almost complete resignation from any concept of a socially responsible, masculine role in society. D became both stringently asocial and patently effeminate in both verbalization and physical actions, while E had moved to alcohol and drugs as an escape.

In each case the two men were fortunate to develop relationships with men who cared for them, saw them as severely handicapped persons, and were most willing to cooperate in any way to enable them to acquire sexual facility.

Primary impotence is overwhelmingly devastating to the involved man, regardless of whether he is homosexually or heterosexually oriented. Not only is he utterly frustrated sexually, but he rarely attains sufficient emotional maturity to function in a masculine role in society. Since an impotent man has no source of psychosocial support for his enforced chastity, his sexual frustrations probably far outweigh those of men who electively choose chastity as a way of life. The primarily impotent homosexual's inherent levels of sexual frustration are compounded by the fact that he usually lives a life in which overt sexual activity surrounds or engulfs him, for in a sexual service role, the homosexual male is constantly stimulated by his pattern of physical interaction with sexually functional men.

But there may be a ray of light at the end of the tunnel. Perhaps the most depressing influence to which the primarily impotent homosexual or heterosexual man has previously been exposed has been relieved. These men have been severely traumatized psychosexually by being forced to accept the popular concept that nothing could be done to relieve them of their gross handicap of sexual inadequacy. Fortunately, this implacable burden has been effectively neutralized and to a large extent removed by the treatment programs that have been developed in this country in the last 10 years.

SECONDARY IMPOTENCE

Forty-nine homosexual men were treated for secondary impotence by the research team during the 10-year clinical control period. Fifteen of these men have been available for follow-up for five years after termination of the acute phase of treatment (see Table 13-1).

The major etiologic influences that moved these homosexual men from full function to varying levels of erective insecurity were primarily psychosocial in character. There have been 2 histories of men experiencing overt physical trauma (including one incident of a sexual attack followed by a brutal beating) that resulted in secondary impotence for the men involved. In addition, 2 men had physical disabilities that probably contributed to their acquired impotence.

Of course, homosexual secondary impotence has many of the traumatic psychosocial aspects that have been described for primary impotence. The three fears of refused treatment by authority, of treatment failure, and above all else, of peer identification of the sexually dysfunctional status are equally present in the secondarily impotent homosexual man.

However, there are additional perspectives that apply to both homosexual and heterosexual men who have previously enjoyed a pattern of successful sexual interaction. Regardless of role preference, when effective sexual function has become an integral part of any man's lifestyle, the prospect that at any time he might become sexually inadequate rarely occurs to him. Yet at a peak of successful performance, he may be experiencing or even initiating influences that well may leave him impotent in the immediate future.

Perhaps the most important additional perspective that secondary impotence carries with it is an additional fear of performance—that of impermanence of symptom resolution. This perspective has rarely been described by previously primarily impotent men.

Once the primarily impotent man has reversed his dysfunctional status, he rarely gives great credence to this level of negativism in concerns for performance. His tendency is to accept the great good fortune of the reversal of his impotence and to totally immerse himself in sexual opportunity with the partner of his choice with far less fear for the future than appreciation of the present.

Not so for the secondarily impotent man. His fears of performance not only focus on the present, he is equally pessimistic about his future (see Chapter 12). While reversal of impotence, when it occurs, is hailed with delight, he immediately tempers his unrestrained pleasure with expressions of anxiety about the future. His reasoning follows a well-established pattern. After all, he had functioned well in the past. If he can move from confident sexual facility to threatening sexual inadequacy and then be reversed and begin functioning again, what is to keep him from repeating the cycle?

So the secondarily impotent man experiences a continuing combination of fears of performance, and whether homosexual or heterosexual, he becomes a spectator at his own bedding. When interacting with any partner, he fearfully watches his own erective status, not the physical reactions of his partner. Even if a completely successful sexual episode is experienced, he immediately is concerned about his functional potential for "the next time." For the secondarily impotent man concerned with the fear of impermanency of sexual performance, a successful sexual episode gives little assurance that the next sexual opportunity will be experienced in an equally rewarding fashion.

But another perspective, this time positive in nature, is more frequently observed in secondary than in primary impotence. The secondarily impotent man, whether homosexual or heterosexual, is usually far more secure in his masculine role in society. Although devastated by sexual dysfunction when it occurs, men usually do not become secondarily impotent in their teens or early twenties. They have more opportunity to develop confidence in the potential of their male role in society and to establish themselves professionally as well as socially because their sexual dysfunctions usually are not millstones around their necks during their formative years. Judd Marmor's well-stated aphorism that "an impotent man is an impotent man" applies far more frequently to the primarily than to the secondarily impotent man.

Successful treatment of secondarily impotent homosexual men is significantly dependent upon whether the dysfunctional man and the research team can elicit full cooperation from the committed or casual partner. The impotent man's fears of performance and his concomitant spectator role in sexual interchange can be reversed far more effectively if the functional partner will interact freely and comfortably with his or her disadvantaged partner.

CASE REPORT: COUPLE 3

F was 42 years old when he and his partner of nine years petitioned the Institute for admission to the therapy program. His had been a distressed, imbalanced home. When he was 7, his seriously ill mother was institutionalized, leaving him and his 5-year-old sister; the mother died a year and a half later. No other woman assumed the maternal role. His father was a beleaguered, apparently insecure man who was unable to cope with the exigencies of the family situation. During F's teenage years there was essentially a total lack of parental control or guidance. His memory of home was of a succession of full- or part-time female help and a father who tried and failed to control his son's quickly asserted social freedom. There was no control of the educational process and no defined religious influence.

At an early age F was involved with drugs, alcohol, and petty crime. He was introduced to sexual activity by a neighbor's wife when he was 13 and thereafter was sexually promiscuous with his peers and with many older women. When F was 18, he was jailed for robbing a grocery store. He was sentenced to one to three years in jail. Within 10 days of his incarceration, he was servicing older inmates either through fellatio or as the penetratee in rectal intercourse. He masturbated regularly, but was given no opportunity to interact sexually with the inmates other than in a service role. Paroled shortly after a year in prison, he found a job working as a house painter. Within a few years he had his own contracting service and was doing well financially.

After serving his prison sentence, F had no further contact with his father or sister.

His sexual cooperation with other inmates had developed at first under the threat of physical punishment, but it continued as a source of pleasure. His sexual activity after release from prison included both indiscriminant homosexual and heterosexual opportunities, always with casual partners. During his late twenties his interest in heterosexual interchange lessened, and he began a series of brief homosexual relationships. At 32 he joined his partner in a committed relationship.

After the first year of their relationship but without his partner's knowledge, F began having occasional casual sexual experiences, usually with homosexual and occasionally with heterosexual partners. It was during one of the casual heterosexual experiences that he first failed to function sexually. He had picked up a girl in a bar and had gone to her apartment. When in bed, he found that he had no real interest in sexual activity and no erection developed. He tried to force the issue, to will an erection, but he could not respond. F panicked, resorted to sexual fakery by feigning illness, dressed, and left quickly. Blaming the girl for his functional failure, it was the last time he ever became involved in heterosexual interaction.

Although he confined his sexual involvement to interacting with his partner and with an occasional casual male partner, he worried increasingly about his erective facility. F began wondering whether his episode of erective failure was really just because he had been with a girl or whether it might recur in a homosexual setting. It was six months before he failed again, once more with a casual bar pickup, but this time it was with a man.

Thereafter F restricted his sexual activity to his ongoing relationship. Despite his self-enforced faithfulness, his fears of performance and his spectator role increased to such an extent that he had been almost completely impotent for approximately three years before treatment was initiated at the Institute.

F was extremely anxious and obviously emotionally unstable when first seen as a client. His partner was most cooperative in therapy, evidencing a sincere commitment to the relationship. The partner, while empathetic with F's dysfunctional sexual status, was also concerned with F's increasingly frequent episodes of acute depression. F was so concerned with his own dysfunctional status that his equally strong commitment to his partner was not fully ascertained during the first week of treatment.

F progressed rapidly in therapy. His fears of performance diminished significantly, and his spectator role was soon neutralized. The couple's acute phase of treatment was terminated in eight days. They have been followed for four years without reported recurrence of F's erective dysfunction with the single exception of an episode of erective failure after an evening of drinking. F was not perturbed by this episode. He simply turned to the therapeutic suggestions that had been made to neutralize his fears of performance, and with his partner's cooperation he continued to function sexually with confidence.

F's recurrent episodes of depression have not been entirely dispelled. Their frequency of recurrence has been markedly diminished, however, and even when depressed, he continues to function effectively sexually. Medication has not been prescribed for the occasional depressed states, since they are being handled well.

This is a case report of a man who was originally fully heterosexual. He became a facultative homosexual during a year in prison and continued as interchangeably homosexual and heterosexual after his release. As time passed, his homosexual orientation assumed dominance. The fears of sexual inadequacy that ultimately severely handicapped him in homosexual interchange originated in a failure to function effectively during a casual heterosexual opportunity. Once initiated by heterosexual failure, his fears of performance and spectator role spread slowly into what had become a full commitment to homosexuality. F's emotional instability probably made him an easy target for debilitating fears of performance.

The uncommitted homosexual male exists in a threatening psychosexual position. He is a man living a life of sexual risk. Moving from one casual partner to the next, he continually places himself in the situation of having to function on demand. The gay bar, public-toilet type of sexual partner solicitation places a man in the position of having to respond to immediate sexual demand.

The subjectively appreciated sexual stimuli necessary to meet this severe functional demand comes from the "grass is greener" concept of a constant stream of new faces and bodies. And for varying lengths of time a multiplicity of partners is often sufficient sexual tonic for most men to respond to the challenge of instant sex.

Many homosexual men do live through a pleasant lifetime of a seemingly unending stream of casual sexual partners and continue to function well sexually. For many others, however, satiation occurs; and with it comes the compelling psychosexual need to force interest, to make erections happen, to evidence objectively an intensity of sexual involvement that simply is not there subjectively. Since men simply cannot force erections, these are times when the erective process is slowed, anxiety creeps in, full penile engorgement falters, performance fears swell, and the erective process is progressively impaired. The following is a report of such a case.

CASE REPORT: COUPLE 4

G was 29 years old when seen in therapy. His partner, a 32-year-old casual acquaintance from the same homosexual community, had accompanied G in treatment both as a favor and in the expectation of enjoying an educational opportunity.

G was an only child; his father had been killed in an accident when the boy was 2 years old. His mother apparently had enough money from her family to support herself and her son. She never remarried.

G's educational experience was a positive one in that he had full support from his mother, who encouraged academic achievement. There were good grades and a number of extracurricular interests. The family religious background was Catholic, but there was little sustained interest in religion.

Childhood and adolescence were essentially uneventful. G did not describe a turbulent household, although he came to expect that an occasional male visitor would spend the night with his mother. Some men even stayed for a few weeks.

After the "playing doctor" stage, G's first overt sexual experience was with a girl in the neighborhood. She was three years older than the 15-year-old boy. She freely joined him in sexual play, during which he learned that if his penis was manipulated effectively, he would ejaculate. Within a few weeks they were having intercourse regularly.

At sixteen G was an apparently well-adjusted young man with many male and female friends. His social life revolved around his high-school peers rather than focusing on family. When he became 16 and obtained his driver's license, G no longer was subject to maternal authority.

G was a counselor in a summer camp when he experienced his first homosexual approach. It was made by a fellow counselor who was the high-school athletic hero. After a few beers the boys joined in an experience of mutual masturbation that led two nights later to participation in an episode of partner manipulation. Although it was G's first homosexual experience, he found himself strongly stimulated both by the physical activity and by the sense of warmth and strength emanating from his partner. He had not had these feelings with his neighborhood girlfriend.

His heterosexual and homosexual partnerships continued actively for another year, and each in turn led to other sexual partners.

G completed two years of college, became interested in the theater, and began living and training in the theatrical community. Sexual opportunities apparently were limitless, but G voluntarily confined himself to homosexual experiences.

There was no background of strong maternal dominance, of social or sexual trauma, of religious orthodoxy, or even of rejection of heterosexuality. G simply found that he preferred the homosexual experience.

He frequented gay bars and sought sexual opportunities with other young men involved in the theatrical world. There was an occasional heterosexual episode, but these occurred with progressively less frequency. Finally, at 27 G openly declared himself homosexual. Moving freely between casual partners, he neither took the opportunity nor expressed the desire to live in a committed relationship.

Early in his twenty-eighth year, G noticed that he seemed to be forcing sexual involvement. His constant array of casual partners became increasingly unappealing, and he voluntarily slowed the frequency of new partners from at least twice a week to perhaps once every two weeks. His erections were progressively slower to develop, did not seem to be quite full, and occasionally were lost during sexual activity.

G became increasingly concerned about his functional facility. Although rarely feeling interested, he increased his sexual cruising. Within a short period of time, there was one sexual episode when G completely failed to achieve an erection. Following this traumatic experience, his anxiety levels increased severely, and he stopped all homosexual activity.

Feeling that possibly he would function better in a heterosexual milieu, G invited a girl he knew casually to spend a weekend. Again there was total lack of erective response as he struggled to force himself into an active sexual role.

After this experience, G was fearful of failure in both homosexual and heterosexual opportunities. Sexual fakery came into play, and he began "concentrating on his career," leaving sexual opportunities to others. He became depressed and sought medical assistance. Medication was given for the depressed state, but there was no attempt to reverse his impotence. He was told that as his mood elevated, his sexual function would probably improve. His mood did respond to the medication; his sexual function didn't.

G contacted the Institute for treatment. He was told that treatment was available but that he would have to provide a partner of choice to accompany him in therapy. G tentatively selected and approached a man who agreed to become his partner in therapy at a time that was mutually satisfactory. This occurred four months later. Meanwhile both men tried to interact sexually a number of times without success on G's part.

In therapy, G's fear of performance and his spectator role were reasonably neutralized, his homosexual orientation confirmed, and his emotional security reinforced. G's partner was fully cooperative through the first week of therapy, but he became restless and progressively less involved the second week. The couple was discharged on the tenth day of treatment.

At discharge G was specifically alerted to the potential complication of continuing to live in his casual sexual lifestyle. It was suggested that he continue in regular sexual activity with his casual partner until he could establish a more permanent relationship. The partner promised full cooperation. The cooperation lasted for about three weeks, when after an argument, the men terminated their relationship.

G contacted the staff and asked for advice. Again, it was suggested that he seek a continuing relationship. The inevitability of increased performance pressures engendered by casual sexual episodes was discussed.

During the acute treatment phase, G had described the possibility of establishing a committed relationship with a specific man of his acquaintance, and after Institute consultation he moved quickly to establish such communication. He was successful in his approach. On the strength of a growing emotional bond with his new partner, G interacted sexually with confidence and effectiveness both before and after the couple began living together.

But within four months after establishing the relationship, G began cruising again and his erective insecurity returned. G found he could function in his relationship but not in sexual opportunities with a casual partner. In time, his committed relationship became jeopardized because he could not or would not discontinue his cruising propensities and his partner did not approve of such license. With repeated failure to function effectively under the cruising demand for immediate sexual performance, G's erective security was slowly destroyed. Five years after participating in the treatment program in St. Louis, G reported that he could function occasionally in a casual sexual opportunity, but that he almost always assumed a service role. He has never attempted to establish another continuing homosexual relationship, nor has he made any attempt to reestablish heterosexual interaction.

This is a case of a man functioning successfully both homosexually and heterosexually as a teenager and finally voluntarily choosing a homosexual orientation. There were no etiologic factors that could be specifically identified as exerting major influences on his choice of lifestyle. His erective insecurity originally may have developed from sexual satiation, and while it was reversed during the acute phase of therapy, he could not maintain his erective security. Probably he could have continued functioning effectively on an indefinite basis had he chosen to support his sexual partnership, but despite sure knowledge that he was gambling with his future as a sexually effective individual, he could not give up his cruising lifestyle with its accompanying severe demands for sexual performance.

Certainly G is a treatment failure. Either the research team was deficient in its communication of the necessity for, or G was deficient in motivation to pursue, a lifestyle that was centered around a committed relationship. For in such a relatively pressureless environment, he would have had his best chance of effective sexual function.

SITUATIONAL IMPOTENCE

Three homosexual men were treated for situational impotence together with their partners. Two of the partners were casual, and 1 was committed. One of the situationally impotent men was also sexually aversive.

Of the three categories of impotence, the situationally dysfunctional man is by far the easiest to treat effectively. As might be expected, the situationally impotent man infrequently seeks professional support. When histories were taken, the 3 men provided strong testimony to support their reluctance to seek treatment. Each man admitted that a situationally impotent homosexual man could easily practice successful sexual fakery (see Chapter 12) and lead a full and reasonably satisfying sex life. In each of the 3 cases, some specific event occurred or an additional sexual distress developed before the sexually handicapped man felt sufficiently pressured to seek treatment.

CASE REPORT: COUPLE 5

He was a 36-year-old Kinsey 5 and his partner a 32-year-old, sexually functional Kinsey 6 when the couple applied to the Institute for treatment of H's combined complaints of situational impotence and sexual aversion. The two men had been living in a committed relationship for approximately four years. A problem that the partners mutually agreed severely handicapped their freedom of sexual expression forced them to treatment. The Institute was the fourth potential source of support contacted by the couple. They had been refused treatment and given no referral by three other professional sources.

H had been committed to a homosexual orientation from his teenage years. He was the youngest of three children in a middle-class family with a fundamentalist Protestant background. He did not remember his father and mother ever evidencing any degree of emotional involvement with each other, but he was fully aware that his parents were completely committed to a life that revolved about their church. He expressed no particular emotional attachment for either parent or their lifestyle, but he did value highly their church affiliation. He also described no particular depth of relationship between himself and his siblings, a brother and sister four and two years older. The siblings had been severely restricted socially as adolescents, since the entire family closely followed church dogma.

At approximately 12 years of age H began masturbating. When he was 13 he joined in a number of mutual masturbational opportunities, sometimes with two and at times with as many as five other boys his own age. Although H did well in school, played on the high-school basketball team, and was quite active in school dramatics, he was rarely involved in social activities. He attributed his antisocial stance both to parental control and to an inherent lack of interest on his part. He far preferred male company. H could not recall any situation that might have created a sense of anxiety with or rejection of female companionship. His stated position was that he had never rejected girls; he simply had no interest in them.

H's first overt homosexual interaction occurred during his senior year in high school. He was with a friend overnight who had been a participant at a number of mutual masturbational episodes in their earlier years. This particular night the boys followed the established pattern of mutual masturbation, but soon each boy was freely manipulating the partner rather than confining himself to self-manipulation. Each boy ejaculated with ease. Apparently they enjoyed the experience, for they continued with episodes of partner manipulation for the rest of the academic year.

H spent two and one-half years in college. There he was moderately active homosexually, confining his sexual activity to the established patterns of mutual masturbation or partner manipulation. He refused cooperation with any other manner of stimulative activity. He left college to work at a steady job that made it necessary for him to move away from home. The only strong connection that he maintained with his previous lifestyle came through his church affiliation. During college and as he moved into an independent, adult existence, his religious commitment became more intense. His tenuous family relationship soon diminished to occasional visits at home during Christmas holidays.

H had a number of social opportunities to interact with women while in college, all but one of which he rejected. He dated one girl three times. The third evening they went to her room, played together sexually, and had intercourse. He left as quickly as possible after he had ejaculated. He experienced no sense of pleasure in this episode, nor did he feel any sense of rejection. The episode was essentially meaningless to him, and he never dated the girl again. He reported this episode as his only overt heterosexual encounter, but he stated that he was glad he had had intercourse for the experience gained. There seemed to him to be no plausible reason for repeating the experience.

His sexual aversion began at 24, when he spent a week in another city on business. He was lonely and sexually aroused, so he began cruising local bars—something he had never done before. One evening he had more to drink than usual and joined a group of men who were leaving the particular bar to go to an apartment for a private party. H described his first experience with fellatio as having a sense of being forced by group pressure to accept a penis, although he denied that there was any implied or real threat of physical retribution. As soon as he accepted the penis orally, he became severely nauseated and vomited. His casual partner was repulsed by the episode, and his host made him leave the apartment.

After this experience, H found himself increasingly anxious about further casual homosexual activity for fear that fellatio would be required. He did try this sexual technique four other times during the next year, always with the immediate response of nausea and, on two occasions, vomiting. Not only was he nauseated when attempting fellatio himself, but he rapidly lost whatever degree of erection he had when approached orally by other men. H never ejaculated in response to fellatio.

The handicap of a sexually objectionable behavioral pattern markedly reduced his number of homosexual partners, since fellatio was a consistently employed interaction technique. He persuaded a number of men to limit sexual activity to partner manipulation, but when oral stimulation or rectal penetration was suggested or even demanded, he always refused. In time, the mere thought of possible oral or rectal penetration was enough to create an anxiety reaction.

H moved from casual to established homosexual relationships to protect himself from demands for fellatio and rectal intercourse. Unlike the other two men who were treated for situational impotence by the research team, his was not a sufficiently dominant personality to successfully impose his sexual restrictions on most casual partners and still maintain their sexual interest. He occasionally attempted to practice sexual fakery, but he was not particularly successful. His obvious levels of anxiety when fellatio was requested apparently alerted his sexual partners. It is one thing to deny interest in a specific sexual technique and request an alternative approach; it is quite another to become overtly anxious or even nauseated when the particular sexual technique is suggested.

Over the years H's increasing anxiety with fellatio slowly encompassed his ability to respond to partner manipulation as well. Initially he found it more difficult to respond to a partner's manipulation of his penis. Then he began to be nauseated when a partner ejaculated in response to his manipulative efforts. In due course, the sight of any seminal fluid other than his own created anxiety responses and occasional nausea.

At 32, H joined a 28-year-old man in what was to become a comfortable, committed relationship. The men had a great deal in common. Neither was a dominant personality. They had similar tastes in music and literature, and each was at approximately the same income level. But most important to both was the fact that they had the same church affiliation. In fact, they initially met during a church-sponsored social activity. H's partner had a level of sexual need that was expressed approximately once every ten days or two weeks. This pleased H tremendously, for by the time these two men became sexual partners, all H could accept in the way of sexual interaction were episodes of mutual masturbation, and he no longer would allow himself to observe his partner's ejaculatory experience. Perhaps once a week H masturbated in private.

For two years this pattern of sexual interchange proved acceptable to both men. Then the partner began expressing increasing need for the warmth of personal contact in sexual interchange. When H tried but could not respond to these requests for partner manipulation or fellatio without becoming extremely anxious, the partner sought occasional sexual opportunities outside the relationship. This outside activity was a source of great concern for H; he agreed to seek professional help initially for his sexual aversion and subsequently for his situational impotence.

As an initial step in treatment, desensitization procedures were instituted that were designed to create a sense of comfort with seminal fluid. Once this was accomplished, the next step was to neutralize the crippling levels of anxiety that H associated with any suggestion of fellatio. When the excessive levels of anxiety were also neutralized, fellatio was accomplished with a rapidly decreasing incidence of nausea. Finally H's fears of erective failure when being fellated by his partner were also reasonably neutralized by following the techniques designed for treatment of fears of performance (see Chapter 12).

H responded to treatment and was functioning well in response to partner manipulation and to fellatio when the acute phase of treatment was terminated.

Two major sources of support were vital to H's progress in treatment. First, his committed partner was most cooperative throughout the demanding acute phase of the treatment program. Second, both men found mutual strength in their active religious commitments. They felt that their shared religious interests added the important dimensions of stability and security to their troubled relationship.

H and his partner were followed for five years after termination of the acute phase of treatment. Occasionally H experienced a return of his anxiety state during sexual interaction and had to terminate a particular episode. But as time passed and with his partner's full understanding and continued support, the anxious moments occurred less and less frequently. The relationship between H and his partner continued to be stable and productive during the entire follow-up period.

This is a case of a man in his midthirties who was prejudicing a committed homosexual relationship of four years' duration by a progressive aversion to sexual interaction. There was no history that could even be used retrospectively to establish an etiologic background for his homosexual orientation. He simply never remembered having the slightest interest in girls sexually or socially. The only evidence of family influence was an active orthodox religious orientation in which he found continuing support. H's positive responses to desensitizing treatment procedures were in large part due to his partner's full support in therapy.

DISCUSSION

The incidence of male sexual dysfunction in the homosexual community is unknown. For a variety of legitimate reasons described earlier in Chapter 12, homosexual men have been loathe to seek clinical treatment for impotence or sexual aversion. Yet adequate treatment for their sexual dysfunctions is available with a treatment failure rate that should not be as high as that previously reported for treatment of heterosexually oriented, sexually dysfunctional men in *Human Sexual Inadequacy* (1970).

The homosexual male always has certain advantages in being able to interact with a same-sex partner. There is a sense of identification and a level of subjective appreciation of fears of performance that perforce are lacking when a sexually dysfunctional man is interacting with an opposite-sex partner. In addition, there is not the inherent performance demand for an erection of sufficient quality to accomplish vaginal penetration that the culture always places on the sexually active heterosexual male. Presuming that the male partners are living in committed relationships, there usually is significantly less performance pressure placed upon the homosexual than there is on the heterosexual male in our culture.

A change in attitude is increasingly evident in the health-care profession. Psychotherapeutic support has recently become available to sexually dysfunctional homosexual men and women in a few clinics. Homosexuals have every reason to request, and to expect, this level of support from the health-care community.

The Institute's failure statistics in treatment programs for homosexual male dysfunctions are reported in Chapter 17.

I4

FEMALE HOMOSEXUAL
DYSFUNCTION

Twenty-five lesbian couples were treated for sexual dysfunction during the Institute's 10-year clinical program. In 23 of these couples only 1 of the partners complained of sexual dysfunction. There were 7 primarily anorgasmic, 13 situationally anorgasmic, and 3 randomly anorgasmic women. There also were 2 couples in which both partners were anorgasmic. The first couple was formed by a combination of a primarily anorgasmic lesbian with a partner who was situationally anorgasmic. The second couple was composed of a situationally anorgasmic lesbian with a partner who was randomly anorgasmic. Thus, a total of 27 homosexual women were treated for anorgasmia by the research team. Six of 27 anorgasmic women also complained of and were treated for sexual aversion (see Table 12-2, Chapter 12).

In the 23 lesbian couples with only one sexually dysfunctional partner, there were 16 committed and 7 casual partners, all of whom were sexually functional. The 2 couples that reported each partner as anorgasmic and requested treatment for both partners were living in firmly committed relationships (see Table 12-2, Chapter 12).

To assume that this chapter reports a treatment approach to anorgasmia would be correct. To assume that it is just another report would be in error. There has been no prior report of treatment of a series of anorgasmic homosexual women in a clinical program of 10 years' duration. Nor has there even been a previous report of five-year follow-up of anorgasmic lesbian clients after the acute phase of treatment has been terminated (see Table 14-1).

The 25 lesbian couples seen over a 10-year period hardly represent a thriving practice. Yet the fact remains that this small sample of what must be an incredibly frustrated segment of society has found the courage to seek professional support. If this totally un-coordinated social movement continues, gathering strength in stead-ily growing numbers and confidence in the health-care professionals' acceptance of its need, this trend will indeed represent a major breakthrough in the health-care field. Homosexual women's frus-trations have come not only from contending with the exigencies of their sexual inadequacies, but also from a widespread concept within the homosexual community that there was nowhere sexually dysfunctional men and women could go or no one they could see to seek relief from their sexual distresses.

The incidence of anorgasmia in the lesbian population in this country is a complete mystery, but the numbers are likely to be of significance. Parenthetically, despite a number of publications on the subject, there also is no secure knowledge of the actual inci-dence of anorgasmia among heterosexual women. We do know, however, that heterosexual anorgasmia is sufficiently widespread to involve millions of women.

Despite lack of research support, it is probably correct to presume that the incidence of anorgasmic states is lower in the homosexual than in the heterosexual female community. If such a discrepancy in the incidence of anorgasmic states exists, and there is in fact less anorgasmia in the homosexual than the heterosexual female populations, it probably is due to a combination of two factors. First, the culture places a markedly increased performance demand on the heterosexual woman to respond at orgasmic levels during in-tercourse, which, as Chapter 6 has shown, is more difficult to respond to than manipulative types of stimulation. Second, the Institute has established divergent definitions of heterosexual and homosex-ual anorgasmia (see p. 312). If a divergence in the incidence of anorgasmia does exist between the two female sexual preferences, the research team does *not* believe that it represents a variation in woman's inherent physiologic capacity to respond to effective sexual stimuli.

DEFINITIONS

The primarily anorgasmic lesbian has been defined by the Institute staff as a woman who has never been orgasmic in response to the techniques of masturbation, partner manipulation, or cunnilingus. The situationally anorgasmic lesbian has been identified as a woman who has responded at orgasmic levels to one or two of these three stimulative techniques, but never to all three. The definition of a randomly anorgasmic lesbian reflects a woman who has been orgasmic at least once in response to each of the three stimulative approaches, but has infrequently reached orgasmic levels of sexual excitation while reacting to any form of sexual stimulation.

It may be recalled that the Institute defines dysfunctional status differently for homosexual and heterosexual men and women because of their established variations in sexual activity. When viewed from this perspective, there should be a major difference in frequency of anorgasmic states between homosexual and heterosexual women. For example, if a heterosexual woman is orgasmic in response to masturbation, partner manipulation, and cunnilingus, she would still be labeled as situationally anorgasmic if she has no history of responding at orgasmic levels during intercourse. On the other hand, the homosexual woman who has a history of responding orgasmically to masturbation, partner manipulation, and cunnilingus would be identified as a fully functional woman. If these definitions are accepted, it will come as no surprise that there is a higher incidence of anorgasmia among women in the heterosexual than in the homosexual community.

CLINICAL POPULATION

During the first year of clinical study, only 2 situationally anorgasmic lesbians were seen in therapy with their partners, 1 of whom was in the committed and the other in the casual category. The second year, a primarily anorgasmic lesbian was treated with her committed partner. This was the only dysfunctional female homosexual couple the research team treated in the entire year. Actually, for the next eight years the clinical facilities were certainly not overrun with applications for treatment. There were only 2 to 4 dysfunctional lesbian couples treated each year (Table 14-1).

TABLE 14-1

Homosexual Female Anorgasmia (N = 27):
Distribution by Year During the 10-Year Clinical Control Period

Type of Anorgasmia	Year Treated										Total
	One	Two	Three	Four	Five	Six	Seven	Eight	Nine	Ten	
Primary	0	1	1	2	0	2	1	0	0	1	8
Situational	2	0	3	1	2	1	2	2	2	0	15
Random	0	0	0	1	0	0	1	1	0	1	4
Total	2	1	4	4	2	3	4	3	2	2	27

1968–1977

Lesbian couples applied for treatment from various metropolitan areas and from academic centers throughout the United States and Canada. Only 1 couple lived in the St. Louis area. Just as was previously reported by the homosexual males who applied for treatment of sexual dysfunctions (see Chapter 13), the lesbian couples' knowledge of the Institute's treatment programs came by word of mouth within the homosexual community.

Every couple entering therapy was self-referred. Of the 27 anorgasmic lesbians treated, 14 had sought and 11 had been refused treatment by other health-care facilities. Of these 11 women, 8 had been refused treatment by more than one health-care source. Each of the 3 sexually dysfunctional lesbians who had previously entered therapy for an anorgasmic state had been treated without a partner, and each of these women had terminated her therapy program as unsatisfactory. None of the women had been referred to another source of treatment by any consulted health-care authority (see Table 12-6, Chapter 12).

These statistics have been repeated here to emphasize the fact that in the past sexually dysfunctional lesbian women have had to contend with the same general fears of social rejection that have haunted homosexual men when considering treatment for their sexual inadequacies. Sexually dysfunctional lesbians fear—and with good reason—that they will not be accepted in therapy when they finally gather their courage and apply for psychotherapeutic support. They also tend to be skeptical of the percentage chance of any treatment program terminating successfully, regardless of the clinical techniques employed. Although they evidence far less anxiety about the problem than do homosexual men, lesbians are traditionally fearful that their homosexual status will be revealed to the general public by the consulted health-care authority or by members of his or her paraprofessional staff.

There also are the various fears for sexual performance that must be dealt with, whether these are culturally or physiologically engendered. Judging only by the sample of both homosexual and heterosexual women who have applied for treatment at the Institute during the last 10 years, the fears of the dysfunctional woman in our culture for her ability to react in a sexually effective manner increase every year. There is, of course, the classic example of the pervasive influence of the printed word upon culturally induced sexual performance fears. Until the hundreds of articles released for public consumption in the last decade emphatically pointed out that every woman has the birthright of effective sexual expression, women's fears of failure to function effectively in sexual interchange were not nearly as incapacitating as they are today. Times certainly have changed—as have attitudes—and not entirely for the better.

This statement must not be construed as a denial of every woman's birthright to be an effectively functional sexual being. Far from it. The research team is fully committed to the contention that every woman should have the privilege of effective sexual expression. Nor is there a problem with the accompanying contention that sexual freedom should be shared equally by the sexes. The problem arises from the implication that is inevitably drawn by the general public once these contentions have been widely accepted. Loosely interpreted, the culture now implies that an anorgasmic woman is less than a woman.

Where have we heard these words before? They remarkably resemble the psychologically devastating cultural accusation that an impotent man is really not a man. So every woman is now hearing in ever-increasing decibels the equally devastating cultural accusation that if she is sexually dysfunctional, she really is not a woman. When this measure of female denigration happens to be combined with the cultural imposition of unworthiness that is frequently associated with a barren state, the pressures may become overwhelming. While it may take just such a preposterous level of public ridicule to bring the anorgasmic lesbian to treatment, it is most unfortunate that she must now bring with her into treatment the additional burden of a culturally imposed fear, disseminated by the popular press, that she is far less a woman than her orgasmically facile sister. Due to current cultural influence, "An impotent man is an impotent man" can be readily paraphrased to suggest that a sexually dysfunctional woman is indeed a dysfunctional woman.

Not only does the anorgasmic woman have to face the culturally derived implication that she is really not a woman in the true sense of the word (whatever that is), but she also must face another cultural implication that is inherent in anorgasmia. It is the fearful question of, "Will I be able to fully satisfy my partner if I don't function effectively?" These fears are as consistently present in dysfunctional homosexual women as they are in dysfunctional heterosexual women. This fear of losing the committed partner, if the partner has been consistently frustrated by inability to provide sexual satisfaction for the dysfunctional individual, was verbalized by a higher percentage of anorgasmic lesbians than impotent male homosexuals, although partner concern certainly was expressed by both sexes.

So freedom of sexual expression, for years the social perquisite of the male in our culture, is now being shared by the female. Unfortunately, with freedom of sexual expression comes the immediate corollary of yet another sexually oriented fear, in this instance the most devastating of all sexual fears, the fear for one's own physiologic capacity to function effectively.

A detailed consideration of male or female fears for sexual performance and the concomitant spectator roles has been presented in Chapter 12. Although the impotent male was used as the primary example, the discussion is equally applicable to the anorgasmic lesbian and therefore will not be repeated.

Both of the anorgasmic homosexual couples who entered therapy with each partner dysfunctional will be considered in detail. When combined, the two couples provide insights into the sexual dysfunctions of primary, situational, and random anorgasmia.

Before presenting case reports, a comparison should be drawn between the sexually dysfunctional homosexual male and female populations. When a dysfunctional lesbian entered therapy, there was a major difference between her approach to treatment and that of the dysfunctional homosexual male. Generally, the anorgasmic lesbian and her partner were significantly more cooperative during the therapy program than were the impotent homosexual males and their partners. The lesbian couples not only tended to follow therapeutic suggestions more conscientiously, but they communicated far more openly and probably more honestly with the therapists.

CASE REPORT: COUPLE 6

J was a 29-year-old Kinsey 6 when she applied to the Institute for treatment of primary anorgasmia. Her committed partner K requested treatment for situational anorgasmia that was further complicated by the existence of sexual anxiety. K was 31 years old, a Kinsey 4, and had a daughter 7 years old. When the women were seen in therapy, their relationship was of almost three years' standing.

J described her childhood as an uneventful but happy time. She had one sibling, a sister two years older. There were no recalled troubles in school. She had a number of friends, both boys and girls. There was no preference for one parent over the other, nor did she feel herself to be the preferred or rejected sibling.

J came from a financially secure background. In retrospect she judged her parents as well-adjusted, well-educated people who appeared to be living comfortably together, although she did not think they were unreservedly committed to each other. She was aware that her father had enjoyed an occasional relationship outside the marriage, and for a period of time when she was about 16 had suspected that her mother was similarly involved. Her background was of Jewish orientation, but the family held formalized religious commitment to a minimum. J's formal education included graduation from one of the well-known women's colleges. She had moved into a banking career after college and was a junior executive at a large bank in an eastern city when seen in therapy. By this time both parents were dead and she was financially independent.

J could not recall any sexual orientation other than homosexual. She had first been taught how to masturbate at age 10 by her sister, and although she described a pleasurable response, she knew nothing of orgasm. After she had started to menstruate at 12, her sister began to exchange episodes of partner manipulation with her. J soon found that it was far more pleasurable to stimulate her sister than to be stimulated by her. She was pleased when her sister experienced orgasm (J didn't know what it was at the time) and approached her sister frequently just to watch what happened. She felt no sense of loss when "it" didn't happen to her.

When her sister began interacting socially with boys, opportunities for sexual play diminished rapidly and soon stopped completely. J then turned to her peers. She described creating opportunities to "play" by her own aggressive approaches. During her high-school years she had two friends, with each of whom she interacted sexually at least once a week. Neither of the friends was attractive physically nor was dating. Both girls apparently became multiorgasmic with J's help. Sexual activity was restricted to partner manipulation. Again J's sexual pleasure came from manipulating her friends; she simply didn't feel very aroused sexually when they stimulated her.

J was an attractive, tall girl with a good figure. She was moderately active in sports, playing competent games of tennis and golf. But, much to her mother's distress, she simply had no interest in social interchange with boys. Throughout high school the total of her overt sexual experience with boys consisted of three episodes of breast play and one experience with penile manipulation. The boy ejaculated, soaking the dress she was wearing, and for five years thereafter there was no further dating.

J had her first and last attempt at intercourse during her senior year in college. She went out on several occasions with an older divorced man who was one of her professors. More from curiosity than any other reason, she agreed to spend a night with him. The entire sexual episode was unappealing from the outset, for she was taken to a dingy motel room and as the night passed she found the experience less and less attractive. On each of three occasions the man ejaculated before he could establish penetration. Again she felt a sense of contamination from the seminal fluid. She could not respond to the man's manipulative attempts and retrospectively rejected the episode as not only of little value, but as a sexual experience in which she had little further interest. Thereafter, her relations with men were held entirely to social interchange.

During college J had three female friends (one a roommate for a year) with whom she interacted sexually. Her total sexual interest was in playing with and satisfying her partners. She became quite facile with manipulative techniques and cunnilingus. Although she allowed her sexual partners full freedom to approach and stimulate her as they wished, she was rarely highly aroused sexually and never orgasmic. She tried to masturbate frequently but continued to be unsuccessful. J became completely convinced that she was incapable of orgasmic experience and that her sexual gratification would come only from exciting and then releasing her sexual partners, during which she could vicariously enjoy their orgasmic experiences. Certainly her highest levels of sexual excitation coincided with observing her partners in orgasm.

J's most frequently employed fantasy patterns involved the mental imagery of wildly excited women who were begging her for sexual release. She also fantasized about seducing married women, a number of whom she personified and each of whom protested vigorously that they didn't want homosexual experience but were powerless to resist her approaches.

At no time did J adopt masculine mannerisms or assume an overtly dominant role with her sexual partners. She encouraged her partners to take as much sexual freedom with her body as she took with theirs. She simply considered herself as a woman who had the permanent sexual handicap of inability to achieve orgasmic levels of sexual response and who was seeking whatever level of pleasure she could achieve in homosexual interaction.

J met K as a member of a lesbian social group. The two women apparently enjoyed a strong mutual attraction, for J moved into K's apartment within three months after they first met.

K's history was more involved. She was the only child in a family of restricted financial means. She remembers that she was very close to her mother and somewhat frightened of her father. Beyond this there are no recalled instances of severe childhood distress. Her mother and father divorced when she was 13 years old. Her mother had a Catholic religious orientation; her father had a Protestant commitment. After the divorce she lived for two years with her mother, who died when she was 15. Her life from then until she finished high school was complicated by brief visits with relatives and/or family friends and longer visits with her father, who lived in the area and had remarried. She despised her stepmother, who she felt had completely rejected her.

As she grew up, K had many friends. She apparently was an attractive teenager, dated regularly, and enjoyed her interaction with and attraction for boys. She began menstruating at 13, first masturbated to orgasm at 14, and started active sex play with boys at 15. After her mother died, K lived with no social control, dated whom and when she pleased, and stayed out as late as she pleased. There were many episodes of genital manipulation, during which her partners frequently ejaculated and she was highly stimulated sexually but not orgasmic. She would usually masturbate at home after such experiences to relieve her sexual tensions.

K was a 16-year-old high-school sophomore when she had her first coital experience in the back seat of a friend's car. There followed many such episodes with many different boys. She was always sexually excited but was never orgasmic. She discovered that her stepmother used a contraceptive foam and began using the same product regularly. Apparently K used sex primarily as a means of identifying with someone, in these instances with her male peers. With her mother dead, her father successfully isolated by her stepmother, and the few relatives or family friends apparently indifferent to her unrestrained promiscuity, she needed some feeling of belonging and she paid the price willingly. During her sophomore and junior years in high school she was constantly in demand as the boys passed her around. At that time, she apparently was quite willing to be passed around, since she rarely raised an objection and sex was a part of almost every date.

During the summer before her senior year at high school, she went out for the evening with a boy she had never met before, and they were soon joined by four other boys who also were strangers to her. K spent the night in a summer cottage with the five boys. At first she was afraid when the boys insisted that she join them in group sexual activity and when they did not respond to her tearful request to go home. Then she was embarrassed in the bedroom, both by her forced nudity and by the requirement that she perform sexually before an audience. But after offering what she stated retrospectively was really only token resistance, she apparently spent the rest of the night as a cooperative sexual partner. After participating in repeated coital episodes, she was introduced to fellatio by the group. When the group changed its sexual approach from intercourse to fellatio, she was overwhelmed with the sense of being used. This was a feeling that she had never experienced during her coital episodes with many different boys in the past two years or, for that matter, even when intercourse had been required by the group members earlier in the night. Hearing what the boys had to say as they watched her fellating their friends had an even greater effect on her sense of personal debasement. Yet, despite the trauma of the verbal denigration and the exhaustion of long-continued physical activity, she was very excited sexually when the boys took her home. The episodes of fellatio had been more arousing than intercourse had ever been. She remembered masturbating several times the next day to relieve her tensions, but her sexual excitation always seemed to return.

Although she thought of little else for weeks, she had no desire to seek retribution for the group-sex episode. Instead, K completely changed her lifestyle after the experience. Still only 17, she was mature enough to realize that once word spread of her group sex experience, and spread it would, what little reputation she might have had left would be destroyed in her male and female peer groups. She also was fearful that she might be pregnant, for no contraceptive had been used. There was an additional six weeks of anxiety before she menstruated. Many boys called her for dates. K refused them all. She transferred to another school in the city, lived with her father, tolerated his wife, and finished high school.

K began living on her own at 19. She went to secretarial school and then moved to another city and got a job in a typist pool for an insurance company. Although she was quite attractive, she refused almost all social opportunities with men. She confined her social activities to interacting with the women she met at work.

K's first homosexual experience was with a woman in her forties who worked for the same company. After several lunches together and one dinner during which K told the woman of many of her past experiences with men, K was invited to spend a weekend with the woman. When she accepted the invitation, she thought she might be approached sexually and was resolved to respond to such an opportunity if it developed. It did. K, who had felt sexually frustrated for over a year, reacted to the woman's manipulative approach with the first orgasmic episode she had ever experienced other than with masturbation.

For the next two months she was with the woman whenever they could meet. Their sex play did not move beyond the level of partner manipulation, to which both women were fully responsive. One night the woman made a cunnilingal approach, and K became quite anxious, somewhat nauseated, and could not cooperate. She vividly recalled the sense of being used during the night when she had fellated boy after boy. The relationship terminated after another month because K consistently refused cunnilingus, but she continued to circulate socially within the homosexual community to which she had been introduced by the woman.

When K was 23, she had intercourse with one of the married executives of the company in a car on the way home from the company Christmas party. It was the first heterosexual activity she had experienced since the night of group sex. She became pregnant. When the pregnancy was confirmed she confronted the man, who agreed to support her through the pregnancy.

She left the company and went to a different part of the country, got a similar type of job, and had the baby—a girl—after an uneventful pregnancy and delivery.

K never had another sexual experience with a man. Her social and sexual activities were completely devoted to lesbian opportunities, which she quickly developed in her new geographic location. She masturbated regularly, manipulated her partners, was as frequently manipulated to orgasm by them, but continued to refuse cunnilingus.

As time passed, she dwelt more frequently in her fantasies on the pseudorape scene of her group-sex experience. As the episodes of fellatio were relived in detail, she usually became somewhat anxious but also found herself so highly excited sexually that she began fantasizing the scene regularly when she masturbated.

But her feelings of anxiety associated with thoughts of oral sex increased and in time were transferred from her heterosexual past and applied to her current homosexual opportunities. She could meet, enjoy, and in time initiate or cooperate in sexual play with a casual partner, but after one or two sexual experiences with a new partner she became anxious and fearful that cunnilingus would be requested or initiated. Over a period of time, her anxieties increased to such a level that she began refusing all physical approaches other than mutual masturbation, an approach that few of her older lesbian acquaintances would accept as a satisfactory pattern of sexual interaction. Although her social life was almost entirely confined to lesbian groups that she helped organize or run and within which she found vital psychosocial support, there was little sexual interaction with the individual group members.

J and K met at such a lesbian social gathering. The women were mutually attracted and immediately began spending a great deal of time together. In three weeks they had told each other of their backgrounds, of their sexual histories, and of their sexual dysfunctions and anxieties. Since J thoroughly enjoyed K's daughter and there seemed no other potential hindrance, the two women agreed to live together. Neither woman had participated in such a living arrangement previously. J reacted to the new relationship by sharing her financial independence with K and her daughter.

Fully cognizant of K's negative feelings, J played a totally nondemanding sexual role, letting K set the pace. On her part, K, although quite anxious, did enjoy masturbating in J's presence even though J, try as she would, could not respond successfully in kind. Within six months' time K had achieved sufficient security in their relationship to allow J to approach her with manipulative techniques, which apparently J enjoyed thoroughly and K responded to freely, although she still had anxious moments. They had lived together for approximately three years in a stable, secure relationship before entering therapy.

The two women entered treatment because they were firmly convinced that they wanted to spend the rest of their lives together. They expressed the hope that J would become fully responsive sexually and that K would lose her anxiety about cunnilingus and become responsive to this sexual approach.

Therapy was initially directed toward K's sexual anxiety. At outset the anxiety seemed of minor moment, particularly in view of the progress K had already made with J's cooperation, but as therapy progressed it was evident that K was still in real conflict.

K was actually at cross-purposes. She had felt totally devalued as a woman by her group-sex experience with the boys, yet she was objective enough to realize that she had practically issued an open invitation to such an experience by her uninhibited promiscuity. Since she had not experienced fellatio before her pseudorape episode, oral sex had come to represent the physical aspect of her complete humiliation. However, she also stated that she had been highly stimulated sexually during and immediately following the fellatio experience and was easily restimulated by reliving the experience in fantasy while masturbating. She had become extremely anxious when cunnilingus was requested because she felt that she might be so sexually aroused by the experience that this might force a return to unrestricted promiscuity, this time of lesbian origin. And, of course, she anticipated further humiliation. She knew she had been used by the teenage boys, and she felt threatened that responding to or initiating cunnilingus would put her in the same position of being used by women. She did not want her female friends to view her as an easy mark, as the boys had done.

K felt no sense of regret in relation to her pregnancy. She had categorized the sexual experience as one of those things that should not have happened but did, and other than some modest financial support for her daughter, had made no demands on the father. She even stopped asking for child support when J was generous financially. At the time the couple was in therapy, the girl had not been told who her father was or given any information about him other than that he and K were permanently separated.

Once the guilt that had resulted from the years of promiscuity was reasonably neutralized, K was encouraged to use her oral sex fantasies, first with masturbation, then during manipulation by J, and finally simultaneously with J's cunnilingal approach. K's sexual anxieties were soon neutralized, and she became freely responsive to J regardless of the manner of stimulation. She reported during follow-up that as her freedom to respond sexually increased, she made less use of her fantasy pattern.

J responded well to the sensate-focus approach, despite her previous lack of involvement in sexual activity. She had usually been approached in a forceful or demanding manner and consistently had used the same type of approach herself when she attempted to masturbate. Little time had been taken in reassurance, and there also had not been a great deal of identification with her partners except as sex objects. She was now fully committed to her relationship with K and was openly pleased that she could play an active part in releasing K from the self-imposed restrictions of her anxiey about oral sex.

J noted that after the first week in therapy she was becoming increasingly excited sexually as she and K became more involved in resolution of K's anxiety. One night, immediately after K had first allowed and then responded orgasmically to cunnilingus, J, highly excited by observing K's orgasmic experience, masturbated to orgasm with little difficulty. It was her first orgasmic experience, and her concept that she was incapable of orgasmic attainment was shattered. She was soon responsive to K's manipulative approaches. Finally K began approaching J with cunnilingus just at the end of the two-week acute phase of treatment, and J was multiorgasmic during the second such approach.

Both women left treatment confident in their sexual responsivity and firmly committed to the expanding dimensions of their relationship. They looked forward to a full life together and seemed equally concerned in giving K's daughter a secure home and full social and educational opportunities. They planned to talk freely with the girl about their own relationship when they considered her mature enough to understand.

This lesbian couple was followed for five years. Their relationship continued as a source of mutual security. Their patterns of sexual interaction continued to be mutually stimulating and completely satisfying for both women. Each woman denied any further interest in sexual experience with other partners. The daughter was denied access to her father both at his request and with K's agreement. J and K's relationship was discussed with the daughter in detail.

After treatment the two women decided to expend their energies on social welfare projects. They have been regularly employed in such endeavor and have broadened their social horizons to include male as well as female friends. They interact socially with a number of married couples, with their own relationship an open book.

This is a study of a firmly committed dyad of two lesbian women, each of whom brought to their relationship the strengths that the other partner needed. Both women matured psychosocially as well as psychosexually within the warmth and security of the relationship. Theirs was a positive response to the treatment program.

The second lesbian couple that applied to the Institute for treatment of anorgasmia with both partners sexually dysfunctional will also be reported in detail and treatment concepts and techniques discussed.

CASE REPORT: COUPLE 7

L was a 44-year-old situationally anorgasmic Kinsey 3 who had been living for nine years in a committed lesbian relationship with her partner M, who was 41, a Kinsey 5, and randomly anorgasmic. L had two children, a daughter 21 and a son 19. She had been married twice, once for six years (during which both children were born) and once for seven months. M had not married. This was the only committed lesbian relationship that L had experienced and the second such relationship for M.

L was born into a family with wealth in both her father's and mother's background. The family religious orientation was Protestant, with obligatory church-school attendance until age 12 and a family record of church attendance that concentrated on religious holidays. Her parents were divorced when she was 16. L did not describe a close relationship with her father either when she was a child or later as an adult. She believed that he had only a perfunctory interest in her as an individual. She had one brother five years older who was killed at age 20 in an automobile accident. He was described as having no significant influence in her life. She did not appear to have a close attachment to either her mother or her father.

L was a reasonably attractive girl with an extrovertive personality. Her formal education included high school and two years of college.

L was conscious of pelvic feelings at a very early age. She could not remember when she first masturbated, but she clearly remembered that her mother had played with her genitals two or three times a week during her preschool years under the guise of helping her "wash well." It was play that L apparently learned to enjoy, looked forward to, and tried to emulate with her own early masturbational attempts. L also could not remember when she was first orgasmic but thought it was at five or six years of age. Throughout her teenage years she usually masturbated at least once and sometimes twice a day. The intensity of her response seemed to increase after onset of menstruation late in her thirteenth year.

At 14, when sex play began with boys, she was freely cooperative but did not experience the sexual release that she had enjoyed for years with masturbation. The boys always seemed clumsy at sex play. She did become sexually excited but had to wait for privacy to gain masturbational release. Intercourse was first experienced at 17, and she continued to be active sexually through casually maintained relationships with seven different men until she married at 22. Despite a variety of sexual approaches, she was never orgasmic with any of the men she knew before her marriage.

She was married for six years and divorced her husband primarily because she had never been sexually satisfied. Her husband was a premature ejaculator and throughout the marriage never evidenced or expressed concern for his wife's sexual needs. L did not have time to respond during coital connection, which she estimated usually lasted for a minute or less, and she also never achieved orgasmic release from other stimulative approaches by her husband. Not until divorce proceedings had been initiated did the husband learn that his wife had been severely frustrated sexually. She not only had not communicated her need, she also had practiced sexual fakery and during many sexual episodes had pretended orgasmic release.

L had continued her almost daily pattern of masturbational release throughout her marriage except when she was pregnant. She found the state of pregnancy to be so sexually stimulating that she usually masturbated two or three times a day. She had always masturbated in private, keeping her husband completely unaware of her level of sexual need and her means of releasing this need.

After the divorce, L was involved with a series of lovers but was unsuccessful in responding to them sexually at orgasmic levels. She married a second time three years after her divorce. With this marriage, L reversed her previous noncommunicative behavior pattern and, deciding that honesty was the best policy, told her husband before they were married that she had what she considered to be a high level of sexual need. She also told him of her lack of sexual relief during her first marriage. Although her honesty was to be commended, the timing of her disclosure could not have been worse. Perhaps the second husband was initially made anxious at the concept of marrying a woman with an overwhelming sexual need that he might not be able to meet. He became impotent 10 days after the wedding when, despite his every effort, L had still not achieved orgasmic release and had begun openly masturbating in his presence. L divorced him after seven months of marriage, a decision with which he was apparently in full agreement.

There were two more brief, sexually frustrating affairs for L, who then deliberately terminated all sexual interaction with men. She continued her daily masturbational pattern, which she now was pleasurably enhancing by fantasizing herself being manipulated despite her objections by various women of her acquaintance, including, at times, her mother.

L found that her unresolved sexual frustrations were altering her personality and making her socially restless. It was apparent that her effectiveness as a mother was being jeopardized, so she made a deliberate decision to completely alter her lifestyle.

When she was 32, L quietly decided to involve herself in homosexual interaction. There had been no prior sexual interaction with women other than her mother's pattern of genital stimulation when she was a child. However, she had lived through two marriages and a number of lovers and had never been orgasmic in response to any male sexual approach. She was still masturbating daily as her only established means of sexual release. As she stated her case for moving into a homosexual orientation, "I felt I had nothing to lose."

Having made a decision to try homosexual interaction, she deliberately went to a gay bar and let herself be "picked up." She responded immediately at orgasmic levels to partner manipulation, but not to cunnilingus. Even so, she was delighted with such a level of response during her first lesbian experience.

Over the next three years, L continued cruising lesbian bars until she had interacted sexually with many partners and tried a variety of different sexual approaches; yet she was orgasmic only with manipulative play. She finally tired of casual sex and began looking for the social stability of a committed relationship. When L was 35 years old, she met M at a married friend's home.

M, who was 32 when she met L, had lived with the personal handicap of what she described as complete lack of sexual interest. She had a history that was almost the exact opposite of L's. She did have in common the fact that hers was a financially secure family background, but there any real similarity ended.

M was an only child in an austere fundamentalist Protestant family. Their religion was the center of the family's social world. The family held long daily prayer meetings, and their lives were socially structured by church dogma. M only learned in her twenties that her mother had forced her father to leave their home for presumed adultery, which he denied, when M was 7 years old. M could not remember another man (other than immediate family) ever visiting the home. When she was 12, her mother told her about menstruation and about sex at the same time. Both were portrayed as woman's burden. Sex was also described as an evil thing, something only men needed, and, of course, only acceptable by women for reproduction.

M believed all that her mother taught her. Although she wasn't quite sure what sex was, as her mother had been quite vague on the details of the subject, she grew up afraid of boys, all of whom she knew would want sex.

M went through high school and college as a good student, but she did not involve herself in extracurricular activities or social interchange. She was an overweight girl with an introvertive personality who considered herself to be unattractive.

Near the end of her junior year in college, M's mother, who was 44 years old, died of peritonitis caused by an illegal abortion. According to the doctors, the mother had been at least four months pregnant. She never identified the abortionist or the man responsible for the pregnancy.

As expected, this was an overwhelmingly shocking episode in M's essentially colorless and certainly uneventful life. Word of the cause of death spread quickly through the family's social circle, and by association, M was made to feel almost as guilty about her mother's sins as if she had been the one who had obtained an abortion. She resolved never to have sexual experience with men because the price that had to be paid was obviously too high.

This resolve lasted about two weeks. M returned to college severely depressed, and one night while aimlessly walking the campus and openly crying, she was stopped by a man who was in a class with her and who asked if he could help. She was caught completely off guard, told him her story, and promptly "fell in love" while they had coffee. M pursued the man constantly until he took notice. She responded to his notice with rapidly developing sexual interest until, two weeks after they met, she spent the night in his room. Although she had never had any kind of sexual experience previously, M was orgasmic with manipulation and with intercourse the first time she experienced either sexual approach. She was overwhelmed with the intensity and the pleasure of her feelings and more than ready for further experimentation when the next night the man told her that he was engaged and was going to be married in six weeks.

M immediately reverted to all of the sexual "thou shalt nots" that her mother had taught her. The single night was all the sexual experience she ever had with any man. The more she involuted socially, the less she was interested in any form of sexual activity. After college she worked irregularly, traveled extensively, and lived alone until she met, quite by accident, a woman she had known in college who had recently moved to her geographical area. This woman was also single, and the two women saw each other a number of times socially.

After a brief period of time M, to combat her loneliness, invited the woman to share her apartment. Before moving in, the woman told M that she was a lesbian. It didn't matter to M, who wasn't really quite sure what a lesbian was and anyway had no interest in sex.

After some months together, the woman, again with M's permission, began bringing an occasional friend home for the night or the weekend. Although M clearly heard the bedroom noises, she did not recall either feeling sexually aroused or even sexually curious. One night, after more than a year of living together, the woman openly moved into M's bed in a direct sexual approach. Despite every effort on the woman's part and despite M's clumsy cooperation, M was not responsive.

In the next few weeks the woman did teach M something of female anatomy and of how to stimulate another woman. Thereafter, M cooperated to release her partner when the partner expressed her sexual need by coming to M's bed. Mutual attempts at releasing each other occurred approximately once a month. In these episodes the partner usually was fully responsive but M was not. It was during this time that, at the partner's suggestion and following her explicit directions, M attempted masturbation for the first time in her life and was orgasmic.

After orgasmic episodes on two other occasions, however, M lost interest in masturbation. During the remaining two years that the couple lived together, M was orgasmic once with cunnilingus and twice with manipulation. Both women agreed that M simply had a low level of sexual interest.

The couple separated because the company for which the woman worked transferred her to another city. Having enjoyed the companionship of the low-keyed relationship, M was left with an even greater sense of social isolation.

After her mother's death and her one night of heterosexual sex, M's only consistently expressed interest was in her religion. Apparently the few homosexual experiences with her roommate were not equated in her mind with sexual sin, or at least they were not considered as sinful as her mother's indiscretion and her own campus episode. After her friend moved to another city, M spent almost a decade in a social vacuum with no male and but a few female acquaintances, most of whom were married and all of whom she met at church functions. M reported no sexual activity of any kind during this time. She did not masturbate and had no sexual fantasies or sex dreams.

M met L one evening in the home of a married woman she had known through her church activities.

What the two women found immediately appealing neither could say, but they did move directly into social interchange. Within a brief period of time the two people, poles apart in social consciousness, sexual experience, and knowledge of the world and the people in it, were fully committed to each other.

L found M's social and sexual naivete completely unbelievable, most appealing, and sexually very stimulating. For M the change was far more dramatic. L turned on a light in her world. She "fell in love" again, this time in a promising, secure relationship.

M began spending long weekends with L in her home, getting to know L's children, who were almost teenagers at the time. The women's mutual social world seemed more secure when they found they had some of the same tastes and so many of the same needs.

Although L was highly excited sexually by her new friend, she was reluctant to aproach M for fear of turning her away. Both women agreed that this problem was solved by M. One night while spending a weekend together, M simply asked L if she could help her with her sexual feelings. Knowing M's sexual history, L was warmed by M's offer but insisted that each should enjoy the other. During their first sexual experience together, L responded freely to manipulation but M could not.

After this weekend of sexual interchange, the women agreed to live together in L's home.

M responded to her new environment with a sense of sexual commitment. She released L almost daily by manipulation but was not successful with many attempts at cunnilingus. Although L also approached M without reservation, M was rarely aroused to orgasmic levels, reporting orgasm perhaps once or twice a year. However, she had no conscious feelings of sexual frustration and thoroughly enjoyed the feelings of physical awareness and, most of all, the physical closeness of sleeping with L.

Both women lived openly but quietly within their homosexual relationship. L's children freely accepted M. Most of L's friends became M's friends. M only regretted that she had so few acquaintances and no friends to share with L.

The two women decided to enter therapy to expand the dimensions of their relationship. L wanted to be able to respond to cunnilingus, and M wanted to feel and respond as openly and freely sexually as she had seen L respond so many times.

There was little difficulty in helping L achieve her goal of orgasmic release with cunnilingus. She had developed real fears of performance and became an immediate spectator whenever cunnilingus was initiated, something she never did when being manipulated or when masturbating. With M's full cooperation and following the concepts outlined in Chapter 12, L's situational anorgasmia was reversed during their first week in therapy.

M was more of a problem. Over the years she had been inundated by feelings of unworthiness. Her social insecurities were reflected in her sexual inadequacies. M had adopted the standard pattern of voluntary social isolation that is frequently employed by such insecure men or women. She was the type of individual who rarely takes social risks or forms close personal attachments and therefore is rarely disappointed by relationships that fail to mature satisfactorily. Her pattern of not venturing personal involvement with social interchange was identically repeated in her pattern of not venturing personal involvement in sexual interaction. When she "didn't feel anything sexually" she was only withdrawing sensually to protect herself against the disappointment of sexual failure.

The key to therapy was to reflect back to M how freely responsive she had been during the one night with her male classmate. Here she identified with the individual, was fully confident and trusting, and gave of herself completely. Supported by her sense of total commitment, she was fully responsive sexually even though it was her first heterosexual experience. When she had found that her sense of commitment was misplaced, she did not have the courage to trust another man or woman fully until L entered her life. Instead she had tried to drown her sense of personal inadequacy in the sea of security provided by her religious commitment.

It was suggested that since she voluntarily had made a major contribution to her current relationship by giving of herself socially without reservation, it was now time to give of herself sexually with confidence. If she could conceive of giving of herself sexually as she had socially, her level of sexual interest inevitably would increase and her ability to respond to sexual stimuli would probably follow the same pattern.

There was, of course, an additional psychosocial hurdle to overcome. If M were to express herself sexually with complete freedom in a continuing lesbian relationship, her "sex is sin" background had to be confronted directly. She had to come to terms with the inevitable clash between the tenets of her religion and her chosen lifestyle. M made a free commitment to the relationship far more readily than the therapists deemed possible under the circumstances.

M had little difficulty in accepting the concept that her voluntary decision to live a life apart socially had been directly reflected in her life apart sexually. She slowly began responding to L's quiet, nondemanding sexual approaches. She was orgasmic once with manipulative and also once with cunnilingal stimulation while in therapy.

During follow-up, M reported increasing sexual involvement in response to L's persistent but low-keyed approaches, and in six months she reached an approximate twice-a-week stage of orgasmic attainment. She also thoroughly enjoyed making sure that L had sexual release on at least a daily basis, using a multiplicity of different stimulative approaches.

These two women are currently living productive lives in a mutually enhancing relationship. They have met and to a significant degree neutralized public resistance to their status by openly stating their relationship but not forcing it upon their peers. M has become far more of a contributor to both the sexual and social aspects of

the relationship since she has been able to join L in mutually responsive sexual interchanges.

The therapy of the 23 couples that applied for treatment of anorgasmia with one partner dysfunctional and the other fully sexually
responsive was conducted using the same general psychotherapeutic
approaches that were employed in the treatment of the two couples reported above. As stated in Chapter 13, a detailed discussion
of the psychodynamics involved will be published separately. Suffice
it to say for the present that, as in the treatment of anorgasmic
heterosexual women, the necessary technical suggestions for more
effective sexual interaction are implemented with the cooperation
of the functional partner. But far more important, the arts of communication are not only taught but are stressed; psychosocial roadblocks are directly confronted; and anxieties are neutralized insofar
as possible. Fears of performance and spectator roles are identified,
discussed with the couple, and treated, again primarily through the
cooperation of the functional partner.

The sexually dysfunctional homosexual woman has a significant
advantage over the similarly dysfunctional heterosexual woman.
She does not have the added cultural requirement of orgasmic response during intercourse. Potentially it is less demanding for a
woman to become orgasmic during masturbation, partner stimulation, and cunnilingus, when the clitoral glans and/or shaft is stimulated by direct manual or oral approaches, than it is during intercourse, when the clitoral shaft usually is stimulated only indirectly
by the tension on the minor labia created by the usual coital thrusting pattern. As was shown in Chapter 6, sexually responsive women
have an increased incidence of failure to function at orgasmic levels in coital interaction as compared to other forms of sexual stimulation. Therefore, when sexually dysfunctional homosexual women
are treated with essentially the same techniques as sexually dysfunctional heterosexual women, the treatment failure rates in terms
of facility of orgasmic attainment should be lower for dysfunctional
homosexual women—and they are. The failure statistics pertaining

to the treatment of lesbian dysfunction are reported in Chapter 17.

For the first time a long-range clinical program for the treatment of lesbian sexual dysfunctions has been presented to the health-care professions. This program is only the first step in a new dimension of health-care growth. Psychotherapists have the responsibility to respond to the requests for support presented by sexually dysfunctional women, regardless of whether the women are homosexually or heterosexually oriented. If a woman is allowed to continue to be sexually dysfunctional on an indefinite basis, in due course she may well become psychosocially dysfunctional, for the culture equates woman's recently acquired sexual equality with a demand for effective sexual performance. It has become increasingly obvious that the pressures for sexual performance are as much directed to homosexually as to heterosexually oriented women. Therefore the culture can no longer afford to ignore the sexually dysfunctional homosexual woman.

15

MALE HOMOSEXUAL
DISSATISFACTION

The homosexually oriented male population that applied to the Institute for reversion or conversion therapy has been described in Chapter 12 and listed in Tables 12-3 and 12-4. Fifty-four men, together with their committed or casual heterosexual partners, were treated over the 10-year period of clinical control (see Table 15-2). Thirty-one of these men were married and entered therapy with their wives, 2 men were living in long-term heterosexual relationships and were listed as married, and 21 men were treated with casual female partners.

The terms *conversion* and *reversion* have been employed by the Institute to connote relative degrees of previous heterosexual and homosexual experience. If a man or woman expressed the desire to move into full heterosexual involvement and described little or no prior heterosexual experience (Kinsey 5 or 6), he or she was classified as requesting *conversion* to heterosexuality. On the other hand, if the man's or woman's degree of prior heterosexual experience ranged decreasingly from dominant to considerable (Kinsey 2 to 4), he or she was identified as requesting *reversion* to heterosexuality.

Providing therapeutic support for the homosexually oriented man or woman who wishes to convert or revert to heterosexuality has been an integral part of the practice of psychotherapy for decades. Some reported treatment results have been acceptable, others have not. Any number of difficulties have been encountered in the treatment of homosexual men and women requesting alteration of sex preference, but the major stumbling block that creates the highest failure rate in any treatment program concerns problems of attitude, both of the therapists and of the sexually dissatisfied men and women.

If the therapist cannot develop and stabilize an objective, personal attitude toward the subject of homosexuality, he or she can easily prejudice the reversal of a sex preference at the very onset of therapy. Therapists have openly taken such biased pretreatment positions as identifying homosexuality as a congenital anomaly, as a major neurosis, as a sexual perversion, or even as a physical illness. In short, therapists have frequently insisted on treating the reversion or conversion applicant for a state of physical, psychological, or social pathology, the clinical existence of which has never been established. This escape from vital professional neutrality under the protective cloak of cultural dictum has usually resulted in the therapist's attempted imposition of his or her own social or sexual value systems on the client. As stated in Chapter 12, it is the Institute's fundamental position that the therapist as a committed professional does not have the privilege of imposing his or her cultural value systems on the client, regardless of whether the client is homosexually or heterosexually oriented.

In therapy, the Institute's *modus operandi* is to identify, evaluate, and then openly discuss the positive and/or negative contributions that the client's social and sexual value systems are making to his or her lifestyle. If an alteration need occur in the client's value systems in order to either instigate or implement the therapy process, the alteration must be accomplished within the psychosocial restrictions imposed by the client's frame of reference—and this frame of reference might not be at all compatible with that of the therapist. A carefully designed treatment program has the best chance for long-range success if it enables the client to live effectively within the encompassing but familiar restrictions of his or her own sexual and social value systems. Of course, established behavior patterns should be modified when necessary, but no attempt should be made to reconstruct the client's basic value systems in a new image (the therapist's). For once the treatment program is terminated, the client will have little chance of enjoying a positive treatment result if he or she is committed by authoritative dominance to interpreting, adjusting to, and living within the social and sexual value systems of the therapist.

A major treatment concern is, of course, the applicant's attitude. Degrees of client motivation are hard to evaluate at any time, and they are particularly difficult to determine when the expressed request for alteration of established behavior patterns encompasses a controversial area. The research team made a determined attempt to identify each applicant's degree of motivation for alteration of sex preference. When there is questionable client motivation, the possibilities of a positive therapeutic result are markedly reduced.

MOTIVATING FACTORS

What are the Institute's methods of evaluating treatment suitability? How does the therapist determine the degree of client motivation for alteration of sexual preference? How does the therapist handle the questionably motivated client?

Much has been learned from the pioneering efforts of other professionals in this field. After considering their reported experiences, the research team decided to give a relatively low priority to the content of the applicant's verbal protestations of interest in sexual preference alteration. It is so easy for any homosexually oriented man or woman to react to psychosocial pressures by claiming, and at the precise moment believing, that he or she is fully committed to heterosexuality, but it is far more difficult to continue living in a heterosexual lifestyle when the psychosocial pressures have been reasonably neutralized or even removed by the passage of time or by an adequate therapy program.

Rather than attempting to determine levels of client motivation merely from the content of a direct interview, it seemed far more equitable to evaluate the factors underlying the presumed motivation. As experience accumulated, criteria developed for evaluating these factors.

If the motivation for sex-preference alteration only developed in apparent response to social threat, the research team felt insecure about the prospects for a permanent therapeutic result and therefore was particularly careful in client selection. When the expressed motivation for change reportedly was stimulated by socially or professionally threatening situations, the involved men and women were judged not so much by what they said when applying for treatment, but by how they had handled their culturally induced anxieties. For example, individuals in socially vulnerable positions, such as teachers in secondary schools or image-conscious public figures, were evaluated far more by their actions in response to the pressured situation than by the content of their verbalizations. Accordingly, the length of time between the client's determined need for change in sex-preference and the first contact with a health-care authority became an important criterion in evaluating motivation levels. If the psychosocially threatened individual or couple sought professional support within approximately three months or less of the first suggestion of public or professional exposure, the motivation for change was presumed to be at a higher level than that of men or women who procrastinated for six months or more before seeking some type of health-care consultation. Many of those who procrastinated verbalized their motivation for alteration of sexual preference in the highest terms, but they had actually given such alteration a less than immediate priority. In other words, if the primary motivation for altering a sexual preference was derived directly from a presumed need for social or professional survival, there seemed to be a better chance of client cooperation if there had been a relatively immediate request for support. If every other means of coping with the situation had been employed before facing what the individual obviously thought of not only as the least attractive but as a finally forced alternative, the therapists had little confidence that attempted conversion or reversion therapy would produce a permanent result.

Of course, a number of other factors were considered in evaluating motivation for alteration in sexual preference. An applicant occasionally expressed open dissatisfaction with his or her homosexuality. Reacting to a significant amount of unfortunate sexual or social experience or both, a few clients not only expressed the desire to alter their sexual orientation but wanted to be relatively certain that the change in role preference would be permanent. These few men and women (there were 7) usually had at hand a desired heterosexual partner (there were 6) with whom they anticipated living in a committed relationship. They had decided that arbitrarily altering sexual preference on their own, without adequate psychotherapeutic support, would be taking an unnecessary risk with the new relationship. They were also intrigued with the concept that they might stimulate a greater degree of support and a higher level of cooperation from their prospective heterosexual mates if the mates were fully informed of the applicants' previous homosexual orientation and, if possible, even of some of the reasons for it.

Couples exemplifying exactly the opposite set of motivating factors were also seen as applicants for reversion therapy. The counterpart to the uncommitted couples who voluntarily sought psychotherapeutic support in altering sex preference before entering marriage was seen in the couples whose existing marriages were threatened by the sexual ambivalence of one partner.

Most of the male and female applicants with a poorly functioning heterosexual commitment admitted to having had a significant amount of both homosexual and heterosexual experience prior to marriage. The marital partner had rarely been informed before the marriage of the mate's ambivalence in sexual preference and had become aware of the dual preference either by accident (a truly traumatic means of enlightenment) or by confronting the individual after suspicions had been raised by the mate's markedly altered heterosexual patterning.

In most instances the couple's immediately expressed need was for relationship support, but also verbalized was anticipation that the dual-preferenced individual could be reverted to full heterosexual commitment. In these situations the factor of motivation was primarily evaluated not by the couple's verbalization of interest in therapy but by their pattern of interaction with the therapists.

If a request for alteration of sex preference was forcefully expressed by the heterosexual partner and was only casually acknowledged or even hesitantly acceded to by the dual-preferenced individual, there was reluctance to accept the couple in treatment. Occasionally there was a deliberate attempt by the dual-preferenced applicant to use the treatment program as a camouflage. For example, several couples applied for reversion treatment with the sexually ambivalent male partner saying one thing in front of his wife and yet another to the therapists in private. When such self-incriminating phrases as "of course I'll need an occasional chance to be with my friends" or "I want to be 95 percent heterosexual" were used in private with a therapist, the couples were refused treatment. The Institute's position was that the male applicants had the right to take any position they wished and to express their sexual value systems as they saw fit, but they did not have the privilege of using the Institute's treatment program as a means of misleading their wives. It must always be borne in mind that the applicant's partner has equal privilege in therapy and the right to equality of protection.

Historically, reversion therapy has rarely been successful if the individual enters a treatment program under duress from a spouse or with the expressed concept that complete reversion is neither possible nor fully desired. However, if the dual-preference partner initially evidenced specific concern for the relationship and then personally requested support in sex-preference limitation and made the request without any stated reservations, the research team was quite willing to accept the couple in therapy.

The highest incidence of questionable motivation occurred in the group of uncommitted homosexual men who, with their casual female partners, applied for conversion or reversion therapy. It was extremely difficult to establish the motivating factors within this group. The uncommitted men had in common with their casual female partners only the factors of sexual curiosity and an apparent freedom from personal commitment.

When evaluating this type of uncommitted homosexual male applicant for conversion or reversion therapy, little priority was given to what was said when requesting treatment. Instead, the research team was far more concerned with evaluating motivation by looking at the potential for gain if treatment were successful. Was the applicant's potential for gain great enough to motivate him or her to cooperate in therapy? If not obviously forced by social pressures and if the applicant evidenced no homosexual dysfunction or dissatisfaction, what positive gain could be anticipated from successful treatment? Since a permanent commitment to the casual female partner was not contemplated, the motivating factors of an anticipated or even a secure relationship could be discounted.

Some of the men were simply concerned with developing confidence in heterosexual function so that their sexual opportunities could be more broadly based. With two exceptions, men with this type of motivation were not accepted in therapy.

The uncommitted male applicants who were selected for therapy with their casual female partners had one motivating factor in common in addition to their concept of having something definitive to gain by moving into a full heterosexual commitment. They had the common factor of anxiety—that of fear of performance in a heterosexual role. Whether the alteration in preference was requested by a Kinsey 2 with a large amount of prior heterosexual experience or a Kinsey 6 with none, there was a universal anxiety among the males accepted for therapy that after their homosexual experience they might not be able to function effectively with their selected female partners. In fact, some of the men had attempted intercourse before applying for treatment and generally had been unsuccessful in heterosexual interchange.

It is probably true that fears of performance keep many more homosexually oriented men from experimenting with heterosexual interaction than we have realized or than might have been admitted if the men had been openly interrogated. Quite possibly the reverse may be equally true. Fears of performance and of social opprobrium keep many men fully restricted to a heterosexual lifestyle who might otherwise have experimented with homosexual opportunity.

Of course, there were the occasionally expressed motivating factors for role alteration that by their very uniqueness intrigued the therapists into acceptance of obligation. For example, a man was accepted who was primarily impotent as a heterosexual. He had married but could not consummate the marriage. He had tried to function with other women and failed and then had turned to homosexual interaction as an ego-salvaging measure. Identified as homosexual four years later by his still-committed wife, he requested support both in neutralizing his established homosexual orientation and in gaining a sexually functional status as a heterosexual.

There was also a Kinsey 6 woman who had been primarily anorgasmic as a homosexual and who, after living approximately 11 years as a sexually active but completely frustrated homosexual, insisted that homosexuality had nothing to offer her. She stated that she wanted to live in a heterosexual relationship with a specifically selected heterosexual partner and to function sexually at orgasmic levels with him. The research team was intrigued not only by her stated motivation for change, but also by the ambiguity of the professional situation. Had she requested support in developing sexual facility as a lesbian, such help would have been freely offered. Instead, her specific request was for therapeutic support in the alteration of her sexual value system, and she was accepted just as openly.

There were also requests for conversion therapy that were based on the simple factor of an openly expressed curiosity for experience with heterosexual interaction, and these were accepted.

Finally, there were 4 couples in which the previously homosexual male partner (Kinsey 5 or 6) was motivated by an in-depth attachment to an opposite-sex individual and was sincerely interested in consummating physiologically the psychosocially committed relationship, even though the consummation had already been tried and had failed repeatedly. These couples were accepted for conversion therapy.

It should be stated that there are a number of other criteria for defining motivation that cannot be openly published. Public identification of these criteria would prejudice the Institute's screening procedures that have been developed over the last 11 years. In the future each individual clinical program, as it is constituted to treat homosexual male or female dissatisfaction and as it gains experience, will develop its own screening concepts and procedures. Methods of screening for motivation are not nearly as important as the *fact* that applicants for the treatment of homosexual dissatisfaction must be screened for motivation in order to maintain a therapy failure rate at reasonably low levels. Of course, regardless of how firmly established the screening procedures might be, a certain amount of latitude in client selection must always be left to the clinical judgment of the therapist.

The distribution of conversion and reversion cases is shown in Table 15-1. A total of 45 male homosexuals were accepted for reversion therapy and 9 male homosexuals for conversion therapy over a 10-year period. Case distribution during this time is indicated in Table 15-2. With the exception of the first two years, approximately 6 cases of homosexual male dissatisfaction were treated each year. Treatment results are presented in Chapter 17.

TABLE 15-1

Dissatisfied Homosexual Male Population
(Total Applicants, N = 70; Applicants Accepted, N = 54)

Applicants	Reversion Candidates			Conversion Candidates		
	Kinsey 2	Kinsey 3	Kinsey 4	Kinsey 5	Kinsey 6	Total No.
No. of applicants *	2	15	40	9	4	70
No. refused †	0	4	8	3	1	16
No. accepted	2	11	32	6	3	54
						(1968–1977)

* No Kinsey 1 men applied for treatment.
† Overall refusal rate, 22.8 percent.

TABLE 15-2

Dissatisfied Homosexual Male Population (N = 54):
Distribution by Year During the 10-Year Clinical Control Period

Dissatisfaction Therapy	Year Treated										
	One	Two	Three	Four	Five	Six	Seven	Eight	Nine	Ten	Total
Reversion	3	2	6	4	5	7	3	5	6	4	45
Conversion	0	2	1	1	0	1	2	0	1	1	9
Total	3	4	7	5	5	8	5	5	7	5	54
											(1968–1977)

REFUSED APPLICATIONS

Male applicants for sex-preference alteration are identified by their Kinsey rating in Table 15-1. Also reported are the number of applicants in the same preference categories who were refused treatment by the Institute. There was approximately a 23 percent rate of application refusal. Those men refused treatment were referred to other sources of therapy, but only after a full explanation had been given not only of the Institute's selection policies but also of the specific reasons for refusal of the individual applicant.

Sixteen homosexual men and their female partners (2 committed and 14 casual) were refused treatment for sexual dissatisfaction during the 10-year period of clinical control (see Table 15-1). There were a variety of reasons for refusing access to the treatment program, but by far the most frequent reason for refusal (9 applicants) was the research team's clinical decision that there was insufficient motivation evidenced by the homosexual applicant for alteration of his sexual preference. Some of the measures by which the team arrived at such decisions have been described earlier in the chapter.

Two of the male applicants were diagnosed as psychotic and referred to other clinical resources. Three were refused therapy because their casual female partners were considered severely neurotic (2) or psychotic (1). The remaining 2 applicants were refused treatment when they were identified as supplying false information during the selection process.

In all probability, mistakes were made in both acceptance and refusal of applications for treatment. In order to ensure consistency in admission policies, the decisions to admit or reject were made by the same individual during the entire 10-year period of clinical control. While the possibility of personal bias in client selection was always present, at least the same level or type of bias existed for the entire clinical control period.

The problem of the health-care professions' refusal to accept into treatment severely distressed homosexual men has been discussed at length for the dysfunctional homosexual male population (see Chapter 13). The same problem has existed (though to a lesser degree) for sexually dissatisfied homosexual men. Of the 54 homosexual men accepted in therapy by the Institute, 36 had previously sought treatment from another health-care facility for their complaints of sexual dissatisfaction (see Table 12-5, Chapter 12). Twenty-one of the 36 men had been refused treatment, 10 of the 21 men more than once. Surprisingly, only 1 of the 21 men refused treatment had been referred to another therapy source. Fifteen men had been accepted in treatment elsewhere, but 12 of these men had terminated their treatment as unsatisfactory. Three men were in active therapy when they applied to the Institute for treatment and were released by their therapists.

It must be acknowledged that a degree of bias exists in these statistics for at least two reasons: First, homosexual men who were successful in obtaining treatment elsewhere were not seen at the Institute; second, these numbers reflect an historical phenomenon of rejection by health-care professionals that probably would not be found to the same extent today.

The prejudice of the health-care professions was not as apparent when support was requested by the dissatisfied homosexual male as it was when the dysfunctional homosexual male asked for help. Since this subject has been discussed in detail (see Chapter 13), there is no need for further exposition.

THERAPEUTIC PROCEDURE

To exemplify the clinical situations encountered, representative case reports are presented. They will be briefly discussed individually and then summarized in principle. A detailed discussion of therapeutic techniques will be presented as a separate publication.

No attempt has been made to describe in detail the general background or the psychosexual status of the heterosexual female partners that were an integral part of the relationships treated by the Institute's staff. But when specific information about the female partner is necessary to complete the clinical picture, it has been provided.

CASE REPORT: COUPLE 8

N was a 37-year-old Kinsey 4 male who had been living for seven years as an unattached homosexual when seen in therapy. Previously, he had been married for two years and divorced because of sexual inadequacy. He was a lawyer whose career was being threatened by rumors that he "didn't like girls," and he sought professional support in reorientation to heterosexuality.

N was the youngest of three children in a family with few or no financial resources. He could only describe his childhood as one of constant turmoil. He remembered whippings from his coal miner father, who was an alcoholic and an uncontrolled tyrant in the home. N described his mother as a woman who lived only to keep the family clothed, fed, and passively protected and who didn't always succeed at these tasks. Fear of the husband-father pervaded the home.

N's siblings were a brother six years older and a sister 17 months older. He had little direct contact with his brother, who began working in the mines after two years of high school and married at age 18. His relationship with his sister was much closer. They shared the insecurities of the home and at times were able to provide each other with some degree of comfort. He felt deserted when she married at 16 in order to leave the home.

N could not recall a single religious direction. He had never been in a church.

N seemed always to be separated from his peer group by necessity. As he grew up, he worked at odd jobs after school, so his opportunities for social interchange were markedly limited. Since his mother also worked, his sister was held responsible for much of the housework. Both N and his sister were whipped repeatedly for what N described as minor offenses, and his mother was subjected to a number of physical beatings that severely traumatized both N and his sister.

After the older brother left home, the father began an open incestuous relationship with N's sister despite both her pleas and those of the mother. About a year later the sister ran away to marry, leaving N alone in the home.

N continued part-time work to contribute to the family's support throughout high school. His grades were excellent, and with the help of the school principal he was granted a full scholarship at a state university. He worked his way through the university and—again with a full scholarship—through law school. Once he entered the university, he never again lived at home. His mother died during his first year in law school.

N's social life was essentially nonexistent throughout his undergraduate years. He worked steadily at part-time jobs to help pay for his room and board and was seriously involved in his course work. His undergraduate academic achievement was of the highest order, and he graduated near the head of a class of many hundreds of students.

N began masturbating at approximately 13 and continued at a rate of once or twice a week through his teens. In his last year in the university, he became involved with a girl who was working with him in a part-time job. After she took the initiative of expressing interest and providing the opportunity, they began a sexual relationship. N had not disliked girls, but he simply had had little time for social interaction as he grew up. Before he met this girl, he had never had a date, kissed a girl, or had any other form of sexual experience with either women or men.

N's social and sexual behavior with his first girl was understandably clumsy and awkward, but since he could not bring himself to admit his virginal status, he was easily misinterpreted by his female partner. He had no concept of female anatomy or, for that matter, of any manner of sexual interaction. Since the girl was quite experienced, at least by comparison, it was not long before she was criticizing his sexual approaches. At first she quietly suggested alternatives and then, when her suggestions apparently fell on deaf ears, she told N specifically that he "wasn't any good" sexually. Soon thereafter she terminated the relationship.

N had occasional sexual experiences with other women during law school and for two years after he graduated, but almost all were of the one-night-stand variety. When he was 26, N was attracted to a secretary in the law firm in which he was a junior member. After a six-month courtship, they married. The sexual aspects of the first few months of the marriage were approximately a repeat of those of his first sexual experience. Again he did not admit his profound ignorance of female sexual needs. His wife began complaining that he hurt her, didn't give her enough time, didn't know how to please her, was only interested in self-satisfaction, and so forth. Probably, all complaints were justified. Finally, there was a very angry scene during which N was told that he simply didn't know how to treat a woman. His wife told him she was "tired of being used like a whore." This statement immediately evoked memories of his father's frequent drunken use and abuse of his mother and sister.

The next time the couple attempted intercourse, N lost his erection shortly after penetration as he thought of his wife's accusation that he was using her like a whore. Within two months N had lost what little sexual confidence he had ever attained. There were no further erections other than when he masturbated. N's wife divorced him after two years of marriage because he no longer could function sexually. He insisted that the divorce complaint read "incompatibility" and was actually relieved to be free of this anxiety-provoking situation. He never attempted further heterosexual interaction until he was in therapy.

Over the next two years N masturbated regularly but had no other sexual experience and buried himself in his career; he also did not take advantage of any opportunities to gain social experience.

When he was 30, N met a man eight years older who was quite successful in business. The man soon became very friendly and saw to it that N was given an opportunity to do a great deal of legal business that otherwise might not have come his way. This man was married, but he was also a very active homosexual. He simply seduced the sexually naive N. The process started with lengthy discussions of sexual problems, proceeded to mutual masturbation, and—in two months—to partner manipulation and fellatio. N consistently refused anal intercourse.

Homosexuality provided an entirely new sexual vista for N. He was no longer accused of being an unsatisfactory sexual partner. When the men were together, usually in N's apartment, sex was quickly initiated and as rapidly and effectively terminated. N was completely satisfied with his homosexual orientation and had no further heterosexual interests. The relationship continued for seven years, during which N's career prospered with his friend's support.

Finally, rumors began to circulate, not about the two men specifically; however, attention was being called to the fact that N never expressed interest in women. The man, by this time fully devoted to N's career and aware of the political threat in the rumors, decided that he and N should no longer be active sexual partners and insisted that N start seeing women socially and even sexually. This N tried to do, but he was quite unsuccessful. He recalled quite vividly the sexual disasters of his failed marriage and with his first sexual partner. Although N could and did learn to meet women at a casual social level with reasonable comfort, he became extremely anxious when circumstances placed him alone with any woman.

Once N began to move in heterosexual social circles, several women openly provided him with sexual opportunity, but this possibility proved too threatening. Finally a woman in her late forties who was widowed and financially independent, whom he met initially through his male sexual partner, also became interested in N. After a brief period of time, both N and his male friend decided that she could be trusted and she was told the whole story of N's failed heterosexual experiences, his complete lack of sexual know-how, and of his subsequent homosexual orientation. After N asked for help, the woman freely agreed to join him as a casual partner in the Institute's treatment program for homosexual dissatisfaction.

N had been accepted in treatment because he had honestly expressed his sexual ambivalence, acknowledged the threat to his professional career, and then made it quite clear that he was very fearful of moving into a heterosexual lifestyle since he was convinced that he was totally sexually inadequate in heterosexual opportunity. He felt that he could not choose objectively between the two sexual preferences in view of his heterosexually oriented fears of performance.

This case is representative of a number of men who turn to homosexual outlets once they have become convinced that, for whatever reasons, they cannot hope to function effectively in a heterosexual role. The most important therapeutic step beyond determining a positive motivation to function heterosexually is to fully understand the reasons for the homosexual orientation. In this case, N moved into homosexuality from psychosexual need, but he was primarily pressured by his overt failures to sexually satisfy the two women with whom he had a continuing sense of sexual commitment. He initially returned to heterosexuality with real reservation, but he was inordinately pleased when his confidence in heterosexual interchange was restored by the full cooperation of the older woman in the treatment program.

At no time was N pressured by the therapists to alter his sexual orientation. Once his heterosexual effectiveness had been restored, his alternatives were explained and it was made very clear that the choice of sexual preference was his alone to decide. He evidenced no indecision in making a full heterosexual commitment.

CASE REPORT: COUPLE 9

Q was a 33-year-old Kinsey 3 who had been married for four years and had one child when seen in therapy. He and his wife requested psychotherapeutic support first to rescue a traumatized relationship and second to alter his role from one of dual sexual preference to that of a full heterosexual commitment.

Q came from a stable, middle-class background. His father was 42 and his mother 39 when Q was born. He was an only child. Apparently a real effort was made by his parents to compensate for their age, but the net result seems to have been a substitution of things for personal warmth. When questioned about childhood memories, Q repeatedly stated that he had never felt close to either parent. As he grew up he felt loved, but as someone or something quite apart from and to a significant degree excluded from their relationship. He did not have a lot of time with his parents in the home, as his father traveled extensively on business and was frequently accompanied by his mother. Yet Q did not describe a sense of loneliness, nor did he recall any feelings of rejection. The parents apparently were able to project a sense of warmth and support, for Q did describe an uneventful, happy childhood.

The family's religious background was Protestant, but religion received only a token acknowledgment in the home.

Despite his single-child status, Q mixed well with his peers. As he grew older, he was encouraged by his parents to have boys stay over for the night and to respond to their return invitations. At 12 he learned to masturbate, and at 14 he was practicing partner manipulation with two different boys over weekends.

Q's first heterosexual experiences also began at 14. They were confined to kissing and breast play. With his parents frequently absent, he had a great deal of privacy in his home, so experimentation continued with a first coital experience with a peer when Q was 16.

For the remainder of his time in high school and through his college years, Q lived a relatively independent and very active sexual life. He responded to both homosexual and heterosexual opportunities as they developed without social hesitation and without sexual reservation.

When he graduated from college, Q started on a business career with his father's support. He had his own apartment and was freely social and openly sexual. He interacted with a number of men and women who also lived without sexual reservation. There were group sex experiences, but Q did not particularly enjoy this means of sexual expression, personally preferring privacy for sexual interchange.

He progressed well professionally and at 28 met the daughter of one of the partners in a competitive firm. She was 24, two years out of college, a devout Catholic and a virgin. These two people developed a strong personal commitment. They were constantly together. By mutual agreement their sexual interchange was limited to manipulation, and when they married nine months later the bride was still a virgin. During the courtship, Q denied himself all sexual outlets other than two isolated homosexual experiences.

After the marriage, the sexual interaction between Q and his wife was severely stylized. His wife controlled their sexual activity by her rigid convictions about what was acceptable sexual conduct and what was not. This was a situation Q had never encountered, and he didn't know how to deal with his feelings. Yet he had no outside sexual activity for more than two years until after his wife was hospitalized with a threatened abortion. For the rest of the pregnancy there was a continuing threat of miscarriage or premature delivery, and intercourse was contraindicated by the obstetrician. To his wife, the obstetrician's interdiction of intercourse meant that any form of sexual expression was unacceptable since it could not culminate in intercourse.

Q became very restless sexually and turned to outside sexual opportunity. His selected opportunities for sexual release were entirely homosexual in orientation. In response to some strange rationalization, Q decided to honor his marital commitment by not turning to another woman, but he did not hesitate to approach other men. After the pregnancy terminated successfully and his wife became fully involved in her new maternal role, Q continued with homosexual activity. When sexual interchange was resumed with his wife, his homosexual experience continued at the same pace.

One of Q's best friends, a business associate, was openly homosexual. The men enjoyed a number of sexual episodes together. They were together in Q's office after business hours early one evening when Q's wife, deciding to surprise her late-working husband and take him to dinner, walked in unannounced.

For almost three months husband and wife lived in separate rooms in their own home. Then, after weeks of religious council for his wife, reconciliation occurred following Q's vow of full marital commitment. This was a vow he found he couldn't keep. Once he denied himself outside sexual experience, he was even more intensely drawn to homosexual interaction. He had a number of homosexual episodes over the next five or six months. Following each episode, he experienced strong guilt feelings, but he still felt a continuing need to pursue his homosexual interests.

Q finally realized that he was at a crossroad in his life. He decided that he could not continue to live a dual-preference life without his wife's knowledge. Over a long weekend he quietly told his wife not only about his inability to keep his vow of marital commitment, but of the sexual details of his past life. He had not given her this information previously. Separation and divorce were seriously considered, but both marital partners felt themselves fully committed to their relationship. They decided to seek professional support in an attempt to salvage the marriage, and they applied to the Institute for therapy.

Both husband and wife clearly stated that their primary concern was for maintenance of the family, while Q specifically asked for help in achieving a full heterosexual orientation. Q's wife offered unreserved cooperation with the treatment program.

With the tremendous therapeutic advantage of working with a committed relationship, and with client motivation at a high level, the therapists were quite free to innovate. Q wanted a complete heterosexual relationship with his wife, but he frankly stated that his homosexual experiences were far more rewarding sexually than most of his recalled heterosexual episodes. This had been particularly true when he was interacting with his uninformed, inexperienced, and sexually very inhibited wife.

The success of the therapy program depended entirely upon constituting the marital bed as the major communicative attraction for both partners. Q's wife was informed of the direction to be taken in therapy. If there was to be a relationship, both partners had to alter their value systems for the other's benefit. It was explained that the therapists had no intention of making her anxious about or fearful of sexual interchange. Rather, they wished her to be particularly receptive to suggestions from her husband. It was emphasized that much of successful sexual interaction between a man and woman depends on two factors. The first factor obviously is the psychosocial security that comes to each individual from the partner's full commitment to the relationship. The second factor is the extensive knowledge each partner has of the other's sexual needs and of the means and measures of fulfilling those needs. Q's wife was not only an apt, but a most cooperative pupil. She openly stated that her marriage was the most important aspect of her life and that no prior sexual reservations, regardless of how ingrained they might be, would be allowed to stand in the way of a functional relationship.

It was suggested to Q that he really had no prior experience with the potential depth of sexual pleasure that could be realized from a committed heterosexual situation. He had only to join his wife without prejudicing the result by recalling her prior sexual rigidity. His inexperienced but most receptive wife quickly convinced him that he wanted his marriage as a way of life. As their mutual sexual comfort increased, so did the communicative base of the relationship. For the first time, Q and his wife found themselves communicating freely without inhibition and without reservation.

In follow-up, Q reports that he has kept his commitment to his wife and family. He consistently works at improving their sexual and social communication in order to contribute to the strength of the relationship. His wife apparently works even harder at the same goals.

This was a relatively easy problem in sorting out sexual preferences. In fact, Q's homosexual orientation really did not pose much of a problem. His wife's personal interpretation of religious orthodoxy was as much if not more of a problem. Fortunately, it was a problem easily solved by the wife when she realized that her interpretation of orthodoxy as well as her husband's dual sexual preference were major obstacles to a functional relationship.

This case was chosen to illustrate the fact that there are instances when the existence of an active homosexual involvement need not be of significant concern to therapists, if they will place the problem in proper perspective. It was not Q's homosexual orientation that needed therapeutic confrontation; it was the potential strength of the relationship that had to be emphasized, and every therapeutic effort was devoted to expanding this potential. Once Q realized what he had in his relationship with his wife, his homosexual orientation was neutralized by his own choice.

CASE REPORT: COUPLE 10

R was a 30-year-old Kinsey 6 when seen in therapy. He was accepted in treatment with his wife of 18 months. They had married after full disclosure of R's prior sexual orientation, but they had been unable to consummate their marriage.

R's family background was one of both security and trauma. R was the third and last child (all boys) in a middle-class family. His brothers were 11 and 8 years older. As a youngster, he remembers feeling either left out or in the way. He could not recall any instance of affectionate interchange between his parents, nor did he feel particularly close to either mother or father. His much older brothers were no source of identification or support. R's was indeed a lonely childhood.

When R was 11, his father died, and when he was 14, his mother remarried. By this time both older brothers had left the home, and R was truly rather than theoretically an only child. During both marriages, R's mother was continuously involved in volunteer work. R recalled that she was rarely at home during the day and was infrequently there in the evenings. R's stepfather accompanied her to the evening meetings and social activities only part of the time. The remainder of the time he was home with R.

R had an introvertive personality, limited social interests, and no sense of social comfort. He had few friends, male or female, while in school. He read a lot, was very much involved in music as a pianist, and earned excellent grades.

R's family was strongly committed to the Jewish religion and were active members of a conservative synagogue. It was in this environment that his mother and stepfather had met, courted, and married.

When R was 15, his stepfather showed him how to masturbate, and shortly thereafter R and his stepfather were actively engaged in mutual masturbation and then in partner manipulation. Their interaction continued on a once- or twice-a-week basis until R finished high school. During this time, R had no social activity with nor could he recall any interest in girls.

When R went to college, his interaction with his stepfather was confined to an occasional weekend or vacation, so R sought out other homosexual opportunities. He was successful in his search, and, fortified by his positive experiences, continued as a completely committed homosexual after he left college. When in need, he cruised the local bars and the public toilets wherever he was located. He thoroughly enjoyed fellatio and on a few occasions was the penetratee in anal intercourse. He never sought the role of penetrator.

R had several jobs, two of which he lost when his ill-concealed homosexual orientation was identified. At 26, he decided to return to academic life for postgraduate work in psychology and was successful in entering a postgraduate program on a fellowship.

His social exposure to women had been negligible. When he thought it necessary as a camouflage, he occasionally took women to dinner or to other social events but never involved himself sexually beyond the level of a goodnight kiss. To protect himself from any possible sexual demands, he rarely had more than two dates with the same woman.

When R was 28 he met a young woman (23) who also was a very

talented pianist. They had so much in common that R broke his two-date rule gladly. In brief, R and the young woman fell in love. But whenever she vigorously pushed for sexual involvement, he just as vigorously retreated. After about three months of steady companionship and of sexual advance and retreat, the young woman confronted R. She told him that she loved him but believed him to be homosexual, and she begged him to seek help, stating that she wanted to marry him.

Overwhelmed with this burst of warmth and offer of commitment, something he had never encountered in his life, R told the woman the details of his sexual orientation. The woman, in turn, reported a moderate amount of sexual experience with four different men. After their mutual confession, the two people decided to try to solve their own problem.

Despite living together for 10 months and then living as man and wife for 18 months, and despite every sexual effort on his wife's part, R could not achieve or maintain an erection of sufficient quality to consummate his marriage.

The couple applied to the Institute for support. When accepted into therapy, R was a sexually functional homosexual and a primarily impotent heterosexual. His wife described herself sexually as a fully functional woman.

From a therapeutic point of view, it was unfortunate that the couple had tried to resolve their own problem. Not only did they fail, but after the repeated episodes of failure with his wife trying time after time to force an erection, R had developed severe fears of performance and had become a constant spectator at every sexual opportunity. His wife had separately developed fears for his sexual performance and had become a confirmed spectator herself.

R also had begun comparing himself negatively with the men with whom his wife had been active sexually, even though he had never met them. Not only was R jealous, but he also developed an acute sense of inferiority in his masculine role socially. He had never had such feelings of inadequacy before.

Treatment was initiated by attempting to neutralize the negative input from the coital failures that had occurred while husband and wife were trying to treat themselves. Both R and his partner became fully involved in sensate-focus experiences. As their nonverbal communication improved, the concept of using the partner's body for one's own pleasure, not to arouse the partner sexually, got through to R's wife. She learned to stop trying to force an erection and so did he. R learned the basics of female anatomy, female sexual physiology, and female psychosexual needs. The information was amplified with his wife's full cooperation.

In addition to his acquired fears of sexual performance, R had other fears that needed confrontation. He had been fearful of the sexual unknown from the outset of his marriage. With his anxieties about woman's sexual responses reasonably resolved, R's performance fears were satisfactorily neutralized and both partners' spectator roles were resolved.

R's wife was a vital element in therapy. She made every effort to support, educate, and interact, but she never ridiculed R's homosexual orientation or joked about his complete lack of heterosexual experience. Through this approach by his wife, R's jealousy and sense of sexual and personal inferiority were rapidly neutralized.

R was never told he must convert to heterosexuality. He was only assured that he could do so if there seemed to be sufficient value for him in the transition. He did convert. He began functioning successfully in intercourse on the tenth day of therapy. The follow-up of this couple has been uneventful. The family has children, R is having a successful career as a clinical psychologist, and both partners describe an effective marriage.

Obviously, this storybook type of history is the exception, not the rule, in any sexual partnership between a Kinsey 6 man and a Kinsey 0 woman. As emphasized before, the limitations in ability to convert or revert to heterosexuality are dependent not only upon the degree to which the client is motivated to become subjectively involved in heterosexuality, but also upon the rewards potentially available from such a conversion.

Lest there be any illusion that therapy for male homosexual dissatisfaction always turns out well, a brief discussion of a complete clinical failure is in order.

CASE REPORT: COUPLE 11

S was 28 years old and a Kinsey 6 when seen in therapy with his casual female partner. He had been accepted in response to his request for psychotherapeutic support during an attempt to convert to heterosexuality.

S was the middle child in a family of three children. He had two sisters, one three years older and another two years younger than himself.

His mother was in full control of the family. The father was described by S in retrospect as both passive and ineffectual. He earned an adequate living for the family but in return was essentially ignored.

The family's religious commitment was Catholic. His mother was very active in her church. His father rarely attended services.

S did not remember his childhood with any sense of pleasure. He was overweight and uncoordinated, and he intensely disliked any manner of physical contact. His mother dressed him carefully, constantly demanding that he not get his clothes dirty. S was essentially rejected by his male peers, who called him a sissy. He responded by withdrawing from male social interchange.

S spent his formative years believing himself to be fully committed to the priesthood. Once past his first year in high school, however, he gave up the idea of a life of religious commitment. During this time he became increasingly afraid of male companionship, yet he secretly admired the muscles of the football heroes. He was labeled a "fairy" long before he understood the connotation of the term. His manners were impeccable, his teachers applauded his academic efforts, and he was generally miserable in school.

Aside from his sisters' friends, he knew no girls. When S finished high school he had had no social or sexual experience. He spent one year in college at a similar asocial level. Then he decided to work in television, left college, and was successful in obtaining a job in the production side of the profession. As the years passed, his career prospered.

S first attempted masturbation at age 16. He was unsuccessful and despite frequent effort was not able to masturbate successfully until just after he graduated from high school. He never approached a girl or a boy sexually while he was in school, nor was he ever approached sexually to his knowledge.

When S was 22 he became strongly attracted to a young man his age who also had a history of serious difficulties with social interaction when he was in school. The two friends filled obvious gaps in each others' lives. After about a year of close companionship, the friend approached S sexually one night and manipulated him to ejaculation. S thoroughly enjoyed the experience, and within a month the two men were living together. The men continued to be active sexually almost on a daily basis, and both were most pleased with the companionship and sense of closeness that neither man had ever experienced previously.

S began interacting with other men sexually about a year and a half after he and his friend started living together. There were no reported sexual difficulties, nor did his friend offer any objection, for he was enjoying the same state of sexual freedom. Both men felt that they had missed a lot socially as they went through school and were determined to make up for some of their lack of sexual experience.

When S was 27 he approached a younger member of the firm where he worked, and this man reported S to the head of the firm. S was terrified that he might lose his employment. He denied all homosexual intent, and to prove his point, he began an active dating pattern with young women in the office. This change in social behavior marked S's first social experiences with women. One night one of the women openly approached S sexually, and this terrified him. Not only was there no erection, but S apparently had what can best be described as a severe anxiety attack.

He realized the need for professional help and applied to the Institute for support. S stated simply that he would have to learn to function heterosexually if he was to survive socially and professionally. He also felt cheated by his lack of prior heterosexual experience. When conversion therapy was requested, it was explained that the Institute did not treat homosexual men without female partners. In addition, it was pointed out that there must be some opportunity for regular sexual activity after the acute phase of treatment was terminated; just the cooperation of a female partner during the acute phase of treatment would be of little value.

S decided to continue an overt heterosexual social life, protecting himself against sexual approaches if possible, until a cooperative partner could be found that he felt he could trust. He had a few homosexual experiences, but they were conducted far from his place of employment. This search for a female partner in therapy with whom he could continue sexual activity afterward took almost a year. When S was 28, he reapplied for therapy with a female partner of choice. His apparent persistence in searching for an available partner distracted the research team from the deeper issues in the case, and he was accepted in therapy.

The acute phase of treatment was completely unsuccessful. S not only had no frame of reference for heterosexual activity, he also became extremely anxious at the thought of any manner of sexual interaction with a woman. He knew unequivocally that he would never be able to function in intercourse and was certainly able to prove himself right. Although he had full cooperation from his female partner, S never had an erection during the acute phase of the treatment program. His fears of performance were never significantly reduced, and if anything, his levels of anxiety increased during therapy. In addition to his sexual dysfunction, he evidenced severe sexual aversion to the female body. This aversion also seemed to increase as therapy continued. The program was terminated by the therapy team at the end of the first week of the two-week acute phase of treatment. It was patently obvious that an error had been made by accepting S into therapy. To continue treatment would have been to threaten S's psychosexual security.

The entire problem was discussed at length with S. The research team's failure in therapy was openly acknowledged, and it was pointed out that his was a far more stable personality when he was psychosexually comfortable as a homosexual than when he was extremely anxious and increasingly aversive as a potential heterosexual. There was no indication that he needed therapeutic support in his homosexual status, but it was suggested that he might profit from short-term professional support for the psychosocial insecurities that had developed as the result of his failure to convert to heterosexuality. He accepted the Institute's offer in this regard.

S returned to homosexuality, and his anxieties disappeared. He followed specific suggestions that he be far less overt in his sexual solicitations and restrict his heterosexual social commitments to business demands only. With a few clearly defined but modest alterations in his lifestyle to protect against any manner of heterosexual pressure, he has had no further social or professional difficulties to date.

While S's theoretical motivation to change his sexual preference may have been strong, his fears of failure and his aversion to the female person were far stronger. Actually, the extreme level of his anxiety about heterosexual involvement had not been correctly determined by the research team during the intake interview. Thus, not only did the therapy fail, it should not have been attempted. Instead, S should have been counseled with suggestions to improve his sociosexual behavior as a homosexual.

This typical case report of a fully oriented Kinsey 6 homosexual man has been presented to underscore the divergence of sexual orientations in our culture. There are any number of Kinsey 0 men who would have anxiety attacks if they thought they might have to interact sexually with another man; and there are also a large number of men who, like S, might have anxiety attacks at the thought of sexual interaction with a woman. Neither should ever be pressured to interact sexually in a manner that poses such a threat to personal security.

DISCUSSION

A brief discussion of the general principles involved in conversion and reversion therapy is in order. Certainly, each case must be individualized and the therapeutic approach frequently drastically altered, not only at outset but at different times during the course of the treatment program. Without this flexibility in therapeutic approach, treatment programs for homosexual dissatisfaction are doomed to a high percentage of failure.

There are a few basic "don'ts" in conversion and reversion therapy that should constantly be borne in mind by the reacting therapist, regardless of his or her level of professional flexibility.

The therapist constantly must be aware that there are any number of good reasons for the individual to seek change in a homosexual orientation. For example, there may be the real or implied threat of social rejection or a constant concern for job security. Of course, the reasons for requesting conversion or reversion therapy must be defined, but in the process, the man's prior sexual experience should never be devalued. His sexual facility as a homosexual is his current security blanket. If the therapist suggests that homosexuality is a psychosocially unacceptable way of life to a man who is in the midst of attempting to alter his sexual value system, the client tends to move to heterosexual expression with a sense that all bridges have been burned. He has the impression that he *must* succeed in therapy in the immediacy of the present or that his life will have little or nothing to offer in the future. Denigration of homosexual preference by the therapist may create unacceptable pressure from a presumed requirement for immediate success in the mind of a man already gravely concerned with his fears for effectiveness of heterosexual performance.

If a man's motivation for alteration in sexual preference is high and there is a cooperative female partner available, reversion to heterosexuality can best be accomplished by concentrating on neutralizing or even removing the psychosocial roadblocks to effective heterosexual interchange. Once functioning with an increasing degree of sexual effectiveness, the man must be allowed to make his own sex-preference decision. By the simple expedient of realizing that he now has two ways to go, he can decide for himself which road offers the greater reward. Such an opportunity for an open, unpressured decision promises far more permanence to the alteration of sexual preference than any attempt at reversion or conversion therapy under the presumed threat of an all-or-nothing approach. A change in role preference has a far better chance of permanence if it comes as the result of the client's decision rather than as the result of a therapist's imposition.

As is true for most men, the homosexual male is made anxious by that which he does not understand or by a situation that makes him feel insecure because of his lack of knowledge or experience. In a quiet, comfortable manner, the therapists must thoroughly educate the male homosexual in female anatomy and sexual physiology and answer any questions he may have about the female's psychosexual attitudes. This information is far more effectively received if it is presented by a female therapist.

The role of the female partner in male conversion or reversion therapy is difficult. The therapist must always keep in mind the trauma she may possibly be experiencing. Her cooperation in therapy depends in large degree on her level of understanding of the treatment process. This is one of the important reasons why the committed or casual female partner typically should be made aware of the homosexual man's background. Once informed, she will not expect the usual level of sexual knowledge from her partner nor anticipate any real evidence of sexual comfort or effective sexual performance at the outset of their relationship or early in therapy. However, the therapist must always individualize the case. In certain situations in which the potential exists for high levels of trauma to the relationship because of disclosure of historical material that may *not* be critical to the progress of therapy, it may be necessary to modify this strategy.

In short, during therapy for reversion or conversion to heterosexuality, the man's prior homosexual orientation is deemphasized. He is never told he must decide between homosexuality and heterosexuality. Only when the psychosexual roadblocks have been reasonably neutralized or even removed, and only when he has been able to function sexually as a heterosexual, is he then encouraged to make his own choice of sexual orientation. After he has had the opportunity to consider the pros and cons of each sexual preference, the therapists stand ready as a reference source to discuss these pros and cons. The therapists never pressure the client for a preference decision.

In response to these treatment principles, some men have returned to homosexuality, some now function with sexual ambivalence, but most of the men treated for conversion or reversion have decided upon a full heterosexual commitment and have apparently maintained that commitment (see Chapter 17).

PARTNERS IN THERAPY

For decades therapeutic effort has been directed toward reversion or conversion of sexual preference on the one-to-one basis of direct interaction between client and therapist. In general, the results have been far less than satisfactory, but valuable lessons can be learned from these published experiences of the pioneers in the field.

The Institute's therapeutic approach has varied significantly from prior techniques. As has been emphasized repeatedly, no homosexual male or female is treated for conversion or reversion without the support in therapy of a partner of the *opposite* sex. These men and women make a vital contribution to the effectiveness of therapeutic procedure.

When the homosexual can immediately put into practice suggestions made by the therapist, when communicative techniques can be practiced in and out of the bedroom, when social or sexual mistakes can be corrected, performance anxieties neutralized, and vital information imparted, all on a daily basis, there is a significantly lower failure rate in treatment.

The casual or committed opposite-sex partner acts as a source of psychosocial support and information, and, if fully cooperative, provides opportunity for the client to react sexually in a nonpressured atmosphere. Since the partner is well aware of the client's problems, a significant portion of the multiple fears of performance is neutralized. These are anxieties that develop when the sexually distressed individual tries to hide his or her performance concerns from a partner.

Potential difficulties in the use of partners in therapy come from two major sources: (1) The therapists must retain adequate control of the casual or committed partner to keep the partner from assuming that he or she is yet another therapist. The distressed homosexual needs a partner in the bedroom as a source of warmth and support, but not as a coach. (2) It also must be constantly borne in mind that a casual partner who is cooperating only for the two-week period of the acute phase of therapy is of limited value. Of course, if another partner is immediately available, a satisfactory transition usually can be accomplished. But once the homosexually distressed client is functioning effectively in a heterosexual orientation, there should be no significant interruption in sexual opportunity for at least a two- or three-month period.

SUMMARY

This report of the treatment of 54 homosexual men for conversion or reversion to heterosexuality has been presented in some detail. Representative case reports have been made available. Specific case discussions and general considerations of the problems of both clients and therapist are reported. The statistical returns from the clinical treatment programs for homosexual male and female dissatisfaction are presented in Chapter 17.

16

FEMALE HOMOSEXUAL
DISSATISFACTION

During the 10-year period of clinical control, 13 homosexually oriented women were accepted by the Institute for treatment of sexual dissatisfaction. Three women were conversion candidates in the Kinsey 5 and 6 categories, while the remaining 10 women who gave Kinsey 3 and 4 preference histories were accepted as reversion applicants (see Table 16-1).

Thirteen is indeed a small number of clients to be treated over a 10-year period, but a total of only 16 lesbians applied for therapy. In fact, the number of women admitted to treatment is so small that the research team has been loathe to formulate any general conclusions in view of its limited experience in treating the sexually dissatisfied lesbian. During the same time period, four times as many men were treated for homosexual dissatisfaction.

The fact that so few women applied for treatment of homosexual dissatisfaction poses a number of questions. Were homosexual women more reluctant to request therapeutic support than men when considering transition to heterosexuality? Were homosexual women generally less interested in moving into a heterosexual orientation than men? When lesbians decided to move to heterosexuality, did they simply initiate heterosexual interaction without feeling any need for professional support?

There is no secure information to answer the questions of whether a lower percentage of active homosexual women than homosexual men decide to move to heterosexuality or whether the women are more reluctant than the men to seek professional guidance. There is some modest support for a positive answer to the question of whether a lesbian who decides to move to heterosexual orientation does so without any considered need for professional support.

The suggested answer is that she probably makes the transition on her own cognizance—unless she has good reason to anticipate complications. Each of the 13 homosexual women who were treated for sexual dissatisfaction had specific reasons to anticipate difficulties. Nine of the 10 women accepted for professional support in reversion therapy had a history of significant sexual dysfunction during prior heterosexual experience (see Table 12-3, Chapter 12). Five of the women had been sexually aversive in prior heterosexual encounters. In addition, 2 women were aversive in both homosexual and heterosexual interaction before requesting reversion therapy. Although the Kinsey 5 client who applied for conversion therapy also had been dysfunctional during prior heterosexual experience, the heterosexual opportunities had been too few in number to label this woman as heterosexually dysfunctional.

Every woman who applied to the Institute for professional support during her active attempt to revert to heterosexuality had a history of prior heterosexual dysfunction, sexual aversion, or a combination of the two distresses associated with heterosexuality. It was not surprising, then, that these women applied for psychotherapeutic support when they made a decision to revert or convert to a heterosexual orientation.

The marital status of the women clients was also a factor in their decision to solicit professional support for reversion attempts. Six women were married, and 1 woman had been living for seven years in a committed male/female partnership and was listed as married for reportorial ease. Four of these 7 married women were among the women described above as aversive to any form of heterosexual activity, and all 7 were heterosexually dysfunctional. All of the married women had been sexually active as homosexuals for periods ranging from two to nine years. Thus, it is apparent that the 10 women who applied for professional support during reversion attempts had reason to anticipate specific psychosexual impediments to heterosexual function.

Of the 3 women who applied for conversion therapy (Table 16-1), one woman, a Kinsey 6, had been living 11 years as a sexually active lesbian but had been primarily anorgasmic during this time. She finally decided that homosexuality had nothing to offer her sexually, found a man she wanted to live with, and asked for professional support during the transition period. Of course, she was fearful that she also would not be sexually responsive in heterosexual interaction.

Each of the other 2 women in the conversion category had been fully responsive sexually as lesbians. One woman (Kinsey 5) had experienced five prior heterosexual episodes during which she described herself as extremely anxious and occasionally nauseated; her comment was that she "felt nothing" during intercourse. The other woman, a Kinsey 6, had decided to try coitus twice but both times, before permitting penetration, withdrew from the sexual opportunity by complaining of nausea and faintness. On the basis of the severe levels of anxiety experienced during their few prior heterosexual opportunities, these women sought help in their conversion attempts. Each woman entered therapy with a male partner of choice.

While the numbers are small, these data suggest that homosexual women without sexual complications either during prior experience as heterosexuals or currently as homosexuals do not seek and probably rarely need professional support when they decide to alter their sex-preference roles.

There is another factor that tends to make female transition to heterosexuality less perilous than male conversion or reversion. The lesbian is not necessarily faced with immediate fears of performance when she voluntarily alters her choice of sexual orientation. She may be anxious, she may be fearful, she may even be aversive, but if she has been sexually responsive as a lesbian she rarely brings crippling fears of performance into the inevitable tensions associated with the alteration of her sexual patterns. Even the women in this report, all of whom had a history of some manner of heterosexual distress, did not exhibit high levels of performance fears.

Generally, the male homosexual, no matter how sexually effective he may have been as a homosexual, immediately reacts negatively to cultural performance pressures when he moves into heterosexual coital opportunity. When a man has lived, as the homosexual does, with the far more realistic concept that he has little, if any, responsibility for his partner's sexual function other than the obvious requirement for a certain amount of mutual cooperation, and then voluntarily moves to heterosexual commitment, the cultural pressures associated with the false concept that the man is primarily responsible for woman's sexual responsivity may prove severely demanding psychosexually; erective insecurity may then develop. Thus, homosexual men may be in greater need of professional support than homosexual women in their attempts to convert or revert to heterosexuality.

MOTIVATING FACTORS

One dominant factor motivated the small group of lesbians who sought assistance from the Institute for alteration of sexual preference. This was the factor of social pressure. For homosexual men, social pressures were evidenced by fear of public identification or the concomitantly implied threat to their job security. Not so for the women. The social pressures were primarily engendered by woman's cultural role in the maintenance of a marriage. Seven of the 13 women who applied for reversion treatment were married, and each of these married women stated that her decision to face alteration of her primary sexual orientation was a specific effort to either reconstitute or provide support for a committed marital relationship. Interestingly, only 1 woman expressed fear of public disclosure of her homosexuality. Lesbianism is usually either openly admitted or easily hidden from the public.

The remaining motivating factors were completely individualized among the unmarried women. One woman was concerned about job security. She had never been publicly identified as a lesbian but was extremely anxious that her homosexual orientation would become common knowledge. Another woman simply felt homosexuality had nothing to offer her and wanted to experiment with heterosexuality. Yet another woman formed a strong attachment to a heterosexual man and, despite a history of severe aversion in previous heterosexual experience, wanted help in reverting so she could live in a committed state with this man.

REFUSED APPLICATIONS

Three women who applied to the Institute for support of attempted reversion to heterosexuality were refused treatment (Table 16-1). One woman (Kinsey 2) was diagnosed as psychotic and referred to appropriate treatment. The Kinsey 3 woman actually did not need professional support to revert to heterosexuality with the man to whom she was fully committed. She wanted very much

TABLE 16-1

Dissatisfied Homosexual Female Population
(Total Applicants, N = 16; Applicants Accepted, N = 13)

	Reversion Candidates			Conversion Candidates		
	Kinsey 2	Kinsey 3	Kinsey 4	Kinsey 5	Kinsey 6	Total No.
Total applicants *	1	3	9	1	2	16
Applicants refused †	1	1	1	0	0	3
Applicants accepted	0	2	8	1	2	13
						(1968–1977)

* No Kinsey 1 women applied for treatment.
† Overall refusal rate, 18.8 percent.

for her desired marriage to succeed and had been pressured into requesting treatment by a concerned family that was fully aware of her previous ambivalence in sexual preference. She was counseled for her family-engendered anxieties and accepted the therapy team's position that further therapy was not really indicated. When the third woman (Kinsey 4) applied for treatment, she was involved in a major personality conflict with her committed lesbian partner of eight years. She had selected a man she scarcely knew as a partner and requested support in converting to heterosexuality. During evaluation it became apparent that she was deeply committed to both a homosexual orientation and to her lesbian partner. She was refused treatment for reversion. Instead, counseling was instituted for the distressed lesbian couple and they were able to resolve their personality conflicts. This woman was basically well adjusted as a homosexual, and once this was determined the therapy team encouraged her to remain committed to that sexual preference.

Of the 13 homosexual female applicants accepted for treatment of sexual dissatisfaction, 5 had requested therapy from other health-care facilities. Two had been refused treatment; 1 of the 2 women had been refused treatment on other occasions. Neither had been referred to another health-care facility. Three of the 13 women had been accepted in treatment, but all 3 terminated their therapy programs as unsatisfactory (see Table 12-6, Chapter 12). These statistics are not as prejudicial as those presented in Chapters 13, 14, and 15, but they do tend to support the Institute's position taken in prior discussions concerning the cultural bias of the health-care professions.

The 10-year case distribution of female homosexuals with complaints of sexual dissatisfaction is outlined in Table 16-2. As indi-

TABLE 16-2

Dissatisfied Homosexual Female Population (N = 13):
Distribution by Year During the 10-Year Clinical Control Period

Dissatisfaction Therapy	Year Treated										
	One	Two	Three	Four	Five	Six	Seven	Eight	Nine	Ten	Total
Reversion	0	2	1	1	2	0	1	2	1	0	10
Conversion	0	0	1	0	1	0	1	0	0	0	3
Total	0	2	2	1	3	0	2	2	1	0	13

(1968–1977)

cated in the table, 8 of the 13 women have been available to follow-up procedures for five years after termination of the two-week acute phase of treatment. A statistical review of the therapeutic results obtained during the acute phase of treatment and the problems of recidivism during the five-year follow-up period are presented in Chapter 17.

THERAPEUTIC PROCEDURE

Two case reports will be presented to exemplify the marked variance in problems that confront the therapist responding to requests made by sexually dissatisfied homosexual women for support in reversion or conversion to heterosexuality. After the case reports have been presented, the individual cases will be discussed briefly and general therapeutic concepts considered. As previously stated in Chapters 13, 14, and 15, there will be separate publication of a detailed discussion of the therapeutic process.

The general background and specific details of the psychosexual status of the two male heterosexual partners will not be presented. When specific information about the male partner is necessary to amplify the clinical picture, it has been provided.

CASE REPORT: COUPLE 12

T was a 31-year-old Kinsey 6 woman who applied to the Institute for professional support in her attempt to convert to heterosexuality. She entered treatment with a partner of her choice whom she expected to marry if the attempted conversion therapy was successful. T had lived an active lesbian life for 11 years and was still primarily anorgasmic. She had voluntarily decided that homosexuality had little to offer and had actively sought male companionship. Ten months later she was involved with a man of her choice and entered therapy.

T came from a middle-class family of modest financial circumstances. She was an only child. Her mother and father lived what T described as a dull marriage. Apparently there were few social outlets. The religious background was Protestant, and her parents maintained a moderately active involvement with the church. As soon as the required years of Sunday-school attendance passed, however, T avoided further religious involvement.

T described her father as warmer and more understanding than her mother. There was also the feeling that the mother was the disciplinarian while the father was obviously the more permissive parent. What T remembered more than anything else about her childhood was that she could not recall ever seeing a spontaneous demonstration of affection between her parents. Even perfunctory goodbye and hello kisses were not exchanged. Nor did she recall any physical contact with her mother. She did remember some occasions of sitting on her father's lap, but they were few in number.

T could not recall any significant amount of sexual interest until she was about 15 years old. She tried masturbating several times, but although it "felt good," she was not orgasmic. There were occasional dates with boys during high school, but she allowed no sexual activity beyond kissing and some breast play, neither of which she found particularly stimulating. She was a moderately successful student, reasonably popular with her peers, but she was not a "joiner."

When T graduated from high school, she worked at odd jobs for more than a year and then decided to enroll in secretarial training. She lived in a small town, so arrangements were made for T to move to a city in another state and live with an aunt while in training. The aunt was in her late thirties, had never married, had a good job, a pleasant apartment, and a number of friends, almost all female.

T worked hard each day in school and enjoyed her new freedom. Her aunt was very active socially and either had friends at the apartment or was out many evenings. T was pleased by the warmth of social acceptance exhibited by several of her aunt's friends.

When T finished secretarial training, her aunt offered her the use of the apartment while she was looking for a job or for as long as she wished to stay if she did not want to move back home. T accepted her offer, soon found a job, volunteered to share some of the expenses, and felt completely at home.

Previously, T had not given any thought to the fact that at least once a week a female friend stayed the night with her aunt. Since it was a two-bedroom apartment, T assumed that the friend who slept with her aunt did so because she (T) occupied the other bedroom.

One day T fell and strained her back, and that night her aunt gave her the first backrub she had ever had. There was welcome relief from the aches of the fall, but when the massages were repeated the next two nights T felt increasing sexual pleasure. She began lubricating so heavily she was afraid her aunt would notice. T offered no protest, so the backrubs continued for another week or 10 days before her aunt moved gently but firmly one night to genital manipulation, despite T's tentative objections. T was highly aroused sexually by the experience, but not orgasmic. In a brief period of time she was returning the backrub favor and responded to her aunt's careful coaching by manipulating her to orgasm. T was pleased when she observed her aunt's orgasmic responses. Her aunt assured her that she would reach a similar level of sexual response shortly, but that never happened.

T lived with her aunt for over two years before feeling the need to express her independence. She moved to her own apartment with the aunt's blessing. Her social life continued to involve the women to whom she had been introduced by her aunt, most of whom were lesbians. In the privacy of her own apartment she saw these women socially and accepted those with whom she wished to interact sexually. During sexual activity, she always became highly excited but was never orgasmic, regardless of the type of or the time spent in stimulative approaches provided by her friends. She repeatedly attempted masturbation but without orgasmic response.

T was consistently frustrated sexually. After one woman commented that she (T) took a long time to "come," she began to fake orgasm by behaving as she had seen her aunt and her friends act in response to her stimulation. As time passed, her pattern became one of applying sexual fakery quickly. This was done in order to cut down the time her casual companions had to spend stimulating her, since she knew she would be unable to respond effectively.

T lived for approximately 11 years as a sexually active lesbian without ever experiencing orgasmic release. For the last three years of this period, she became increasingly restless. In addition to her continuing sexual frustrations, she was also disturbed with what she felt was an entirely too restricted social life.

During the 11-year period, T's heterosexual experiences consisted of a few dates with several different men. When approachd sexually, she froze and would not cooperate. With her lack of sexual confidence T did not attract many men, and those that she occasionally did attract quickly withdrew after being overtly rejected sexually.

Finally, at age 30, T decided to abandon her familiar lesbian social structure and to move into heterosexual society for as long as it would be necessary to form some objective evaluation of the heterosexual lifestyle. It took several months of looking and some very anxious moments sexually before she met and was immediately attracted to a man in his late thirties who was recently divorced. He had two children who lived with their mother.

The couple soon were spending all of their time together. After a number of sexual approaches were made and parried, the man expressed concern. T, deciding to take a risk, told the man she was a virgin and then agreed to spend a weekend with him. She did not tell him of her lesbian orientation. Over the weekend the man, appreciating her obvious anxiety and presuming her fearful of loss of virginity, was as gentle as possible, but he could not penetrate. T was quite disturbed when the man finally ejaculated after a long-continued play period.

With the failure of a desired relationship at stake, T took an even greater risk, told the man her entire story, and begged his cooperation in helping to change her sexual orientation. The man, who by this time was fully committed to T, offered help in any way he could. The couple tried to consummate their relationship sexually on two other weekends but were unsuccessful. T was increasingly disturbed whenever the man ejaculated, and on the last occasion she became nauseated.

After their third failure at consummation, T asked the man if he would join her in treatment at the Institute. He agreed without reservation.

When seen in therapy, T was a primarily anorgasmic woman who also had a moderately severe degree of vaginismus. In addition, she described a sense of discomfort with seminal fluid.

The therapists' great advantage in treatment was, of course, the cooperative, committed, sexually experienced man T picked to accompany her in therapy. He was devoted to T and stated that despite her position that she would marry him only if treatment were successful, he wanted to marry her regardless of the outcome of the therapy program.

With T's full agreement, the man was made completely aware of the last 11 years of T's life. At first he found it very hard to believe she had never been fully responsive sexually as a lesbian, but he was most receptive to supporting the attempted sex-preference transition in every way possible.

The initial step in therapy was to draw T's attention to her aunt's backrub approach, and she was questioned in great detail. What had pleased? Had she been anxious or frightened? If so, of what and when? How did she resolve her conflicts, if any?

The full story was that she had loved the backrubs, was highly excited sexually, confused by the strength of her sexual feelings, but then terrified when her aunt insisted on playing with her genitals. She felt ashamed and guilty that she had liked what happened and felt morally weak when she continued to cooperate with repeat performances. T apparently became quite anxious when pressured into approaching her aunt physically, but she was openly intrigued when the aunt was readily multiorgasmic and freely verbalized her orgasmic attainment.

With this information, T was introduced to sensate-focus therapy with the man's full cooperation. Initially, the genitals of both partners were declared off limits. T's return to sensual pleasure began by using her partner's body for her own pleasure and allowing the partner access to her body for his pleasure.

When confidence and pleasure in sensate focus had been attained, the genitals were included in the touching and the vaginismus was treated as described in *Human Sexual Inadequacy* (1970). First T and then her partner inserted the plastic dilators in graduated sizes until the involuntary vaginal spasm was overcome.

The entire process of neutralizing both her dislike of seminal fluid and her vaginismus took 10 days, during which T and her partner slowly increased their degree of mutual sexual involvement by nondemanding approaches to the genital organs. On the afternoon of the tenth day, after T had finished inserting the vaginal dilators, she lay on the bed resting. There was no sexual activity at the time, but she suddenly experienced her first orgasm. She was frightened, did not know what had happened to her, but fortunately was with a sexually experienced man who thought he recognized the signs of orgasm. T was in tears when later reassured by the female therapist that she had simply experienced her birthright of sexual expression.

That night T tentatively approached her partner sexually and had intercourse for the first time without any distress. She was orgasmic in response to manipulation the next day, and about three weeks after termination of the acute phase of treatment was orgasmic during intercourse.

Although by definition the man had to be labeled a casual partner, since the couple had no formal commitment, he was far from casual in his approach to T. He was quiet, confident, and comforting. Without his full cooperation a positive therapeutic result would have been most unlikely.

Aside from her most cooperative partner, T's support in her altered preference role came from the female therapist. Every step of the treatment program was explained in detail. Such questions as what was to be looked for and what was to be gained were answered in detail. Fears were analyzed, anxieties explained, and female anatomy and sexual response patterns discussed repeatedly. T's fears of performance, both homosexual and heterosexual, were approached directly. Her problems of vaginismus and dislike of seminal fluid were also dealt with primarily by the female therapist.

As the treatment program progressed, training in the arts of communication posed no problem for the couple, particularly since the bedroom aspects of the communicative interchange went so well. The male therapist's responsibility was to keep the male partner informed as to the details of the treatment process, suggest attitudinal approaches to the complexities of T's transition process, evaluate treatment progress, and educate and explain as the therapy program unfolded. Every effort was expended to maintain the male partner as an effective adjunct in therapy. Care also was taken to be sure that he did not become a third therapist.

Understandably, the debate in this case might center on whether T was ever fully homosexually oriented. As is usual in most reversion and in a few conversion cases, a good argument could be made for either side of the fence. On the one hand, T had freely interacted sexually on many occasions with a number of women using and responding to every type of homosexually oriented physical approach. She had thoroughly enjoyed releasing her female partners and was sexually excited by the process. For years she was fully involved socially in a lesbian orientation and had no interest in male companionship. She had never been sexually responsive to men. She had found male company socially unstimulating, and, on a few occasions, sexually threatening. In fact, she had developed vaginismus and a dislike of seminal fluid.

On the other hand, she had been quietly but firmly seduced into homosexual activity and had never been fully sexually responsive to women. After 11 years, she had openly rejected a female-oriented society and voluntarily sought heterosexual experience.

In any event, T ultimately chose heterosexuality and, despite her inexperience, was extremely fortunate in her choice of the man with whom she was to share her life.

Follow-up information records that T is freely responsive sexually. The couple has married and T has had her first child. She does not describe the slightest interest in homosexual activity.

CASE REPORT: COUPLE 13

V was a 32-year-old Kinsey 4 woman who had been married for over three years when seen in therapy. Her husband was reluctant to accompany her in treatment because he felt that the relationship was at an end. He entered therapy only as a favor to his wife.

V's family history was that of a turbulent home. Her mother and father were constantly at war. She recalled that her parents never seemed to agree on any subject. As a young girl she frequently got conflicting messages from her parents and also noted that there were different directions given to her brother who was three years younger. Her father increasingly spent longer time periods out of the home and when V was 12, filed for a divorce and married another woman. He rarely saw his children after the divorce and remarriage. Two years later he moved to a different section of the country and had little continuing contact other than minimal financial support. There was no identifiable religious influence in the home.

V's mother started working, frequently at two jobs. V, as the older sibling, at 13 was left in charge of the home and her brother. Since having to keep house and care for her brother severely restricted her social opportunities while in high school, V usually had girlfriends coming to her house. With no supervision, there was unlimited sexual freedom. V and two of her friends frequently showed each other how they masturbated and in time began manipulating each other.

V thoroughly enjoyed the sex play and, in addition, continued to masturbate frequently in private. She didn't remember when she was first orgasmic, but she was fully responsive during the play episodes. Actually, during her socially deprived years, masturbation was her principal source of entertainment and was enjoyed on at least a daily basis.

V was an attractive girl. When she did date a boy and allowed petting, the boy could never satisfy her as she did herself or as her two friends were doing. At 16 she had her first coital experience. It not only was unanticipated, it was unappreciated. There had been a petting session during which she had not been aroused sexually. The boy suddenly forced his penis into the vagina and ejaculated. There was some physical distress, but she was more enraged than pained. However, her anger turned to anxiety when she bled and continued to bleed during the night. The next morning, her bed soaked with blood, she told her mother what had happened. She was taken to the hospital, and a small bleeding site in the ruptured hymen was sutured.

The surgery was minor in character. The trauma was not. Her angered mother confronted the boy's parents to no avail, but as a consequence word of the event soon spread through her peer group. She was severely embarrassed and resolved never to let "that" happen again. It didn't—for many years.

After this episode, V refused all dates until the boys stopped calling. At 17 she dropped out of high school half-way through her junior year and began working at odd jobs during the day. After leaving high school, she only interacted socially with the women who worked with her. She became more aggressive sexually, learned to be carefully selective, and usually had at least one available friend with whom she could interact sexually.

By the time V was 20 years old, she was living in a rooming house, providing her own support, and cruising gay bars for sexual partners when in need.

As she grew older, she entered three separate, continuing lesbian relationships that lasted significant lengths of time. In each instance, she felt fully committed to the other woman at the outset of the relationship. The briefest commitment lasted about six months, the longest for over four years.

During this time, most of the few social relationships she had with men were with homosexual men. She did recall that two different half-hearted attempts at intercourse with one man were unsuccessful; she could not cooperate for fear she might be hurt and bleed again. The two fiascos left her with even less interest in sexual interaction with men.

When V was 28 years old, she met a junior executive in the manu-facturing firm where she was working. Their relationship was at first casual, for a few weeks quietly social, and then, with real apprehension on V's part, overtly sexual. The man could not penetrate when attempt-ing intercourse. V told him of her traumatic coital episode as a teenager, but not of her lesbian orientation. The man suggested a visit to a doctor, and V complied. She was told that there was no physical reason why she couldn't have intercourse. Again, the couple tried intercourse, but the man still could not penetrate. They attempted to terminate the relationship but soon found that they were too strongly attracted to each other to separate, so they decided that things would work out sexually if they took their time.

They married six weeks later. It took another four weeks to consum-mate the marriage. During the first three months of the marriage V was extremely anxious every time they had intercourse. There was no real pain, but since she lubricated poorly, there was a good deal of vaginal irritation. V found herself hoping each coital episode would terminate quickly. She felt little sexual stimulation and, in a matter of months, was regularly using artificial lubrication and had assumed a completely passive role physically during intercourse. She frequently masturbated in private, but this didn't seem to bring sufficient relief to her sexual tensions.

Her husband, aware that V was experiencing little sexual pleasure during intercourse, frequently tried to develop sexual release through manipulation or cunnilingus, but these approaches also failed to provide sexual satisfaction.

V was severely frustrated sexually, and after six months of marriage began to visit gay bars occasionally. Whenever she had a cooperative woman as a partner, sexual release was readily accomplished and V was fully satiated.

The marriage continued in this manner for about three years. V was frequently depressed, and there were increasingly longer intervals be-tween the marital unit's sexual episodes.

Approximately four months before requesting therapy, V was seen entering the apartment of a known lesbian by a friend of her husband's who told him of the occasion. When quietly confronted, V not only freely admitted the episode but then told her husband that she was fully committed to a lesbian orientation. They agreed to divorce and separated.

A month later V asked her husband to accompany her in treatment so that she could learn to function sexually as a heterosexual woman. She said that she was fearful of being unable to alter her lesbian status, but also felt handicapped in being without freedom of choice, since she had no history of a satisfactory heterosexual experience.

Reluctant to enter therapy, the husband agreed to accompany V as a last gesture to a marriage that he understood was to be terminated by mutual consent. Although the therapists were concerned that the husband might not cooperate fully, V's plea that if hers was to be a lesbian orientation, she wanted it to be by choice, not by default, was considered sufficient motivation for the Institute to accept the couple in treatment.

At first, the treatment program did not progress satisfactorily. As feared, the husband was not fully cooperative; despite the therapists' suggestions and appeals, he seemed to be just going through the motions. V, sensing this, was as unresponsive to his stylized sexual approaches as ever. Near the end of the first week in therapy, after preliminary attempts to alter this pattern had proved unsuccessful, the couple was directly confronted; it was suggested that they either spend the next week in an all-out attempt to provide V with the freedom of choice she sought or that they withdraw from the treatment program.

Thereafter the husband became far more cooperative, and V, recognizing the crucial nature of her situation, apparently altered her psychosexual attitudes almost overnight. The couple spent hours talking about their past lives—something they had never done—and V took the initiative of showing her husband what pleased her. She made a number of suggestions to improve his sexual techniques, which again was something she had not had the courage to do previously. She had always been afraid that he would raise the question of where she had acquired her sexual expertise if she coached him in his sexual approaches. He proved an apt pupil, for V was orgasmic with manipulation two days later.

This breakthrough pleased V and delighted her husband. It was the first time that he had seen his wife obviously sexually involved and fully sexually responsive. His mental picture of V had been of an initially somewhat anxious and subsequently completely passive sexual partner who was intent only on providing sexual service as a "good" wife should. He told V how personally rejected he had felt by her sexual behavior patterns. She had no idea that he had felt denigrated as a person by her "let's get it over with" attitude.

Her feelings of rejection had not been directed to him as an individual but to his sexual clumsiness in comparison to the sexual effectiveness of her lesbian partners. He, of course, had no idea of the fact that he was living with direct sexual competition, nor of the nature of the competition.

After the manipulative orgasmic experience, V's performance fears and spectator roles that previously had been such constant companions during intercourse could be approached with some hope of therapeutic reversal.

Within 48 hours V was feeling comfortable with intercourse, lubricating well, and "feeling something." When therapy terminated, V was orgasmic regularly with manipulation, occasionally with cunnilingus, and was responding pleasurably during intercourse.

The couple moved back together a week later. Their sexual involvement has continued to prove satisfactory to both partners. V has only been orgasmic occasionally with intercourse, but she frequently initiates sexual interaction and plays a very active role. Her husband has been consistently receptive to her requests for sexual release. Occasionally he needs direction when approaching her sexually. She gives it freely, and he accepts it gracefully. V states that she has no interest in further lesbian experience. Since the full five-year follow-up period has not yet been completed, no final conclusions can be drawn in this regard.

This case report has been selected as reasonably representative of the majority of the women who asked the Institute for professional support during requested reversion therapy. Eight of the 13 applicants accepted in therapy had a Kinsey 4 preference rating. There was a history of a significant amount of heterosexual experience, but it usually was considered of little value by the women involved or actually had been a series of traumatic episodes. There was considerable variation in whether lesbian opportunity had been experienced as an original sexual outlet or lesbian interests had been kindled when the heterosexual aspects of the women's lives resulted in sexual and/or social disappointments.

DISCUSSION

Generally, the women seeking reversion to heterosexuality have been unresponsive to or fully rejecting of heterosexually oriented stimuli in prior sexual experience. This lack of heterosexual responsivity has been created by a variety of factors. The most frequently stated factors were: (1) psychosocial rejection of the particular men in whom the woman had been interested; (2) lack of sufficient male sexual expertise in providing the woman with effective sexual opportunity; (3) apparent disinterest on the man's part in providing his female partner with sexual release; (4) male use of the female partner sexually with little or no regard for either her personal or sexual needs; (5) long-continued physical or psychological abuse of the woman; and (6) either lack of sexual interest on the man's part or deliberate withholding of sexual opportunity from the woman as a means of punishment.

Of course, there were many other etiologic factors leading to the rejection of a heterosexual role. The lesbian role was described as preferable because women reported that it was not only more sexually stimulating, but it was psychosocially more enhancing to the individual. Women in this study consistently reported that they experienced far more freedom for self-expression during their commitment to a lesbian orientation.

Therapy for those who wished to convert or revert to heterosexuality was primarily directed toward providing each female client with some opportunity for the self-expression she had grown to appreciate in her experience with lesbian society. By improving the communicative skills of both partners, the woman's inherent privilege of expressing herself as an individual was either initiated or enhanced, depending upon the psychosocial values preexistent within the relationship. If it was a committed relationship, the woman was usually extremely encouraged by her husband's altered receptivity to communicative exchange. If it was a casual relationship, the woman was pleased with the opportunity to be heard, to be given full freedom of self-expression, and, in short, to practice communicative interchange.

Emphasizing the potential advantages in woman's role as a fully social as well as an effective sexual partner has been the cornerstone of effective reversion therapy. It has given the female client the freedom of expressing her social and sexual value systems in a heterosexual partnership just as she consistently had been accorded this privilege in a homosexual relationship.

The therapeutic process has been one of pointing out the potential psychosocial advantages of and the specific psychosexual opportunities in the relationship brought to treatment. Both men and women have responded well to the Institute's controlled educational programs. The men had little frame of reference for appreciating woman's psychosexual needs. The women usually were contending with a background of objectionable heterosexual experience, and they had to have their negative sexual impressions neutralized and the usual "men are all alike" concepts dispelled.

Further detailed discussion of the advantage of working with a couple when one member of the unit seeks treatment for sexual dissatisfaction is superfluous. Nor is there further need to point out the distinct advantages of having a dual-sex team in control of the treatment program in these circumstances. These discussions have been presented previously to the health-care professions in other publications and reviewed in previous chapters of this clinical section. Suffice it to say that from a clinical point of view the use of the dual-sex team in treating problems of homosexual dissatisfaction as well as homosexual dysfunction represents a significant improvement over other therapeutic approaches.

Most homosexual women who applied for support in attempts to convert or revert to heterosexuality opted for an ongoing heterosexual relationship if within the relationship their status could be established as that of a partner, not merely a provider of sexual service. If the women who requested support in attempted reversion or conversion were satisfied psychosocially as well as psychosexually, they usually remained committed to a heterosexual lifestyle.

17

CLINICAL STATISTICS

From an academic point of view no investigative program, particularly one involving new clinical concepts and techniques, is considered complete until the investigators have made a reasonably detailed report to the health-care professions. As an integral part of this report, there must be appropriate discussions, not only of concepts and techniques, but of results returned from the therapeutic process. For these reasons, a brief statistical review is presented of the results of treatment of homosexual men and women for sexual dysfunction or dissatisfaction.

Before attempting statistical evaluation of the treatment programs, the Institute's position relative to the inherent value of statistics published in the field of psychosexual therapy should be restated. Statistics mean little in physiologic or psychological research if the statistician is attempting to establish levels of subjective responsivity to objective stimuli. Since the clinical interpreter cannot define with exactitude subjectively appreciated points A, B, or C, claims of statistically significant therapeutic success are unjustified when evaluating the interrelationships of these variables. On the other hand, treatment failures always loom large on any clinical horizon. If the clinical research errs on the side of conservatism, declaring as a treatment failure every unit involved in the program about which the slightest question of effective therapeutic progress exists, failure statistics become increasingly important. Therefore, statistical evaluation of therapeutic procedure in the 10 years of treatment for homosexual dysfunction or dissatisfaction will be considered only from the point of view of failure rates.

The preceding paragraph, a free quote from *Human Sexual Inadequacy* (1970), reiterates the Institute's position on the statistical

379

evaluation of treatment programs devoted to the reversal of human sexual inadequacies.

There always remain two unresolved questions when psychotherapists of any persuasion attempt to report therapeutic successes. First, what does constitute success in treatment for a particular psychosexual dysfunction, and second, who is to be the judge of successful treatment? Not only are criteria for judging clinical success ill-defined, but an even greater problem centers around the anointing of authority.

The therapist is the least acceptable authority to define levels of successful treatment in his or her own clinical program. There inevitably is uncontrolled judgmental bias if the therapist and the individual who evaluates the progress and records the successes of any therapy program are one and the same individual. What the therapist may see as a successfully completed treatment program, the client may consider in a different light. Has he or she really achieved what was wished for in treatment? Has the projected goal been reached? Or has the result been judged in the light of what the therapist told the client or clients was within the realm of treatment probability?

Nor should the client be the sole judge of success or failure of the therapeutic process. What real frame of reference, either theoretical or clinical, does he or she have in goal attainment? How can he or she have any objective perspective on the effectiveness of the therapeutic program? If the client wants the moon and stars from treatment and gets only the moon, the therapist may consider with professional justification that the therapeutic accomplishment was a job well done. With equal justification, the client may consider it a job half done.

If neither the therapist nor the client is consistently capable of providing an unbiased, objective report of therapeutic success, who is to evaluate clinical treatment programs? It must and should remain for professional peers to provide the ultimate evaluation of the success potential of any clinical treatment methodology. Can they reduplicate the effort with reasonable parallelism in results? This is the acid test of new or divergent clinical programs. Therefore, it is of utmost importance that the reported results of any clinical research program be made interpretable with relative ease.

If the subjective aspects of any particular psychotherapeutic process cannot be interpreted as treatment success with statistical security (and they cannot), what of treatment failure? Are we always sure of the extent and degree of our failures? *Emphatically not*— but there usually is more agreement between therapist and client on what constitutes failure than what constitutes success in the treatment process. What the therapist knows is almost unbelievable progress in treatment may be termed by the client as unsatisfactory— "not what I anticipated." What the client is delighted with as effective therapeutic progress, the authority may well realize is but a short-term gain at best. But both authority and client usually are in reasonable accord as to what constitutes either immediate or long-term treatment failure.

For these reasons, the Institute will follow the precedent it originally established in 1969 when reporting the results of the clinical research programs designed to develop treatment techniques for heterosexual inadequacies. The results of treating homosexual dysfunction or dissatisfaction will be described in terms of treatment failures rather than as estimates of therapeutic success. It must be emphasized that a 20 percent treatment failure rate should not automatically be converted into the suggestion that the therapy program was blessed with an 80 percent success rate. A 20 percent treatment failure rate means just that—and nothing more.

The same format employed in presenting and discussing therapy failures incurred during the heterosexual treatment programs will be used to report results of the homosexual treatment programs. But only a superficial comparison can be presented of results returned from treating men and women of the two sexual orientations, because there were too many clinical variables. For example, the patient population treated for homosexual inadequacies was far smaller than the total number of men and women treated for heterosexual distresses. In addition, sexual behavior patterns inherent in homosexual and heterosexual orientations necessitated separate definitions of sexual dysfunctions and dissatisfactions (see Chapter 12). Thus, similarities and differences between the therapy results returned from the two clinical populations can be generally appreciated from selective scrutiny but not with statistical security.

There are a number of other factors that must be taken into consideration in analyzing treatment failure data. The treatment of homosexual distresses has certainly been facilitated by the Institute staff's years of prior clinical experience with treatment of heterosexual inadequacy. It also is generally true that with one exception, the sexually dysfunctional homosexual man or woman does not face as difficult a problem in returning to effective sexual function as does the heterosexual. The one exception to this general rule, the primarily impotent homosexual male, will be discussed in context in the next section.

TREATMENT FAILURE STATISTICS
(DYSFUNCTION)

In reporting the clinical statistics returned from treating dysfunctional homosexual men and women, consideration will be given first to the failure rate encountered during the initial or rapid-treatment phase of the program. Second, the incidence of failure during the required five years of the follow-up program will be reported. And third, the overall treatment failure rate will be presented. This statistic has been established by combining the number of men and women who have initial treatment failures during the acute phase of therapy with the number of individuals who returned to dysfunction during the first five years after treatment.

When reporting initial treatment failures, N represents the total number of clients treated for the specific sexual distress; F, the number of immediate treatment failures with the rapid-treatment method; and IFR, the initial failure rate. For reference convenience, data will be summarized in numbered lists.

MALE DYSFUNCTION

1. *Primary Impotence:* $N = 5$; $F = 0$; $IFR = 0\%$.

The Institute treated 5 primarily impotent homosexual males during the rapid-treatment phase of the clinical program. Despite the lack of initial treatment failure, it generally has been more difficult to treat primary impotence of homosexual than heterosexual orientation. While he does not have the added burden of functioning effectively during intercourse, the homosexual is usually the more psychosexually devastated of the two types of primarily impotent men, since by Institute definition he has not even been able to achieve and consistently maintain a full erection with masturbation and has never experienced orgasmic release in response to any form of direct sexual stimulation by self or partner. His only ejaculatory experience (if any) has been during nocturnal emissions. The primarily impotent homosexual client has not only been psychosexually dysfunctional, but he has consistently evidenced a significant degree of psychosocial pathology.

2. *Secondary Impotence:* $N = 49$; $F = 4$; $IFR = 8.2\%$.

The failure rate in the rapid treatment of secondarily impotent homosexual men is at an acceptable level. If the distressed man is seen with a cooperative partner, there is reason to expect an initial failure rate below 10 percent when treating this category of homosexual dysfunction. Levels of motivation are particularly important in treating secondary impotence, for they usually determine whether the impotence stays reversed during the posttreatment years of the follow-up period. Men frequently have more of a problem in maintaining their functional status after treatment than in regaining it during therapy.

3. *Situational Impotence:* $N = 3$; $F = 0$; $IFR = 0\%$.

Only 3 cases in this category of impotence were treated by the therapy team. There should be only a rare failure in this category of homosexual impotence. The additional distress of sexual aversion, which occasionally accompanies this type of male potency dysfunction, usually presents more problems in treatment than does reversal of this form of impotence. The category of situational impotence was not established during the heterosexual treatment program. At that time clients in this category were incorrectly identified as secondarily impotent.

4. *Ejaculatory Incompetence:* $N = 0$.

Although this complaint of sexual inadequacy must exist in the homosexual community, it was not encountered in the 10-year period of clinical control. Had the problem been presented, it would have been approached with the techniques originally described for the treatment of ejaculatory incompetence of heterosexual orientation.

The ejaculatorily incompetent homosexual should not be confused with the primarily impotent homosexual. While neither man has an orgasmic experience during overt sexual activity with a partner, the man with ejaculatory incompetence has the facility to maintain erections indefinitely; the primarily impotent homosexual does not. The ejaculatorily incompetent man can and does ejaculate during masturbation; the primarily impotent man cannot.

5. *Premature Ejaculation:* $N = 2$; $F = 0$; $IFR = 0\%$.

The treatment of premature ejaculation in the homosexual male population has not been presented or discussed in any detail. As noted in Chapter 12, homosexual men rarely registered the complaint of premature ejaculation with the research team. If too-rapid ejaculation is believed to be a functional problem by male homosexuals, it was not considered of enough importance to bring men to treatment. The complaint is reversed so easily that it does not necessitate the usual two-week, acute-treatment program. The reversal techniques employed are identical to those developed for treating the far more functionally handicapped heterosexual premature ejaculator. Usually, two or three counseling sessions will serve to resolve a problem of too-rapid ejaculation that might exist for a homosexual male. The same usually cannot be said for the heterosexual rapid ejaculator and his usually psychosexually traumatized female partner.

Because the complaint was rarely registered and its reversal easily accomplished without requiring admission to the formalized treatment program, the dysfunction will not be discussed further, nor will treatment results be included in the Institute's overall report of treatment failures. This material is only presented for reader information and reference convenience.

FEMALE DYSFUNCTION

6. *Primary Anorgasmia:* $N = 8$; $F = 1$; $IFR = 12.5\%$.

The most difficult problems in treatment are the client's extremely low levels of self-esteem, her overwhelming sense of inadequacy as a woman, and, of course, her fears of sexual performance.

These problems are present regardless of whether the primarily anorgasmic woman is homosexually or heterosexually oriented.

But the primarily anorgasmic lesbian has a better chance of complete symptom reversal than her heterosexual counterpart because she does not have the added requirement of orgasmic return during intercourse. In primary homosexual anorgasmia a low initial failure rate should be anticipated. There may be an additional complication, however: A high incidence of sexual aversion has been associated with primary anorgasmia in the Institute's small series of cases.

7. *Situational Anorgasmia:* $N = 15$; $F = 1$; IFR $= 6.7\%$.

An occasional situationally anorgasmic client presents approximately the same complications in treatment as that of primary anorgasmia, but generally the complaint is reversed with less difficulty. In fact, if there is an accompanying secondary diagnosis of sexual aversion, the latter clinical problem usually represents more of a therapeutic challenge than the problems associated with reversal of the basic complaint.

8. *Random Anorgasmia:* $N = 4$; $F = 0$; IFR $= 0\%$.

Random anorgasmia in the small series of lesbian clients was also frequently associated with the secondary complaint of sexual aversion. Presuming an adequate level of client motivation for alleviation of the random anorgasmic state and a cooperative partner in therapy, initial failure rates in treatment should be quite low.

9. *Vaginismus:* $N = 2$; $F = 0$; IFR $= 0\%$ (not treated).

Vaginismus was identified as a secondary diagnosis on only two occasions in the treatment of anorgasmic lesbians. The diagnosis can be firmly established only by adequate pelvic examination. Since its presence was of little consequence to anorgasmic lesbians, the condition was not treated directly when identified. In both cases of homosexual vaginismus, the women were also sexually aversive, so therapy was primarily directed toward the aversive state. As is true for the concerns of premature ejaculation, the presence of the distress in sexually dysfunctional lesbians is noted for reference ease, but since treatment was not indicated, these statistics will not be included in the overall treatment report.

SEXUAL AVERSION

There was a significant incidence of sexual aversion as a second-ary diagnosis during the treatment of male and female homosexual dysfunction. This sexual problem is not classified as a dysfunction, however. The statistics recorded below reflect the incidence of therapy failure in symptom reversal during the rapid-treatment pro-gram. N represents the number of cases of diagnosed sexual aver-sion; F, failure to reverse the symptoms; and FR, the failure rate during follow-up in the 10-year period of clinical investigation.

The numbers in parentheses represent the cases of each type of homosexual dysfunction treated as the primary diagnoses.

    10. *Male Sexual Dysfunction*   *Aversion*
        a. Primary impotence (5): $N = 1; F = 0; FR = 0\%$
        b. Secondary impotence (49): $N = 2; F = 0; FR = 0\%$
        c. Situational impotence (3): $N = 1; F = 0; FR = 0\%$

    11. *Female Sexual Dysfunction*   *Aversion*
        a. Primary anorgasmia (8): $N = 3; F = 0; FR = 0\%$
        b. Situational anorgasmia (15): $N = 1; F = 0; FR = 0\%$
        c. Random anorgasmia (4): $N = 2; F = 0; FR = 0\%$

Four instances of homosexual male sexual aversion and 6 in-stances of homosexual female sexual aversion were identified as sec-ondary diagnoses during treatment of the primary complaints of sexual dysfunction. There was a far higher incidence of sexual aver-sion identified in the sexually dysfunctional lesbian population than in the dysfunctional male clients. The aversive symptoms were re-versed without treatment failure. Since statistics from this category of sexual distress were not recorded during the investigation of het-erosexually oriented sexual inadequacy reported in *Human Sexual Inadequacy*, the failure-rate statistics will not be included in those of the overall treatment program for homosexual inadequacy.

SUMMATION STATISTICS (DYSFUNCTION)

The totals of the initial treatment failures and the failure rates in the rapid-treatment phase of the therapy programs for homo-sexual dysfunction are listed below. For reference convenience, the totals are separated first by sex and then recorded as a total research population.

12. *Total Male Dysfunction:* $N = 57$; $F = 4$; $IFR = 7.0\%$.

13. *Total Female Dysfunction:* $N = 27$; $F = 2$; $IFR = 7.4\%$.

Accumulation of the initial failure rate statistics supports the Institute's 21-year contention that there should be no significant clinical difference in the overall failure rates returned from treating sexually dysfunctional men and sexually dysfunctional women. This position presumes that the dual-sex team is employed as a basic ingredient of the treatment program and that the sexually dysfunctional individual is accompanied in therapy by a partner of choice. This lack of a clinically significant differential in treatment failure statistics between the two sexes was first reported in *Human Sexual Inadequacy.*

14. *Total Male and Female Dysfunction:* $N = 84$; $F = 6$; $IFR = 7.1\%$.

The initial failure rate of 7.1 percent in the treatment of dysfunctional homosexual men and women is an acceptable figure. The initial treatment failure rate should not rise above a theorized 10 percent level and probably will be lowered to the 5 percent area as more clinical experience is acquired. It must be emphasized that this figure only represents the treatment failures that developed during the acute phase of the therapy program. To these failures of clinical treatment must be added those incidences of treatment reversal that occurred during the required five-year follow-up period before an overall treatment failure rate for homosexual dysfunction can be determined.

In order to present significant follow-up information, there should be a large number of cases available that can be carefully evaluated to determine rates of treatment reversal. The Institute cannot provide such information at this time. The fault is not that of lack of effective follow-up procedures, though there are always difficulties in any program of continuing clinical control. The Institute's basic difficulty is lack of numbers. There have been only a small number of male and female applicants for treatment of homosexual dysfunction and dissatisfaction. Over the 10-year period of clinical control the number of homosexual men treated for sexual dysfunction has only totaled 57; the corresponding figure for females is 27. Those treated for sexual dissatisfaction have totaled only 54 male and 13 female applicants. Since the applicant populations were small, every effort was expended to maintain adequate follow-up procedures for those men and women who were not immediate treatment failures.

Immediate treatment failures were referred directly to other sources of professional support. Since follow-up attempts might have proved distracting to the client's new treatment program and because the information returned could not be used statistically after other treatment modalities had been involved, no attempt has been made to follow the initial treatment failure group of male and female clients.

Statistics cited below refer to the number of clients who have reversed treatment gains and returned to their prior sexually dysfunctional status during the 10-year clinical control period. It is important to emphasize that since the final years of follow-up have not been completed, there may be other instances of return to a prior sexually dysfunctional state. Also recorded are the numbers of men and women lost to follow-up.

In Lists 15 and 16, N represents the number of men or women treated for sexual dysfunction over the 10-year control period. F identifies those men and women who were immediate treatment failures during the acute phase of therapy; TR, the known instances of treatment reversal during the required five-year follow-up period; and LF, the number of clients lost to follow-up in each of the dysfunctional categories.

15. *Male Sexual Dysfunction*
    a. Primary impotence: $N = 5; F = 0; TR = 1; LF = 1$
    b. Secondary impotence: $N = 49; F = 4; TR = 1; LF = 2$
    c. Situational impotence: $N = 3; F = 0; TR = 0; LF = 0$

One primarily impotent man became secondarily impotent and refused to continue follow-up one year after his acute treatment phase terminated.

One secondarily impotent man had the return of prior erective inadequacy and refused further treatment or referral to another professional source, but he has cooperated in routine follow-up procedures. Two secondarily impotent men have been lost to follow-up four and three years, respectively, after the acute-treatment phase. They reported functioning well sexually when last contacted.

16. *Female Sexual Dysfunction*
    a. Primary anorgasmia: $N = 8; F = 1; TR = 0; LF = 0$
    b. Situational anorgasmia: $N = 15; F = 1; TR = 1; LF = 1$
    c. Random anorgasmia: $N = 4; F = 0; TR = 0; LF = 0$

Among the original 27 women treated for homosexual dysfunction, 2 have experienced immediate treatment failures and there has been 1 instance of posttreatment return of symptoms when the woman lost a committed partner and turned to casual partners for sexual release. One previously situational anorgasmic woman was lost to follow-up two years after the rapid-treatment phase. She reported effective sexual function when last contacted.

FOLLOW-UP (DYSFUNCTION)

Only 3 homosexual men and 1 woman have been lost to follow-up in 57 male and 27 female cases of sexual dysfunction. Since a total of only 3 men and women reverted to prior states of sexual dysfunction during the same observation period, a significant return to dysfunction would not be anticipated among the 4 cases lost to follow-up. One individual, at the most, might be expected to have returned to dysfunction. One additional treatment failure would not alter the statistics to a clinically significant degree (from 10.7 percent to 11.9 percent).

As a statistical summary, the overall therapy failure rates that developed from treating homosexual men and women for sexual dysfunction are recorded in Table 17-1. The overall failure rate is a combination of the faliures that occurred during the acute treatment phase and those incurred during the required five years of follow-up observations after termination of the rapid-treatment program.

The program statistics reported in Table 17-1 are encouraging when it is realized that this level of treatment failure was attained in a pilot clinical program. The vast majority of cases were seen in therapy by the research team, which treated 78 of the total of 81

TABLE 17-1

Male and Female Homosexual Dysfunction:
Treatment Failure Statistics

Gender and Complaint	N	F	IFR (%)	TR	OFR (%)
Male					
Primary impotence	5	0	0	1	20.0
Secondary impotence	49	4	8.2	1	10.2
Situational impotence	3	0	0	0	0
Male total	57	4	7.0	2	10.5
Female					
Primary anorgasmia	8	1	12.5	0	12.5
Situational anorgasmia	15	1	6.7	1	13.3
Random anorgasmia	4	0	0	0	0
Female total	27	2	7.4	1	11.1
Male and female total	84	6	7.1	3	10.7

N = number of clients; F = initial treatment failures; IFR = initial failure rate; TR = treatment reversals; OFR = overall failure rate.

sexually dysfunctional homosexual couples. The remaining 3 couples were treated by other staff teams at the Institute.

Since there had been no prior professional experience with such treatment programs, mistakes were made that would not be repeated today. A great deal has been learned about patient management. For example, the ill-concealed levels of antagonism that the secondarily impotent man frequently exhibits toward the therapists are far easier to cope with since the devastating level of his social and sexual performance fears has been recognized. At least 2 of the 4 initial treatment failures to reverse secondary impotence (see List 2) should have been avoided. The therapists found real difficulty in maintaining their vital state of professional neutrality in the face of deliberate lack of cooperation with the therapy program. These professional mistakes were made early in the 10-year period of clinical control. It is not expected that they would be repeated at this time.

The overall failure rate (10.7 percent) for the treatment of homosexual male and female sexual dysfunction is perhaps higher than it should be. Once the dysfunctional homosexual is reasonably sure that he or she will be openly received by the health-care professional and has confidence that his or her sexual distress can be alleviated in a high percentage of cases, there should be a marked increase in applications for treatment, and far better client cooperation in therapy. Consequently, failure rates for treatment of homosexual dysfunction should shrink. When sufficient professional experience has been acquired, an overall failure rate of 5 to 8 percent can be safely anticipated for similarly constituted treatment programs.

TREATMENT FAILURE STATISTICS
(DISSATISFACTION)

The initial failure rate during the 10-year period of clinical control for treatment of homosexual dissatisfaction is at a much higher level than that found in treating dysfunctional homosexuals. This higher failure rate had been anticipated for a variety of reasons. There has been a long-established belief among health-care professionals that attempting to support a homosexual applicant in his or her stated request to move to heterosexual orientation entails a frighteningly high level of therapy failure. It has also been openly stated that among the men and women who have converted or reverted to heterosexuality in response to various treatment programs, there has been a high percentage of return to homosexuality. The homosexual community has also adopted and freely propagandized these cultural concepts.

Other attitudes or concepts exhibited by both clients and therapists have been severe handicaps to any treatment program. Potential homosexual clients have presumed a professional bias on the part of the therapist and, more often than not, such a bias may have existed. Therapists exhibiting bias have tried to move their clients to a "better way of life" (heterosexuality) or have approached clients with preconceived ideas of the origin or development of homosexuality. Clients have sometimes requested professional support in sex-preference alteration without any real motivation for change.

If treatment of homosexual dissatisfaction is to be effective, therapists must attempt and attain a reasonable degree of professional neutrality in conducting the treatment programs, and the clients must demonstrate sincere levels of motivation for altering their sexual orientation.

At the outset of this discussion of the results of the treatment program for homosexual dissatisfaction it must be made quite clear that the Institute is reporting statistics on a highly selected treatment population. As discussed in Chapter 12, there was careful screening of prospective clients with reference to their levels of motivation for alteration of sexual preference roles. For, regardless of the etiology of the demand for the role change, without sufficient client motivation therapeutic attempts at conversion or reversion have markedly reduced chances of success. Therefore, no applicant was accepted in treatment unless he or she passed the scrutiny of the Institute's evaluation techniques for treatment motivation as described in Chapter 12. Since this was a pilot project and the therapy team was without prior experience in the field, retrospectively it is obvious that mistakes were made both in accepting and in rejecting candidates for reversal of preference roles. The overall screening procedures have proved reasonably effective, however, and are being improved on a year-to-year basis.

In reporting the clinical statistics pertaining to the treatment of homosexual men and women for sexual dissatisfaction, consideration will be given first to the failure rate encountered in the rapid-treatment phase of the program. In succession, the incidence of treatment reversal during the required five years of the follow-up program will be reported and then the overall treatment failure rate will be presented.

Finally, the overall failure rates of men and women treated for homosexual dissatisfaction will be combined with similar statistics developed from those treated for homosexual dysfunction to provide some concept of the composite clinical failure rate of the Institute's 10-year treatment program for homosexually distressed men and women.

MALE DISSATISFACTION

17. *Conversion Clients:* $N = 9$; $F = 2$; $IFR = 22.2\%$.

Given the low number of conversion clients and the rigorous selection process, which eliminated 4 clients (see Table 15-1, Chapter 15), this is a lower immediate failure rate than might have been anticipated from prior publications on the subject. Had the screening process been more effective, 1 of the treatment failures, a Kinsey 6, would not have been accepted in therapy. Although there is little clinical difference in the initial treatment failure rates, the conversion clients were generally far more cooperative in therapy than were the reversion clients. It was anticipated that the conversion clients' fears of the sexual unknown would work against their free acceptance of heterosexuality, and this proved to be true.

18. *Reversion Clients:* $N = 45$; $F = 9$; $IFR = 20.0\%$.

This is the initial failure rate that most surprised the research team, since an initial failure rate of 50 to 60 percent had been anticipated from prior professional communication. Again, the statistics were significantly aided by the Institute's screening process, for 12 of an original number of 57 reversion candidates were refused admission to the treatment program (see Table 15-1, Chapter 15).

The initial failure rates for male conversion and reversion clients are quite comparable statistically. Prior to outset of the treatment program, the research team evidenced their own bias, anticipating that for homosexual males conversion might be more difficult than reversion. This presumption was based on the fact that, by definition, all of the reversion clients had a significant degree of prior experience with heterosexual interaction. It was theorized that this familiarity with heterosexuality could be used to therapeutic advantage. What the team had not taken into account in its theorizing was the fact that a significant number of reversion clients were severely handicapped by negative rather than positive or even neutral prior heterosexual experiences. In fact, a number of reversion clients had originally moved to a homosexual orientation when their heterosexual experiences had been, at best, unrewarding and, at worst, repulsive. Therefore, prior heterosexual experience and its attendant fears for effective heterosexual performance were usually hurdles that the reversion client had to surmount, rather than an aid to his treatment progress.

19. *Conversion Clients:* $N = 3$; $F = 0$; $IFR = 0\%$.

There were only 3 homosexual women who underwent conversion therapy. No conversion applicants were rejected during screening episodes (see Table 16-1, Chapter 16). None of the 3 women treated by the research team failed to convert to effective heterosexual function.

There have not been enough clients to allow the therapists the privilege of drawing secure conclusions on the subject. In at least 3 instances, the previously expressed concept that no Kinsey 5 or 6 woman could or would convert effectively to a full heterosexual orientation has proved incorrect. No further comment is indicated at this point in time.

20. *Reversion Clients:* $N = 10$; $F = 3$; $IFR = 30.0\%$.

While the initial failure rate is high, it is lower than had been anticipated at the outset of the program. Three women were refused admission to reversion programs by the screening process (see Table 16-1, Chapter 16).

The staff have not had enough clinical experience in treating female conversion or reversion to undertake any professional discussion other than this brief statistical report. The therapy team anticipates that publication of this material will provide impetus for women to seek treatment who previously have not dared to request conversion or reversion therapy.

Paralleling the histories of the male reversion clients, there was a high incidence of prior unsuccessful or even repugnant heterosexual experiences. Again, such negative heterosexual experiences had originally turned some of the reversion clients to homosexuality.

21. *Vaginismus:* $N = 5$; $F = 0$; $IFR = 0\%$.

Vaginismus was identified in 5 of the 13 women who applied for treatment of homosexual dissatisfaction. One conversion client and 4 reversion clients were diagnosed as vaginismic during physical examinations. They were treated without incident and with the aid of their male partners of choice, in the same general manner as described in Chapter 16 and in *Human Sexual Inadequacy*. Following the reporting pattern established in the section of this chapter devoted to problems of sexual dysfunction, the incidence of this secondary diagnosis is presented for reference but will not be included in the overall treatment statistics.

SEXUAL AVERSION

Just as was noted previously in the statistics for male and female homosexual dysfunction, the incidence of sexual aversion as a secondary diagnosis for homosexually dissatisfied men was high and for homosexually dissatisfied women even higher. The statistics recorded reflect the incidence of therapy failure in symptom reversal during the rapid-treatment program.

N represents the number of cases of diagnosed sexual aversion; F, failure to reverse the symptoms; and FR, the failure rate.

The numbers in parentheses represent the cases of each type of homosexual dissatisfaction treated over the 10-year period of clinical control.

22. *Male Homosexual*   *Aversion*
    Dissatisfaction
    a. Conversion clients (9): $N = 1; F = 1; FR = 100\%$
    b. Reversion clients (45): $N = 7; F = 1; FR = 14.3\%$

23. *Female Homosexual*   *Aversion*
    Dissatisfaction
    a. Conversion clients (3): $N = 1; F = 0; FR = 0\%$
    b. Reversion clients (10): $N = 6; F = 0; FR = 0\%$

There is little to discuss in these statistics. The only clinical failure to reverse a sexual aversion was in the case of primary impotence that also was a treatment failure in a therapeutic attempt at role reversal.

The high incidence of the diagnosis of sexual aversion in both male and female clients undergoing reversion therapy has been commented upon previously in the discussion of the results of male reversion therapy. Since these statistics were not recorded during the program for heterosexually oriented sexual inadequacy, the failure rate statistics will not be included with those of the treatment program for homosexual functional inadequacy.

SUMMATION STATISTICS (DISSATISFACTION)

The initial therapy failures and the initial failure rates in treatment of homosexual dissatisfaction are listed below. They have first been separated by gender, then recorded as a total research population.

24. *Total Male Homosexual Dissatisfaction:* $N = 54$; $F = 11$; IFR $= 20.4\%$.

25. *Total Female Homosexual Dissatisfaction:* $N = 13$; $F = 3$; IFR $= 23.1\%$.

Again, these statistics support the Institute's contention that there should be little significant clinical difference in the results obtained from treating male and female sexual inadequacy. In this case, the initial failure rates in treatment of male and female homosexual dissatisfaction were in the same general clinical range. The same essential equality between the sexes in initial failure rates was demonstrated earlier in the chapter when the failure rate statistics were presented for the treatment of male and female homosexual dysfunction (see Lists 12 and 13). In addition, the same lack of a major differential between sexes in initial failure rate statistics was reported for the treatment of heterosexually dysfunctional men and women in *Human Sexual Inadequacy.*

26. *Total Male and Female Homosexual Dissatisfaction:* $N = 67$; $F = 14$; IFR $= 20.9\%$.

An initial failure rate of 21 percent in the treatment of highly selected male and female clients for conversion or reversion therapy is three times higher than the 7.1 percent initial failure rate recorded from treatment of homosexual men and women for sexual dysfunction (see List 14), but the figure is still lower than the original expectation.

Again, emphasis must be placed on the fact that these statistics only represent the initial treatment failure rates. To these totals must be added the statistical incidence of treatment reversal during the follow-up period before the overall failure rates for homosexual dissatisfaction can be determined.

If there is to be adequate follow-up information, there must be full cooperation from the clients treated during the two-week rapid-treatment program. It had been presumed by the research team that men and women who had undergone therapy for sex-preference alteration at their own request and had moved psychosexually into a different pattern of sexual orientation would be willing to help others accomplish the same purpose by occasionally relaying information as to their current status, describing their problems and providing insight into their vastly altered lifestyles. The reverted and converted clients have not been that cooperative.

During the entire 14 years of investigation into various aspects of homosexuality, this is the only segment of the clinical or laboratory populations that, as a group, evidenced a high percentage of refusal to continue informational interchange with the Institute. There were a number of reasons for the generalized lack of cooperation, but by far the most important was fear of disclosure of the past orientation.

As indicated in Table 12-3 (see Chapter 12), 33 of the 54 men and 7 of the 13 women were married or living in long-term committed relationships when seen in treatment for homosexual dissatisfaction. They were seen with their spouses, not only to secure partner involvement and support during the therapeutic effort, but to reconstitute the relationship. But when there was no immediate treatment failure and the relationship had been revitalized, the couple frequently did not want to be reminded of the past. There were expressions of fear that continuing contact with the Institute might rekindle prior homosexual interests or place an undue strain on the relationship by invoking memories of prior traumatic experiences.

There also was an openly expressed fear of identification. Most couples, particularly those with children, wanted no possibility of outside sources identifying their prior involvement in treatment programs at the Institute. Telephone calls were not particularly welcome and, in some instances, even mail in unmarked envelopes was considered to be threatening.

There was an additional fear that had not been anticipated by the research staff. This fear has been reflected by applicants who at the time of therapy were not seen in committed relationships. There were 21 men and 6 women in this group. A number of these men and women have not only continued in their converted or reverted roles to heterosexuality, but have married and/or are living entirely different lifestyles. The Institute staff are aware that very few of these men and women have confided the details of prior homosexual orientations to partners in the new relationships. To these men and women, any continued communication with the Institute poses a threat to their new relationship in that they have no desire to have their prior sexual preference identified even in retrospect.

There have been a number of other difficulties in maintaining adequate follow-up procedures. To the surprise of the research team, the conversion and reversion treatment population proved to be far more migratory in character than the homosexually dysfunctional group. Also, a significant number of the members of this group had hardly been cooperative during the acute phase in therapy, and despite the fact that they had accomplished the preference alteration they had requested, they continued to be almost as uncooperative after therapy as they had been during treatment. For these reasons, it proved very difficult to maintain contact with the conversion and reversion clients.

In short, the follow-up program for the 54 men and 13 women treated at their request for conversion or reversion to heterosexuality represents the Institute's disaster area statistically. During the 10-year contact period, 16 of the 54 men and 3 of the 13 women have been lost to continuing communication with the Institute. In comparison, it should be noted that during the same 10 years of clinical control, 57 homosexual men and 27 homosexual women were treated for sexual dysfunction. Only 3 of these 57 men and 1 of the 27 women have been lost to follow-up in an identical time period.

In essence, the follow-up procedures, at least as currently constituted, basically cannot be faulted. Probably there should have been some early alteration in follow-up techniques to compensate for the particular social problems of the conversion and reversion clients, but the widespread lack of cooperation in this particular population had not been anticipated, so satisfactory research-team reaction to the problems was delayed until a disconcerting number of clients had already been lost to follow-up.

The following statistics present the Institute's current level of knowledge of the treatment reversal rate incurred during the treatment program for homosexual dissatisfaction. In Lists 27 and 28, N represents the number of men and women who were clients in conversion or reversion therapy during the 10-year control period. F identifies those men and women who were immediate treatment failures during the acute stages of therapy; TR, the instances of known treatment reversal during the required five-year follow-up period; and LF, the number of clients lost to follow-up procedures.

27. *Male Homosexual Dissatisfaction*
    a. Conversion clients: $N = 9$; $F = 2$; $TR = 1$; $LF = 2$
    b. Reversion clients: $N = 45$; $F = 9$; $TR = 3$; $LF = 14$

There have been 4 known reversals to prior homosexual status. One client was a prior Kinsey 5, and the remaining 3 men were in Kinsey 3 and 4 categories before attempting reversion therapy. All 4 of the reversion clients known to have returned to prior homosexual commitment were married men. With the loss to follow-up of 16 cases, further incidences of treatment reversal would be anticipated but cannot be documented.

28. *Female Homosexual Dissatisfaction*
    a. Conversion clients: $N = 3$; $F = 0$; $TR = 0$; $LF = 1$
    b. Reversion clients: $N = 10$; $F = 3$; $TR = 1$; $LF = 2$

One reversion client returned to her prior homosexual orientation. She was a married Kinsey 4 when seen during the acute phase of therapy. One conversion and 2 reversion clients have been lost to follow-up procedures.

It should be pointed out that of the combined total of 67 male and female cases of sexual dissatisfaction, 52 clients were treated by the research team and 15 by other therapy teams on the Institute's staff.

As a statistical summary of the homosexual dissatisfaction program, the overall therapy failure rates developed from treating homosexual men and women for sexual dissatisfaction are listed in Table 17-2.

TABLE 17-2

Male and Female Homosexual Dissatisfaction:
Treatment Failure Statistics

Gender and Complaint	N	F	IFR (%)	TR	OFR (%)
Male					
Conversion	9	2	22.2	1	33.3
Reversion	45	9	20.0	3	26.7
Male total	54	11	20.4	4	27.8
Female					
Conversion	3	0	0	0	0
Reversion	10	3	30.0	1	40.0
Female total	13	3	23.1	1	30.8
Male and female total	67	14	20.9	5	28.4

N = number of clients; F = initial treatment failures; IFR = initial failure rate; TR = treatment reversals; OFR = overall failure rate.

FOLLOW-UP (DISSATISFACTION)

As noted in Table 17-2, there was a known overall failure rate of 28.4 percent in the treatment of homosexual male and female sexual dissatisfaction. These are misleading figures, however, for 16 men and 3 women were lost to follow-up. Although these individuals had been supported without treatment failure during the acute phase of therapy, a small number of these individuals could be expected to return to their prior homosexual orientation during the five-year follow-up period.

The male statistics in Table 17-2 can be used to estimate the unrecorded level of male client treatment reversal. Fifty-four men were originally treated for sexual dissatisfaction, and there were 11 immediate treatment failures. Of the remaining 43 men, 16 were lost to follow-up. There remain 27 men who have been followed for varying lengths of time ranging from one to five years. Four of these 27 men returned to prior homosexual orientation. Assuming the same reversal proportion (15 percent), it must be anticipated that 2 or possibly 3 more among the 16 men lost to follow-up may have returned to homosexual activity. Presuming 3 men returned to their prior homosexual orientation, such a theorized return would leave an overall failure rate for the treatment of male homosexual dissatisfaction of approximately 33 percent.

The statistics on the female side are too meager to support presumption. There has been 1 return to prior homosexual status among the 10 women who did not experience acute-treatment failure. But 3 of the 10 women have been lost to follow-up. At least 1 of these 3 women lost to follow-up may be presumed to have reverted to homosexual orientation. Such a reversal would provide an overall treatment failure rate of 40 percent for female conversion or reversion clients.

Yet another factor remains. The treatment program reported in this text was initiated in January, 1968, and terminated in December, 1977. Therefore, at current writing (January, 1979), the Institute staff have completed only six years of five-year follow-ups. Four years of observation remain. There may be additional conversion or reversion clients who return to homosexuality. However, an overall treatment failure rate of more than 45 percent for homosexual dissatisfaction is considered unlikely.

Ominous as these statistics appear, they are encouraging. For the first time we can be sure of a relatively low immediate treatment failure rate. Improved follow-up procedures with increased post-treatment support may reduce the treatment reversal rate. The current concept that the sexually dysfunctional or dissatisfied homosexual male or female cannot be treated without an 80 to 90 percent overall failure rate is simply erroneous.

Regardless of the obvious inadequacies of these follow-up statistics, the overall failure rate for the treatment of homosexual dissatisfaction over the 10-year period of study is a positive return. To a major degree, the positive results can be attributed to the rigorous selection procedures for clients, the vital use of opposite-sex partners in therapy, and the multiple advantages inherent in the use of the dual-sex therapy teams in treatment of human sexual inadequacy.

Finally, the current overall failure rate for the entire clinical therapy program directed toward treatment of homosexual dysfunction

TABLE 17-3

Program Failure Statistics

Gender and Complaint	N	F	IFR (%)	TR	OFR (%)
Homosexual dysfunction population (male and female)	84	6	7.1	3	10.7
Homosexual dissatisfaction population (male and female)	67	14	20.9	5	28.1
Total treatment population	151	20	13.2	8	18.5

N = number of clients; F = initial treatment failures; IFR = initial failure rate; TR = treatment reversals; OFR = overall failure rate.

and dissatisfaction should be considered. In Table 17-3, the overall statistical returns from the two treatment programs are combined. The two programs have been conducted simultaneously by the same research team.

As stated in the discussion of Tables 17-1 and 17-2, problems of loss of follow-up and of possible further treatment reversal might add another 9 or 10 failures to the overall failure rate reported in Table 17-3, thus raising the total program failure rate to a level of approximately 25 percent. Such an estimate is, of course, conjectural.

While the statistics reported in this chapter are of interest, no secure conclusions can be drawn. The statistics support two tentative impressions. First, the popular concept that the treatment of homosexual dissatisfaction has little chance of being effective is certainly open to question. Second, there is real potential of a professional breakthrough in the treatment of homosexual dysfunctions.

Selected positive and negative aspects of the entire treatment program will be discussed in Chapter 18.

18

CLINICAL DISCUSSION

Fourteen years of laboratory and clinical investigation of human homosexual function and dysfunction have provided broad-based support for the Institute's major premise that from a functional point of view homosexuality and heterosexuality have far more similarities than differences. Yet today, many decades after cultural dictum originally introduced the concept that important functional differences do exist between the two sexual preferences, the overwhelming pressure of public opprobrium still blindly reinforces this false assumption. The general public as well as many segments of the scientific community remain convinced that there are marked functional disparities between homosexual and heterosexual men and women.

This cultural precept was originally initiated and has been massively supported by theologic doctrine. The Institute has no point of contention with the relatively well-defined position of theology on the subject of homosexuality. It is not our intention to assume a role in interpreting or implementing moral judgment. These privileges and their accompanying awesome responsibilities are not within the purview of a research group devoted to psychophysiologic aspects of human sexuality.

Actually, interviews have provided tentative support for the cultural concept of physical differences. Kinsey 0 men or women have unhesitatingly contended that homosexuality was without any semblance of psychosexual appeal because "they (homosexuals) are different," while Kinsey 6 individuals have been just as adamant in rejecting any possible personal interest in heterosexual interaction—and for the same reason. Unfortunately, many individuals have loosely interpreted the "they-are-different" doctrine as meaning physically different in sexual response. Men and women representing both ends of the Kinsey spectrum have based their intractable belief in the existence of physical differences in sexual interaction entirely upon culturally engendered impressions, for they have had no personal experience with which to support or deny their socially reinforced opinions.

The bioethical problem in evaluating supposed physical differences has centered on the fact that until 15 years ago cultural prejudices were so powerful that their precepts could not even be challenged in the research laboratory. Therefore, subjective opinions, the basic fodder of cultural dictum, have neither been supported nor denied by objectively developed investigative material. Fortunately, the culture can no longer dictate this degree of blind obeisance from investigative science.

When we admit to judging the physical aspects of sexual preference on the shaky foundation of subjective impression rather than from relatively secure research objectivity, there is another and far less appealing pattern of human behavior that has consistently developed as a cultural consequence. In order to lend credence to our personal preference for a particular sexual orientation, we not only categorically deny value in "the other way," we insist on attempting to discredit it completely. It frequently follows that those individuals who adhere to opinions and practices that are contradictory to our own in this controversial area are personally rejected.

Meanwhile, the small voice of reason has gone unheeded. For decades, Kinsey 2, 3, and 4 men and women who have had a significant amount of both homosexual and heterosexual experience have consistently contended that there was not any difference in the functional aspects of the two preference roles. These individuals may indicate a personal bias for either homosexual or heterosexual encounter, but any cultural concept of physical difference in sexual interaction has been replaced by the more pragmatic process of enjoying sensual aspects of the sexual encounter, regardless of the gender of the partner.

We are genetically determined to be male or female and, in addition, are given the ability to function sexually as men or women by the physical capacities of erection and lubrication and the inherent facility for orgasmic attainment. These capacities function in identical ways, whether we are interacting heterosexually or homosexually. When a man or woman is orgasmic, he or she is responding to sexual stimuli with the same basic physiologic response patterns, regardless of whether the stimulative technique is masturbation, partner manipulation, fellatio/cunnilingus, vaginal or rectal coitus—and also regardless of whether the sexual partner is of the *same* or the *opposite* gender.

Of course, the "they-are-different" doctrine has had many interpretations other than the concept that homosexuals and heterosexuals function differently sexually. The Kinsey 0 considers the Kinsey 6 vastly different in many ways because he or she expresses sexual interest in a same- rather than an opposite-sex partner.

The Kinsey 0 man or woman who identifies with an opposite-sex individual as a sex object does so on an individual basis. The identification does not extend to all members of the opposite sex. In fact, although he or she might never admit the interest level openly, the Kinsey 0 man or woman is occasionally committed far more closely psychosexually with a same-sex individual than he or she ever is with many opposite-sex acquaintances. The same behavior pattern is followed by Kinsey 6 men and women, who often identify far more closely with an opposite-sex individual than with same-sex acquaintances.

In the middle of the spectrum are many men and women (Kinsey 2, 3, and 4) who closely identify with partners of both the same and opposite sex and find them equally stimulating sex objects. When responding to these partners, they react in the same physical manner regardless of the gender of the particular partner.

Finally, there are ambisexual men and women. They simply do not care whether the partner is male or female, for the gender of the partner is not an important source of sexual arousal. As abundantly demonstrated in the laboratory, ambisexuals respond in identical fashion regardless of the gender of the partner or the mode of sexual activity. Therefore, it appears that the "they-are-different" doctrine is also consistently interpreted as "they do not feel precisely as we do about a potential sex object." When making this "they-are-different" social judgment, it is always convenient to overlook the fact that we usually feel differently about a potential sex object from day to day. We tend to require consistent sexual focus on one partner or a specific type of sex object from other individuals, but not from ourselves.

Over the last 15 years, it also has become apparent that the individual's sexual orientation does not significantly alter his or her problem of sexual dysfunction. Impotence and anorgasmic states have just as devastating an effect on homosexual as on heterosexual men or women. Fears of performance and spectator roles can make a sexual cripple out of any sexually dysfunctional individual, homosexual or heterosexual. Sexual fakery is freely practiced by representatives of both sex preferences. Therefore, the Institute strongly supports the concept that sexual dysfunction be treated with the same therapeutic principles and techniques regardless of the sexual orientation of the distressed individual.

If therapeutic procedures are carried out effectively, differences in the clinical failure statistics should be minimal. Generally, there may be a lower failure rate in treating the dysfunctional homosexual than the dysfunctional heterosexual because the sexually dysfunctional homosexual does not have the extra demand for effective function during coition that is inherent in heterosexual interaction. In support of these statements a comparison of the overall failure rates in treating homosexual and heterosexual dysfunction is indicated.

Overall treatment failure rates have been compiled from a combination of acute treatment failures and both recorded and theoretical instances of renewed dysfunction during the required five-year follow-up period after termination of the acute treatment phase (see Chapter 17). The combined (male and female) overall treatment failure rate for homosexual dysfunction was approximately 12 percent. The corresponding heterosexual statistic published in 1970 (*Human Sexual Inadequacy*) was approximately 20 percent.

The lower overall failure rate returned from treating dysfunctional homosexual men and women not only reflected the fact that effective function during intercourse was not required, but also the additional influence of another important factor. The research team had the enormous advantage of a decade of clinical experience treating heterosexual dysfunction before it initiated the homosexual treatment program. From a clinical point of view, a significant differential between the two estimated overall failure rates was to be expected.

Therapy for sexual dissatisfaction represents the "disaster area" in the Institute's treatment program for sexually distressed homosexuals. The overall combined (male and female) failure rate was estimated at approximately 35 percent (see Chapter 17). Actually, a significantly higher failure rate was anticipated for the treatment of homosexual dissatisfaction than that developed from treating homosexual dysfunction, but the marked differential in the failure rates was not expected. The overall failure rate for homosexual dissatisfaction was approximately three times that recorded for sexually dysfunctional homosexual men and women. This poor clinical return developed despite the fact that there was careful screening of clients in every case of sexual dissatisfaction accepted into the therapy program.

In brief, approximately one in three homosexual men and women treated for sexual dissatisfaction either failed to convert or revert to heterosexuality during the acute phase of the treatment program or actively or theoretically returned to overt homosexual interaction during the required five-year follow-up period. In comparison, approximately one in 10 homosexual men and women had a similar report of a failed therapy program for sexual dysfunction (see Chapter 17).

The elevated overall failure rate for the treatment of homosexual dissatisfaction is, of course, unacceptable. There should be no overall failure rate higher than 20 percent for treatment of any form of either homosexual or heterosexual inadequacy.

An important factor that has contributed significantly to failures in treating male homosexual dissatisfaction in the past should prove far less of a barrier to effective therapy in the future. It is anticipated that the degree of cooperation with the therapeutic process by those homosexual men requesting reversion or conversion therapy will improve markedly. The clients' increased confidence in the treatment modalities and, subsequently, their higher levels of clinical cooperation should come from two sources. First, the homosexual community will soon realize that there are improved therapeutic procedures available to the dissatisfied as well as the dysfunctional homosexual. This realization should, in turn, increase confidence in and cooperation with the therapeutic process. Second, there also should be a better rapport between client and therapist when there is unmistakable evidence of the health-care professional's full assumption of its professional responsibility toward the treatment of sexually distressed homosexual men and women.

There is a discrepancy between treatment programs involving sexually inadequate homosexual and heterosexual populations. This imbalance revolves about the clinical problems of dissatisfied homosexual men and women who entered treatment with the expressed interest of converting or reverting to heterosexuality (see Chapters 15 and 16). The problem is that there is no facet of the treatment program for the sexually distressed heterosexual population corresponding to the section for homosexual dissatisfaction. Over the 20-year period during which the Institute has been treating sexually distressed heterosexual men and women, there have only been 2 men asking for professional help in converting to homosexuality, and they were primarily impotent as heterosexuals to start with (see Chapter 13).

With this discrepancy in mind, the only statistics that remain of more than passing interest are those that provide an open comparison between the overall failure rates of the treatment programs for all forms of heterosexual inadequacy and those for all forms of homosexual inadequacy. The overall failure rate for the heterosexual dysfunction program was estimated at a combined (male and female) total of approximately 20 percent (*Human Sexual Inadequacy*), and the overall combined failure rate for the treatment programs for homosexual dysfunction and dissatisfaction was estimated at approximately 25 percent (see Chapter 17).

Of necessity, these are estimated statistics, for as previously stated, they are a combination of the numbers of acute treatment failures and the number of actual and theoretical failures during the required five-year follow-up program. Yet, the figures are in such close clinical parallel that they lend support to the concept of similarity, not difference, between the sexual functions and dysfunctions of the two sexual preferences.

The parallelism in overall failure rates also underscores the fact that the treatment techniques, which were essentially identical in concept and format, were generally as effective in treating homosexual as heterosexual inadequacies. Regardless of the distressed individual's sexual preference, the research team insisted upon the use of dual-sex therapy teams and requested that the sexually inadequate individual be accompanied in therapy by a partner of choice. A detailed discussion of the psychotherapeutic principles involved in the treatment of homosexual dysfunction and dissatisfaction by the dual-sex team techniques will be published at a later date.

HORMONES AND HOMOSEXUALITY

In the last decade, research interest has been rekindled in the quest to identify biologic factors important in the genesis of homosexuality. Since the Institute's endocrine section under the direction of Robert C. Kolodny has been active in this area, we would be remiss if the current status of these research programs were not summarized.

Investigative endocrinologists have been aided by technologic advances such as radioimmunoassay techniques, which for the first time have permitted precise quantification of various hormones related to reproduction and sexual functioning. Such work has also been stimulated by related advances clarifying embryologic mechanisms of sexual differentiation—with increasing evidence that in certain instances the fetal hormonal environment may predispose individuals toward particular patterns of sexual behavior.

A large body of experimental literature, only briefly mentioned here, documents the fact that in a variety of animal species hormonal manipulation during critical phases of sexual differentiation can produce subsequent alterations in adult sexual behavior that have been interpreted as paralleling homosexual behavior in humans. While it is difficult to decide if interspecies comparisons of these behaviors provide accurate etiologic insights or, indeed, whether such behavior patterns are truly homologous, there are additional findings stemming from isolated studies of clinical situations involving humans that lend credence to the observations derived from animal studies. These diverse situations, including females with the adrenogenital syndrome (exposed in utero to high levels of androgen), men with Klinefelter's syndrome (usually marked by both a fetal and adult relative deficiency of androgen), and instances of prenatal exposure to exogenous hormonal intake (principally progestins and estrogens) seem to be associated with a higher incidence of subsequent homosexuality than would occur by chance alone.

In 1970, Margolese reported that the urinary excretion of androsterone and etiocholanolone was different in homosexual and heterosexual men. That same year, Loraine and his colleagues reported that urinary excretion of testosterone was low in two homosexual men and elevated in four homosexual women. Subsequently, work by Kolodny and his colleagues from the Institute (1971–1972)—undertaken with a degree of skepticism about such hormonal variations in homosexuals—found that plasma testosterone levels were significantly lower in young men who were either exclusively or almost exclusively homosexual (Kinsey 5 or 6) than in an age-matched group of heterosexual controls. These investigators carefully stated: "There is no suggestion that endocrine abnormalities will be found in the great majority of homosexuals. . . . In fact there must be speculation that the depressed testosterone levels could be the secondary result of a . . . depressive reaction relayed through the hypothalamus from higher cortical centers."

Following this study, a large number of additional reports have appeared with considerable disagreement in results. While Evans (1972) and Margolese and Janiger (1973) separately found further evidence of altered urinary hormone metabolites in homosexual men, others have not confirmed this difference. Similarly, while Starká and co-workers (1975) described lower circulating testosterone in homosexual men than in heterosexual controls, and Rohde and his colleagues (1977) found significantly lower free plasma testosterone in 35 homosexual men than in 38 heterosexual men, studies by other investigators—including Brodie et al. (1974), Birk et al. (1973), Friedman et al. (1977), Doerr et al. (1973, 1976), Tourney and Hatfield (1973), Pillard et al., and Barlow et al. (1974)—found no differences in circulating testosterone between homosexual and heterosexual men. To further complicate the situation, Doerr and his colleagues (1973) noted that there were significant differences in estrone and dihydrotestosterone between homosexual and heterosexual men; significant differences in luteinizing hormone secretion in these same groups were also observed by Doerr's group (1976), by Kolodny and his colleagues (1972), and by Rohde and his co-workers (1977). Similar controversy exists in hormonal studies of homosexual women, although this topic has not received such intensive investigative scrutiny.

What conclusions or inferences can be drawn from the available evidence? First, it is apparent that all of these reports are significantly handicapped by methodological limitations ranging from relatively small sample size to problems in sampling intervals. Until these problems are remedied, it is difficult to assess the evidence with any security. Second, it is apparent that homosexuality is no more a unitary phenomenon than is heterosexuality: Until it is possible to separate specific subgroups of homosexuals and heterosexuals by precise classification criteria, the heterogeneity that cuts across the basic lines of homosexual versus heterosexual—supported by the heterogeneity found in the physiologic and clinical studies reported in this text—complicates the identification of significant hormonal differences even if these exist. Third, until more is known about the origins of heterosexuality, it is difficult to believe that meaningful insights will be reached regarding the origins of homosexuality. Finally, in view of the current lack of secure information in this field, we must maintain an intellectually open stance acknowledging that in at least some instances—though clearly not in most cases—hormonal predispositions may interact with social and environmental factors to lead toward a homosexual orientation.

There is little need for further detailed comment. A start has been made. Far more sophisticated basic research in the neurophysiology of human sexual function is next in order. In time, the neuroendocrinology of sexual response must be established. Newer and more effective variations in the basic therapeutic techniques for sexual dysfunction and dissatisfaction must be developed. These techniques must also be combined with improved applicant screening and more effective follow-up procedures. In response to such investigative efforts, there will be progressive lowering of the overall failure rates for the treatment of both homosexually and heterosexually oriented sexual inadequacy.

BIBLIOGRAPHY

Most successful collections of multidimensional bibliographies on the subject of homosexuality have been accomplished by Martin Weinberg and Alan Bell, by Arno Karlen, and by William Parker. There isn't the slightest indication for further reduplication of their massive efforts. Therefore, the bibliography presented in the following pages only represents reading conducted in conjunction with the Institute's basic science investigation of homosexual function and its clinical programs designed to treat homosexual dysfunction and dissatisfaction.

Since there have been no previous reports on the subject of human homosexual physiology and in the last year just two reports of treatment of homosexual dysfunction, there are really a negligible number of applicable bibliographic references. The treatment of homosexual dissatisfaction by dual-sex teams incorporating partners of the opposite sex in the therapy program also has not been previously reported. And with the exception of Harold Lief's pioneering effort, there have been no reports in the literature of five-year follow-up of homosexual males or females treated for sexual inadequacy.

Thus, aside from those references pertaining to statistical evaluation and to endocrinology, the bibliography represents only the Institute's general scan of the literature devoted to problems of the homosexual and, of necessity, has little applicability to material presented in this text.

Achilles, N. Development of the Homosexual Bar as an Institution. In *Sexual Deviance* (J. H. Gagnon and W. Simon, Eds.). New York: Harper & Row, 1967.

Adler, A. *The Individual Psychology of Alfred Adler* (H. L. and R. R. Ansbacher, Eds.). New York: Harper Torchbook, 1964.

Allen, C. The treatment of sexual abnormalities. *Med. Press* 210:23–25, 1943.

Allen, C. Homosexuality: The psychological factor. *Med. Press* 218: 222–223, 1947.

Allen, C. *The Sexual Perversions and Abnormalities: A Study in the Psychology of Paraphilia* (2nd ed.). London: Oxford University Press, 1949.

Allen, C.   On the cure of homosexuality. *Int. J. Sexol.* 5:148–150, 1952.

Allen, C.   The problem of homosexuality. *Int. J. Sexol.* 6:40–42, 1952.

Allen, C.   *Homosexuality: Its Nature, Causation, and Treatment.* London: Staples, 1958.

Allport, G.   *The Nature of Prejudice.* Cambridge, Mass.: Addison-Wesley, 1954.

Altman, D.   *Homosexual: Oppression and Liberation.* New York: Dutton, 1971.

Alverson, C. A.   A minority's plea—U.S. homosexuals gain in trying to persuade society to accept them. *Wall Street Journal* July 17, 1968.

Asprey, R.   *The Panther's Feast.* New York: Putnam, 1959.

Aubrey, J.   *Brief Lives* (O. L. Dick, Ed.). Ann Arbor: University of Michigan Press, 1957.

Bailey, D. S.   *Homosexuality and the Western Christian Tradition.* London: Longmans, Green, 1955.

Barlow, D. H., *et al.*   Plasma testosterone levels and male homosexuality: A failure to replicate. *Arch. Sex. Behav.* 3:571–575, 1974.

Beach, F. A.   Sex reversals in the mating pattern of the rat. *J. Genet. Psychol.* 53:329–334, 1938.

Beach, F. A.   *Hormones and Behavior.* New York: Hoeber, 1948.

Beach, F. A.   *Sexual Behavior in Animals and Men* (*Harvey Lectures,* 1948, 254–280). Springfield, Ill.: Thomas, 1950.

Beach, F. A.   The descent of instinct. *Psychol. Rev.* 62:401–410, 1955.

Beach, F. A.   Factors Involved in the Control of Mounting Behavior by Female Mammals. In *Perspectives in Reproduction and Sexual Behavior* (M. Diamond, Ed.). Bloomington: Indiana University Press, 1958.

Beach, F. A. (Ed.).   *Sex & Behavior.* New York: Wiley, 1965.

Beach, F. A., *et al.*   Coital behavior in dogs: Effects of estrogen on mounting by females. *J. Comp. Physiol. Psychol.* 66:296–307, 1968.

Becker, H. S.   *Outsiders.* New York: Free Press, 1963.

Becker, H. S. (Ed.).   *The Other Side: Perspectives in Deviance.* New York: Free Press, 1964.

Becker, R. de.   *The Other Face of Love* (M. Crosland and A. Daventry, Trans.). New York: Grove, 1969.

Begelman, D. A.   Homosexuality and the ethics of behavioral intervention. *J. Homosex.* 2(3):213–219, 1977.

Beigel, H. G.   The Meaning of Coital Postures. In *Sexual Behavior and Personality Characteristics* (M. DeMartino, Ed.). New York: Grove, 1966.

Bell, A. P., and Weinberg, M. S.   *Homosexualities: A Study of Diversity Among Men and Women.* New York: Simon & Schuster, 1978.

Belot, A. *Mademoiselle Giraud, My Wife*. Chicago: Laird & Lee, 1891.

Bem, S. L. The measurement of psychological androgyny. *J. Consult. Clin. Psychol.* 42:155–162, 1974.

Bem, S. L. Sex-role adaptability: One consequence of psychological androgyny. *J. Pers. Soc. Psychol.* 31:634–643, 1975.

Bene, E. On the genesis of female homosexuality. *Br. J. Psychiatry* 3:815–821, 1965.

Bene, E. On the genesis of male homosexuality: An attempt at clarifying the role of parents. *Br. J. Psychiatry* 3:803–813, 1965.

Benson, R. O. D. *In Defense of Homosexuality*. New York: Julian, 1965.

Bergler, E. *Homosexuality: Disease or Way of Life?* New York: Hill & Wang, 1956.

Bergler, E. *1000 Homosexuals*. Paterson, N.J.: Pageant, 1959.

Bieber, I. Clinical Aspects of Male Homosexuality. In *Sexual Inversion: The Multiple Roots of Homosexuality* (J. Marmor, Ed.). New York: Basic Books, 1965.

Bieber, I., *et al.* *Homosexuality: A Psychoanalytic Study of Male Homosexuals*. New York: Basic Books, 1962.

Birk, L. Group therapy for men who are homosexual. *J. Sex Marital Ther.* 1:29–52, 1974.

Birk, L., *et al.* Serum testosterone levels in homosexual men. *N. Engl. J. Med.* 289:1236–1238, 1973.

Bowman, K. M., and Engle, B. A psychiatric evaluation of the laws of homosexuality. *Temple Law Q. Rev.* 29:273–326, 1956.

Brill, A. A. *Freud's Contribution to Psychiatry*. New York: W. W. Norton, 1962.

Brodie, H. K. H., *et al.* Plasma testosterone levels in heterosexual and homosexual men. *Am. J. Psychiatry* 131:82–83, 1974.

Brown, J. S. A comparative study of deviations of sexual mores. *Am. Sociol. Rev.* 17:135–146, 1952.

Burgess, E. W. The Sociologic Theory of Psychosexual Behavior. In *Psychosexual Development in Health and Disease* (P. H. Hoch and J. Zubin, Eds.). New York: Grune & Stratton, 1949.

Bychowski, G. The ego and the object of the homosexual. *Int. J. Psychoanal.* 42:255–259, 1961.

Cantor, D. J. Deviation and the criminal law. *J. Crim. Law, Criminol., Polit. Sci.* 55:441–453, 1964.

Cappon, D. *Toward an Understanding of Homosexuality*. Englewood Cliffs, N.J.: Prentice-Hall, 1965.

Caprio, F. *Variations in Sexual Behavior*. New York: Grove, 1955.

Caprio, F. S. *Female Homosexuality*. New York: Citadel, 1954.

Carpenter, E. *The Intermediate Sex: A Study of Some Transitional Types of Men and Women.* London: Allen & Unwin, 1908.

Carpenter, E. *Love's Coming of Age.* New York: Liveright, 1911.

Carrier, J. Participants in urban Mexican male homosexual encounters. *Arch. Sex. Behav.* 1:279–291, 1971.

Carrier, J. Urban Mexican male homosexual encounters: An analysis of participants and coping strategies. University of California Ph.D. Thesis, 1972.

Carrier, J. Cultural factors affecting urban Mexican male homosexual behavior. *Arch. Sex. Behav.* 5:103–124, 1976.

Carrier, J. M. "Sex-role preference" as an explanatory variable in homosexual behavior. *Arch. Sex. Behav.* 6:53–65, 1977.

Catlin, G. Illustrations of the Manners, Customs, and Condition of the North American Indians. Cited in *The Origin and Development of the Moral Ideas* (E. Westermarck). London: Macmillan, 1908.

Chang, J., and Block, J. Study of identification in male homosexuals. *J. Consult. Psychol.* 24:307–310, 1960.

Churchill, W. *Homosexual Behavior Among Males: A Cross-Cultural and Cross-Species Investigation.* New York: Hawthorn, 1967.

Clemmer, D. *The Prison Community.* New York: Holt, Rinehart & Winston, 1958.

Coates, S. Clinical Psychology in Sexual Deviation. In *The Pathology and Treatment of Sexual Deviation: A Methodological Approach* (I. Rosen, Ed.). London: Oxford University Press, 1964.

Cory, D. W. *The Homosexual in America: A Subjective Approach.* New York: Greenberg, 1951.

Cory, D. W. (Ed.). *Homosexuality: A Cross-Cultural Approach.* New York: Julian, 1956.

Cory, D. W. *The Lesbian in America.* New York: Citadel, 1964.

Cory, D. W., and LeRoy, J. P. *The Homosexual and His Society: A View from Within.* New York: Citadel, 1963.

Cotton, W. L. Role-playing substitutions among homosexuals. *J. Sex Res.* 8:310–323, 1972.

Cotton, W. L. Social and sexual relationships of lesbians. *J. Sex Res.* 11:139–148, 1975.

Croft-Cooke, R. *The Verdict of You All.* London: Warburg, 1955.

Crowley, M. *The Boys in the Band.* New York: Farrar, 1968.

Curran, D., and Parr, D. Homosexuality: An analysis of 100 male cases seen in private practice. *Br. Med. J.* 1:797–801, 1957.

Dank, B. M. Coming out in the gay world. *Psychiatry* 34:180–195, 1971.

D'Arcangelo, A. *The Homosexual Handbook.* New York: Ophelia, 1969.

Darwin, C. *The Descent of Man and Selection in Relation to Sex* (2nd ed., rev. and augm.). New York: Appleton, 1909.

Davenport, W., and Davenport, P. Sexual Patterns and Their Regulation in a Society of the Southwest Pacific. In *Sex and Behavior* (F. A. Beach, Ed.). New York: Wiley, 1965.

Davis, A. Sexual assault in the Philadelphia prisons and sheriff vans. *Trans-Action* 6(2):8–13, 1968.

Davis, K. B. *Factors in the Sex Life of Twenty-Two Hundred Women.* New York: Harper & Brothers, 1929.

Davison, G. C. Homosexuality and the ethics of behavioral intervention: Homosexuality, the ethical challenge. *J. Homosex.* 2(3):195–204, 1977.

Davison, G. C. Not can but ought: The treatment of homosexuality. *J. Consult. Clin. Psychol.* 46:170–172, 1978.

Davison, K., et al. A male monozygotic twinship discordant for homosexuality. *Br. J. Psychiatry* 118:675–682, 1971.

Dean, R. B., and Richardson, H. Analysis of MMPI profiles of 40 college-educated overt male homosexuals. *J. Consult. Psychol.* 28:483–486, 1964.

DeFries, Z. Pseudohomosexuality in feminist students. *Am. J. Psychiatry* 133:400–404, 1976.

DeLuca, J. N. Performance of overt male homosexuals and controls on the Blacky test. *J. Clin. Psychol.* 23:497, 1967.

Devereaux, G. Institutionalized Homosexuality of the Mohave Indians. In *The Problem of Homosexuality in Modern Society* (H. Ruitenbeek, Ed.). New York: Dutton, 1963.

Diethelm, O. *Treatment in Psychiatry.* Springfield, Ill.: Thomas, 1950.

Doerr, P., et al. Plasma testosterone, estradiol, and semen analysis in male homosexuals. *Arch. Gen. Psychiatry* 29:829–833, 1973.

Doerr, P., et al. Further studies on sex hormones in male homosexuals. *Arch. Gen. Psychiatry* 33:611–614, 1976.

Donnelly, R. C., et al. Consensual Homosexual Acts Between Adults in Private—A Crime: A Problem for the Legislature? In *Criminal Law: Problems for Decision in the Promulgation, Invocation, and Administration of a Law of Crimes.* New York: Free Press of Glencoe, 1962.

Dörner, G. Hormonal induction and prevention of female homosexuality. *J. Endocrinol.* 42:163–164, 1968.

Dörner, G. *Hormones and Brain Differentiation.* Amsterdam: Elsevier, 1976.

Dörner, G., and Hinz, G. Induction and prevention of male homosexuality by androgen. *J. Endocrinol.* 40:387–388, 1968.

Douglas, J. D. *American Social Order: Social Rules in a Pluralistic Society.* New York: Free Press, 1971.

Dunbar, J., et al. Attitudes toward homosexuality among Brazilian and Canadian college students. *J. Soc. Psychol.* 90:174–175, 1973.

Edwards, D. A. Neonatal administration of androstenedione, testosterone, or testerone propionate: Effects on ovulation, sexual receptivity and aggressive behavior in female mice. *Physiol. Behav.* 6:223–228, 1971.

Eisinger, A. J., et al. Female homosexuality. *Nature* 238:106, 1972.

Elliott, R. H. Enforcement of laws directed at homosexuals: A typical metropolitan approach. *Drum* 26:10–13, 26–28, 1967.

Ellis, A. *Homosexuality: Its Causes and Cure.* New York: Lyle Stuart, 1965.

Ellis, A. The right to be wrong. *J. Sex Res.* 4:96–107, 1968.

Ellis, H. *Studies in the Psychology of Sex.* New York: Random House, 1936. Vols. 1 & 2.

Evans, R. B. Childhood parental relationships of homosexual men. *J. Consult. Clin. Psychol.* 33:129–135, 1969.

Evans, R. B. Physical and biochemical characteristics of homosexual men. *J. Consult. Clin. Psychol.* 39:140–147, 1972.

Farber, L. H., and Fisher, C. An Experimental Approach to Dream Psychology Through the Use of Hypnosis. In *Contemporary Psychopathology* (S. S. Tomkins, Ed.). Cambridge, Mass.: Harvard University Press, 1943.

Feldman, M. P., and McCulloch, M. J. A systematic approach to the treatment of homosexuality by conditioned aversion: Preliminary report. *Am. J. Psychiatry* 121:167–171, 1964.

Feldman, M. P., and McCulloch, M. J. Aversion therapy in management of 43 homosexuals. *Br. Med. J.* 2:594–597, 1967.

Féré, C. *Sexual Degeneration in Mankind and in Animals* (U. van de Horst, Trans.). New York: Anthropological Press, 1932.

Ferenczi, S. On the Part Played by Homosexuality in the Pathogenesis of Paranoia. In *Contributions to Psychoanalysis* (E. Jones, Trans.). New York: Brunner, 1950.

Ferenczi, S. The Nosology of Male Homosexuality. In *The Problem of Homosexuality in Modern Society* (H. M. Ruitenbeek, Ed.). New York: Dutton, 1963.

Fisher, P. *The Gay Mystique: The Myth and Reality of Male Homosexuality.* New York: Stein & Day, 1972.

Fletcher, G. F., and Cantwell, J. D. Continuous ambulatory electro-cardiograph monitoring: Use in cardiac exercise programs. *Chest* 71: 27–32, 1977.

Fonzi, G. J. *The Furtive Fraternity.* San Francisco: Pan-Graphic, 1963.

Ford, C. S., and Beach, F. A. *Patterns of Sexual Behavior.* New York: Harper & Brothers, 1951.

Forel, A. *The Sexual Question* (English adapt. from 2nd German ed., rev. and enl. by C. F. Marshall). New York: Rebman, 1908.

Freud, A. Homosexuality. *Bull. Am. Psychoanal. Assoc.* 7:117–118, 1951.

Freud, S. *The Problem of Anxiety* (H. A. Bunker, Trans.). New York: W. W. Norton, 1936.

Freud, S. Three Contributions to the Theory of Sex. In *The Basic Writings of Sigmund Freud* (A. A. Brill, Ed. and Trans.). New York: Modern Library, 1938.

Freud, S. Letter to an American mother. *Am. J. Psychiatry* 107:786–787, 1951.

Freud, S. *Collected Papers* (E. Jones, Ed.). New York: Basic Books, 1959. Vols. 1–5.

Freud, S. *The Ego and the Id* (J. Strachey, Ed. and J. Riviere, Trans.). New York: W. W. Norton, 1961.

Freud, S. *New Introductory Lectures on Psychoanalysis* (J. Strachey, Ed. and Trans.). New York: W. W. Norton, 1965.

Freud, S. *Three Essays on the Theory of Sexuality* (J. Strachey, Trans.). New York: Avon, 1965.

Freud, S. *An Outline of Psychoanalysis* (rev. ed., J. Strachey, Ed. and Trans.). New York: W. W. Norton, 1970.

Freund, K. A note on the use of the phallometric method of measuring mild sexual arousal in the male. *Behav. Ther.* 2:223–228, 1971.

Freund, K., *et al.* Heterosexual aversion in homosexual males. *Br. J. Psychiatry* 122:163–169, 1973.

Freund, K., *et al.* The phobic theory of male homosexuality. *Arch. Gen. Psychiatry* 31:495–499, 1974.

Friedman, R. C., *et al.* Psychological development and blood levels of sex steroids in male identical twins of divergent sexual orientation. *J. Nerv. Ment. Dis.* 163:282–288, 1976.

Friedman, R. C., *et al.* Hormones and sexual orientation in men. *Am. J. Psychiatry* 134:571–572, 1977.

Friedman, R. C., *et al.* Plasma prolactin levels in male homosexuals. *Horm. Behav.* 9(1):19–22, 1977.

Frumkin, R. M. Early English and American Sex Customs. In *Encyclopedia of Sexual Behavior* (A. Ellis and A. Abarbanel, Eds.). New York: Hawthorn, 1967.

Gagnon, J., and Simon, W. Homosexuality: The formulation of a sociological perspective. *J. Health Soc. Behav.* 8:177–185, 1967.

Gagnon, J., and Simon, W. Femininity in the lesbian community. *Soc. Probl.* 15:212–221, 1967.

Gagnon, J. H. Sexual Behavior: Sexual Deviation: Social Aspects. In *International Encyclopedia of the Social Sciences* (D. E. Sills, Ed.). New York: Macmillan, 1968.

Gagnon, J. H., and Simon, W. Perspective on homosexuality. *Dublin Rev.* 241:96–114, 1967.

Gagnon, J. H., and Simon, W. (Eds.). *Sexual Deviance.* New York: Harper & Row, 1967.

Gartrell, N. K., *et al.* Plasma testosterone in homosexual and heterosexual women. *Am. J. Psychiatry* 134:117–119, 1977.

Gebhard, P., *et al.* *Sex Offenders: An Analysis of Types.* New York: Harper & Row, 1965.

Gebhard, P. H. Situational Factors Affecting Human Sexual Behavior. In *Sex & Behavior* (F. A. Beach, Ed.). New York: Wiley, 1965.

Gebhard, P. H. The 1965 Kinsey Report: Our dangerous sex laws. *Ladies Home Journal* 82:66–67, 121, and 82:42–44, May and June, 1965.

Gebhard, P. H. Homosexual socialization. *Excerpta Medica Int. Congr. Ser.* 150:1028–1031, 1966.

Gebhard, P. H. Incidence of Overt Homosexuality in the United States and Western Europe. In *National Institute of Mental Health Task Force on Homosexuality: Final Report and Background Papers*, Publ. No. HSM 72–9116 (J. M. Livingood, Ed.). Washington, D.C.: U.S. Government Printing Office, 1972.

Geller, J. J., and Rouslin, S. A psychoanalytic view of homosexuality: An interview with Joseph J. Geller, M.D. *Perspect. Psychiatr. Care* 16(2):76–79, 1978.

Gerassi, J. *The Boys of Boise: Furor, Vice, and Folly in an American City.* New York: Macmillan, 1966.

Giallombardo, R. *Society of Women: A Study of a Women's Prison.* New York: Wiley, 1966.

Gittings, B. B. The Homosexual and the Church. In *The Same Sex* (R. Weltge, Ed.). Philadelphia: Pilgrim, 1969.

Gittings, B. B. *A Gay Bibliography.* Philadelphia: Task Force on Gay Liberation, American Library Association, 1974.

Glass, S. J., et al. Sex hormone studies in male homosexuality. *Endocrinology* 26:590–594, 1940.

Goffman, E. *Stigma*. Englewood Cliffs, N.J.: Prentice-Hall, 1963.

Goode, E., and Haber, L. Sexual correlates of homosexual experience: An exploratory study of college women. *J. Sex Res.* 13:12–21, 1977.

Goode, E., and Troiden, R. R. (Eds.). *Sexual Deviance and Sexual Deviants*. New York: William Morrow, 1974.

Green, R. *Sexual Identity Conflict in Children and Adults*. New York: Basic Books, 1974.

Greenblatt, D. R. Semantic differential analysis of the "triangular system" hypothesis in "adjusted" overt male homosexuals. University of California Ph.D. Thesis, 1966.

Griffiths, P. D., et al. Homosexual women: An endocrine and psychological study. *J. Endocrinol.* 63:549–556, 1974.

Gross, A. A. *Strangers in Our Midst: Problems of the Homosexual in American Society*. Washington, D.C.: Public Affairs Press, 1962.

Gross, M. J. Changing attitudes toward homosexuality—or are they. *Perspect. Psychiatr. Care* 16(2):71–75, 1978.

Gundlach, R. H., and Reiss, B. F. Self and Sexual Identity in the Female: A Study of Female Homosexuals. In *New Directions in Mental Health* (B. F. Reiss, Ed.). New York: Grune & Stratton, 1968. Vols. 1 & 2.

Gunnison, F. *An Introduction to the Homophile Movement*. Hartford, Conn.: Institute of Social Ethics, 1967.

Hadden, S. B. Group psychotherapy of male homosexuals. *Curr. Psychiatr. Ther.* 6:177–186, 1966.

Hadden, S. B. Treatment of male homosexuals in groups. *Int. J. Group Psychother.* 16:13–22, 1966.

Hadden, S. B. A way out for homosexuals. *Harper's* 234:107–108, 114–120, Mar., 1967.

Hadden, S. B. Group psychotherapy for sexual maladjustments. *Am. J. Psychiatry* 125:327–332, 1968.

Hadfield, J. A. The cure of homosexuality. *Br. Med. J.* 1:1323–1326, 1958.

Hagmeier, G., and Gleason, R. Homosexuality. In *Counseling the Catholic*. New York: Sheed & Ward, 1959.

Hagmeier, G., and Gleason, R. Moral Aspects of Homosexuality. In *Counseling the Catholic*. New York: Sheed & Ward, 1959.

Hampson, J. L., and Hampson, J. G. The Ontogenesis of Sexual Behavior in Man. In *Sex and Internal Secretions* (W. C. Young, Ed.). Baltimore: Williams & Wilkins, 1961.

Harlow, H. F.   Of love in infants. *Natural History* 69:19–23, 1960.

Hart, M., *et al.*   Psychological adjustment of nonpatient homosexuals: Critical review of the research literature. *J. Clin. Psychiatry* 39:604–608, 1978.

Hatterer, L. J.   *Changing Homosexuality in the Male.* New York: McGraw-Hill, 1970.

Hauser, R.   *The Homosexual Society.* London: Bodley Head, 1962.

Havemann, E.   Homosexuality in America: Scientists search for answers to a touchy and puzzling question—why? *Life* 56:76–80, June 26, 1964.

Hefner, H. M.   The legal enforcement of morality. *Univ. Colo. Law Rev.* 40:199–221, 1968.

Heilbrun, A. B., Jr., and Thompson, N. L., Jr.   Sex role identity and male and female homosexuality. *Sex Roles* 3(11):65–79, 1977.

Hemphill, R. E., *et al.*   A factual study of male homosexuality. *Br. Med. J.* 1:1317–1323, 1958.

Hendin, H.   *Black Suicide.* New York: Basic Books, 1969.

Hendin, H.   Homosexuality: The psychological dimension. *J. Am. Acad. Psychoanal.* 6:479–496, 1978.

Henry, G. W.   *Sex Variants: A Study of Homosexual Patterns.* New York: Hoeber, 1948.

Henry, G. W.   *All the Sexes: A Study of Masculinity and Femininity.* New York: Holt, Rinehart & Winston, 1955.

Hess, E. H., *et al.*   Pupil response of heterosexual and homosexual males to pictures of men and women. *J. Soc. Abnorm. Psychol.* 70:165–168, 1965.

Hirschfeld, M.   *Men and Women.* New York: Putnam, 1935.

Hirschfeld, M.   *The Sexual History of the World War.* New York: Cadillac, 1946.

Hirschfeld, M.   *Sexual Anomalies.* New York: Emerson, 1956.

Hoffman, M.   *The Gay World: Male Homosexuality and the Social Creation of Evil.* New York: Basic Books, 1968.

The homosexual: Newly visible, newly understood. *Time* 94:56–67, Oct. 31, 1969.

Homosexual wedding. *Newsweek* 70:59, July 17, 1967.

Homosexuality: Coming to terms. *Time* 94:82, Oct. 24, 1969.

Hooker, E.   A preliminary analysis of group behavior of homosexuals. *J. Psychol.* 42:217–225, 1956.

Hooker, E.   The adjustment of the male overt homosexual. *J. Proj. Tech.* 21:18–31, 1957.

Hooker, E.   Male homosexuality in the Rorschach. *J. Proj. Tech.* 22: 33–54, 1958.

Hooker, E.   What is a criterion? *J. Proj. Tech.* 23:278–281, 1959.

Hooker, E.   The case of El: A biography. *J. Proj. Tech.* 25:252–267, 1961.

Hooker, E.   *Male Homosexual Life Styles and Venereal Disease.* Washington, D.C.: Department of Health, Education, and Welfare, 1961.

Hooker, E.   Review of Hervey Cleckley's "the caricature of love." *J. Crim. Law, Criminol., Polit. Sci.* 52:12–13, 1961.

Hooker, E.   Male Homosexuality. In *Taboo Topics* (N. L. Farberow, Ed.). New York: Atherton, 1963.

Hooker, E.   *The Male Homosexual* (Venereal Disease Control Informational Report No. 8). Sacramento: California State Health Department, 1964.

Hooker, E.   An Empirical Study of Some Relations Between Sexual Patterns and Gender Identity in Male Homosexuals. In *Sex Research: New Developments* (J. Money, Ed.). New York: Holt, Rinehart & Winston, 1965.

Hooker, E.   Male Homosexuals and Their "Worlds." In *Sexual Inversion: The Multiple Roots of Homosexuality* (J. Marmor, Ed.). New York: Basic Books, 1965.

Hooker, E.   The Homosexual Community. In *Sexual Deviance* (J. H. Gagnon and W. Simon, Eds.). New York: Harper & Row, 1967.

Hooker, E.   Homosexuality. In *International Encyclopedia of the Social Sciences.* New York: Macmillan, 1968.

Hooker, E.   Sexual Behavior: Homosexuality. In *International Encyclopedia of the Social Sciences.* New York: Macmillan, 1968.

Hooker, E.   Parental relations and male homosexuality in patient and non-patient samples. *J. Consult. Clin. Psychol.* 33:140–142, 1969.

Hooker, E., *et al.*   Problems of Sex Ethics: Homosexuality. In *Foundations for Christian Family Policy* (E. S. Genné and W. H. Genné, Eds.). New York: National Council of Churches, 1961.

Hopkins, J. H.   The lesbian personality. *Br. J. Psychiatry* 115:1433–1436, 1969.

Horney, K.   *New Ways in Psychoanalysis.* New York: W. W. Norton, 1939.

Howard, W. L.   Sexual perversion in America. *Am. J. Derm. Genito-Urinary Dis.* 3:9–14, 1904.

Hudson, B.   *Christian Homosexuality.* North Hollywood, Calif.: New Library Press, 1970.

Humphreys, L.   *Tearoom Trade: Impersonal Sex in Public Places.* Chicago: Aldine, 1970.

Hunt, M. *The Natural History of Love.* New York: Knopf, 1959.

Hunt, S. P. Homosexuality from a contemporary perspective. *Conn. Med.* 42:105–108, 1978.

Hyde, M. H. *The Love That Dared Not Speak Its Name.* Boston: Little, Brown, 1970.

Jacobs, H. Decoy enforcement of homosexual laws. *Univ. Penn. Law Rev.* 112:259–284, 1963.

James, S., et al. Significance of androgen levels in the aetiology and treatment of homosexuality. *Psychol. Med.* 7:427–429, 1977.

Jennings, T. W., Jr. Homosexuality and Christian faith: A theological reflection. *Christian Century* Feb. 16, 1977, pp. 137–142.

Johnson, V. E., and Masters, W. H. Intravaginal contraceptive study: Phase I. Anatomy. *West. J. Surg. Obstet. Gynecol.* 70:202–207, 1962.

Johnson, V. E., and Masters, W. H. Intravaginal contraceptive study: Phase II. Physiology (a direct test for protective potential). *West. J. Surg. Obstet. Gynecol.* 71:144–153, 1963.

Johnson, V. E., and Masters, W. H. A product of dual import: Intravaginal infection control and conception control. *Pacif. Med. & Surg.* 73:267–271, 1965.

Johnson, V. E., et al. The Physiology of Intravaginal Contraceptive Failure. In *Manual of Family Planning and Contraceptive Practice* (2nd ed., M. E. Calderone, Ed.). Baltimore: Williams & Wilkins, 1970.

Jones, H. K. *Toward a Christian Understanding of the Homosexual.* New York: Association Press, 1966.

Judson, F. N., et al. Screening for gonorrhea and syphilis in the gay baths—Denver, Colorado. *Am. J. Public Health* 67:740–742, 1977.

Jung, C. G. *Collected Works* (H. Read et al., Eds.). New York: Pantheon, 1953–1970.

Kallmann, F. J. Comparative twin study on the genetic aspects of male homosexuality. *J. Nerv. Ment. Dis.* 115:283–298, 1952.

Kallmann, F. J. Twin and sibship study of overt male homosexuality. *Am. J. Hum. Genet.* 4:136–146, 1952.

Kameny, F. E. Gay Is Good. In *The Same Sex* (R. Weltge, Ed.). Philadelphia: Pilgrim, 1969.

Kardiner, A., and Ovesey, L. *The Mark of Oppression.* New York: Meridian, 1962.

Karlen, A. *Sexuality and Homosexuality: A New View.* New York: W. W. Norton, 1971.

Katz, S. The homosexual next door. *Maclean's Magazine* 77:10–11, 28–30, Feb. 22, 1964.

Kauffmann, S. Homosexual drama and its disguises. *New York Times* Jan. 23, 1966.

Kauffmann, S. On the acceptability of the homosexual. *New York Times* Feb. 6, 1966.

Kaye, H. E., *et al.* Homosexuality in women. *Arch. Gen. Psychiatry* 17:626–634, 1967.

Ketterer, W. A. Venereal disease and homosexuality. *J.A.M.A.* 188: 11–12, 1964.

Kinsey, A. C. Homosexuality: Criteria for a hormonal explanation of the homosexual. *J. Clin. Endocrinol.* 1:424–428, 1941.

Kinsey, A. C., *et al. Sexual Behavior in the Human Male.* Philadelphia: Saunders, 1948.

Kinsey, A. C., *et al.* Concepts of Normality and Abnormality in Sexual Behavior. In *Psychosexual Development in Health and Disease* (P. H. Hoch and J. Zubin, Eds.). New York: Grune & Stratton, 1949.

Kinsey, A. C., *et al. Sexual Behavior in the Human Female.* Philadelphia: Saunders, 1953.

Kitsuse, J. I. Societal response to deviant behavior: Problems of theory and method. *Soc. Probl.* 9:247–256, 1962.

Kolodny, R. C., *et al.* Plasma testosterone and semen analysis in male homosexuals. *N. Engl. J. Med.* 285:1170–1174, 1971.

Kolodny, R. C., *et al.* Plasma gonadotrophins and prolactin in male homosexuals. *Lancet* 2:18–20, 1972.

Krafft-Ebing, R. von. *Psychopathia Sexualis* (H. E. Wedeck, Trans.). New York: Putnam, 1965.

Krich, A. M. (Ed.). *The Homosexuals: As Seen by Themselves and Authorities.* New York: Citadel, 1954.

Lanahan, C. C. Homosexuality: A different sexual orientation. *Nurs. Forum* 15:314–319, 1976.

Lawrence, J. C. Gay peer counseling. *J. Psychiatr. Nurs.* 15:33–37, 1977.

Lemert, E. *Social Pathology.* New York: McGraw-Hill, 1951.

Leznoff, M. Interviewing homosexuals. *Am. J. Sociol.* 62:204, 1956.

Leznoff, M., and Westley, W. A. The homosexual community. *Soc. Probl.* 3:259–260, 1956.

Licht, H. *Sexual Life in Ancient Greece.* New York: Barnes & Noble, 1963.

Liddicoat, R. Homosexuality: Results of a survey as related to various theories. *Br. Med. J.* 2:1110–1111, 1957.

Liebow, E. *Tally's Corner.* Boston: Little, Brown, 1967.

Lief, H., and Mayerson, P.   Psychotherapy of Homosexuals: A Follow-up Study of Nineteen Cases. In *Sexual Inversion: The Multiple Roots of Homosexuality* (J. Marmor, Ed.). New York: Basic Books, 1965.

Lief, H. I., et al.   Psychoendocrinologic studies in a male with cyclic changes in sexuality. *Psychosom. Med.* 24:357–368, 1962.

Lim, K. S., et al.   Role of sexual and non-sexual practices in the transmission of hepatitis B. *Br. J. Vener. Dis.* 53:190–192, 1977.

Lindner, R. M.   Homosexuality and the Contemporary Scene. In *Must You Conform?* New York: Holt, Rinehart & Winston, 1956.

Linton, R.   Marquesan Culture. In *The Individual and His Society* (A. Kardiner, Ed.). New York: Columbia University Press, 1939.

Littler, W. A., et al.   Direct arterial pressure, heart rate and electrocardiogram during human coitus. *J. Reprod. Fertil.* 40:321–331, 1974.

Livingood, J. M. (Ed.).   *National Institute of Mental Health Task Force on Homosexuality: Final Report and Background Papers*, Publ. No. HSM 72–9116. Washington, D.C.: U.S. Government Printing Office, 1972.

Livingstone, I. R., et al.   The effect of luteinizing hormone releasing hormone (LRH) on pituitary gonadotropins in male homosexuals. *Horm. Metab. Res.* 10:248–249, 1978.

Löfgren, L. B.   Difficulties and ambiguities in using "results" as an evaluating norm in psychiatry. *Br. J. Med. Psychol.* 33:95–103, 1960.

London, L. S.   Homosexual panic with hallucinations—a case study. *Med. Times* 92:175–189, 1964.

Loraine, J. A., et al.   Endocrine function in male and female homosexuals. *Br. Med. J.* 4:406–408, 1970.

Lorenz, K.   *Evolution and the Modification of Behavior.* Chicago: University of Chicago Press, 1965.

Lowry, A. S.   Entry into homosexual lifestyles: A trimodal formulation. Goddard University M.A. Thesis, 1973.

Lucas, D. S. (Ed.).   *The Homosexual and the Church.* San Francisco: Mattachine Society, 1966.

Ludovici, A.   Homosexuality, the law and public sentiment (commentary by C. Allen). *Int. J. Sexol.* 5:143–150, 1951–1952.

MacAlpert, L.   East coast homophiles discuss the great society. *Tangents* 1:13, 1965.

McGuire, R. J., and Vallance, M.   Aversion therapy by electric shock: A simple technique. *Br. Med. J.* 1:151, 1964.

McIntosh, M.   The homosexual role. *Soc. Probl.* 16:182–192, 1968.

McWhirter, D. P., and Mattison, A. M.   The treatment of sexual dysfunction in gay male couples. *J. Sex Marital Ther.* 4:213–218, 1978.

Magee, B. *One in Twenty: A Study of Homosexuality in Men and Women.* New York: Stein & Day, 1966.

Malthus, T. R. *On Population* (G. Himmelfarb, Ed.). New York: Modern Library, 1960.

Marcus, F. *The Killing of Sister George.* New York: Random House, 1967.

Margolese, M. S. Homosexuality: A new endocrine correlate. *Horm. Behav.* 1(2):151–155, 1970.

Margolese, M. S., and Janiger, O. Androsterone/etiocholanolone ratios in male homosexuals. *Br. Med. J.* 3:207–210, 1973.

Marks, I. M. Aversion therapy. *Br. J. Med. Psychol.* 41:47–52, 1968.

Marmor, J. (Ed.). Male Homosexuals and Their Worlds. In *Proceedings of the XIVth International Congress of Applied Psychology and Personality Research.* Copenhagen: Munksgaard, 1962. Vol. 2.

Marmor, J. (Ed.). *Sexual Inversion: The Multiple Roots of Homosexuality.* New York: Basic Books, 1965.

Marmor, J. Homosexuality. *Stud. Pers. Newsl., State Univ. Coll., Buffalo* 1(3):15–34, 1967.

Marmor, J. Homosexuality and objectivity. *S.I.E.C.U.S. Newsl.* 6(2): 1, 3–4, 6, 8, 10–12, Dec. 23, 1970.

Marmor, J. Homosexuality in males. *Psychiatric Ann.* 1:44–59, 1971.

Marmor, J. "Normal" and "deviant" sexual behavior. *J.A.M.A.* 217: 165–170, 1971.

Marmor, J. Notes on Some Psychodynamic Aspects of Homosexuality. In *National Institute of Mental Health Task Force on Homosexuality: Final Report and Background Papers,* Publ. No. HSM 72–9116 (J. M. Livingood, Ed.). Washington, D.C.: U.S. Government Printing Office, 1972.

Marmor, J. Homosexuality—mental illness or moral dilemma? *Int. J. Psychiatry* 10:114–117, 1972.

Marmor, J., and Green, R. Homosexual Behavior. In *Handbook of Sexology* (J. Money and H. Musaph, Eds.). New York: Elsevier/ North Holland Biomedical Press, 1977.

Maslow, A. H. Love in Self-Actualizing People. In *Sexual Behavior and Personality Characteristics* (M. F. DeMartino, Ed.). New York: Grove, 1966.

Maslow, A. H. Self-Esteem (Dominance-Feeling) and Sexuality in Women. In *Sexual Behavior and Personality Characteristics* (M. F. DeMartino, Ed.). New York: Grove, 1966.

Maslow, A. H., *et al.* Some Parallels Between Sexual and Dominance Behavior of Infra-Human Primates and the Fantasies of Patients in

Psychotherapy. In *Sexual Behavior and Personality Characteristics* (M. F. DeMartino, Ed.). New York: Grove, 1966.

Masters, R. E. L. *The Homosexual Revolution: A Challenging Expose of the Social and Political Directions of a Minority Group.* New York: Julian, 1962.

Masters, W. H., and Johnson, V. E. The artificial vagina: Anatomic, physiologic, psychosexual function. *West. J. Surg. Obstet. Gynecol.* 69:192–212, 1961.

Masters, W. H., and Johnson, V. E. *Human Sexual Response.* Boston: Little, Brown, 1966.

Masters, W. H., and Johnson, V. E. *Human Sexual Inadequacy.* Boston: Little, Brown, 1970.

Masters, W. H., and Johnson, V. E. *The Pleasure Bond.* Boston: Little, Brown, 1975.

Mattachine Society of Washington. *Federal Employment of Homosexual American Citizens.* Washington, D.C.: Mattachine Society, 1965.

Max, L. W. Breaking up a homosexual fixation by the conditioned reaction technique. *Psychol. Bull.* 32:734, 1935.

Mead, M. Cultural Determinants of Sexual Behavior. In *Sex and Internal Secretions* (W. C. Young, Ed.). Baltimore: Williams & Wilkins, 1961.

Meyer, R. G., et al. A social episode model of human sexual behavior. *J. Homosex.* 2(2):123–131, 1976–1977.

Meyer-Bahlburg, H. F. L. Sex hormones and male homosexuality in comparative perspective. *Arch. Sex. Behav.* 6:297–325, 1977.

Mildvan, D., et al. Venereal transmission of enteric pathogens in male homosexuals: Two case reports. *J.A.M.A.* 238:1387–1389, 1977.

Moll, A. *Perversions of the Sexual Instinct: A Study of Sexual Inversion* (M. Popkin, Trans.). New York: Julian, 1931.

Moll, A. *Libido Sexualis.* North Hollywood, Calif.: Brandon House, 1966.

Money, J. Components of Eroticism in Man: Cognitional Rehearsals. In *Recent Advances in Biological Psychiatry* (J. Wortis, Ed.). New York: Grune & Stratton, 1960.

Money, J. Sex Hormones and Other Variables in Human Eroticism. In *Sex and Internal Secretions* (W. C. Young, Ed.). Baltimore: Williams & Wilkins, 1961.

Money, J. Factors in the Genesis of Homosexuality. In *Determinants of Human Sexual Behavior* (G. Winokur, Ed.). Springfield, Ill.: Thomas, 1963.

Money, J. Psychosexual Differentiation. In *Sex Research: New Developments* (J. Money, Ed.). New York: Holt, Rinehart & Winston, 1965.

Money, J. (Ed.). *Sex Research: New Developments*. New York: Holt, Rinehart & Winston, 1965.

Money, J. The genetics of homosexuality. N.Z. Med. J. 66:745–748, 1967.

Money, J. *Sex Errors of the Body*. Baltimore: Johns Hopkins Press, 1968.

Money, J. Sexual dimorphism and homosexual gender identity. *Psychol. Bull.* 74:425–440, 1970.

Money, J. Pubertal Hormones and Homosexuality, Bisexuality and Heterosexuality (Appendix B). In *National Institute of Mental Health Task Force on Homosexuality: Final Report and Background Papers*, Publ. No. HSM 72–9116 (J. M. Livingood, Ed.). Washington, D.C.: U.S. Government Printing Office, 1972.

Money, J. Statement on antidiscrimination regarding sexual orientation. *J. Homosex.* 2(2):159–161, 1976–1977.

Money, J. Bisexual, homosexual, and heterosexual: Society, law, and medicine. *J. Homosex.* 2(3):229–233, 1977.

Money, J., and Alexander, D. Psychosexual development and absence of homosexuality in males with precocious puberty. *J. Nerv. Ment. Dis.* 148:111–123, 1969.

Money, J., and Daléry, J. Iatrogenic homosexuality: Gender identity in seven 46, XX chromosomal females with hyperadrenocortical hermaphroditism born with a penis, three reared as boys, four reared as girls. *J. Homosex.* 1(4):357–371, 1976.

Money, J., and Ehrhardt, A. *Man & Woman, Boy & Girl: The Differentiation and Dimorphism of Gender Identity From Conception to Maturity*. Baltimore: Johns Hopkins Press, 1972.

Money, J., and Hosta, G. Negro folklore of male pregnancy. *J. Sex Res.* 4:34–50, 1968.

Money, J., and Wang, C. Human figure drawings: II. Quality comparison in gender-identity anomalies, Klinefelter's syndrome, and precocious puberty. *J. Nerv. Ment. Dis.* 144:55–58, 1967.

Morin, S. F. Heterosexual bias in psychological research on lesbianism and male homosexuality. *Am. Psychol.* 32:629–637, 1977.

Neumann, H. H. Urethritis caused by anal coitus. *Med. Aspects Hum. Sex.* 10:73–74, 1976.

Nichols, J., and Clarke, L. *I Have More Fun With You Than Anybody*. New York: St. Martin's, 1972.

Oswald, I.   Induction of illusory and hallucinatory voices with considerations of behaviour therapy. *J. Ment. Sci.* 108:196–212, 1962.

Ovesey, L.   The homosexual conflict: An adaptational analysis. *Psychiatry* 17:243–250, 1954.

Ovesey, L.   The pseudohomosexual anxiety. *Psychiatry* 18:17–25, 1955.

Ovesey, L.   Pseudohomosexuality, the paranoid mechanism, and paranoia. *Psychiatry* 18:163, 1955.

Ovesey, L.   Masculine aspirations in women. *Psychiatry* 19:341–351, 1956.

Ovesey, L.   Fear of vocational success. *Arch. Gen. Psychiatry* 7:30–40, 1962.

Ovesey, L.   Pseudohomosexuality and Homosexuality in Men: Psychodynamics as a Guide to Treatment. In *Sexual Inversion: The Multiple Roots of Homosexuality* (J. Marmor, Ed.). New York: Basic Books, 1965.

Ovesey, L.   *Homosexuality and Pseudohomosexuality.* New York: Science House, 1969.

Parker, W.   *Homosexuality: A Selective Bibliography of Over 3000 Items.* Metuchen, N.J.: Scarecrow, 1971.

Parsons, T.   *The Social System.* New York: Free Press, 1951.

Perloff, W. H.   The role of hormones in homosexuality. *Albert Einstein Med. Cen.* 11:165–178, 1963.

Pillard, R. C., Rose, R. M., and Sherwood, M.   Plasma testosterone levels in homosexual men. *Arch. Sex. Behav.* 3:453–458, 1974.

Ploscowe, M.   *Sex and the Law* (rev. ed.). New York: Ace Books, 1962.

Poe, J. S.   The successful treatment of a 40-year-old passive homosexual based on an adaptational view of sexual behavior. *Psychol. Rev.* 29: 23–36, 1952.

Pomeroy, W. B.   Human Sexual Behavior. In *Taboo Topics* (N. Farberow, Ed.). New York: Atherton, 1963.

Pomeroy, W. B.   Homosexuality. In *The Same Sex* (R. Weltge, Ed.). Philadelphia: Pilgrim, 1969.

Prosin, S.   The concept of the lesbian, a minority in reverse. *Ladder* 6(10):5–22, 1962.

The psychoanalytic treatment of male homosexuality (Eng. abstr.). *J. Am. Psychoanal. Assoc.* 25:183–199, 1977.

Ranier, J. D., *et al.*   Homosexuality and heterosexuality in identical twins. *Psychosom. Med.* 22:251–259, 1960.

Rao, C. R.   *Advanced Statistical Methods in Biometric Research.* New York: Wiley, 1952.

Rees, J. T., and Usill, H. V. (Eds.). *They Stand Apart: A Critical Survey of the Problems of Homosexuality.* London: Heinemann, 1955.

Regelson, R. Up the camp staircase. *The New York Times* Mar. 3, 1968.

Reik, T. *A Psychologist Looks at Love.* New York: Farrar & Rinehart, 1944.

Reik, T. *The Psychology of Sex Relations.* New York: Farrar & Rinehart, 1945.

Reik, T. *Myth and Guilt: The Crime and Punishment of Mankind.* New York: George Braziller, 1957.

Reiss, A. J., Jr. Sex offenses: The marginal status of the adolescent. *Law Contemp. Probl.* 25:319, 1960.

Reiss, A. J., Jr. The Social Integration of Queers and Peers. In *The Problem of Homosexuality in Modern Society* (H. M. Ruitenbeek, Ed.). New York: Dutton, 1963.

Riess, B. A new psychology of women or a psychology for the new woman, active or passive. *Int. Ment. Health Res. Newsl.* 14(4):1–4, 1971.

Ritchey, M. G. Venereal disease among homosexuals (letter to the editor). *J.A.M.A.* 237:767, 1977.

Ritchey, M. G., and Leff, A. M. Venereal disease control among homosexuals: An outreach program. *J.A.M.A.* 232:509–510, 1975.

Robinson, V. *Encyclopedia Sexualis.* New York: Dingwall-Rock, 1936.

Robinson, W. J. *Woman, Her Sex and Love Life.* New York: Eugenics, 1931.

Roesler, T., and Diesher, R. W. Youthful male homosexuality: Homosexual experience and the process of developing homosexual identity in males aged 16–22 years. *J.A.M.A.* 219:1018–1023, 1972.

Rohde, W., *et al.* Plasma basal levels of FSH, LH and testosterone in homosexual men. *Endokrinologie* 70:241–248, 1977.

Rosen, I. (Ed.). *The Pathology and Treatment of Sexual Deviation.* London: Oxford University Press, 1964.

Rosen, I. The basis of psychotherapeutic treatment of sexual deviation. *Proc. R. Soc. Med.* 61:793–796, 1968.

Rubington, E., and Weinberg, M. *Deviance: The Interactionist Perspective* (2nd ed.). New York: Macmillan, 1973.

Rubinstein, L. H. Psychotherapeutic aspects of male homosexuality. *Br. J. Med. Psychol.* 31:74–78, 1958.

Ruitenbeek, H. (Ed.). *The Problem of Homosexuality in Modern Society.* New York: Dutton, 1963.

Saghir, M. T., and Robins, E.   Homosexuality: I. Sexual behavior of the female homosexual. *Arch. Gen. Psychiatry* 20:192–201, 1969.

Saghir, M. T., and Robins, E.   *Male and Female Homosexuality: A Comprehensive Investigation.* Baltimore: Williams & Wilkins, 1973.

Saghir, M. T., *et al.*   Homosexuality: II. Sexual behavior of the male homosexual. *Arch. Gen. Psychiatry* 21:219–229, 1969.

Saghir, M. T., *et al.*   Homosexuality: III. Psychiatric disorders and disability in the male homosexual. *Am. J. Psychiatry* 129:1079–1086, 1970.

Saghir, M. T., *et al.*   Homosexuality: IV. Psychiatric disorders and disability in the female homosexual. *Am. J. Psychiatry* 127:147–154, 1970.

Schmerin, M. J., *et al.*   Amebiasis: An increasing problem among homosexuals in New York City. *J.A.M.A.* 238:1386–1387, 1977.

Schmidt, G.   Letter to the editor. *Arch. Sex. Behav.* 7:73–75, 1978.

Schofield, M.   *The Sexual Behavior of Young People.* London: Longmans, Green, 1965.

Schofield, M.   *Sociological Aspects of Homosexuality.* London: Longmans, Green, 1965.

Schott, W.   Civil rights and the homosexual. *New York Times* Mar. 3, 1966.

Schur, E. M.   Homosexuality. In *Crimes Without Victims.* Englewood Cliffs, N.J.: Prentice-Hall, 1965.

Scott, P. D.   Definition, Classification, Prognosis and Treatment. In *The Pathology and Treatment of Sexual Deviation: A Methodological Approach* (I. Rosen, Ed.). London: Oxford University Press, 1964.

Secor, N. A.   A Brief for a New Homosexual Ethic. In *The Same Sex* (R. W. Weltge, Ed.). Philadelphia: Pilgrim, 1969.

Siegelman, M.   Parental background of male homosexuals and heterosexuals. *Arch. Sex. Behav.* 3:3–18, 1974.

Siegelman, M.   Psychological adjustment of homosexual and heterosexual men: A cross-national replication. *Arch. Sex. Behav.* 7:1–11, 1978.

Simmel, G.   Soziologie. In *Behavior in Public Places* (E. Goffman, Ed.). New York: Free Press, 1963.

Simon, W., and Gagnon, J. H.   The Lesbians: A Preliminary Overview. In *Sexual Deviance* (J. H. Gagnon and W. H. Simons, Eds.). New York: Harper & Row, 1967.

Simon, W., and Gagnon, J. H. (Eds.).   *Sexual Deviance.* New York: Harper & Row, 1967.

Simon, W., and Gagnon, J. H. Homosexuality: The Formulation of a Sociological Perspective. In *The Same Sex* (R. W. Weltge, Ed.). Philadelphia: Pilgrim, 1969.

Socarides, C. W. *The Overt Homosexual.* New York: Grune & Stratton, 1968.

Socarides, C. W. Homosexuality and medicine. *J.A.M.A.* 212:1199–1202, 1970.

Society for Individual Rights. *The Armed Services and Homosexuality.* San Francisco: Society for Individual Rights, 1968.

Society for Individual Rights. *The Military Discharge and Employment Experiences of 47 Homosexuals.* San Francisco: Society for Individual Rights, 1969.

Sonnenschein, D. Homosexuality as a subject of anthropological inquiry. *Anthropol. Q.* 39:73–82, 1966.

Sonnenschein, D. The ethnography of male homosexual relations. *J. Sex Res.* 4:69–83, 1968.

Stahl, F., *et al.* Significantly decreased apparently free testosterone levels in plasma of male homosexuals. *Endokrinologie* 68:115–117, 1976.

Star, J. The faces of the boys in the band. A changing view of homosexuality? *Look* 33:62–68, Dec. 2, 1969.

Starká, L., *et al.* Plasma testosterone in male transsexuals and homosexuals. *J. Sex Res.* 11:134–138, 1975.

Stein, R. A. The effect of exercise training on heart rate during coitus in the post myocardial infarction patient. *Circulation* 55:738–740, 1977.

Stephan, W. G. Parental relationships and early social experiences of activist male homosexuals and male heterosexuals. *J. Abnorm. Psychol.* 82:506–613, 1973.

Stevenson, I., and Wolpe, J. Recovery from sexual deviations through overcoming non-sexual neurotic responses. *Am. J. Psychiatry* 116:737–742, 1960.

Stoller, R. J. The "bedrock" of masculinity and femininity: Bisexuality. *Arch. Gen. Psychiatry* 26:207–212, 1972.

Stow, M. Closet queens. *Vector* 7:4, 1971.

Sturgis, E. T., and Adams, H. E. The right to treatment: Issues in the treatment of homosexuality. *J. Consult. Clin. Psychol.* 46:165–169, 1978.

Sullivan, H. S. *The Interpersonal Theory of Psychiatry* (H. S. Perry and M. L. Garrel, Eds.). New York: W. W. Norton, 1953.

Swerdlow, H. Trauma caused by anal coitus. *Med. Aspects Hum. Sex.* 10:93–94, 1976.

Szasz, T.   *The Myth of Mental Illness.* New York: Hoeber, 1961.

Szasz, T.   *Law, Liberty and Psychiatry.* New York: Macmillan, 1963.

Szasz, T.   Legal and Moral Aspects of Homosexuality. In *Sexual Inversion* (J. Marmor, Ed.). New York: Basic Books, 1965.

Szmuness, W., *et al.*   On the role of sexual behavior in the spread of hepatitis B infection. *Ann. Intern. Med.* 83:489–495, 1975.

Tarnowsky, B.   *Pederasty in Europe.* North Hollywood, Calif.: Brandon House, 1967.

Taylor, G. R.   *Sex in History.* New York: Vanguard, 1960.

Thielicke, H.   The Problem of Homosexuality. In *The Ethics of Sex* (J. W. Doberstein, Trans.). New York: Harper & Row, 1964.

Thompson, C.   Changing concepts of homosexuality in psychoanalysis. *Psychiatry* 10:183–189, 1947.

Thompson, N. L., *et al.*   Parent-child relationships and sexual identity in male and female homosexuals and heterosexuals. *J. Consult. Clin. Psychol.* 41:120–127, 1973.

Tiger, L.   *Men in Groups.* New York: Random House, 1969.

Tourney, G., and Hatfield, L. M.   Androgen metabolism in schizophrenics, homosexuals, and normal controls. *Biol. Psychiatry* 6:23–26, 1973.

Tripp, C. A.   Who is a homosexual? *Soc. Prog. J. Church Soc.* 58(2): 13–21, 1967.

Tripp, C. A.   *The Homosexual Matrix.* New York: McGraw-Hill, 1975.

Tylor, E.   *Primitive Culture.* London: Oxford University Press, 1963.

United Church of Christ, Council for Social Action.   *Civil Liberties and Homosexuality: An Issue in Christian Responsibility.* Lebanon, Pa.: United Church of Christ, 1967.

United Presbyterian Church in the U.S.A. Office of Church and Society of the Board of Christian Education.   *What About Homosexuality?* Lancaster, Pa.: United Presbyterian Church, 1967.

United States Department of Health, Education, and Welfare. National Institute of Mental Health.   *Final Report of the Task Force on Homosexuality* ("The Hooker Report"). Oct., 1969.

Vaisrub, S.   Homosexuality—a risk factor in infectious disease (editorial). *J.A.M.A.* 238:1402, 1977.

Vander Veldt, J. H., and Odenwald, R. P.   Homosexuality. In *Psychiatry and Catholicism* (2nd ed.). New York: McGraw-Hill, 1957.

Vanggaard, T.   *Phallos: A Symbol and Its History in the Male World.* New York: International Universities Press, 1972.

Ward, D. A., and Kassebaum, G. G.   *Women's Prison: Sex and Social Structure.* Chicago: Aldine, 1965.

Watson, J. B. *Behaviorism* (rev. ed.). Chicago: University of Chicago Press, 1930.

Weinberg, G. H. *Society and the Healthy Homosexual.* New York: St. Martin's Press, 1972.

Weinberg, M., and Bell, A. (Eds.). *Homosexuality: An Annotated Bibliography.* New York: Harper & Row, 1972.

Weinberg, M. S., and Williams, C. J. *Male Homosexuals.* New York: Oxford University Press, 1974.

Welch, P. Homosexuality in America: The "gay" world takes to the city streets. *Life* 56:68–74, June 26, 1964.

Weltge, R. W. (Ed.). *The Same Sex: An Appraisal of Homosexuality.* Philadelphia: Pilgrim, 1969.

West, D. J. Parental figures in the genesis of male homosexuality. *Int. J. Soc. Psychiatry* 5:58–97, 1959.

West, D. J. *Homosexuality.* Chicago: Aldine, 1968.

West, L. J., and Glass, A. J. Sexual Behavior and the Military Law. In *Sexual Behavior and the Law* (R. Slovenko, Ed.). Springfield, Ill.: Thomas, 1965.

Westermarck, E. *The Origin and Development of the Moral Ideas.* London: Macmillan, 1908.

Westermarck, E. *The History of Human Marriage.* New York: Allerton, 1922. Vols. 1–3.

Westwood, G. *Society and the Homosexual.* New York: Dutton, 1953.

Westwood, G. *A Minority: A Report on the Life of the Male Homosexual in Great Britain.* London: Longmans, Green, 1960.

Whitam, F. L. Childhood indicators of male homosexuality. *Arch. Sex. Behav.* 6:89–96, 1977.

Whitam, F. L. The homosexual role: A reconsideration. *J. Sex Res.* 13:1–11, 1977.

White, J. Those others: A report on homosexuality. *Washington Post* Jan. 31–Feb. 4, 1965.

Wildeblood, P. *Against the Law.* London: Weidenfeld & Nicolson, 1955.

Wille, L. Chicago's twilight world—the homosexuals. *Chicago Daily News* June 20–23, 1966.

Williams, C. J., and Weinberg, M. S. *Homosexuals and the Military.* New York: Harper & Row, 1971.

Willis, S. E., II. *Understanding and Counseling the Male Homosexual.* Boston: Little, Brown, 1967.

Woetzel, R. K. Do our homosexuality laws make sense? *Saturday Rev.* 48:23–25, Oct. 9, 1965.

Wolfenden, J. *Report of the Committee on Homosexual Offenses and Prostitution.* New York: Stein & Day, 1963.

Wolpe, J. *Psychotherapy by Reciprocal Inhibition.* Stanford, Calif.: Stanford University Press, 1972.

Wolpe, J., and Lazarus, A. *Behavior Therapy Techniques.* New York: Pergamon, 1966.

Wood, R. W. *Christ and the Homosexual.* New York: Vantage, 1960.

Wysor, B. *The Lesbian Myth.* New York: Random House, 1974.

Yale Cross-Cultural Index. New Haven, Conn.: Yale University Library.

Yalom, I. D., *et al.* Prenatal exposure to female hormones. *Arch. Gen. Psychiatry* 28:554–561, 1973.

Young, W. C. (Ed.). *Sex and Internal Secretions.* Baltimore: Williams & Wilkins, 1961.

INDEX

initiation of mounting process, 79–80

in married couples, 79–81

as mutual experience, 214–215

rectal. *See* Rectal intercourse

and responses of ambisexuals, 162–163, 164, 165, 169–170, 203

female, 169

male, 167

risk of failure in, 122, 208, 209

and sexual functional efficiency, 200, 201, 207–209

Coloration

labial, in homosexuals, 136

penile, in homosexuals, 139

Committed couples

acclimation to laboratory, 54

heterosexual, 10, 211, 217–221. *See also* Married couples

homosexual, 10, 13–16, 211, 212–216. *See also* Homosexual study group

and sexual functional efficiency, 209

sexual interactions compared to assigned couples, 210

Communication

in homosexual committed couples, 73, 213, 215, 230

lack of, in heterosexual couples, 79

in assigned couples, 221

in married couples, 68, 69, 74

need for, in heterosexual couples, 218–219, 220–221, 350

Comparative patterns in sexual behavior, 61–91, 212–226

in ambisexuals, 165–169

in coition

in assigned couples, 81–82

in married couples, 79–81

in committed couples, 64–65

in cunnilingus, 75–77

in dildo usage, 86–89

and fantasy patterns, 177–185

in fellatio, 75

and functional efficiency, 92–123, 198–204. *See also* Functional efficiency of study subjects

in masturbation, 62–64

in partner stimulation, 66–74

and postorgasmic behavior, 82–83

in rectal intercourse, 83–86

in vocalization of sexual tensions, 89–90

Concerns of study subjects, 45–46. *See also* Fears

and security measures, 6, 45, 48–49

Contraception

in ambisexual subjects, 140

intravaginal agents in, evaluation of, 47

Conversion clients, 240, 333

failures in therapy

in females, 394, 399, 400

in males, 393, 399, 400

sexual aversion in, 395

Cross-preference encounters, as fantasy material, 178, 186–188

in females

heterosexual, 184

homosexual, 180

in males

heterosexual, 182

homosexual, 179

Cultural concepts

and attitudes of health-care professionals, 247–250, 251, 272, 276, 314, 334, 342, 366, 391

and fears of performance, 267, 314

and female view of fellatio, 76–77

and male dominance in coition, 170

and male view of cunnilingus, 76, 77

and men as sex experts, 122, 219–220, 227

and performance pressures, 260–271

and physical aspects of sexual preference, 403–405

and public opprobrium of homosexuals, 227, 228–230, 272, 403

Cunnilingus, 6

failure incidence in, 199

in ambisexuals, 203

in female homosexuals, 94, 97

in committed vs. assigned couples, 120

in group A females, 99, 101

in homosexual couples, 75–76

in married couples, 76–77

and responses of ambisexuals, 157, 158, 160, 161, 162, 164, 165, 203

and sexual functional efficiency, 199, 205–208

Desensitization procedures, in male homosexual dysfunction, 307

Dildo usage, 12, 86–89

by female homosexuals, 87–88

by married couple, 88–89

in masturbation, 88

number of subjects studied, 48

Dissatisfied homosexuals, 240, 243–246. *See also* Sex-preference reversal